The Million-to-One Team

The Million-to-One Team

Why the Chicago Cubs Haven't Won a Pennant Since 1945

GEORGE CASTLE

10/28/00

George B. Castle

DIAMOND COMMUNICATIONS, INC.

South Bend, Indiana

The Million-to-One Team
Why the Chicago Cubs Haven't Won a Pennant Since 1945
Copyright © 2000 by George Castle

10 9 8 7 6 5 4 3 2 1

Manufactured in the United States of America

Diamond Communications, Inc.
Post Office Box 88
South Bend, Indiana 46624-0088
Editorial: (219) 299-9278
Fax: (219) 299-9296
Orders Only: 1-800-480-3717
Website: www.diamondbooks.com

Library of Congress Cataloging-in-Publication Data

Castle, George
    The million-to-one team : why the Chicago Cubs haven't won a
pennant since 1945 / George Castle
        p. cm.
    ISBN 1-888698-31-4
    1. Chicago Cubs (Baseball team)--History. I. Title.
GV875.C6 C29 2000
796.357'64'0977311--dc21

                                                00-029479

Contents

To Nina and Laura

Acknowledgments

I have to thank a lot of people for putting up with me as I gathered a *War and Peace* length collection of information and interviews for this work.

Top thanks must go to Jay Rand, formerly of the Chicago Cubs' publications department, Paula Blaine of *Chicago Sports Profiles* magazine, and Richard Babcock of *Chicago Magazine* for helping go through back articles to glean some vital material.

I'll thank former *Times of Northwest Indiana* David Campbell for letting me run with a feature on sports odds in the fall of 1997 that helped inspire this book. More thanks go to Campbell successor Mike Sansone and *Times'* staffer Ruth Smith for help.

Then a nod of gratefulness goes to Benjie de la Fuente and Chuck Wasserstrom of the Cubs' media relations department for helping with the task of crunching information and numbers. Alyson Footer of the Houston Astros also was helpful on short notice. Additional assistance in this area was dutifully provided by Don Zminda of STATS, Inc., and Stuart Shea of Publications International in Lincolnwood, Illinois.

Thanks for access to the Cubs, White Sox, St. Louis Cardinals, and Lansing Lugnuts media relations departments. And there's appreciation for both working microfilm machines and helpful staff at the Harold Washington Library in Chicago and the public library in Skokie, Illinois.

Jack Kuenster of *Baseball Digest* was invaluable in tapping his memories of covering the Cubs in days of yore and directing me to some interesting old articles in the 1950s. I could have written two more books if I had more time to talk to such old-timers such as Moe Drabowsky, Glen Hobbie, Bob Anderson, George Altman, Buck O'Neil, and Gene Handley. And here's tribute to Dick Bertell, who died not long after he gave me his own special trip into Cubs history.

I will always appreciate the long, candid sit-down interview sessions with Jim Dowdle, Andy MacPhail, Jim Hendry, Andy McKenna, Mark Grace, Dick Balderson, and a host of other key figures in recent Cubs history.

Using an analogy of a pitcher trying to make it through a tough nine innings, I appreciate the ongoing encouragement of Jill Langford, who kept coming out to the mound to say everything was all right when I thought I was running out of gas. And the cheerleading from the dugout of Jim Langford, who knew all too well the road I was traveling.

And appreciation and love to my wife, Nina, and daughter, Laura, who allowed me to hole up in my office to crank out *The Million-to-One Team* day after day, week after week during the off-season of 1999-2000.

—*George Castle, February 2000*

Introduction

Following the Cubs, becoming emotionally involved with pro sports' most spectacular championship drought, is most often an involuntary act. You usually have no choice in the matter. You're a conscious human being one minute, usually in early elementary school, minding your own business. The next minute, you're part of Cubdom.

My own connection was generational, in the same manner as for countless Cubs fans. I have a vivid memory of a sunny day in the Wrigley Field center-field bleachers somewhere around 1960 or 1961, and the feeling of climbing over people sitting on those hard wooden benches. It was my first game at the Friendly Confines. My grandfather, Morris H. Zutz, was my guide, but he was emptying his pockets at this moment of nickels and dimes, my sweet tooth getting the better of me as I descended to the concession stand below.

These must have been moments of pleasure for Grandpa. He had not enjoyed an easy life. Other family members said he related stories of ducking into basements in Kiev, Ukraine, at the turn of the century as horse-borne Cossacks charged through the streets looking for Jews. Well, Morrie Zutz ended up better off than the Cossacks even as he struggled for a living as an electric supplies salesman. He raised a family in Albany Park, on Chicago's Northwest Side. He took his vacations in the Wrigley Field bleachers. That was a simple yet triumphant pleasure. Morrie Zutz could watch Hack Wilson and Rogers Hornsby in complete freedom in the Wrigley family's little ballpark. A world away, those ol' Cossacks had to worry about Uncle Joe Stalin, then Hitler's marauding armies, and later Stalin again.

Grandpa enjoyed the pennant-every-three-years routine from 1929 through 1938, and no doubt exulted in the wartime flag of 1945. By the early 1960s, his own emotional brow must have been furrowed at the thought of the laggard Cubs, permanently entrenched in the National League's second division. No number of five-year plans, trades with the Dodgers or colleges of coaches were going to make a bit of difference in their fortunes. And yet Morrie Zutz was still going out to the bleachers, this time with his first grandchild. That sounded like a nice routine for a retirement that loomed in 1963, just after his 65th birthday.

He didn't get that chance for multi-generational Wrigley Field trips. An operation late in 1962 found widespread stomach cancer. Too far gone, the surgeon sewed him up and sent Grandpa home to spend his last months. He died in mid-season 1963 as the Cubs struggled to stay in contention in a rare foray into the first division.

But the seed had been planted. It bloomed ripe and full in 1967, when the Cubs shook off their 20-year stupor to tie the St. Louis Cardinals for first place on several occasions in July. Morrie Zutz would have loved the scene, but not the decibels that Monday night, July 3, when the Cubs, reaching for the top of the NL, launched a barrage of homers against the Braves at Fulton County Stadium in Atlanta. I ran through the house yelling war whoops. Irv Kupcinet wrote in the *Sun-Times* that if the Cubs and White Sox, also flirting with first place, played in a Subway Series, Ed Sullivan would bring his CBS-TV variety program to Chicago to mark the occasion.

The Big Shew never did arrive in town in '67 or future years, but that didn't dim the enthusiasm for Chicago's own version of the ol' Brooklyn Dodgers. These were the "Boys of Summer" for a multitude of kids: Banks, Santo, Williams, Kessinger, Beckert, Hundley, Jenkins, Hands, and Holtzman. The best team that never won the pennant.

In 1971, I forged a note, trying to match my mother's handwriting, to cut classes at Mather High School to attend my first Cubs opener at Wrigley Field. Great game, Jenkins vs. Gibson, Cubs beat the Cards 2-1 in 10 innings on a Billy Williams' homer, the glorious result and one-hour, 59-minute gametime reviving the numbness of 10 frozen fingers in the 39-degree cold. School disciplinarians never caught me. I pulled it off again in 1973. In 2000 I had planned to attend my 30th straight Cubs opener.

Back in the first Nixon administration, sportswriters Jerry Holtzman, Jim Enright, Ray Sons, and others kept predicting the Cubs would win the NL East. They'd always make some good early progress toward that prediction, yet invariably something bad would happen in June or September. It didn't matter when, but it kept happening.

All the while, reading all the sportswriters and columnists, I started to pick up stuff about the game. There was a common analysis that a conservative, low-key Cubs bossman named John Holland was slow to rebuild the Cubs, that he kept the core nucleus together even as the players grew dangerously old, which by early 1970s standards was 32 or 33. I started noticing how the game's best minds said the Cubs were too one-dimensional, relying on power to win in Wrigley Field while the game's successful franchises were integrating speed into their lineups. And I started to hear talk about how maybe a few night games at Wrigley Field might keep the team a little fresher through the dog days of summer.

The nuances of strategy were next. The basic lefty-vs.-lefty match-ups, things like that. "You've got to lose honestly," a cigar-chomping bleacher character told me one day.

That philosophy didn't apply one August afternoon in 1976. The Cubs had somehow built up a 10-1 lead on the powerful Big Red Machine. But, true to form against the soft Chicago bullpen, the Reds had shaved the lead to 10-8 with two outs in the ninth, a runner on first, Ken Griffey, Sr., up to bat and Joe Morgan in the on-deck circle. Sidearming righthander Joe Coleman was on the mound for the Cubs, while lefty Darold Knowles heated up in the bullpen.

A crony and I screamed in vain from the right-field bleachers at Cubs manager Jim Marshall. Why didn't he bring in Knowles to face the lefty-swinging Griffey? Who was he saving him for? Morgan? He had to go lefty vs. lefty *now*. You've got to lose honestly. Coleman, huffing and puffing from a long relief outing, stayed in. Griffey smashed a 440-foot drive to the center-field concession stand to tie the game 10-10 while Knowles continued to warm up in the bullpen. Maybe Griffey also would have homered off Knowles, but at least Marshall would have lost honestly, lefty vs. lefty. He lost the game, too, 13-10 in extra innings.

The Question with No Answer

Something strange was in the air, and people verbalized their puzzlement about the Cubs. "Why do the Cubs always lose?" my grandma, Cele Zutz, then 73, who along with Grandpa had seen a bevy of pennants in their younger days, asked me in 1976.

My only response was, "If I had the answer, I'd be the richest man in the world."

I never quite found the answer, but I didn't stop trying to learn the game from the bleachers and grandstands. Any average fan can learn a lot about the game by daily observation, by osmosis. Even my wife, Nina, not a dyed-in-the-wool fan, could see the obvious in a trip out to the ballpark. On one of our first dates in 1980, she saw a Cubs outfield of Larry Biittner in right, Scot Thompson in center, and Bill Buckner in left—a pitcher's defensive nightmare. Biittner stumbled about in pursuit of extra-base hits. "These guys don't look like ballplayers; they look like they work in offices," Nina said.

The notion that writers and fans don't know the game is uttered often by players and baseball executives. I've heard that often since I worked my way out to Wrigley Field for frequent baseball feature and column assignments for various publications by the mid-1980s, turning an avocation into a vocation. I developed that into a full plate of baseball in 1994, starting what developed into a nationally-syndicated weekly baseball radio show called *Diamond Gems*. That same year, I began daily beat coverage of the Cubs at home, spring training, and a few road games for *The Times of Northwest Indiana*.

No matter where you work, or how adeptly you analyze the game, a lot of baseball insiders' logic is that if you haven't strapped on the jock at a high level, preferably professionally, or you haven't worked the front-office inner-sanctum, you don't know the game inside out. The fact you'd watch anywhere from 40 to 90 games a year in person, as a fan, or as a sports journalist, doesn't seem to count in their eyes. Not every professional scout played at a high level, yet their knowledge, gleaned from personal observation at games, is considered vital to any franchise's artistic and financial well-being.

Maybe I don't know the exquisite thrill of gripping Louisville's finest ash while it connects with a 98-MPH heater, or throwing the ball three times in a rundown play (sometimes botching it), or split the fingers wide over a ball and made it dive away from the bat like in the movie *It Happens Every Spring*. No, fate said that those who can, end up playing. Those who can't, try to write about the ones who play. Some of those who can't end up as top baseball executives instead of writers.

I always tried to learn more about the game directly from the players, coaches, and managers. Almost every day, I'd work the locker room, getting to know the Cubs as people, finding out about the little nuances of the game and what motivates them. I'd take the extra time compared to the cut-and-run journalists or others, particularly the blow-dried TV types and sports-talk show hosts who never worked the locker room. Much of the time was just casual conversation, not formal note-taking and tape recording for print stories or my radio show. In the majority of cases players appreciated that. Just a few others seemed perturbed about my presence.

What the players, managers, and honchos often lack is a sense of history. And that's particularly critical with the Cubs. Their history is not only chock full of management mistakes, but also misunderstandings about Wrigley Field, the playing environment in and around the ballpark, and the factors that have been proven to work in helping and that could help the Cubs halt their endless journey between pennants.

A few years back, I'd get into some vocal and funny locker-room debates with Mark Grace over which team was better—the 1969 Cubs or the 1989 Cubs, the latter of which Grace served as a second-year first baseman. I maintained the overall talent level of the '69ers was better, with three Hall-of-Famers in Banks, Billy Williams, and Fergie Jenkins and a third baseman who has been jobbed out of enshrinement in Cooperstown, Ron Santo. Grace retorted that that '89 Cubs finished first and featured two Hall of Fame-bound players of their own, Andre Dawson and Ryne Sandberg. Grace realized quickly, though, that any published putdowns of the '69 Cubs would get him run out of town.

Actually, a lesson can be learned from the 1984 Cubs. The first Cubs team to top their division since 1945 led the league in runs scored. Six players had at least 80 RBI. The two top hitters in the lineup, Bob Dernier and Ryne Sandberg, totaled 77 stolen bases, blending speed with the power that followed. Meanwhile, the pitching, ranked in the middle of the pack at season's end, actually had been the best in the NL in the season's second half, cutting the team ERA by one-quarter of a run from June 1 onward. It was as close to a perfect team as has been created in Cubdom since 1945, and fell just three innings short of that long-awaited World Series berth.

In the middle of the 1999 season, then-Cubs manager Jim Riggleman, a true gentleman, proclaimed that a Cubs lineup needed to be stocked with power to win in Wrigley Field. Riggs fell into the 30-year-old trap about home runs being vital in the Friendly Confines.

Another longtime canard about Wrigley Field concerns the outblowing winds supposedly combining with the short fences to always make it tough on pitchers. But statistics have been kept by the Cubs since 1982 showing that the wind actually blows in, on aggregate, two-thirds of the time. Even in the hot months of July and August, the homer-bearing southwest gales were in evidence only a minority of games. That's been a many decades-long trend, with former players who were left-handed hitters stating they had changed their swings to hit to the opposite field and avoid winds that consistently blew in from right field.

Apparently, no one bothered to tell present-day Cubs folks about the wind trends. When a shaky Cubs pitching staff utterly collapsed in

June 1999, Riggleman said one reason was the wind turned around to blow out with the onset of hot weather. Well, sure, the wind will come from the southwest for a few days in a row, but it always turns around.

One of the oldest adages is that those who forget or ignore history are condemned to repeat it. Cubs history is filled with triumph and tragedy, but too many with the power to change the timeline for the better haven't experienced it. Pretending the past doesn't exist is wrong, and helps put the solution to the reigning dilemma in team sports further off into the future. Not emulating the most successful organizations in the game also will hurt the effort to win. Mix all the negative factors in, and you'll understand why the Cubs have defied one million-to-one odds against them avoiding a World Series since 1945.

The blueprint is basic. A productive farm system produces a core of winning-attitude players onto which costly free agents can be added. Speed and power is blended in the lineup. Management seeks out pitchers with control who aren't freaked out by the days when the wind blows out, and actually can take advantage of the more frequent occasions when the wind comes in. Enough depth and team spirit exists to survive the inevitable injuries to some key performers. An aggressive management is outgoing in collective personality, trying to verbalize a championship atmosphere and putting its money where its mouth is by sometimes taking financial gambles on player contracts that could backfire. It's all supported by an ownership that allows baseball people to make the baseball decisions without constant interference or second-guessing.

Why this blueprint has rarely been duplicated in more than a half-century, and how close the Cubs actually are to following it as the 21st century commences, is the essence of *The Million-to-One Team*. It's a book that shouldn't have been 54 years in the making. The grist for the sequel, on how the Cubs finally made it to a World Series, logically should take a tiny fraction of that short lifetime-period to compile if the right management practices are followed. The folks at Clark and Addison just need to add two-plus-two to equal four, as their friends in New York, Atlanta, and a few other less deserving towns annually do.

A Lifetime without a Pennant?

One of the great characters I met in the right-field bleachers in the summer of 1974 was Caleb "Chet" Chestnut.

Chet Chestnut was a blustering, husky white-haired African-American, always making proclamations about baseball and cackling when the Reds or another visitor tattooed Tom Dettore, Oscar Zamora, or some other hapless Cubs hurler. Mississippi-born Chet, pushing 80 by the mid-1970s, apparently had moved north to work construction in Chicago around World War I. He walked with a limp; his right foot was artificial. The original limb was lost to a construction accident. "My foot's gone to heaven," Chet said. He also was a longtime baseball fan, and enthralled us Baby Boomers with stories of life in and out of the ballpark 'way back when. To the best of his recollection, Chet began attending games at Wrigley Field in 1919. He claimed he was in attendance when Babe Ruth gestured at the 1932 World Series, giving rise to the legend of the Bambino's "called shot" homer against the Cubs' Charlie Root.

Chet got irritated by our rationalizing about the Cubs. "If" Bonham develops, "if" Harris can learn to hit rankled him. "'If' is not a word," he said, setting it in stone. We kept paying our way in as Cubs management raised bleacher ticket prices from $1.25 to $1.50 while the players got paid well and the team didn't improve. "Fans are the biggest fools in the world," proclaimed Chet. "They [players] deserve more than they used to make, but now it's too much. The average man can't afford to come to the park."

Then Chet kicked hope out of its front-and-center perch at Wrigley Field. "P.K. Wrigley doesn't know a thing about baseball, and the son [Bill Wrigley] is worse than the father," he'd bellow. He'd explain why the gum magnate hung on to the team despite his apparent disinterest in the game: "P.K. Wrigley made a promise to his daddy on his deathbed that he'd never sell the team." Perhaps Wrigley himself overheard Chet as he passed by in the back row. The owner reputedly paid his own way occasionally into the bleachers dressed in plain clothes, looking like any other senior-citizen fan, his desire for anonymity fulfilled, his trademark shyness not overwhelmed by a torrent of media and eager-to-please Cubs employees.

One day Chet produced the ultimate putdown for the ever-optimistic Cubs fan. He turned to me and said, "The Cubs will never win a pennant in your lifetime." This brash prediction demanded I disrespect my elder. I waved at Chet and told him he was full of it. I was 19. I had a ton of lifetime left. And surely, as bad as the Cubs played in '74, as bad as they were run, some Cubs team of the foreseeable future would coalesce into a contender and make the World Series. After all, they almost did in the just-concluded Leo Durocher era and could do it again.

Sure, there's lots of time, lots of opportunities. Any team can get lucky in any given year, right?

P.K. Wrigley preceded Caleb "Chet" Chestnut in death by a few weeks in the spring of 1977. He lived long enough to see that the tale about the owner's promise to William Wrigley, Jr., never to sell apparently had been kept. The Cubs were not dealt away until Bill Wrigley, buffeted by $40 million in inheritance taxes, was forced to unload the team to white-knight purchaser Tribune Co. in 1981. And if Chet had rejoined his long-gone foot in the hereafter, he could put forth that familiar cackle as my teens turned into my 20s, then matured into my 30s, and merged into my 40s without a Cubs entrée into the World Series. First-place finishes, to be sure, in 1984 and 1989, but no pennant. A wild-card playoff berth in 1998, but again, post-season elimination short of a Fall Classic invitation.

The Odds That Don't Compute

Somehow, Chet's prediction stayed in the back of my mind all those years, but moved forward a little bit one winter day in 1993. On assignment from *Sport* magazine in Las Vegas, I was to interview Greg Maddux, freshly signed to a $29 million contract with the Atlanta Braves after the Cubs had bungled away several eminently achievable openings to re-sign their young ace of aces. That was yet another seminal event in the Cubs' endless walk in baseball's wilderness. While I waited for Maddux to confirm a time to come over to his home on the west side of Vegas, I wandered through the sports book at Bally's hotel. One idea clicked with another, and I mentally time-tripped back to Chet. Sports books offer odds on practically everything in sports. With the Cubs screwing up royally again, what would the odds be against the Cubs going from 1945 to 1992 without appearing in a World Series?

I finally tracked down John Avello, head of Bally's sports book, and explained the situation. Without hesitation, Avello concocted an outwardly preposterous computation. "It's got to be a million to one," he said. "It would be off the board. That's a long time to go without appearing in a World Series. You'd figure a team would have a lot of chances to make a World Series in 47 years."

Why not present those odds to Maddux, whose departure was one of the big reasons the Cubs staggered about for a half-century while a gaggle of newcomers to the game like the New York Mets win 82 games and still make the World Series. Besides, odds were related to the Maddux family professionally. His father, Dave, was a blackjack dealer at a 'Vegas casino. So I brought my tape recorder to Maddux' house. We talked baseball over pizza in his living room, the whole recrimination over the contract that involved the Cubs, Braves, and New York Yankees. Finally, it was time to leave, and Maddux and a buddy, going out on a Friday night beer run, offered me a ride back to Bally's.

"So what do you think about the odds against the Cubs avoiding a World Series since 1945?" I asked the once and future Cy Young Award winner.

In his deadpan style, Maddux didn't take long to respond. "About 200,000 to 1," he said.

I got back to the hotel, and now Avello's million-to-one shot competed for memory space with Chet's never-in-your-lifetime prediction. Neither sounded logical, but it was happening in real life. The Cubs had a streak of championship failure that seemed to feed on itself, that was self-perpetuating.

The facts were black and white. Of the 16 Major League teams in existence in 1945, only the Cubs had not appeared in a World Series in the intervening decades. Only one other team, the White Sox, had played in as few as one Fall Classic. Of course, the Pale Hose had to play in Chicago, too, giving an appreciative baseball town the ultimate loser's complex and making the odds even more staggering: two teams, one town, one World Series (1959) since 1945. The Detroit Tigers had appeared in just two. The Boston Red Sox, whose fans and media cry over the "Curse of the Bambino" and the lack of a world's championship since 1918, had played in four World Series since '45. At the other extreme were the New York Yankees with 20 through 1997 and the Brooklyn-Los Angeles Dodgers with 15.

I had not been the first ink-stained wretch to wonder about the Cubs' World Series drought odds. In the September 30, 1991 issue of *Sports Illustrated*, Rick Telander had commissioned the Elias Sports Bureau, Major League Baseball's No. 1 statistical service, to compute the odds against the stretch without October baseball since 1945. Elias came up with 130-1 as Telander listed all sorts of woeful odds figures for baseball's post-season also-rans.

The clock moved forward a tad to 1994. The Cubs lost their first 12 games at Wrigley Field, requiring Sam Sianis' billy goat to parade about

Wrigley Field to lift the "hex" that now was as much a part of team folklore as the College of Coaches and the smoky link cart. After the ruinous players strike halted the season, mercifully in the Cubs' case, corporate master Tribune Co. decided to overturn the furniture again, one of the constants of their management style since Dallas Green was cashiered in 1987. In came golden-boy president Andy MacPhail, two World Series triumphs in Minnesota close behind in his rear-view mirror. MacPhail now possessed more power to end the walk in the wilderness than anyone running the Cubs since Phil Wrigley himself. He had the support of top corporate management and vowed that player payrolls, sometimes pinched by Tribune Co. under the stewardships of general managers Jim Frey and Larry Himes, would not be an issue under his administration.

I did not mention the million-to-one angle in my first lengthy interview in the winter of 1994-95 with MacPhail, a cerebral, thoughtful, and deliberate man. But he already had picked up on the crazy-quilt trend he had inherited.

"The perception of the Cubs would have been a lot better had they gone further, to the World Series, in 1984. Same as in 1989," he said of the two NL East divisional titles that still fell short of the Fall Classic.

The perception didn't improve in 1995, 1996, and 1997 as a moribund Cubs farm system failed to produce a homegrown core of talent, while MacPhail and Ed Lynch, his general manager, refused to throw around $6 million contracts on premium free agents. Taking the middle-ground in an attempt to stay competitive—"patching," in MacPhail's own words—with a lot of second-tier free agents and middle-level veterans acquired in trades only condemned the Cubs to .500, or sometimes a lot worse. The Cubs lost 14 of their last 16 in 1996 to finish 10 under .500 for the season. They topped that slump by starting out a record 0-14 in 1997, fulfilling a lot of negative talk in spring training about the rigors of starting the season on the road against the powerful Atlanta Braves and Florida Marlins.

After the embarrassing 68-94 finish of 1997, year No. 52 without a World Series and a full dozen years longer than Moses wandered in Sinai, I expanded on the million-to-one concept. Casting about for an interesting off-season story, I pitched David Campbell, sports editor of *The Times of Northwest Indiana*, for whom I covered the Cubs since

1994, on computing the odds against Chicago teams avoiding championships. The package of stories still centered on the Cubs, though.

I asked Dan Troy, a mathematics professor at Purdue-Calumet University, to figure out the laws of probability regarding the Cubs. Ditto with STATS, Inc., the Morton Grove, Illinois-based sports and statistical service employed by Major League Baseball. And I made another call to Avello at Bally's in Las Vegas.

Coming up with 99-1 odds against the Cubs avoiding a World Series since 1945, Troy employed the concept of "binomal distribution," defined as "the number of times I should have success in a group of independent trials, given that I should have a certain probability of success on each trial. Like how many times should I have heads come up if I flip a coin 500 times." Troy added that any team should play in a World Series at least once every 12 years, with both leagues having averaged 12 teams in operation annually through 1997.

STATS, Inc., whirled its computers to come up with 206-1, based on the laws of probability along with the number of teams in each sport in each season as the factors used in the numbers.

Avello repeated the million-to-one analysis based on a bit of mental time-travel.

"If I was bookmaking back in 1945, and if you said the Cubs would not make the World Series through 1997, I could not make the number high enough for you," he said. Avello would not have taken such a bet.

Two other sets of odds were computed in 1999 by Cubs historian Ed Hartig, who contributes to the team's monthly newspaper, *Vine Line*. One is 219-1, while the other is 221-1. Hartig, who likes to fool around with mathematical formulas, explains it this way:

"The first way is more mathematical," he said. "Start with 1946 when there were eight National League clubs. The chance of not making it is 7/8, then multiply that by number of years there were eight teams. Then it became 9/10 when the league expanded to 10 teams. That goes from 1962 to 1968. It was 11/12 from 1969 to 1992 following another expansion. Then 13/14, and 15/16 after more expansions. Through it all, you leave out 1994, because the World Series was canceled due to the strike.

"By purely mathematical odds, you'd have expected the Cubs to be in World Series five times total since 1945, purely assuming equal probability."

"The second method is calculating 574 seasons in NL since 1946. Give the Cubs 53 sheets of paper, along with all other teams, leaving out 1994 again. Throw 'em in a hat, mix it up, and never end up picking the Cubs."

Hartig throws in an important caveat in Formula No. 1: the practical odds in many years would have been far higher, given the dreadful quality of the Cubs' roster. "In most years in the 1950s and early and mid-1960s, it would have been 50-1 against making the World Series," he said.

To be sure, safety-first, sometimes eccentric management under both the Wrigley family and Tribune Co. ownerships, centering around talent misevaluation at the big-league level, the lack of consistent scouting and player development, and too much front-office regime upheaval under Tribune Co., accounts for the bulk of the Cubs' problems. But some logical entry points to a World Series through the decades, in which the Cubs assembled competitive teams and had some good momentum going toward the Promised Land, also have contributed greatly to the million-to-one concept.

Most dramatic was 1984, when the Cubs, man for man the best team in the NL and the best Chicago franchise since 1945, went into the seventh inning of the final Game 5 of the National League Championship Series with a 3-0 lead against the San Diego Padres. Leon "Bull" Durham's error on a Tim Flannery grounder that opened the floodgates for the Padres' winning rally in the 6-3 victory is one of the single most infamous events in Cubs annals. But consider that the Cubs took a two-games-to-nothing lead in that series, needing just one win in three games in San Diego to wrap it up.

Both math professor Troy and STATS, Inc., computed the odds at 7-1 against a Padres comeback from that 2-0 hole. Avello said he would have made the Cubs a 3 1/2-1 or 4-1 favorite to win the NLCS after winning the first two games at Wrigley Field. The odds don't seem staggering when measured against the fact that a handful of teams in the past three decades, the latest being the Red Sox against the Cleveland Indians in 1999, have come back from two games down in a five-game series. Still, the wild comeback came at the Cubs' expense, just when the sun, moon and stars were aligned properly for the expected rock 'em, sock 'em World Series matchup against the powerful Tigers.

"Nineteen eight-four was our chance," said Steve Friedman, executive producer of CBS-TV's new morning extravaganza, *The Early Show*, which stars fellow Cubs fan Bryant Gumbel. Friedman lived through a lot of lean years in the 1950s and 1960s, watching the Cubs in the right-field bleachers with future author and screenwriter Barry Gifford. "Twice in 15 years, San Diego was the worst team to make it to the World Series. I really feel that was our chance. Things were going our way."

Just as painful to the majority of Cubs fans middle-aged and over is the foldup of 1969, which more properly should be classified as a once-in-a-generation stretch run by the Miracle Mets. Amid all the recriminations over Leo Durocher's mishandling of the Cubs' regulars and pitching staff, the fact remains that the Mets, winners of just 73 games in 1968, were rated 100-1 longshots to make the World Series going into the '69 season.

Loaded with great young pitching led by Tom Seaver, Nolan Ryan, and Jerry Koosman, but with a somewhat mediocre lineup, the Mets should have made a logical improvement to, say, 86 or 87 wins, maybe 90 at the outside. Even with their September fade, the Cubs would have survived as NL East titlists with their 92 victories and probably beaten the Braves, a team they had dominated in the regular season, in the NLCS. But the Mets picked 1969 to improve to 100 wins, totally overwhelming the Cubs down the stretch. New York never even came close to its feat in future years, never winning more than 86 games with the Seaver-led cast.

The Cubs' and Mets' fortunes dovetailed again in 1973. Most of the core of the '69 Cubs were still in the lineup as Chicago broke out to a 46-31 record, eight games ahead in the NL East at the end of June. Inexplicably, the Cubs then got old all at once, a team hitting slump the major component in a 10-33 downslide that dropped the team to 56-64, in fifth in mid-August. The Mets, dragging their feat in the cellar most of the season, rallied with a 22-9 finish at the end to sport an 82-79 record, a record-low winning percentage for a first-place team. Lo and behold, the Mets upset the Cincinnati Reds in the NLCS and actually took a 3-games-to-2 lead in the World Series before succumbing to the Oakland Athletics.

Dan Troy's odds on the 46-31 Cubs not winning at least 83 games in '73: 999-1.

Another mega-collapse took place in 1977. The Cubs again were eight games up in first place at the end of June, this time with a sparkling 47-22 record. "You can kiss the .500 mark good-bye this season,"

Cubs radio color announcer Lou Boudreau said in exultation on the air at the time.

I asked then-Cubs manager Jim Riggleman in the middle of the 1999 season what he would expect a team's record to be in mid-August if it had been 25 games over .500 on June 29. "Forty games over .500," Riggleman said with cold logic, which unfortunately doesn't apply to the blue-pinstriped brigade. Cubs GM Lynch, who had grown up in New York and Miami and whose family were longtime Brooklyn Dodgers fans, said he had been unaware the Cubs had been that far above break-even at any point in '77.

But the Cubs pulled it off, all right. In spite of injuries to Bruce Sutter and other key players, the Cubs still should not have collapsed all the way to an 81-81 record at season's end, making a mockery of Boudreau's prediction. To end up at break-even, the Cubs still had to lose their final five games in a row. Dan Troy's odds of the Cubs not finishing with a winning record after reaching 47-22: two billion-to-one.

The '73 and '77 mid-season collapses were only the most outstanding examples of a strange series of monstrous mid-summer or September nosedives that had afflicted the Cubs since 1955. If the team wasn't fated to win the pennant, at least the boys in blue could have finished with an above-.500 season. In many years they were on pace to comfortably end up on the positive side of the won-lost ledger. But the hot-weather and post-Labor Day collapses ruined these ambitions in 1978, 1979, 1985, 1987, 1988, and 1991, 1992, and 1996. The mother of all collapses, of course, took place in 1999, when a 32-23 record on June 9 pulled a 180-degree turn to a 67-95 season finish, featuring a 10-40 July-through-September death march that dwarfed all other collapses. As a result of all these collapses, the Cubs have sported just 13 seasons above .500 since 1945.

I did not obtain odds on three other years: the NL wild-card team of 1998, the 1989 NL East champions, and the 1970 second-place finishers. The latter team featured another abrupt change-of-fortune: a 35-25 first-place record in June melted away in two weeks due to a 12-game losing streak. The Cubs were unable to get a full head of steam going the rest of the season as the Pittsburgh Pirates won the NL East with an 89-73 record, an achievable mark for Chicago "if"—sorry, Chet—not for the June swoon.

When I approached GM Lynch with the series of odds-defying collapses, he said the repeated failures were the independent events with just one possible connection: the energy-draining effect of all-day base-ball schedule at Wrigley Field prior to the 1988 installation of lights. But even then, how do you explain the 20-games-above.500 improved performance, particularly the pitching staff, in the second half of the 96-win '84 Cubs? Or fine second halves in seasons like 1968, 1972, and 1982?

Maybe the explanation is simply an extreme form of snake eyes of the type you'd see in Avello's casino. Jack Brickhouse himself once ver-balized the worst fear: "The Cubs are the most unlucky team in sports." And both Avello and Troy concede that there are rare instances when your unlucky number keeps coming up.

"The [Cubs' pennant-less] streak could go another 50 years," Avello theorized. "It's very possible to coin-flip 50 tails in a row. Tails could come up for another 20. Things happen. The question is: Do they hap-pen for a reason?"

"You can have rare events, and one will continue to happen," Troy said. "I would tell any of my classes that these results are unusual."

"A phenomenon," is what Pirates coach Lloyd McClendon, a Cubs fan growing up in Gary, Indiana before he played left field for the '89 NL East champs, called the endless journey through also-ran status. He is among a prominent group of baseball types—including Hall-of-Famer Billy Williams and all-time Cub Mark Grace—who agree with the million-to-one analysis. Williams, in fact, looks at his fingers and wonders where the couple of World Series rings went.

If a futurist had gone to Phil Cavarretta, Most Valuable Player of the NL in 1945 for the league champion Cubs, and projected ahead to a barren half-century, he would have not been quoted odds, as Avello would have done. He simply would have been waved away as a crackpot.

"That's a lot of years," Cavarretta, now 83, said. "It's not only hard to believe, but it's sad. I'm disappointed."

A member, like Williams and Grace, of the Cubs' All-Century team, ol' Philabuck watches the Cubs daily on cable TV at his retirement abode in Villa Rica, Georgia, south of Atlanta, and remains puzzled. He played for the Cubs for 20 seasons, longer than anyone else in the 20th century, and he still doesn't have the answers.

"I liked that 1969 club," Cavarretta said. "They should have won at least one [pennant]."

The Cubs' long, strange trip sounds like science fiction or fantasy.

Sure enough, the epic pennant drought has become fodder for Hollywood producers and scriptwriters.

Centuries between Pennants?

A Cubs' dynasty of the mid-21st century was envisioned in the 1995 Fox space opera *Space:Above and Beyond*. U.S. Marine Paul Wang, played by Joel de la Fuente (whose brother Benjie is an ace media-relations official for the present-day Cubs), receives a book from his parents and a clump of Wrigley Field sod while fighting hostile aliens way out there. The book is entitled *Back to Back to Back*, chronicling three consecutive World Series winners.

"The frequent references to the Cubs [and other sports teams] on *Space:Above and Beyond* stemmed mainly from the creative minds and dispositions of the show's creators, Glen Morgan and James Wong," said Joel de la Fuente, who grew up a Cubs fan. "Natives of San Diego, they were hardcore Padres and Chargers fans. Can you imagine how hard it was to swallow, hearing about the 1984 NLCS from your bosses?

"The character of Paul Wang was not developed in the pilot episode. They wanted to build his character off of the actor who played him. After many a sports conversation during the pilot shoot, Wang began having more and more sports references in his vocabulary as the season progressed. There is another Cubs moment, when Wang tries to run after a squad of enemy Chigs [the hostile aliens] after they yell, 'Cubs suck.'"

De la Fuente wasn't the only Chicago expatriate involved in the episode "Dear Earth" that contained the dynastic Cubs references. Windy City emigres stock Hollywood's creative ranks from top to bottom.

"In addition to Hollywood's general sense of kinship with tough-luck and hard work and Glen and Jim's sports-loving nature, 'Dear Earth' was written by a Chicago native, Richard Whitley," de la Fuente said. "There are many Chicago natives in Hollywood—a huge reason for the popularity of the Cubs' out West. I believe it was Richard who took great glee in creating a Cubs' dynasty in the future [and giving Wang a piece of Wrigley Field sod]. Also, the props master of *Space* was a man named Jimmy Wagner, a Chicago native and *huge* Chicago sports fan. It was he who designed the book cover: *Back to Back to Back*.

If the Cubs don't win until around 2065, most of us won't be around to see it. In another video timeline, our great, great grandchildren will be the lucky ones. The 1993 syndicated sci-fi show *TimeTrax* featured Dale Midkiff playing a late-22nd century cop, Darien Lambert, who went back exactly two centuries to catch bad guys who used a time machine to escape justice. One of the storylines was a "vintage" Cubs hat Midkiff's character wore. It was from 2145, the year the Cubs had finally won a pennant. The team had gone a cool 200 years since Cavvy's 1945 club without winning, according to the script.

In yet another bit of celluloid speculating about the Cubs, we have a chance to witness glory in our lifetimes. Michael J. Fox stares at a 2015 video message board in the 1989 movie *Back to the Future II*. It advertises a Cubs' World Series.

Meanwhile, the literary world has an interesting reference to the Cubs' winning—at the end of time. W.P. Kinsella, author of *Shoeless Joe* and the inspiration for the movie *Field of Dreams*, penned a short story in 1984 entitled *The Last Pennant Before Armageddon*. Kinsella's plot: A Cubs manager, with his team about to play the Dodgers in the NLCS, experiences a series of dreams in which deceased Cubs fans appeal to God to allow the Cubs to win the pennant. After a number of appeals, God finally announces the Cubs will indeed capture the pennant—right before time's end game, Armageddon, commences. The Cubs find themselves playing Game 5 (at the time of the Kinsella work the final game of the NLCS) as American and Soviet forces prepare to clash over the latter's occupation of Sri Lanka.

The sci-fi angle even invades the daily byplay of life on the baseball beat.

I had authored three books, on Harry Caray, Sammy Sosa, and the Cubs-Cardinals rivalry, that had been published within an 10-month span in 1998 and 1999. Cubs GM Lynch was interviewed in all three works. An avid reader who was capable of an extremely cutting wit, Lynch, sitting in the dugout, remarked one day in '99 that I was "writing more books than Isaac Asimov."

Delighted to be named in the same breath with one of the most prominent sci-fi authors of all time, I aimed a return zinger at Lynch, a tactic deemed fair in the bench-jockeying baseball world. "You must be a fan of science fiction. Then you also must believe the Cubs are going to win a pennant." Lynch grinned slightly and nodded his reluctant approval of the comeback; baseball etiquette says it's fair game to get somebody back verbally, even if he's 6-foot-6 and once threw a spectacular brushback pitch at Keith Moreland that precipitated a famous Wrigley Field brawl.

No matter in which medium the tale of the Cubs' defiance of odds and the calendar is told, if the million-to-one streak continues well into the new millennium, time will indeed play a factor in the team's loyalists' patronage of hope, still entrenched front-row and center at Wrigley Field. That emotion can't outlast the ravages of old age. The fans will simply not be able to outlive the streak if dramatic action isn't taken by management or the Cubs' best crop of young homegrown kids since the mid-1980s doesn't develop into productive big leaguers.

A precious few are prepared to become modern-day Methuselahs.

"My sentiment is I will not die until the Cubs are in the World Series," CBS morning-show honcho Friedman, 54, said. "I won't die. The Cubs are keeping me alive."

But most others can't dodge the Grim Reaper's calling. It doesn't wait for Cubs pennants. Right-field bleacher fan Marvin Rich kept taking October vacations every year, hoping he'd watch the Cubs play in a World Series. Thwarted, he lazed on a Florida beach instead. Rich died early in the 1989 season, having seen only that one half-pennant (1984) after 46 years of sitting in the same bleacher seat. Fate couldn't even oblige to let Marvin live to see the second half-pennant later in '89.

My grandmother, Cele Zutz, witnessed the pennant in 1945. She did not live to see another flag. She died at 83 in 1986, never having her question answered about why the Cubs don't win.

The literal lifetime, and perhaps beyond, of the million-to-one streak was perhaps summed up best by the late *Chicago Sun-Times* sports lyricist, Jack Griffin.

"An entire generation has grown up on Chicago's North Side...and championships are strictly old men's tales or something out of the story books, like maybe the gingerbread house," Griffin wrote in a column.

"Boys have grown to be men, and fought wars, and traveled the world to come home to raise families, and paid off half the mortgage, and never in all that time dared the impossible dream.

"Children have sat at the knees of their grandfather and listened to him tell of the time the Cubs were in the World Series. And they have marked it off to just another fantasy by the old gaffer, like the depth of the snowfall in the year of the great blizzard."

Griffin composed the ode to the ever-loyal in the August 31, 1969, *Chicago Sun-Times*.

The 24-year gap since the last pennant seemed an eternity then. That has since been doubled, and then some.

And now the task of breaking the million-to-one streak is more difficult. For the first 23 years, the Cubs had to beat out the entire NL to gain entrée into the World Series. Then, for the next 27 years, excepting 1994, they had to survive first a five-game, then a seven-game, NLCS. Now they have to plow through the minefield of a second-round of playoffs, the Division Series, in the age of the wild card. A team can be all dressed up and ready to go, like in 1984, and find its dreams dashed in a short series against an inferior foe. All kinds of powerful teams, rated the best in baseball during the regular season, have crashed on the rocks of the division and league championship series throughout the 1990s.

Somehow, someway, the management team running the Cubs has to answer the moral imperative to make the team as strong and efficient as the Yankees or Atlanta Braves. Neither team has significantly more financial resources than the Cubs. Neither team has fans who care as much, or whose patience has been tested more, or who have been taken for granted more.

Listen to the voice from Cubs' World Series past, not only the last one in 1945, but also 1935 and 1938. He's the last living link to the era of greatness, and he feels the pain. As the millennium turned, time was in its own footrace with his own desire to witness pomp, ceremony, and the traditional bunting.

"The fans in Chicago are the best," Phil Cavarretta said. "They deserve a winner. They lose, and lose, and ballpark is still packed."

It will take a lot of money, any way you cut it, spent both at the major-league and player-development levels. But returning the Cubs to the World Series also will require a goodly amount of passion, mounted on a not-inconsiderable base of ego, by the men with the power. They possess the blueprints to win, and also the warning guideposts on how not to fall again into all the million-to-one traps. Whether they're willing to study the past and take resolute action in the present in order to map the future and win prior to the 21st and 22nd century cinematic lifetimes of Paul Wang and Darien Lambert seemingly is on a par with "What's the meaning of life?"

Chapter 1

WHEN IT STARTED OUT ONLY TWO-TO-ONE

REVERSE THE clock seven years from 1945. For Cubs fans, the concept of decades of prolonged losing seemed to be more fantastic that Orson Welles "War of the Worlds" radio shocker that panicked thousands of Americans on Halloween, 1938, a few weeks after the Yankees swept the Cubs four straight in the World Series.

That year, the Cubs kept on their pennant-every-three-years schedule with the near-miracle September rally over the Pittsburgh Pirates, sparked by Gabby Hartnett's "homer in the gloamin'" on September 28 at Wrigley Field. By now the Cubs could win on their winning tradition, built lovingly and with an open checkbook a decade earlier. Then, the dynamic management tandem of owner William Wrigley, Jr., and team president William Veeck, Sr., had assembled what Cubs shortstop Woody English later called "The Yankees of the National League."

Starting in the mid-1920s, Wrigley—who had become majority Cubs owner in 1921—and Veeck began adding on to a small talent nucleus of catcher Gabby Hartnett and first baseman Charlie Grimm. Hiring manager Joe McCarthy to pilot the Cubs, the team honchos quickly acquired the game's best outfield: left fielder Riggs Stephenson, center fielder Hack Wilson, and right fielder Kiki Cuyler. English came up, only 20, to take over shortstop in 1927. A reliable starting rotation headed by Charlie Root was established by 1928. The crowning touch was Wrigley's appropriation of a then-stupendous $200,000, paid to the Boston Braves as part of a blockbuster six-player trade to acquire Rogers Hornsby, the NL's best hitter, before the 1929 season.

The Cubs now boasted star power at almost every position, and Wrigley gloried in every moment. He loved his status as a successful owner and allowed no barrier, financial or otherwise, to stand in the way of building a winner. He spoke of his passion and love of baseball and the

1

Cubs in particular. "No man is qualified to make a genuine success of owning a big-league ball team who isn't in it for his love for the game," he said. Wrigley was dynamic and outgoing, in contrast to his introverted son, Philip, who took over the presidency of the Wrigley Gum Co. in the mid-1920s. The elder Wrigley was the classic, old-fashioned definition of a "sportsman," the upfront symbol of his franchise.

Fans within streetcar or L train commuting distance of the newly-expanded Wrigley Field—the upper deck had been added just before the inflow of talent—responded as never before. A big-league record 1,485,166 flocked to Clark and Addison in 1929 to watch the power-laden Cubs carve up the NL on their way to a World Series date with Connie Mack's Philadelphia Athletics. The only downer was the Athletics' upset of the Cubs in the Fall Classic amid Hack Wilson's infamous misplay of a flyball and A's pitcher Howard Ehmke's heroics.

But the first warning bell for the future sounded January 26, 1932 when Wrigley died at 70 in Phoenix. The ballclub was passed on to Philip K. Wrigley, but with Veeck running day-to-day operations, the momentum continued with another pennant in 1932. The Cubs still kept the flow of good talent coming with the new double-play combo of second baseman Billy Herman and shortstop Billy Jurges, third baseman Stan Hack, first baseman-outfielder Phil Cavarretta, and others. Jack Doyle, along with longtime Cubs functionary Clarence "Pants" Rowland, headed the team's scouting efforts.

"Jack Doyle was a great scout," Cavarretta recalled. "He brought up Jurges, Herman, Galan, and Demaree. We used to call him the 'Million Dollar Scout.'"

The Big Ones Get Away

But the forward momentum of the Cubs began to grind to a halt. William Veeck, Sr., died after the 1933 season. Suddenly, Philip K. Wrigley had to put his own stamp on the Cubs.

A lifetime of bad decisions on talent had begun. And the first one was a whopper. A story long in circulation stated that in 1935, the Cubs had the first crack at a talented but gimpy outfielder with the San Francisco Seals of the Pacific Coast League. His name was Joe DiMaggio.

"Joe had an extremely bad knee," Cavarretta recalled. "At times he could hardly walk. I think that was one of the reasons the Cubs backed off on him. Joe always wore a [knee] brace. Also, I think Joe didn't want to come to Chicago."

Obviously, the New York Yankees weren't scared off by DiMaggio's knee. They plucked him out of the Bay Area, dressed him in pinstripes for the 1936 season and the rest is history.

Much closer to home, another talented young player had an overriding urge to play for his favorite team. Multi-sport star Lou Boudreau, out of the south Chicago suburb of Harvey, dreamed of playing for the Cubs. A leader of the famed "Flying Clouds" state basketball champions at Thornton High School, Boudreau had a chance to play both basketball and baseball at the University of Illinois.

He discussed that opportunity and his goal of signing with the Cubs with Charlie Grimm. The manager suggested Boudreau get his college education, with the Cubs committing to sign him in a few years. Boudreau took the advice—and a Cleveland Indians scout came to Champaign-Urbana in 1937 with an offer Boudreau couldn't refuse.

By 1939, Boudreau had started his Hall-of-Fame shortstop career in Cleveland while the Cubs began 15 years of instability at the position until Ernie Banks' arrival. Boudreau would not work for the Cubs again until a too-short tenure as manager in 1960 that preceded the infamous "College of Coaches" fiasco. He had actually traded jobs with Grimm, coming down from the WGN-Radio broadcast booth to manage while Grimm went upstairs to work the mikes as baseball color analyst.

Could the Cubs have missed out on two great shortstops in a row? Another story circulated, later denied by Pants Rowland, that in 1939 the Cubs had a chance to select one of two young shortstops out of the St. Louis Cardinals' organization—Marty Marion for $25,000 or Bobby Sturgeon for $35,000. The Cubs took Sturgeon. Marion, of course, went on to a stellar career with four St. Louis pennant winners in the 1940s while Sturgeon was part of an overhyped group of Cubs kids who largely flopped in the same decade.

"Sturgeon and [fellow middle infielder] Lou Stringer came highly recommended," Cavarretta said. "They thought they'd be better than Herman and Jurges. No way."

Phil Wrigley himself ignored the warnings of most sane minds in the game when, emulating his father's strategy with Rogers Hornsby, he paid $185,000 to the Cardinals in a huge deal to snare sore-armed ace pitcher Dizzy Dean just before the 1938 season. Dean had injured his arm after coming back too quickly from a broken toe, suffered in the 1937 All-Star Game. In spring training 1938, almost everyone who watched Dean pitch in Florida said he had lost his best fastball. But Wrigley plowed ahead, figuring Dean would recover. He never did, although he did contribute in a limited role in 1938-39, pitching on guile and control.

By the end of the 1930s, after a four-game World Sweep at the hands of the Yankees in 1938, the Cubs were stuck in full reverse. The decade's mainstays began to be traded off one by one. At that time, both Cavarretta and Boudreau both said they noticed the dropoff in quality of incoming talent. Cardinals' Mahatma Branch Rickey set up the game's first extensive farm system, putting 600 minor-league players under contract by 1940 while the Cubs had just 34. Phil Wrigley's lieutenants continued a longtime practice of purchasing players from independent minor-league teams rather than developing them in an organized Cubs style. Rickey soon moved to the Dodgers and duplicated his farm-system success, and the Yankees also built up their minor-league teams.

"The Dodgers could have fielded four teams with the players they had," former Cubs pitcher Warren Hacker said. "We continued buying players from independent clubs."

"The farm systems started by the Dodgers, Cardinals, and Yankees enabled those teams to get a leg up on everyone else," former Cubs shortstop Roy Smalley said. "It was very difficult for anyone else to do as good of a job. It sort of fed on itself. A lot of kids wanted to play for those clubs. Look at me—I almost signed with Brooklyn."

"In 1949, we had 500 to 600 players under contract," former Dodger Paul Minner, a lefthander who enjoyed some success with the Cubs in the early 1950s. "In spring training, we didn't have names, we had numbers. For the first week in camp we did nothing but fundamentals."

Throughout the 1940s, the Cubs were run by general manager Jim Gallagher, a former sportswriter hired by Phil Wrigley, perhaps figuring he'd emulate the success his father had in summoning William Veeck, Sr., also a sports scribe, to run the team.

Gallagher's tenure as GM got off to a bad start on May 6, 1941, when he dealt a still-potent Herman to the Dodgers for two lesser-light players and $65,000. Another legend grew up around this deal: Brooklyn boss Larry MacPhail, grandfather of present-day Cubs president Andy MacPhail and a noted imbiber, tried to get Gallagher drunk, better to wheedle Herman out of his grasp.

While Gallagher supposedly was getting tipsy, Larry MacPhail would excuse himself to go to the bathroom. Each time, he poured the booze down the drain in order to remain sober and heist Herman.

"I guarantee you that's not a true story," said Lee MacPhail, Larry MacPhail's son and Andy MacPhail's father. "And I can prove it by one thing: There's no way my father would ever pour liquor down the drain. It was a great trade for the Dodgers, so I can understand it [the story]."

Cubs brass had to be drunk to make many of the moves they did. Or at least incompetent, which is what Cavarretta thought of the team's scouting staff as the years progressed.

"I think we had good scouts up to about 1942 and 1943," he said.

The good salaries paid to the William Wrigley, Jr.-era Cubs also were a fading memory. Wrigley and Gallagher cut pay scales. Cavarretta, an 11-year veteran in his Most Valuable Player season of 1945, made just $20,000 as one of the better-paid Cubs. Six years later, when he was named player-manager, Cavarretta had risen to just $25,000.

The parsimonious pay continued well into the 1950s under Gallagher's successor Wid Matthews—with a special incentive common for baseball executives then.

"Wid Mathews told me Mr. Wrigley gave him $300,000 to sign all the players," Warren Hacker said of the 1953 payroll. "Wid would keep whatever was left over after he signed them all, so he tried not to spend all $300,000.

"I got $8,500 when I went 15-9 with a 2.58 ERA [second in the NL] in 1952. The next year, they offered me $9,500."

The Cubs delayed the onset of the million-to-one skein by squeezing one more pennant in 1945 out of old standbys Cavarretta and Hack, ably supported by Nicholson, Passeau, and one prime young player, center fielder Andy Pafko. Most of the top Cubs had avoided the wartime draft for various reasons, including injuries or other physical ailments that enabled them to be deferred.

But even this flag would not have been hoisted over Wrigley Field had the Cardinals' Stan Musial not missed the 1945 season due to Navy service, the only World War II season in which Musial was absent. Even without Stan the Man, the Cardinals won 16 of 22 games from the Cubs in '45. The pennant winners survived by cleaning up on the NL's second-division clubs, especially Cincinnati. And Larry MacPhail, now running the New York Yankees, paid back Gallagher for the Billy Herman trade by selling ace starter Hank Borowy for $100,000 in a mid-season waiver deal. The Cubs needed every ounce of production from Borowy's 11-2 record in Chicago the remainder of '45.

Other teams' top players returned in full force in 1946, with the Cardinals returning to their accustomed spot atop the NL. The Cubs finished third. That only delayed the inevitable as the team's veterans began drifting into retirement or part-time roles. By 1947, the Cubs started on the steep, slippery slope downward, this time for good, the neglected player development system hitting full force. In 1948, the Cubs settled into the cellar of the eight-team NL, their image as an incompetent franchise overwhelming whatever good feelings the contenders of the previous decade had left behind.

"It was very discouraging in the late 1940s," Cavarretta said. "We could see it. They [young players] just weren't coming up. Our scouting system was bad. Our instructors weren't doing the job. You didn't have to be an Einstein to look at the players to see the talent wasn't there."

Wrigley finally attempted some changes in 1949, but they only made matters worse. He replaced longtime managerial warhorse Charlie Grimm with former Cardinals Gashouse Gang manager Frankie Frisch, who had been warned by friends against taking the Cubs' job. His Cubs players wish he hadn't.

"He was the worst manager I had ever seen,' said Hacker. "Frisch belittled everyone on the club. He had a $500 fine for talking with opposing players."

Double-teaming the players and fans with woe was Wid Matthews, who had been named the de facto general manager in '49 when Gallagher was moved sideways to business manager.

Brooklyn West

Matthews ended up setting up an auxiliary farm system for the Dodgers from the Cubs' roster.

The former top aide to Branch Rickey in Brooklyn, Matthews figured the abundant Dodgers farm system would supply some of the Cubs' needs, too. But he ended up acquiring a slew of Rickey rejects.

Cavarretta soon became manager, replacing Frisch, but his appointment came too late to stop one of the more horrific deals in Cubs history. Lusting after his old Dodgers players, Matthews dispatched center fielder Pafko, then in his prime and coming off a 36-homer season, on June 15, 1951 for outfielder Gene Hermanski, infielder Eddie Miksis, left-handed pitcher Joe Hatten, and catcher Bruce Edwards. None of the imports were Dodgers regulars. None became significant Cubs contributors as the team continued to wallow in the second division.

"That deal was horseshit," Cavarretta said.

"Matthews believed he could get some of the good players from Mr. Rickey. Instead he got Hermanski, Miksis, Hatten, and Edwards. Hatten had a bad arm. So did Edwards, who had started out as a good catcher. Our scouts should have seen it. Matthews thought these players were great players. It was hard to believe. You make a deal like the Brooklyn deal, you're lost."

"We were the Dodgers' 'B' team," Hacker said.

Actually, Matthews did acquire some legitimate talent from the Dodgers. In 1949, he snared starting pitcher Minner. In another deal, in 1950, Dee Fondy, who capably held down first base through most of the first half of the 50s, came to the Cubs. Another player in the Fondy deal was lanky first baseman Chuck Connors, later of *Rifleman* fame and other TV shows and movies. Later, in 1956, Matthews landed hard-hitting Walt "Moose" Moryn, who produced as a Cub after being stuck behind entrenched stars in the Dodgers' outfield.

If Matthews was a bumbling wheeler-dealer, he was an even worse handler of players. Pitcher Hacker recalls several injuries that Matthews choose to ignore. That signaled a disturbing trend in which Cubs executives and team physicians seemed to soft-pedal, if not look the other way, when their players informed them of maladies.

"I had a bad blister in 1954," he said. "Nowadays, I wouldn't have pitched. But Matthews said you've got to pitch and hold your turn [in the rotation]. I also had a planter's wart on my left foot. It was like stepping on a needle. I took my cleats off my spikes. I couldn't stride. I wanted to have it cut out. But Wid said I'd lose my spot in the rotation if I didn't pitch. They didn't care in those days.

"You played hurt, otherwise you didn't play. It was a whole different era. You didn't pop off to sportswriters."

Hacker, who had a hard, natural sinker, began losing prodigiously. Pressured to win by the front office's attitude, he changed his style and tried to "strike out everybody." That only made matters worse.

Meanwhile, the few promising Cubs coming up through the farm system were mishandled. Most prominent in that predicament was Roy Smalley, Jr.

Famed for his errors, Smalley displayed maddening alter egos on the field in 1950 after being rushed up to start at shortstop two years previously. Smalley slugged 21 homers and drove in 85 runs, but also hit just

.230 while leading the NL in strikeouts. He led the league with 541 assists, while pacing the NL's shortstops with 332 putouts and 115 double plays. But the overriding number was an astounding 51 errors. He gave rise to a legendary ditty that had no relation to "Tinkers to Evers to Chance." This time it was "Miksis to Smalley to Addison Street."

"Maybe this is where more experience in the minors might have helped," Smalley said. "It was inconsistency. I found it hard to maintain the confidence to be productive.

"At least I had a strong enough arm to get it to Addison Street."

All the while, as his production declined, the Cubs had a logical replacement for Smalley in their own farm system. Shortstop Gene Baker was stuck at Triple-A Los Angeles since he signed with the Cubs in 1950. Baker was better than Smalley and the other ex-Dodgers. But he was the Cubs' first African-American signee. Wrigley and Matthews were overcautious in breaking the color line. In hindsight, their refusal to promote Baker until Ernie Banks' signing in September 1953, in effect providing Banks with a road roommate, angered prominent Cubs of the day.

By the early 1950s, the Cubs were in such disarray that an earlier commitment to breaking the color line might not have turned the franchise into a contender, given what was developing into benign neglect at the ownership level by Phil Wrigley and Matthews' bumbling. The team was entrenched as a 90-loss, seventh- or eighth-place team with little pitching and not much power beyond Sauer's "Mayor of Wrigley Field" home-run feats that netted packets of chewing tobacco, tossed onto the warning track from grateful bleacherites. Only a 77-77 season in 1952, sparked by uncommonly good starting pitching, punctuated the losing tedium.

Cavarretta, sensing that his club was on a treadmill to nowhere, candidly informed Phil Wrigley in the spring of 1954 that the Cubs were bottom feeders. Tolerating no dissent in his ranks, Wrigley then cashiered Cavvy after 20 loyal years of service, the only manager until the Toronto Blue Jays' Tim Johnson in 1999 ever to be fired in spring training. Stan Hack took over as manager.

The Cubs couldn't even win a consolation prize for their losing ways. One story had Matthews, always looking at the Dodgers' system for talent, supposedly eyeing a young Puerto Rican outfielder named Roberto Clemente. The Dodgers tried to hide Clemente from the post-season minor-league draft. The team with the NL's worst record would get first dibs at drafting Clemente. The Cubs had wallowed in the cellar most of '54, behind the seventh-place Pirates. But near season's end, Chicago put on a mild spurt and overtook Pittsburgh for seventh. Guess who the Pirates drafted by virtue of their last-place finish?

Another brief uptick took place in the first half of the 1955 season. Banks emerged as a world-class slugger, while an outfielder named Bob Speake had a sensational May. Sam Jones, the Cubs' third African-American player, pitched a no-hitter against the Pirates that included a ninth-inning strikeout of Clemente after Jones had loaded the bases with nobody out. The Cubs actually climbed to second place with a 46-37 record in early July.

But then the first of a long series of startling, almost interminable mid-season collapses that would mark the million-to-one era wrecked the '55 campaign. The Cubs suffered through an Eastern roadtrip to hell, going through a 1-19 stretch to drop to the bottom of the NL standings. Cosmetically, the Cubs seemed a little improved with a final 72-81, fifth-place record, but had really gone nowhere with the exception of Banks' 44 homers, including five grand slams.

The bell was tolling for Wid Matthews despite a revival of the talent flow in the farm system. After the Cubs finished in the NL basement with an all-time worst 60-94 record in 1956, Wrigley uncharacteristically conducted a front-office housecleaning within weeks of the final pitch. Matthews, Hack, and Jim Gallagher were fired.

Taking the places of the cashiered trio was the management team that had guided the Los Angeles Angels to a Pacific Coast League championship—general manager John Holland and manager Bob Scheffing, a former Cubs catcher. The team even changed uniform design, adopting the blue pinstriped style used today.

But, like everything else in the million-to-one era, the fresh faces and new look would only provide a false dawn.

Chapter 2

PHILIP K. WRIGLEY
The Contrarian Man and His Deputies

SOON AFTER HE was first called up by the Cubs in September 1972, young, promising outfielder Pete La Cock strolled down Chicago's Magnificent Mile. Approaching the Chicago River, he noticed the white Wrigley Building and its giant clock, teaming with Tribune Tower as twin sentinels of Chicago's power and wealth at either side of Michigan Avenue.

Always a free spirit, the son of *Hollywood Squares* host Peter Marshall decided to walk into the building and call on the boss. La Cock must have astounded himself when he was admitted to Philip K. Wrigley's private office. Here was the 77-year-old patriarch of the Cubs and the William Wrigley, Jr., gum company meeting with the shaggy-haired, carefree kid who had won the American Association's Triple Crown. How many other jeans-and-T-shirt-clad guys could be admitted to the inner sanctum of such a titan of commerce and industry merely by knocking on the door?

"I walked into the office, I told him I was Pete La Cock, one of the new players in 1972," said La Cock, now co-owner of a youth baseball academy in the Kansas City suburb of Olathe, Kansas. "A minute later, the secretary takes me to his office. I talked to Mr. Wrigley for an hour and half.

"He knew about my dad, Aunt Joanie [actress Joanne Dru] and [singer] Dick Haymes. We sat there and talked, and I asked him why he doesn't come out to the ballpark. He said writers gave him such much grief.

"And then Mr. Wrigley leaned over and lowered his voice, almost in a whisper like he wanted to tell me a secret. He said he got out, dressed pretty causally, paid $1 and sat in the bleachers. He loved to sit in the left-field bleachers. He said he did it often. It cracked me up."

The whispered secret was astounding. Wrigley, famed for his apparent apathy toward baseball, notorious for his absence from Wrigley Field, confessed that he blended in with the crowds, virtually in disguise, to watch his Cubs play. The whole idea was preposterous, but then long-time ballpark business and concessions manager E.R. ("Salty") Saltwell suggested the story had credibility.

"I'd get a phone call, and he'd raise a question about something about the ballpark, and then he'd end the conversation," said Saltwell, now retired and a Park Ridge, Illinois resident. "I got to thinking about how he's aware of it, not being at the ballpark. He had to have known about it through personal observation. I asked him about it, and he would chuckle and say 'I have my ways.' He might have had some spies at the ballpark, but I'm not sure.

"So I approached his chauffeur, and asked him if he ever dropped Mr. Wrigley off at the ballpark. He said not at ballpark, but several blocks away."

Although Wrigley was noted for his absence from Wrigley Field in favor of watching the games on TV—he had missed the 1945 World Series and 1962 All-Star Game—he previously had admitted that he worked his way into the ballpark virtually incognito.

In 1959, Wrigley was quoted in a baseball media guide as insisting that he arrived at Cubs games in the late innings after starting out watching on TV in his office at the Wrigley Building.

"Generally I sit up in the grandstand where the real fans are," he said. "I don't like any special treatment. I haven't sat in the Wrigley box for years—ever since they put in an outlet for an electric blanket. That's when I moved out."

Wrigley was so anonymous that, earlier in the 1930s, an usher tried to bar him from a World Series game. Another time, a vendor, not recognizing Wrigley as the ultimate boss, insisted upon sitting on his lap as he held a pot of coffee.

Imagine the sight of Philip K. Wrigley, sitting in the bleachers in 1969, adorned with sunglasses, floppy hat and casual shoes like any of the hundreds of senior-citizen fans that used to populate the sunny seats. You hope he used sunscreen. He could have watched the famed Left Field Bleacher Bums party, guzzling beer, draining flasks, smoking pot, and ogling the babes. Despite such behavior 180 degrees opposite of his own, at the end of August 1969, Wrigley paid a $9,000 tab to send 50 of the Bums on an all-expenses-paid trip to a Cubs' weekend series in Atlanta.

The secret trips to Wrigley Field alone would have backed up the analysis of Wrigley by Jerome Holtzman, now Major League Baseball's official historian after decades as dean of Chicago baseball writers, that the mogul was a "contrarian." Wrigley was out and about among the fans, soaking up their undying loyalty, no doubt hearing countless pleadings to his spirit to spend some money to boost the Cubs out of their doldrums. If Wrigley truly was out and about, a man of the people in disguise, he would have picked up the thirst, the lust, for winning. But most of his actions in running the Cubs proved it went in one ear and out the other, or somehow got jumbled in the interim. He constantly tried to improve the fans' comfort at Wrigley Field with wider seats and off-season maintenance, but never gave the folks what they so dearly desired—a winner, built upon a consistent baseball organization.

The Cubs' dilemma was simple. Philip K. Wrigley did things contrary to baseball and business norms while often contradicting himself and his beliefs in his actions.

He was not revolutionary or cutting edge. He was simply different, often edging into the wacky category in a sport that usually played it straight and used clowns like Max Patkin for sideshows, not the main act.

"To tell the truth, I don't know what Phil Wrigley is likely to do in a given situation," wrote *Chicago Tribune* columnist Robert Markus on October 1, 1975. "Except that whatever it is it's probably wrong. He may be a great gum man but when it comes to baseball he's made only two sensible decisions in the last 20 years. The first is when he hired Leo Durocher. The second is when he fired him."

Different, But Not Better

Wrigley himself stated his desire to go against the flow when young Cubs media relations director Chuck Shriver visited him in his Wrigley Building office during the off-season of 1967-68.

The Cubs always had produced their media guide, then called a roster book, in a five-by-seven inch booklet-size form. But the National League wanted to standardize all team media guide sizes to five-by-nine, certainly not a radical change. The NL desired to incorporate all the guides into a loose-leaf binder for reporters' convenience.

"We were the only club that didn't conform right away," recalled Shriver, who was the Cubs' media relations chief during the infamous 1969 season and later headed the White Sox media relations department during the 1983 AL West division title season. He now is chief night-shift news copy editor for the Arlington Heights, Illinois-based *Daily Herald*, Illinois' third-largest newspaper.

Both Cubs business manager Bill Heymans and general manager

John Holland passed the buck up to Wrigley. In the meantime, Shriver checked on printing costs, discovering there would be little extra expenditure for the enlarged media guide.

"We went into his corner office overlooking Michigan Avenue," Shriver said. "Mr. Wrigley said, 'What is this, young man? You want to change the shape of the press guide?' He had only one question: 'What's the additional cost?' He looked at the figures I had written down. There was a pause of 10 minutes as he thought about it. Nothing was said.

"Then he spoke: 'Well, you know I don't like to do things that conform to the rest of the league.'"

Wrigley did OK the change, but the fact that he liked to be different, not necessarily better, was the death knell for championship-calibre baseball at Wrigley Field.

More than any other man, Wrigley is the one responsible for the Cubs defying million-to-one odds against avoiding a World Series berth since 1945. He had absolute power to bring the endless seasons of losing to a close with a couple of capital expenditures here, a couple of key hires there, and the reconciliation of his tepid—if that much—interest in baseball twinning with his desire to tinker and meddle to the reality of letting dynamic baseball men run his team.

But the transformation of the Cubs from stumblebums into the proud powerhouses worthy of the stewardship of his father, William Wrigley, Jr., never took place because of the unique, eccentric, and singular personality that Philip K. Wrigley possessed.

The Cubs could never get a head of steam up because of the contrarian nature of Wrigley's personality, expressed in so many different ways:

• He was an intensely private, shy man with admittedly few close friends, without even a guest bedroom at his Phoenix mansion because he believed there was no need for anyone to stay overnight. He would have been repulsed had he entered his ballpark as Philip K. Wrigley, owner, with notebooks being filled, flashbulbs popping, cameras whirring and microphones thrust his way. Yet he was astoundingly accessible for his stature in business and baseball, with La Cock walking in off the street to see him, baseball writers easily reaching him at the office and home in Lake Geneva when he answered his own phone, and Wrigley responding with long written treatises to fan and media criticism.

• He increased the profitability and reach of the William Wrigley, Jr., gum company that his father had first built into prominence. Wrigley held a chokehold on the gum market with lavish expenditures on marketing and advertising, the broadcast gum jingles among the most memorable of all time. But as well-managed as the gum company was, the Cubs were run in Alice In Wonderland style. The team was starved for a decent operating budget while mossified executives, virtually assured of lifetime employment by Wrigley, ignored the blueprints for winning available right under their noses. The team tried the oddball and the unusual, but never did the basic baseball player-acquisition and development processes better than its competitors. The contrast between the gum company's efficiency and profitability, and the Cubs' eternal ineptness was the most striking and makes the least amount of sense, even generations later.

• He kept lights out of Wrigley Field even after planning to introduce night games for the 1942 season; he had donated the steel for the towers to the war effort. All other big-league teams had lights by 1948. The lack of lights helped doom the Cubs to mediocre season attendance counts for much of the 1950s and 1960s, spurring a downward cycle of financial losses that fed on itself when Wrigley insisted the ballclub be self-supporting.

• He believed that one strong man couldn't possibly run an effective business organization, that delegation and specialization was needed. Yet he was executive general manager of the Cubs, with no major player or financial move permitted unless he approved it. His employees were not empowered to act independently or with any ingenuity.

• Wrigley's favorite all-time Cubs player was Ernie Banks, an African-American, and he loved Jose Cardenal, a colorful, Afro-adorned Cuban. Wrigley himself went on record opposing discrimination on his Catalina Island property. But his organization was particularly hard on African-American players who had indiscretions in their personal lives or spoke out about their salaries and playing conditions. They were dispatched in relatively quick order in trades or released. All the while, few Latin players became Cubs on his watch, and scouting in the Caribbean was thin at best.

• But perhaps the biggest contradiction was Wrigley's maintenance of Cubs ownership through all the aggravation and financial losses and brickbats from players, fans, and media, while continually spurning offers to purchase the franchise. It made little sense that self-described hermit Wrigley continued to own the Cubs, his every move subject to public scrutiny unlike the gum company, his burden never lifting as the team continued to lose.

A Deathbed Vow?

The only logical explanation would have been a solemn vow made to William Wrigley, Jr., on his deathbed to keep the Cubs in the family, like a treasured heirloom, maintaining it to fend off the ravages of time, but not fiddling with it or improving it. Phil Wrigley kept the Cubs out of an old-fashioned sense of duty, not out of a passionate urge to restore the near-dynastic status of the 1920s-1930s teams. Ol' Chet Chestnut obviously proclaimed in the bleachers in 1974 what was common knowledge in the 1930s, but whose impact had become blurred with the passage of decades.

On January 26, 1932, the dynamic William Wrigley, Jr., died at age 70 in Phoenix. In his will, the elder Wrigley bequeathed the Cubs directly to his son.

"The club and the park stand as memorials to my father," Phil Wrigley was quoted in 1933 as proclaiming. "I will never dispose of my holdings in the club as long as the chewing-gum business remains profitable enough to retain it."

Decades later, he re-confirmed this position in a conversation with *Chicago Sun-Times* columnist Irv Kupcinet: "I inherited the Cubs from my father and I feel an obligation to carry on in respect to him. But I'll leave the team to my son Bill and he can do whatever he pleases."

Bill Veeck, who had worked as a jack-of-all-trades for Phil Wrigley throughout the 1930's, said in his 1962 book *Veeck: As in Wreck* : "Phil Wrigley assumed the burden out of his sense of loyalty and duty. If he has any particular feeling for baseball, any real liking for it, he has disguised it magnificently."

Phil Wrigley had spent his time running the gum company as president starting in 1925 while his sportsman father busied himself building the Cubs into the National League's strongest franchise. The heir to the family fortune, which had grown to $40 million at the time of William Wrigley, Jr.'s, death, had not been interested in sports. To be sure, he engaged in the passions of the idle rich, such as polo. But displaying his contrarian nature, he enjoyed working with his hands, fixing car engines, watches, and radios. In 1955, Wrigley even fixed the broken-down pitching machine at the Cubs' spring training field in Mesa, Arizona. He said he would have been a garage mechanic had he not been born a blue blood. Phil Wrigley also skipped a privileged education at Yale University after graduating from Phillips Andover Academy prep school. Instead, he traveled to Australia to help build a new chewing gum factory.

In spite of his privileged background, he never grew up to be an old-school, corporate robber-baron or monopolist. In spite of the dominance of the Wrigley Co. in the chewing gum market, he opted not to squeeze out competitors.

"The Wrigley Co. owned some of the chicle forests in South America," said Chuck Shriver. "He could have put the other chewing gum companies out of business because he was selling the raw materials to them. But he chose not to do it.

"Phil Wrigley said that when a pack of chewing gum was a nickel, two cents were for manufacturing, two cents were for marketing and the last penny went into his pocket."

The mogul's accessibility to visitors and callers, combined with some of his attitudes toward business and life, should have made him a hero to Cubs fans. Pete La Cock continued to call on Wrigley in his office as the 1970s proceeded.

"At least once a month, I visited him," La Cock said. "I'd always drop in unannounced. He'd give me gum. We talked about baseball, we talked about how team was playing. We talked about certain players. He'd always asked me how I was doing."

Jack Kuenster, then covering the Cubs for the now late, lamented *Chicago Daily News*, got inside Wrigley's head in a one-on-one interview in his Wrigley Building office in the fall of 1959. The story was published on Wrigley's 65th birthday on December 5, 1959. The against-the-flow Wrigley must have subliminally influenced the placement of the story in the big Saturday weekend edition of the *Daily News*. The piece appeared at the bottom of the TV-radio page.

"I don't know, maybe I'm a socialist," Wrigley told Kuenster, the latter's ears perking up. "But I think the more people we have in the middle class, who own homes and so forth, the better off we'll be.

"They'll take more interest in government, because they'll have more to lose if they don't."

He opened a window to his own contrarian mind with another train of thought about the need to de-centralize authority in business. He described the gum company, but the reality of his Cubs stewardship was just the opposite in which all decisions flowed through him.

"We've got to have experts in taking inventory, packaging, taxation, office machine operation, pension plans, legal problems," Wrigley said.

"If one man tried to take over by himself, he'd flop. You've got to have a team. The most valuable man is the one who doesn't try to run it all by himself.

"My biggest trouble is finding people who say, 'I don't know.'"

Kuenster then wrote that in "looking back on his business career, Wrigley admits he hasn't been a builder." The mogul's quote following up on this statement: "My experience has been to take something and keep it rolling."

Wrigley never ended up building the Cubs, and maybe that wasn't possible given his inherent nature. Having not grown up around the game and with his shy personality, Wrigley was uncomfortable around the gregarious, often coarse, tobacco-chewing-and-spitting baseball people. He didn't know how to mix and blend in, despite his common-man interests. A man who once remarked that he'd like to live in a cave to get away from everyone wasn't going to survive in the backslapping—and backstabbing—world of baseball. Flushed into the spotlight due to the ultimate sense of family obligation, he dutifully kept the Cubs' door open for business, but certainly didn't dive into it with the passion required of an owner who wanted to win more than anything else. Passion and desire are like balls and strikes in the game. They're central to everything.

"You have to understand where Phil Wrigley was coming from," Shriver said. "He was not a baseball person. His approach to the Cubs was like being the main sponsor of a Chicago symphony orchestra. It was a Chicago resource to be maintained, but you don't waste a lot of money on it. It's entertainment, you keep it in business. That was his approach."

"The worst thing that tore down the Cubs were the Wrigleys," said 1960s' Cubs catcher Dick Bertell a few months before his death in 1999. "The Wrigleys weren't passionate baseball people."

"It seemed like when Wrigley owned the Cubs, the feeling was it would be super if you won the pennant, but if not, no big deal," said Bertell batterymate Glen Hobbie.

Wrigley, of course, always denied he was disinterested.

"It always amazes me," he said in another 1959 interview. "Sure, I'm interested. Some of the fans develop the darndest ideas. 'If you come up with three 20-game winners, you'd be all right,' they tell me. Who the hell wouldn't?

"It's pretty hard to do anything right in baseball. If you don't butt, in you're not interested; if you do, it's front office interference. My job is planning ahead. I'm generally working with the future, rather than with the present. I'm out ahead somewhere like an advance man for a circus. I supposed that's why people don't think I'm interested in things—because I don't hang around."

But the Cubs eventually turned into a circus, with Wrigley as ringmaster. Without a strong, willful baseball personality, he was susceptible to all kinds of wacky ideas, like the College of Coaches, an athletic director, and an "evil eye" to put hexes on Cubs opponents.

Appearances Are Everything

Meanwhile, the owner sweated the small stuff, including the appearances and personal behavior of players, rather than the big picture—building a consistent contender.

When some Cubs wore stylish blue socks obtained from the Dodgers, Wrigley ordered equipment chief Yosh Kawano to immediately replace the socks with the traditional stirrups. Players' desire to wear high insteps on their socks became a minor bone of contention on the Cubs in the early 1960s.

Around the same time, Dick Bertell had to pay close attention to his shinguards when he came to bat.

"Usually, when you're in the on-deck circle with two out, you keep your shinguards on to save the trouble of taking them off and putting them back on if the batter makes the third out," Bertell said. "But the word came on down from upstairs to take the shinguards off. It looks bad, you showed no faith in your hitter if you kept them on."

Wrigley even had his peculiar ideas about how his own headquarters building on Michigan Avenue should appear to the public.

"I often had lunch at the Wrigley Building restaurant," said veteran sports columnist Bill Gleason of the *Daily Southtown*. "The head waiter told me about a classic Phil Wrigley decision. He had a round table where the [gum company] executives gathered. Rarely would you see a baseball person there because there was no merging of the baseball business with the gum business. Wrigley was like a feudal lord sitting there. He didn't throw his weight around, but his presence was very important to everyone there.

18

"One day a fellow in the group ordered a double martini. Phil asked, 'How's your martini?' The man said, 'It's fine, but it's not a double martini.' Wrigley was not a martini drinker and called the head waiter. He asked him to bring him two single martini glasses. He had a double martini poured into the two glasses. It was only a martini and a half. He then ordered all of the double-martini glasses broken and thrown away, and a whole new consignment of double-martini glasses ordered. That's a special kind of human being."

Gleason felt that, all along, Wrigley was playing a kind of joke on Chicago baseball fans with his ownership dictums.

With eccentric schemes and the cosmetic appearance of the players and ballpark taking center stage, basic player development and scouting became a neglected part of the Cubs' organization. Although his personal fortune was estimated to be $100 million with $50,000 weekly dividends from the gum company, Wrigley chose not to pour money into the team in an era when much lower costs prevailed. In the cottage industry that was Major League Baseball in the first two-thirds of the 20th century, Wrigley could have outspent most, if not all, other owners by a wide margin. He did not choose to.

And the family fortune grew only bigger. Just before the death of only son Bill Wrigley in 1999, *Fortune* magazine estimated his holdings at $2.7 billion. Staking out global markets years ahead of many other top U.S. companies in the early 1960s, Bill Wrigley's stewardship of the gum company enabled annual sales to rise from almost $900 million to $2 billion from the late 1980s to the late 1990s.

Even before these windfalls, the Wrigley family had enough resources to operate several teams. But Phil Wrigley, molding his son in his same conservative, publicity-shy style, allowed too many rivals with much thinner checkbooks to outflank and outsmart him in baseball.

The Brooklyn-turned-Los Angeles Dodgers under first Branch Rickey's, then Walter O'Malley's ownership were held up as the model franchise in producing players. The Dodgers at one time employed between 50 to 60 scouts. Their "Dodgertown" spring-training complex in Vero Beach, Florida—which is still operated after nearly five decades—was the largest of its kind with eight fields and fine facilities for players, team employees and media. Minor league instructors were paid major-league salaries instead of the pittance that farm-system employees normally receive. That all cost lots of money, then and now. The Dodgers willingly spent it, but Wrigley could have put $5 down for every $1 O'Malley had in building facilities and hiring the right people.

"Walter O'Malley had far less money than Wrigley," author Peter Golenbock said of the astute Dodgers owner. Golenbock authored a 1996 narrative book called *Wrigleyville* after penning nostalgic books profiling the Brooklyn Dodgers and Boston Red Sox. He can make comparisons among these three clubs and others in the good ol' days.

"O'Malley had made his money as a lawyer for banks who foreclosed on bankrupt people in the Great Depression," Golenbock said. "The worse the country did, the better O'Malley did. When Branch Rickey sold out his share of the Dodgers to O'Malley, it was $1 million.

"But a lot of baseball owners at the time didn't have money. The team was their only source of income. Connie Mack had some fabulous teams with the Philadelphia Athletics, but lost most of his wealth in the Depression. He sold off his players and ran the team on a shoestring until 1950. Sam Breadon of the Cardinals had millions, but not lots of millions. He always was very concerned with losing the money he had. That's one of the reasons Branch Rickey had started the successful Cardinals farm system. You sign hundreds of guys, pay them $50 a month, and hope a handful are successful. The Griffith family with the Washington Senators had little money, and they succeeded or failed based on their attendance."

A few owners besides Wrigley were loaded. One was Tom Yawkey of the Boston Red Sox, who was passionate about the game. When he was younger, Yawkey used to suit up and shag flyballs in spring training. The Yankees' ownership of Del Webb and Dan Topping also was affluent.

But when Yawkey assembled a roster of highly paid players who became also-rans to the Yankees in the late 1940s and early 1950s, Wrigley used the Red Sox as an example that money doesn't buy happiness.

"I think Tom Yawkey did a great thing for baseball," he said in 1959. "He came in and spent unlimited sums and proved you can't buy a pennant. But the average fan thinks that if you have money you can do anything."

Wrigley left out one key fact. The Red Sox had a good baseball organization, their scouts and farm clubs always producing a steady flow of homegrown players even while they were the last major-league franchise to break the color line, with infielder Pumpsie Green in 1959. When Boston stumbled in the late 1950s into the 1960s, the decline wasn't as prolonged or as deep as the Cubs. The Red Sox's dark ages lasted less than a decade, broken by the "Impossible Dream" pennant in 1967, and the team has never strayed far from contention ever since.

"Remember, the Red Sox had Ted Williams and plenty of great players," author Golenbock said. "They had better scouts and they spent money. Yawkey loved baseball, and he desperately wanted to win."

Despite his massive fortune, Wrigley early on displayed nickel-biting proclivities. While a prep-school student, he had a $30-a-month allowance, which he tried to bank. William Wrigley, Jr., ordered his son to spend the stipend or lose it. Decades later, he offered his own best explanation of his philosophy. At his annual luncheon with Cubs employees one day in the late 1960s, Chuck Shriver remembered Wrigley stating he really didn't care if the Cubs made a profit; he just wanted to break even.

The owner confirmed that fact in 1964 when he rejected another in a series of attempts to purchase the Cubs.

"They're not exactly a money-maker as you now, but I'm not in baseball for the money," he said. "Neither was my father before me."

No Subsidy, by Gum

Not being in for the money meant Wrigley simply was not going to spend money to make money. The Cubs were just not central to his being.

"I don't ever remember him putting any personal money into the ballclub," former concessions chief Salty Saltwell said. "Mr. Wrigley felt his entities should be self-sustaining. We had a line of credit at a downtown bank, and sometimes there was a period, when cash flow was down, when we would tap that credit line during the winter."

The players sensed they were in it by themselves, employees of a rich man who kept a padlock on his bulging wallet. The Cubs had to win to make money. If not...

"I was assistant player representative when Larry Jackson was player rep," the late Dick Bertell said. "Bill Wrigley told me they would only spend the money that came into the ballclub (from gate receipts and concessions). You know that if you didn't bring it up [win], you wouldn't get it."

Wrigley did not have to spent all that much, compared to today's mega-millions, to jump-start the Cubs.

"In the late 1950s and early 1960s, the net profit from our concessions was enough to cover the player payroll," said Salty Saltwell. "We had no middleman in concessions like the White Sox, so that kept costs down and we kept more revenue."

"If Wrigley had just spent a couple of hundred thousand more, we could have picked up a couple of star players who could have helped us," Bertell said. "I never saw us bringing in that kind of talent from the outside."

"The Cubs seemed to operate at a Mom and Pop store level," Jack Kuenster said. "They operated at a level below everyone else."

The Milwaukee Braves, which at times in the 1950s drew three times the Cubs' attendance in a market one-fifth the size of Chicago, reaped the benefits in their ledger books. By the standards of the day, the Braves raked in the cash like few others: an average $364,517 annual profit for their first four seasons in Brewtown from 1953 to 1956. Top net revenue was $682,511 in '53, an enormous figure for the times. The Braves were a solid first-division NL team each season and contended to the very end of the season in '56, before winning back to back pennants in 1957-58. The relatively modest investment in player development and scouting, and hiring of good baseball men to snare the likes of Henry Aaron, Eddie Matthews, and their teammates paid off handsomely in the limited number of revenue centers available to teams of the Eisenhower Era.

The artistic and financial success of the Cubs' "country cousins," as *Chicago Tribune* beat writer Ed Prell called them in 1957, apparently had no impact on Wrigley just 90 miles down the road. Spending money to make more money wasn't in his gameplan. He lost tens of millions of dollars of potential revenue after the pennant in 1945 by not installing lights and practically giving away his TV rights.

The absence of night games was Wrigley's most distinguishing characteristic off the field. Stereotypes about Wrigley's philosophy on day baseball prevailed for decades: That if he couldn't be first with lights, he wasn't interested, and that he didn't want to disturb the nighttime peace and tranquility of the surrounding Lake View residential neighborhood.

In reality, Wrigley was all set to install lights for the 1942 season, seven years after the first lights were erected in Cincinnati. Cubs season attendance had dipped sharply, to 534,878 and 545,159 in 1940 and 1941, both years featuring mediocre teams. The attendances were far under the low points of turnstile counts at the trough of the Depression from 1933 to 1935. In fact, the Cubs had weathered the Depression at the gate better than most teams. But now, as the economy improved with increased war orders, the fans desired winners.

The original lights plan was dashed by Pearl Harbor. All the raw materials for the light towers were donated to the war effort. A second, brief attempt to install lights with wooden poles failed. Wrigley didn't have the neighborhood in mind in the whole issue. A series of boxing and wrestling shows, and even a Harlem Globetrotters' exhibition basketball game, were played at night at Wrigley Field with the help of portable lights from the 1930s through 1954. Drawing good crowds, these events certainly did not lower the decibel level on Waveland, Sheffield, Addison and Clark, and surrounding streets.

Wrigley did not revive the lights plan after World War II, and for good reason. Crowd counts skyrocketed in the post-war baseball-wide attendance boom, with the Wrigley Field crowds returning to levels achieved only in the 1929-30 period despite the steeply-declining on-field fortunes. The owner had no reason to tamper with the success of day games as season attendance climbed to more than 1.3 million in both 1946 and 1947. Attendance stayed above 1.1 million through 1950, when the post-war era of good feelings in baseball began to fade. Any owner's dream in this era was to crack the one-million attendance mark.

The push for lights was absent as the 1950s proceeded and a general malaise settled over the entire Cubs organization. Attendance followed the general pattern of baseball in general with an overall decline, especially after 1952. Entrenched as one of baseball's sad-sack teams while the White Sox sported a consistent contender at old Comiskey Park, the Cubs suffered at the gate. Only in 1958 and 1963 did season crowds exceed 875,000. The crowds dropped almost to 600,000 in 1962, 1965, and 1966—an embarrassing total for the No. 1 baseball team in what was then the nation's second largest market. Ten miles south, White Sox attendance stayed above one million most seasons, thanks partly to night baseball. Clearly, the Cubs needed at least some night games to boost attendance.

Several market rules of thumb were at work here. Wrigley disdained selling season tickets, preferring that fans be able to walk up to the gate on game day and buy a good box seat, while always keeping 22,000 grandstand and bleacher seats for sale on the day of the game only, a fact advertised daily by Jack Brickhouse on his WGN-TV game broadcasts. But without the assured income from pre-sold seats, the Cubs were at the mercy of the weather, the team's won-lost record, and the identity of the opponent. Baseball teams in the '50s and '60s typically drew good crowds when they played well, or when a top visiting individual attraction—

Jackie Robinson with the Brooklyn Dodgers, Willie Mays with the New York/San Francisco Giants, and Sandy Koufax with the Los Angeles Dodgers—came to town.

In addition, as America settled into its workaday schedule in the post-war, the average working man (or woman, to a much lesser extent) had much less flexibility in schedule, vacation benefits and discretionary income used for entertainment compared to the 1980s and 1990s. A far greater percentage of the work force was employed in the industrial sector. Industrial workers often were docked a day's pay if they called in sick. Vacation benefits across the board were a lot less liberal than at the end of the 20th century; two weeks off with pay was generous (compared to four in many companies now), and many workers had to settle for one week off. Heads of families were not going to use precious off days to attend a weekday baseball game.

Life for the majority in the post-war fell into this routine: working a day shift Monday through Friday, or sometimes additional work on Saturday. Retail stores were generally closed on Sundays and all nights except for Mondays and Thursdays, not so coincidentally the times big-league teams usually slotted off days. Shopping usually was crammed into Saturdays and one of the two open nights. Other household tasks had to be done on Saturdays. That precluded daytime baseball attendance in significant numbers unless there was a powerful lure of a contending Cubs team to take the risks of playing hooky from work or school.

The regional draw of the Cubs wasn't as strong compared to the last two decades, despite the longtime interest of Midwest baseball fans in no small thanks to a far-flung Cubs radio network. Travel to Wrigley Field was more difficult in the pre-interstate highway era. To journey to Chicago from downstate Illinois, Iowa, Indiana, and Michigan required a dawn-to-after-dark commitment possible only on Sundays, and then only one or two times a season.

You Had to Win to Draw

Between 1952 and 1967, Cubs mid-summer weekday crowds rarely climbed over the 10,000 mark, unless a doubleheader lured more fans through the turnstiles. Saturday daytime crowds usually did not exceed 20,000. Only Sundays and holidays, many featuring scheduled double-headers, enabled the Cubs to thoroughly populate the upper deck, which was shuttered for many weekday games. From June through Labor Day,

Sunday and holiday crowds usually topped 20,000, and sometimes inched above 30,000 in the 36,000-capacity Wrigley Field even when the Cubs were at their lowest ebb. Of course, no matter what the composition of the team, April, May, and September weekday figures ensured Phil Wrigley would take a bath of red ink just by opening the ballpark gates. Crowds under 2,000, on several occasions dipping into the hundreds, were common at the bookends of each season.

Wrigley did have proof that whenever the Cubs flirted with contention, the crowds returned in full force, at least on Sundays and for weekday doubleheaders.

On the strength of a slugging veteran lineup, the Cubs were one of baseball's surprises in the first half of the 1958 season. The attendance pattern of modest crowds continued. On Friday, July 11, 1958, with the blue-pinstriped gang playing .500 ball, the Cubs-Pirates affair drew a paid crowd of 8,070 on Ladies Day, when all females were admitted free. The total crowd count was several thousand higher. Then, on Saturday, July 12, 1958, with the Phillies in town, the gate climbed to 17,114. The Sunday doubleheader on July 13 jumped to 30,413.

The Cubs swept the Cincinnati Reds in a Wednesday, July 16, 1958 doubleheader to sport a 45-41 record, two and one-half games out of first place. That was the closest the Cubs had inched to the NL lead that late in the season since 1945. The bonus twin bill drew 30,412. But with only a single game the next day, the crowd dropped to 13,186.

The arch-rival Braves then hit town for a titanic three-game series. The combination of Ladies Day and the Hank Aaron-Eddie Matthews-Warren Spahn gate attraction swelled the gate to a total of 43,173, including 15,916 freebie females, on July 19, 1958. The massive throng spilled out of the bleachers, with dozens of fans standing on the steps leading down to the catwalk. All but the modest number of Braves fans in attendance were rewarded when crowd favorite Moose Moryn slugged a two-run homer into the teeming masses in right field to give the Cubs a 5-3 lead and a 46-42 record, two games out.

That turned out to be the high-water mark of 1958 as the Cubs began one of their typical mid-summer slumps. The Braves won 3-2 and 4-2 the next two days, Saturday, July 20, and Sunday, July 21, before respective capacity throngs of 37,918 and 35,328. The five biggest crowds in this stretch represented a healthy chunk of the Cubs' total 1958 season attendance of 979,904, highest of the 1952 to 1968 period, lured by the first-half heroics that cooled off to a season final 72-82, fifth-place record.

Meanwhile, the best team in the Cubs' second-division decades was the 1963 entry that finished 82-80, seventh place in a 10-team league. Such a record normally was good enough for fifth, but the expansion New York Mets and Houston Colt .45's (now the Astros) lost so prodigiously that most established teams were able to play .500 or better cleaning up on the new clubs. The Cubs had climbed to first place in early June and, just like 1958, briefly excited the city. The pitching-savvy team managed to bump along in third or fourth place for the next two months, marginally in contention.

On Friday, July 26, 1963, a game against the Cardinals drew 17,917, decent for the time but no way comparable to late 20th century Friday crowds for the arch-rival Redbirds. The Saturday gate, with many potential fans committed to supermarket, other errands, and work, climbed to 23,589. "If you're in the neighborhood, come out out," Jack Brickhouse would implore early in the game when thousands of seats remained available.

Finally, on the old-time Day of Rest, Sunday, July 28, 1963, the Cubs drew 40,222 for a doubleheader, sweeping the Cardinals, 5-1 and 16-11. The throng was the largest since the '58 gates-storming affair against the Braves and the largest paid crowd since a 1952 date with Jackie Robinson and the Brooklyn Dodgers. The huge twin-bill house no doubt included some Redbird rooters and many Cubs fans on their one summer pilgrimage to Chicago. All witnessed Lou Brock belting two homers and a triple, driving in five runs in the nitecap, the young outfielder attracting the attention of Cardinals manager Johnny Keane and GM Bing Devine in the process. The sweep increased the Cubs' record to 55-47, six and one-half games behind in fourth place.

But the dependence almost solely on walk-up crowds for day games did not mean a bonanza at the gate despite the improved team. Wrigley Field attendance in mid-July 1963 prior to the Cardinals series inched up only into the 10,000 to 15,000 range from the poor crowds of the 1962, 59-103, ninth-place disaster (a post-war low attendance of 609,802 for a full season).

The following weekend, Willie Mays and the Giants were the attraction. On Friday, August 2, 18,698 saw the Cubs outslug the visitors 12-11. But a Saturday crowd of 25,149 and a Sunday gate of 33,289 were disappointed by Cubs losses.

Then the Dodgers and Koufax hit town. A Tuesday, August 6, game drew 15,276. With Koufax dueling Cubs ace lefty Dick Ellsworth on Wednesday, August 7, the crowd jumped to 27,180. But on Thursday, August 8, the attendance dipped back to the typical mid-teens at 16,408.

The Cubs, though, had started a slump which knocked them out of contention for 1963. The team fell from fourth during early August to eighth with a 64-62 record on August 20. Attendance reflected the slide. The geographical rival Milwaukee Braves drew two mid-week crowds of just more than 15,000 on August 20-21. But a Friday game against the woeful New York Mets on August 23 attracted 9,634. On Sunday, August 25, 15,137 showed up to watch Ellsworth pitch. Then, the next weekend, the Labor Day holiday, just 8,279 and 9,027 passed through the gates to watch Cubs play the Houston Colt .45's. The disparity in attendance proved that Cubs fans were willing to watch their team on their off-hours at night, even if it meant an hour-and-a-half drive to do it. The loyalists while unwilling to journey the much shorter distance to the so-called "Friendly Confines" during a weekday. That was the fact of life of baseball attendance in the mid-20th century. The phenomenon of consistent 30,000-plus crowds for all weekday games in the three prime summer attendance months did not show up until after the Cubs finally finished in first with the NL East title in 1984.

Absolute proof that the Cubs needed some night home games in the middle of the 20th century was displayed on Friday, August 27, 1965 at Milwaukee County Stadium. The Braves, playing out the string as a lame-duck team in Wisconsin just prior to their move to Atlanta, drew their third largest season crowd—20,723. Edgar Munzel of the *Chicago Sun-Times* reported that the crowd included 77 busloads of Chicago-area fans. When Billy Williams slugged a fifth-inning grand slam for the Cubs, Richard Dozer of the *Chicago Tribune* noted a roar for the feat, concluding the crowd was "heavily laden with Chicago constituents."

With the Cubs bumping along 10 games under .500 at the time, languishing in eighth place, fans simply were not going to take off work or use up precious late-summer, pre-school opening vacation time to make the short trip to watch day games at Wrigley Field. But on their TGIF off time on Friday night, they gladly made the 90-minute trip to County Stadium to cheer on the Cubs for the 8 PM gametime.

That contrasts with crowds one week previously in Wrigley Field. A Thursday, August 19, 1965 doubleheader with the Reds, in which fireballing Jim Maloney no-hit the Cubs in Game 1, fanning 10 and walking 10 in 10 innings, drew just 11,342. Another doubleheader on Friday, August 20, with the faceless Astros playing the 58-68 Cubs, drew just 7,936 paid. The Saturday, August 21, crowd was even lower at 6,362. And on Sunday, August 22, in the middle of giant Chicago, only 9,106 passed through the turnstiles to watch the Cubs and Astros.

The Cubs' poor crowds put to the lie Wrigley's theory about selling baseball in the sunshine in "beautiful Wrigley Field." The owner always believed that a team needed a fallback position to draw crowds when the team didn't win. That strategy offered the supposed sun-splashed atmosphere of his father's treasured ballpark, where fans could come out, enjoy a picnic, and, by the way, watch a ballgame.

The problem was, that's all Wrigley offered. No giveaways, no Bill Veeck-style promotions and stunts. Gametime 1:30 PM, sunny day, plenty of available cheap seats, hot dogs, peanuts, Cracker Jack, smokie links, and Frosty Malts. With apologies to Salty Saltwell, the concessions menu paled in variety and quality to White Sox games at Comiskey Park. The average Cubs fan could get a lot of what Wrigley Field offered at even lower cost at the beach or forest preserves. They most wanted what every other rooter in baseball dearly desired—a contending team. Without one, there was no motivation to come out to Wrigley Field other than a selected few weekend or holidays dates per season, if that many.

In contrast, the "Go-Go" White Sox of the same era, tapping into a smaller, more geographically confined and far more fickle fan base compared to the Cubs, drew more than one million fans in all but three seasons between 1952 and 1968. Friday night and some other selected weeknight games at old Comiskey Park proved to be a success for the perennially contending Sox. During several seasons between 1952 and 1968, the Sox drew almost twice as much as the Cubs.

Fans Square Off vs. Owner

For much of the first part of the million-to-one era, the fans cast their vote on Wrigley's management through the seas of empty seats. They'd come out a couple of times a year, but no more, to Wrigley Field when the team wallowed in the second division. And they often made the owner aware of their feelings. They may not have spun the turnstiles, but they were always close at hand. Most owners would have been moved off Square One by the combination of the fans' angry reaction and their informal boycott of the ballpark, but not Phil Wrigley, always ensured of his gum-company financial cushion.

A disgruntled fan named "Guido II"—no doubt a forerunner of the nickname-laden callers to sports-talk radio four decades hence—aired a laundry list of complaints about Wrigley and the Cubs in a letter to the *Chicago Daily News* in July 1959. Guido II lambasted the owner's aversion to night baseball, his apparent tolerance of his baseball management's "stand pat" attitude, and the longtime feeling that Wrigley retained the Cubs as a tax deduction.

The newspaper submitted the letter to Wrigley for his reaction. As was his custom, Wrigley wrote a long response. On July 21, 1959, both the Guido II letter and Wrigley's reaction were published as the lead story on the *Daily News*' lead sports page.

Wrigley, for one, suggested Guido II was expending too much energy worrying about the Cubs. In the process, he displayed he did not understand the mindset of his fans. Did he simply expect the fans to come on out, sheeplike, to have a picnic in the sunshine at Wrigley Field? The answer may be obvious.

"The writer of this letter if fortunate that we still live in a comparatively free country where he was the right to limit his visits to Wrigley Field," Wrigley penned, "but what puzzles me is feeling the way he does, why doesn't he direct his time and attention to something else that would not get him so stirred up?"

Wrigley sloughed off 14 years' of failure by stating that other teams had lost for longer periods of time.

"It is true that it has been 14 years since the Cubs won their last pennant, and none of us is very proud of that. But there are a lot of clubs that have been trying even longer and their owners are not in the gum business.

"No one connected with the Cubs has ever had a 'stand pat' attitude in spite of of any articles that might have been written about it, and no one is satisfied with .500 ball [the Cubs' pace in mid-season 1959]."

Wrigley also threw off the notion that he believed the Cubs played better in the daytime, citing the team's .512 winning percentage for night games vs. .451 for day games in 1958, and .524 for night games vs. .475 for day games through the All-Star break in 1959. He also stated that night games at Ebbets Field in Brooklyn and the Polo Grounds in New York led to the decline of the surrounding neighborhoods, conveniently ignoring that white flight to the burgeoning suburbs of the 1950s was the real reason.

The Cubs a tax writeoff? Wrigley's view: "I have heard this voice before, and I would love to know how anyone can take a ballclub as a tax deduction as I have never found anyone who could figure this out, and I am sure that the Bureau of Internal Revenue would take a very dim view of anyone who thought he could."

A torrent of angry letters was received by the *Daily News* from fans reacting to Wrigley's response. They were published about a week later.

Bob Springer of Chicago wrote that Wrigley didn't answer the tax and "stand pat" questions, sarcastically adding that the owner "didn't say a word about the man who drills for oil at third base." Mildred Walker of Bellwood, Illinois, said Wrigley "does not care if his club draws people and if he doesn't want a winning ballclub as much as any one of his fans, then I would say that he had better stick to making gum." Anita Petita Gonzalez of Cicero reasoned that "it doesn't take eons to build up at least a competent first division ballclub."

A few days later, a small-scale Cubs stockholder wrote in, getting lead *Daily News* sports-page play. The stockholder said he had been stonewalled on some of the same questions during the annual shareholders meetings.

"He excuses failure by stating other clubs have gone without winning a flag. Nuff said," wrote the stockholder.

"If he can explain to me why no ball club has ever abandoned night baseball I might listen with more attention to his claim there is no 'stand pat' attitude...It makes sense if your team is able to play winning baseball at night even on the road, perhaps they might do even better in night games at home."

Wrigley could be criticized on a lot of counts. And he continued to field the torrent of complaints for the rest of his ownership tenure. For a shy man who'd rather be alone, that must have been pure torture. But he bore the burdens, the 1932 vow to keep the Cubs unbroken despite the flak.

To his credit, Wrigley did one important thing right as owner. He kept a regular schedule of ballpark upkeep that preserved Wrigley Field for decades to come. Salty Saltwell supervised many of the off-season remodeling and reconstruction projects that included turning entire sections of grandstand seats down the foul lines to an angle facing homeplate. In contrast to old Comiskey Park, which began falling down in the 1970s and 1980s due to maintenance neglect by cash-strapped ownerships, Wrigley Field was adequately rehabbed so that its lifespan, which began in 1914, could reach its 100th birthday in 2014 if the demands of baseball economics doesn't overwhelm it in the interim.

"When the club had a good year [financially], Mr. Wrigley put an awful lot into the physical structure of the ballpark," Saltwell said. Left out of all the construction projects, of course, were up-to-date and comfortable quarters for the players in the form of a larger clubhouse and dugout.

Free Lunch for WGN-TV?

With attendance held down by bad teams and the no-lights policy, the Cubs' cash flow further was hampered by Wrigley's before-his-time policy on television coverage of the team.

Other owners began clamping down on the number of games televised, fearing a negative impact on the gate, after an initial burst of video coverage at the dawn of TV in the late 1940s. Braves owner Lou Perini, in fact, forbade any coverage, home or road, of games in the Milwaukee market. The only time Braves fans got to see their team on TV was during the 1957 and 1958 World Series, when the NBC-TV rights superseded the local deal, permitting broadcasts of home games.

But Wrigley opened the doors wide open to the camera's lenses—lots of them. In 1948, two stations, WGN-TV and WBKB-TV, each used their own equipment to televise the entire Cubs' home schedule. Brickhouse was at the mike for WGN while "Whispering Joe" Wilson handled play-by-play for WBKB, which had been Chicago's first commercial TV station. In 1949, the brand-new ABC-owned station, WENR-TV (now WLS-TV) joined the orgy of televised baseball with the irascible Rogers Hornsby announcing the games. There were times when the Cubs game was the only telecast on the three channels on summer afternoons in '49. Wrigley believed in exposing his product in the new video medium, and he did it more prolifically than any other owner.

Soon WENR and WBKB, the city's first CBS affiliate, dropped out due to mounting production costs and the encroachment of network daytime programming. WGN had exclusivity. Problem was, the Tribune Co.-owned station did not have to pay through the nose in rights fees. Wrigley opted not to strike a hard bargain. Some called it a "sweetheart deal" for WGN. Saltwell admitted "the radio-TV rights were undervalued, compared to what other clubs were getting. We probably should have gotten more."

Financial records could not be obtained, but longtime WGN-TV director-producer Arne Harris estimates that the station paid the Cubs around $5,000 a game (multiply that by 77 games in the old 154-game schedule) in the 1950s. "I heard we were paying the Blackhawks $10,000 a game in the early 1960s, and I don't think the Cubs were getting more than that," Harris theorized. Ward Quaal, then WGN's general manager, also cannot remember specifics of TV rights-fees numbers, but confirms he got a near-bargain. "It is true that it was modest, but Mr. Wrigley saw the value of TV exposure to build fans among kids and women," said Quaal, who now runs a Chicago consulting firm a stone's throw from Tribune Tower.

Without rancorous rights-fees negotiations, the WGN-Cubs relationship became so close that many fans thought the two entities were under common ownership. They might as well have been, and it was made official when Tribune Co. bought the team in 1981.

WGN and the Cubs had further cemented their marriage in 1958 when the former's 50,000-watt clear-channel AM station landed the radio rights from longtime Cubs carrier WIND-Radio. With morning disc jockey Howard Miller helping make WIND the No. 1-rated station in Chicago at the end of the 1950s, the station was a 5,000-watt outlet that had built up a huge Midwest network for baseball broadcasts to compensate for lack of signal reach. WIND had paid the Cubs $75,000 a year for rights. Jack Brickhouse, who negotiated sports contracts on behalf of WGN at the time, had lobbied Quaal to fork up the modest amount of cash Wrigley wanted. The Cubs and the radio station settled for a five-year, $150,000-per year deal. "You might lose money the first year," Brickhouse later recalled telling Quaal, "but then you'll make money forevermore."

That was not a difficult prophecy. In a nearly one-way deal, Wrigley was providing a profit center and countless hours of reliable programming for WGN-TV and radio. The ratings enabled the stations' sales staffs to stock the commercial timeslots during games with name sponsors.

Despite the Cubs' losing ways, the fans proved to be never further away from their TV's and radios. Brickhouse broadcast sidekick Vince Lloyd said he was astounded to find that in the early 1960s, a losing Cubs team had higher ratings comparable to the contending White Sox club that WGN-TV also aired. Wrigley's decision to act contrary to most owners in televising all home games did build up a loyal following that translated into increased attendance decades down the line. Near-saturation TV coverage in almost all sports has proven to be a marketing a financial boon in recent decades, with only a couple of holdouts like Blackhawks owner Bill Wirtz in the NHL still not getting it.

New fans were created for the future, to be sure. But the Cubs' ledger books suffered during Wrigley's ownership due to the near-giveaway to WGN. The true market-value of rights fees, the team's just-due part of the healthy cash flow the broadcasting operation raked in, never came back to the team. And many still wonder if the same holds true under the Tribune Co. umbrella.

Rejecting the logical forms of cash flow and unwilling to subsidized the Cubs, the team was operated a lot more leanly than most major-market franchises. The financial squeeze often put on the Cubs by Wrigley and his son, Bill, privately exasperated some who worked under them. Fearing the price of dissent, they had to keep their feelings to themselves.

But the statue of limitations does run out. And so, twice in the late 1990s, Bob Kennedy, who had served father and son Wrigley as manager and general manager, rued the fact that the Cubs operated at the whims of multi-millionaires who would not use a fraction of the interest on their earnings to improve the team. And when Bill Wrigley was buffeted by $40 million in inheritance taxes after his father and mother, Helen Wrigley, died within two months of each other in 1977, the economic pressure was heightened just when the onset of free agency demanded more budget flexibility.

"I wish the Cubs had been owned by the gum company instead of the individual. Then there would have been more money available to it," Kennedy said as he watched spring training games and workouts near his retirement home in Mesa, Arizona. His wish would have never come true. Phil and Bill Wrigley kept the Cubs and the gum company separate, even to the point of not selling Wrigley's gum at the ballpark.

For all his egalitarian and pro-consumer stances, Wrigley did not believe in free speech for his staff or players. Dissidents were spun out of the organization.

In a quirky way, true to his contrarian personality, Wrigley virtually bought his players' silence in the 1960s by increasing the pay scales after keeping a lid on salaries under Wid Matthews in the early 1950s. The Cubs typically had very few holdouts in spring training. By 1968, players throughout the National League remarked how Wrigley treated his players better than any other team. But the happy, satisfied crew didn't last long into the 1970s with the coming of $100,000 salaries, agents, and free agency. Wrigley opposed salaries heading into the healthy six-figure range in multi-year deals. Players complained about their pay, and Wrigley dispatched them to the detriment of his ballclub.

All along, those who zipped their lips and dutifully carried on were rewarded. Loyalty to the owner and the organization seemingly was prized over creative thinking and initiative. Like a long-running TV show, the owner kept an ensemble of employees, some with ability, but always the same cast in an industry where change is often the byword. The end result was an inbred style of management that fell far behind the most progressive baseball organizations.

Former trainer Gary Nicholson, who worked for the Cubs from 1972 to 1976, summed up the Wrigley-era front-office attitude the best: "Don't rock the boat, do things as we've always done."

If an executive's, manager's or coach's time was up in one job, Wrigley often would lateral him to another position in the organization, no matter whether the man merited continued employment. When Phil Cavarretta was fired as Cubs manager in spring training 1954, Wrigley offered him the manager's job at the Triple-A Los Angeles Angels. But with his pride wounded, Cavarretta rejected the position, going crosstown to play one more season for the White Sox. Despite Cavvy's 20 years of loyal service to the Cubs as player and manager, he never worked for the team again while other lesser lights found employment with the Cubs.

"If you ever left the organization [on your own], quit on the organization and then wanted to come back, he wouldn't take you," Salty Saltwell said of Wrigley. "If you were fired by him, he would take you back."

The Wrigley cast of characters who worked the majority of their career lifetimes for him included general manager John Holland, vice presidents Charlie Grimm and Clarence "Pants" Rowland, farm director Gene Lawing, business chief Bill Heymans, Salty Saltwell, ticket manager Jack Maloney, top scout and sometimes-coach Vedie Himsl, and minor-league functionaries Lou Klein, Freddie Martin, and Walt Dixon. Ernie Banks joined the group after he retired as a player in 1971. Mr. Cub served as first-base coach, roving minor-league hitting instructor, group-ticket sales official, and team speaker until new general manager Dallas Green lopped his $25,000 salary off the payroll in 1982 for allegedly not fulfilling his job description.

Wrigley even gave his retired chauffeur, Gus Settergren, a paycheck and title as "assistant traveling secretary." No team in the turn of the century, let alone the 1960s, employed an assistant traveling secretary.

When the owner described himself as a "socialist," he wasn't kidding when it came to those who displayed him fealty. He kept his own form of the dole for his core group of employees, on whom he bestowed unusual titles.

He did not like the term "general manager," so Holland was a vice president. His business manager was called "secretary and treasurer." Shriver was not a media-relations chief, but a "director of information and services." Contrarian here, too. If the William Wrigley, Jr., company had been run in the same manner, we'd all be chomping on Beechnut now, with Wrigley an antediluvian brand name from a far-off time.

"That's not the way he ran the gum company," Cavarretta said. "You make a mistake in the gum company, you get another chance. You do it again, and you're out. Not with the Cubs. He just kept these guys on for years who should have been gotten out of there."

Saltwell and Himsl proved their worth on their own; they continued working for the Cubs in key roles under Tribune Co. ownership, after Green cleaned out many of the Wrigley family holdovers in the front office. Martin and Dixon had been much-praised by their minor-league players; Dixon stayed on as a scout under Green. Yet the work style of others simply kept the Cubs running by the process of inertia. Major decisions had to filter up to Wrigley for approval.

John Holland, the Loyal Servant

The one man who logically could have moved Wrigley off square one was Holland, in his role as general manager for 19 years, from 1956 to 1975. But Holland was the absolute wrong man to play off Wrigley. His low-wattage personality, innate conservatism, blundering trades, mishandling of homegrown players, and fear of offending Wrigley made him a close second to the owner in establishing the losing tradition that led the Cubs to million-to-one status.

"Wrigley easily could have spent $1 million to boost scouting and the minor-leagues, but he would have had to have someone to direct that money in the right direction," said Peter Golenbock.

Holland was not the right man for the job. He was decades behind the times. Yet he stayed on as Cubs GM until his retirement at 65, never once fielding a Cubs team that didn't have at least two major holes. Holland would have been fired by the majority of teams after his few years of failure, but he stayed subservient to Wrigley, and thus was rewarded with lifetime employment. If anything, he was even more conservative and cautious than Wrigley.

Holland did not act independently of Wrigley. When the owner took out an ad in Chicago newspapers defending embattled manager Leo Durocher on September 4, 1971, he said that he and his general manager were close. "John and I are like one," Wrigley said. "We don't do anything without talking it over."

Wrigley would make the final decision on whatever they were talking about with the ballclub. Holland said when he began with the Cubs that Wrigley gave him "carte blanche" in decisions involving player personnel. But in 1975, Salty Saltwell later revealed who had the last say: "Mr. Wrigley, of course, gives final approval on trades." Despite his lack of knowledge of the game's nuances and people, Wrigley also reportedly wanted Holland to call him after the end of every game, no matter what the time.

Holland was as nondescript as baseball executives go, and from the same southern and western roots of many of the game's mainstays. He was born in 1910 in Wichita, Kansas, and grew up in St Joseph, Missouri. Briefly a minor-league catcher in 1929-30, Holland went to work for the Oklahoma City minor-league team owned by his father, John Holland, Sr. He took over as president in 1936 after his father died, selling the team in 1942, when Holland went to work at an aircraft factory in Los Angeles.

He linked up with the Cubs to run their Visalia team in the California League in 1946. Two years later, Holland took the helm of the Cubs' Double-A Des Moines franchise. He was moved up to general manager of the Triple-A Los Angeles Angels of the Pacific Coast League in 1955. After the Angels won the PCL pennant in 1956 with Bob Scheffing as manager, Holland was promoted to the de facto general manager's post in Chicago with Scheffing in tow as manager on October 10, 1956.

He was cast in the classic mode of the baseball executive of the time. Holland did not shy away from his cigarettes and liquor. "John liked his Scotches," Salty Saltwell said. Holland also played poker with his players, the pots running up to $200, at the back of the team's chartered flights, a practice that was criticized by outfielder Moose Moryn in 1959 as part of a mid-season blow-up, and which eventually was clamped down upon by Wrigley.

Initially, Holland seemed like a breath of fresh air after the Wid Matthews' regime. *Chicago Tribune* writer Robert Cromie called him a "stocky, friendly man" on the day of his appointment as GM. Three years later, *Tribune* baseball writer Ed Prell recalled in an article how Holland first "took the reporters into his confidence and it was a happy association."

But Holland was transformed from an open, amenable honcho to a GM who was "secretive," by Chuck Shriver's description, in his first three years on the job. Prell wrote a particularly scathing piece by the standards of the late '50s during the 1959 winter meetings, claiming that Holland had "gradually withdrawn into his shell, so that now press relations are at a low ebb. It is almost as though the Cubs want it that way." Prell looked back at how Holland stayed in the background when Wrigley unexpectedly fired Scheffing as manager on September 28, 1959, after helping the Cubs overachieve with mediocre talent.

"He did the talking," Prell wrote of Wrigley's actions at the press conference announcing Scheffing's firing. "Holland sat in the corner sipping coffee. He let Wrigley carry the ball after the announcement that Charlie Grimm was succeeding Scheffing as manager.

"It seemed that Holland might have expressed himself as a strong Scheffing supporter, despite the surprising ouster of the man who had done a good job, considering the tools at his command. If Holland had fought for retention of Scheffing, it is a Cub secret."

Prell apparently caught on to the Wrigley style of management and Holland's fealty to the owner.

"It becomes more evident with each passing year that Wrigley does not want a 'strong man' at the head of his club," he wrote.

A year later, Wrigley fired manager Lou Boudreau, who had requested a two-year contract. The dismissal ushered in the College of Coaches.

"He was intensely loyal and backed him all the way," Boudreau said. "He never did tell me if he agreed with Mr. Wrigley's decision to dismiss me and hire a coaching system to manager. Holland would agree with Mr. Wrigley's thoughts."

Holland had one creative idea that he dared run by Wrigley. Around 1960, he tried to deal Ernie Banks for four or five players.

"I don't know which team it was, perhaps the Braves," said Jack Kuenster, then turning over Cubs furniture for the *Daily News*. "John told me he had a deal in the works that could get the Cubs into contention with all those players for Banks. But he also said the 'Old Man' [Wrigley] didn't want to do it."

Holland was almost a mirror image of Wrigley's personality.

"John was shy by nature," said Blake Cullen, who worked under Holland as traveling secretary starting in 1965 before becoming Holland's de facto assistant general manager in the early 1970s. "Part of the reason for his shyness was that he was a terrible stutterer as a child."

No wonder the fans rarely heard Holland talking in broadcast interviews.

"John didn't like TV or radio interviews," recalled Chuck Shriver. "He was always concerned what Wrigley's reaction would be to anything that he said. He could always say he was misquoted in the paper. He was very, very careful. He did Lou Boudreau's pre-game radio show because he knew Lou wasn't going to throw him any hardball questions."

"John was always afraid to put his foot in his mouth, afraid to offend Wrigley. He was very loyal to Wrigley," said Cullen.

"I think he was uncomfortable in the major-league role. He probably would have made a good farm director. He liked going down to the minor-league clubs to watch the kids."

But despite his minor-league background, Holland wasn't going to push for more money to build up the Cubs' often-lagging player development system. If he thought Wrigley put the screws to the budget, he kept his opinions to himself.

"I never heard John say we don't have the money to do what we needed to do," Salty Saltwell recalled.

"John was a product of when baseball didn't have a lot of money," Shriver said. "He was tight."

Holland also had an impatient streak. Instead of providing an upward path for homegrown Cubs prospects, grooming them with proper development at both the minor- and major-league level, Holland had an itchy finger on the trade button. He always seemed to believe the grass was greener with other teams, that he could receive better players via trade than the ones he already possessed.

Holland himself provided a hint at the folly of his management style back in 1956, when he was appointed GM. He ignored the tried-and-true method of player development employed by the Dodgers.

"The farm system is the lifeblood of any ballclub," he said, "but I don't believe that any ballclub can be built successfully entirely from the farm system. You need balance and experience, which comes through trades with other major league clubs."

On one end, Holland rushed players up to the majors without adequate minor-league experience. On the other, he became dissatisfied when they didn't produce. He always believed the grass was greener on the other side, condemning the Cubs to even more losing seasons in the process.

Lou Brock was promoted to the Cubs after one year in Class C. Oscar Gamble came up at 19 without a full season in Double-A. Bonus-baby outfielder Danny Murphy became a Cub at 17, upsetting the veterans at the sight of the green teenager. A long parade of pitchers like Dick Ellsworth, Ken Holtzman, Rich Nye, Joe Niekro, and Bill Stoneman were called up to the Cubs without any high minor-league seasoning. Only Holtzman avoided taking his lumps in the majors as a result. When these young players stumbled on the job, Holland quickly soured on them, reaching for the phone to trade them. Many of the deals, led by Brock-for-Ernie Broglio in 1964, backfired spectacularly on Holland.

But he was so old-fashioned that he couldn't even bear to say the word "trade" when he called Brock with the bad news.

"He said he had made an 'arrangement.' He said he had 'transferred my contract,'" Brock recalled.

Cubs Easy Mark for Cards, A's

The Brock deal was the most high-profile of a merry-go-round of trades with both the St. Louis Cardinals and the Oakland Athletics.

In 19 years on the job, Holland made 22 deals with the Cardinals, the majority with GM Bing Devine.

"John and Bing were very similar types," Blake Cullen said. "There was no bullshit, they said they wanted tit for tat. It wasn't like when I was on an elevator at the winter meetings, and Al Campanis of the Dodgers asked about Billy Williams. I said we'd be interested in the left fielder [Bill Buckner] and the catcher with glasses [Steve Yeager]. I had heard guys talk like that making trades, talk without naming names. Campanis said that ploy might work with Spec Richardson [Astros GM], but not with him. So John and Bing were direct with each other."

Devine, back for his third tenure with the Cardinals as a scout in his mid-80s, confirmed that view. "We understood each other," he said.

When word first surfaced in late May 1964 that Holland was trying to peddle Brock to the Cardinals for a pitcher, the GM actually said the two teams benefited each other in deals. "We've helped each other in the past and we may do it again," he said. Any top Cubs exec who admitted these days that he's trying to help St. Louis would be strung up from the highest yardarm. Sure enough, just one Cubs-Cardinals trade has been consummated since 1980.

A's owner Charlie Finley, a shrewd judge of talent, apparently found an easy mark in Holland. From 1970 to 1975, Finley made 12 trades with the Cubs. "Charlie knew our team better than his own," Cullen said. "With Finley being in Chicago, it made trades easier with him. And we also made a whole bunch of trades with the teams we played against in spring training in Arizona. It was easier being with them."

Holland did make a series of good deals that rounded out the Leo Durocher-led contenders of the late 1960s and early 1970s. But he became as cautious as ever as his retirement loomed, the organization going into a tailspin as a result. He also could not handle the onset of a new baseball economic system, represented by the first appearances of agents.

"The minor-league system began to deteriorate at that time," Chuck Shriver said. "The dollars started getting bigger. The Cubs figured if they hold the line, everyone else will hold the line."

Agents began representing players, and the latter's demands infuriated old-timers like Holland. Ken Holtzman came in one day to talk contract, and Holland threw an ashtray at him.

The aging executive could scarcely comprehend players, now adorned with flowing locks and facial hair, marching to their own drummer with interests not in the classic baseball booze-and-broads mold.

Pete LaCock practiced yoga to prepare himself for games. Along with pitchers Bill Bonham and Bob Locker, LaCock performed the yoga routines out on the field, in full view of fans and players. Not for long, as the dictum from the front office came down hard.

"They said it was too freaky, too hippie-like," LaCock said. "We had to do it somewhere where we can't be seen. We found a room in the ballpark, but it was cramped."

A large part of John Holland emotionally resided in the 1940s, in the little family business of baseball. He could hardly deal with the present and had no vision for the future.

As the Cubs broke all their attendance records during the memorable 1969 season, broadcaster Vince Lloyd sat one day with Holland in the Pink Poodle press dining room, Lloyd told Holland that if the Cubs won the pennant, they could draw two million in each of the following few seasons. Holland told Lloyd he didn't believe him.

40

"One million was considered a lot in those days," Shriver said. "Two million was almost beyond the ability to conceive."

Lloyd's prediction would come true 15 years later. When the Cubs finally finished in first during the 1984 NL East title season, attendance for the all-daytime schedule finally cracked the two-million mark. The season-ticket count jumped from 6,000 in 1984 to 25,000 in 1985. The Cubs have drawn fewer than two million only once since for a full, non-strike shortened season.

Holland would not have lifted a finger to promote attendance. By the early 1970s, he conducted his job defensively to protect his retirement income.

"In those days in baseball, there was no such thing as employment benefits," Shriver said. "The benefit was that you were paid, you worked there.

"When a GM retired, he was put on a retainer as a 'consultant.' That was his retirement benefit. John was in a no-rock-the-boat mode his last couple of years. He didn't want to get fired and lose his retirement deal."

Kept on as a vice president when he left the job at 65 in 1975, Holland stayed on as a vice president. He died on July 15, 1979, drawing tributes from several ex-Cubs.

"He was tough," former second baseman Glenn Beckert said. "He had his own ways. But he was a nice man, a gentleman. He felt something for the players."

"He was a common-sense executive, probably the best GM I ever had," ex-pitcher Milt Pappas said. "He was very intelligent about baseball."

But whatever intelligence Holland possessed couldn't properly surface to help the Cubs due to his own low-key personality, set-in-his-ways style and deference to Wrigley. The combination of the owner and GM was a bad one to break the million-to-one mold.

"If Wrigley really wanted to have a winner, he had to push John or get another GM," Shriver said. "It was the kind of combo that was locked up in a slow step. The two of them together weren't going to change."

Wrigley had kept Holland on the job so long he did not know where to turn for a replacement GM. He did not possess the social skills and connections in the game to effectively snare an outsider. Wrigley always had promoted or recycled from within the organization with the major exception of Leo Durocher. And once Durocher established himself as a near-savior of the Cubs in the late 1960s, Wrigley adopted him as one of his own. He even toyed with the idea of bringing Leo The Lip back as general manager to succeed Holland in 1976, and even turning over day-to-day operation of the Cubs to broadcaster Jack Brickhouse, a member of the Cubs' board of directors. Brickhouse wisely opted to retain the lifetime security of the broadcast booth.

Wrigley's Salty Tastes

A more likely scenario focused on Blake Cullen. He thought he was in line to replace Holland. After all, he had served as Holland's right-hand man for the previous few years, recommending trades and negotiating some contracts. He was led to believe he was Holland's successor by the GM's own words and in a conversation with Wrigley. Cullen had been approached by Lee Stern for a job with the latter's new pro soccer team, the Sting, in 1974. He told Holland of the offer.

"John said he was grooming me for the [GM] job," Cullen said. In another conversation with Wrigley, he was told there was no one else in the picture. Believing he was the next GM, Cullen turned down Stern.

But Cullen, his co-workers, and fans and media alike were soon in for a surprise.

"As the 1975 season ended, John said he had bad news for me," Cullen said. "Salty Saltwell had the job."

"We all thought he'd get the job," Shriver said of the front-office employees' opinions of Cullen. "We thought it was a foregone conclusion. He was much younger and had a different way of thinking. He was not hidebound by old baseball traditions. He would have made changes, as best he could. We were all shocked when he didn't get the job.

"Maybe Blake was perceived as being from the hotel business [his employer prior to the Cubs], not the baseball business. I don't think John recommended him, and I don't think Wrigley would have made the decision on his own."

Cullen speculated he was too high-profile for Wrigley's tastes. His name had appeared in a gossip column when he attended a play, and had been the subject of other articles. "Wrigley apparently didn't like people promoting themselves," Cullen said. "That wasn't the case with me, but to Wrigley maybe that's how it appeared."

Wrigley himself gave a contrarian explanation for passing up Cullen and Whitey Lockman, then director of player development. "They were too close to the present management," he said. Interesting. Wrigley had kept that "present management" intact for nearly two decades.

Chicago sports media members were in near-shock with the news that Saltwell, who had worked on the business side of the Cubs for the previous two decades, was named GM.

"It must be pointed out that he has watched the Cubs play ball every day for the last 10 years, both at home and on the road," the *Chicago Tribune*'s Robert Markus wrote of Cullen, contrasting that with Saltwell's desk-bound job at Wrigley Field that prevented him from watching entire games live. "He's seen every ballplayer in the National League and is well-acquainted with the Cubs' own personnel. So the fact he started life running a hotel doesn't mean he couldn't do a decent job wheeling and dealing players. After all, Charlie Finley, the most successful GM in the game, began as an insurance salesman."

Through the decades, the ranks of GM's have been rounded out by men who hadn't played professionally. Cubs president Andy MacPhail, for one, went directly into front-office work right out of college without any playing experience. Other GM's, like former Dodgers chief Fred Claire, had begun as their team's media relations director. The Wrigley family themselves had hired two GM's—William Veeck, Sr., and Jim Gallagher—directly from the ranks of sportswriters.

"I can't guarantee you that Cullen would have been a successful general manager," Markus wrote. "But he at least has acquired the first-hand baseball knowledge that Saltwell obviously lacks."

Critics and fans called Saltwell a "peanut vendor" because he headed concessions. That had been his bailiwick since he joined the Cubs in 1958. Previously, though, Iowa native Saltwell had worked in baseball operations in the minor leagues. He had been executive vice president of the old Class A Western League, before joining the Des Moines farm club in 1955 after John Holland had been promoted to Triple-A Los Angeles.

So why did Wrigley pick a GM who wasn't familiar, day to day, with big-league personnel?

"Mr. Wrigley sensed what was happening in baseball with free agency coming around," Saltwell said. "His thinking was that somebody with a little business background was needed to work on the player end. He approached me. I had an interest in it. If he expressed enough confidence in your ability to do the job, you went along with it. I had no trepidations."

Wrigley also believed that Saltwell's no-nonsense style could stir an underperforming club—and duel the newly-empowered agents to a standstill.

"I told him to get rough," the owner said. "And I think he will."

Wrigley cited the example of Leo Durocher's imperious tenure as manager.

"The closest we came to winning was under Durocher in 1969," he said. "The players hated him.

"Maybe we're being too nice."

Saltwell's alleged toughness aside, he was an astute man, with a penchant for details, of how the Cubs ran as a business. But at a crucial juncture in baseball history, the Cubs lost more by not promoting Cullen. He had worked his way up to the job.

"I still have notebooks that I compiled then on how to play the game in Wrigley Field," Cullen said. "Also about the type of pitcher you need to win in that ballpark—big, tall, right-handed pitchers with sinkers. The left-handed pitcher seems to struggle there, and it has something to do with the angle of the ball coming out of the bleachers. High fastballs don't work in Wrigley Field.

"With free agency coming in, I had a real door set up with agents. Dealing with them never bothered me. I almost liked dealing with agents. You had to jump on the free-agent bandwagon, and it got away from the Cubs."

In picking Saltwell, Wrigley simply chose someone else from his longtime cast of characters, as per custom. But the Saltwell rein was brief, notable only for another disastrous trade (Andre Thornton to the Indians), the callup of Bruce Sutter and Saltwell being forced to get an unlisted number at his Park Ridge home when teenage girls called to plead with him not to trade Rick Monday.

Business-operations chief Bill Heymans left in the middle of the 1976 season for health reasons. "I got the whole bundle of wax, baseball and business end, because I was the only one in the front office with experience," Saltwell said. "After the end of the season, I told Mr. Wrigley that there was no way I could continue as general manager and business manager. I could do one or the other."

Wrigley gave him the choice. Saltwell selected business operations, but was asked to help choose his successor and work in negotiating baseball contracts.

"He asked if I had anyone in mind," Saltwell said. "Bob Kennedy had been trying to get back into the organization. He had been doing a good job evaluating players for Seattle, which was then just starting as an expansion team. Mr. Wrigley asked me about what Kennedy was doing."

Kennedy, Cubs manager from 1963 to 1965, was hired as Phil Wrigley's last general manager. He hired Herman Franks as manager to replace Jim Marshall. Kennedy had worked for Franks as manager of the Triple-A Salt Lake City team Franks had owned back in 1962. Franks himself was a recycled Cub. He had served as a coach under Leo Durocher in 1970. Later, after quitting as Cubs manager with a week to go in the 1979 season, Franks returned again as a caretaker general manager to succeed Kennedy as Bill Wrigley sold the team to Tribune Co.

Happy to get back to his native Chicago, Kennedy was not going to counter Phil Wrigley's dictums when stars Bill Madlock and Rick Monday wanted hefty raises for 1977. Wrigley ordered both traded. The Madlock deal was another long-run stinker. By this time, the 82-year-old Wrigley felt lost. The world had turned. "I have outlived my usefulness. Everything has changed," he said as salaries exploded and free-spending owners like George Steinbrenner reaped immediate benefits in the won-lost column.

Thou Shalt Not Sell the Cubs

The aggravation at the end of his life causes the question to be asked again: What pleasure, what ego-satisfying process did Phil Wrigley derive from continued ownership of the Cubs? The team lost for so long. Red ink flowed. Wrigley believed he tried everything to turn the franchise around. Nothing worked. Why not make the team someone else's burden, despite the commitment to his father's memory?

Wrigley did not lack for ways out of his predicament. He was always approached to sell the Cubs by some of the biggest names in sports, business, and entertainment.

McDonalds impresario Ray Kroc, a dyed-in-the-wool Cubs fan, made Wrigley offers he could refuse. When he had the chance to buy the San Diego Padres in 1973, Kroc enlisted George Halas as an intermediary in another purchase attempt. Wrigley said "no," and Kroc went ahead with the Padres deal.

Halas, who rented Wrigley Field for his Bears from William Jr. and Phil Wrigley from 1921 to 1970, said he had approached Wrigley in the 1950s to buy the Cubs for himself. That would have been an emotional buy. Halas had played briefly in the majors for the New York Yankees and had long lived on Chicago's far North Side, not far from the ballpark.

"At the time, he said he would give me not the first refusal but the last refusal," Halas said in 1977. "But nothing came of it."

Chicago radio talk show host Chet Coppock, whose family was close to Halas, said Papa Bear continued loving baseball through his decades of Bears stewardship. Halas had a drawing on one of his office walls at 233 W. Madison St. of Babe Ruth pointing before his "called shot" homer in the 1932 World Series at Wrigley Field.

Frank "Trader" Lane, the frantic baseball executive who once was general manager of the White Sox, reportedly made a $7 million bid to buy the Cubs.

Saltwell said he heard rumors that Bob Hope, who at one time had an ownership interest in the Cleveland Indians, had made an offer to Wrigley.

Jack Brickhouse expressed interest in buying the club in several conversations while driving in his car with Coppock and his father, Charles.

The younger Coppock also remembered "a vivid conversation" among a group of moneyed men around the grill at North Shore Country Club in Glenview in the late 1950s.

"They all talked about what it would take to buy the ballclub," Coppock said. "They were all very moneyed people, some very strong family money. Each of them individually could have bought the team. Financially, it would have been very easy to buy Cubs at this time. Bill Veeck bought his share of the White Sox for $2.5 million at the beginning of '59."

Veeck himself never made a formal bid to buy the Cubs. He knew of Wrigley's familial commitment to retain the team first-hand as the owner's young aide-de-camp in the 1930s. But his desire to come home to Wrigley Field always stayed with him in subsequent decades. After all, Veeck's father had been Cubs president during their glory years, and Veeck's first accomplishment in the game was supervising the planting of the ivy and construction of the present-day bleachers and scoreboard in 1937. In 1967, when asked about any future ownership plans, Veeck said the only teams in which he'd be interested were the Cubs and Washington Senators.

Wrigley seemed unperturbed by most sales overtures. He got aggravated, though, on one dog-day afternoon when not one, but two groups of parties approached him to buy the Cubs. One group consisted of a pair of 20-year-old Cubs fans who called on Wrigley at his Lake Geneva estate.

Livening up an otherwise slow August 25, 1964 was a telegram to Wrigley from Harvey Walner and David Rosner, two 28-year-old Chicago attorneys. Representing a syndicate of eight investors headed up by Edwin Miller, president of the Yale Insurance Agency, Walner and Rosner wired Wrigley with a $4.3 million purchase offer.

"We feel the club lacks a top-notch front office and we want to bring an aggressive management to the Cubs similar to what the Phillies [then pacing the NL in first place] have," Rosner said. "We have a group of civic-minded Chicago sports fans who are well-heeled and interested in bringing a winner to Chicago. We feel 18 years since we've had a first-division team on the North Side is much too long.

"This isn't a capricious thing with us. We know the approximate value of the Cubs stock and the value of the park. We also know they have lost money for several years running."

Rosner envisioned installing "young, aggressive Bill Veeck" type management. The ownership syndicate would have immediately installed lights for night games.

But Wrigley rejected the offer.

"I wouldn't care if they offered me $40 million, the Cubs aren't for sale," he said.

One of the college-age kids journeying to Green Gables in Lake Geneva was Jim Anixter, who later would make two offers to buy the Cubs when he ran a cable-TV equipment supply firm, Skokie-based Anixter Brothers. A maniacal lifelong fan who stocks the basement of his Highland Park, Illinois mansion with Cubs memorabilia and clippings, Anixter and a friend drove up to Lake Geneva after stopping at Wrigley Field, where he was told by John Holland that the owner was out on holiday for a month.

When the pair of impetuous youths rang the doorbell, Helen Atwater Wrigley answered. Overhearing the conversation, Phil Wrigley came to the door and told them the Cubs weren't for sale.

"I said I didn't care if they represented John D. Rockefeller, the Cubs were not for sale.

"Here a couple of young punks pull up in a sports car and want to buy the Cubs. This is ridiculous. I have a waiting list of people who want to buy the team. People who would be good for baseball."

"Do you think I'm going to sell to a couple of strangers who just walk up and ring the doorbell? Those two...they would have been a couple of dandies to have in the National League.

"I don't understand why so many people think they can buy anything."

Obviously, a lot tried to buy the Cubs, listening to Phil Wrigley's own words. "He probably had 25 serious offers and 1,500 inquiries about buying the team," Chet Coppock said.

Maybe Wrigley didn't understand the passion of Cubs fans. He should have if he was slipping into the ballpark incognito. The gap between the owner's desire to win and that of his fans was light years wide. The frustration of the fans was so great by 1964 that they concocted fantastic, but fruitless schemes to seize the team from the man who refused to take action to win pennants.

In addition to the apparent William Wrigley, Jr., deathbed vow not to sell the Cubs, perhaps there was some influence within the Wrigley household to retain team ownership. Helen Wrigley apparently liked the family heirloom.

"Mrs. Wrigley got to like the Cubs very much and I think it was because of her that he would not dispose of the Cubs," George Halas theorized in 1977.

"Mrs. Wrigley was a bigger fan than her husband," Phil Cavarretta said.

Of all the rich guys who could have owned the Cubs, put their heart and soul into the tradition-dripping franchise, the fans ended up drawing the short straw with Phil Wrigley. Part of him had the attitude of ultimate privilege. Another part of him didn't mind getting down and dirty, tinkering with engines, dodging spilled beer cups incognito in Wrigley Field. Either part on its own should have brought the Cubs a winner.

Maybe 100,000 to one against a man with Phil Wrigley's resources not bringing at least one pennant to the North Side between 1946 and 1976? A lot of factors go into compiling million to one odds. The modest man who wanted to live in a cave could claim a lion's share of the credit. What a legacy.

Chapter 3

THE LOST CONTENDER, 1957-1964

DICK DROTT AND Moe Drabowsky, great fastballs and knee-buckling curves. Glen Hobbie, hard sinker. Bob Anderson, he can really bring it.

"We had our horses," Jack Brickhouse once said.

"And they came up lame."

The million-to-one era really got rolling when promising right-handers Drott, Drabowsky, Hobbie, and Anderson offered the promise of lifting the Cubs up from their 1950s malaise. Here was a quartet of young starters that any team would drool over to acquire, to build an entire franchise around.

They all broke down. What the Cubs missed as their shoulders, elbows, and backs went awry was staggering. Bad mechanics, bad coaching, bad medical treatment, and just plain bad luck would form a witch's brew of negativity that had a domino effect on Cubs history for years to come.

"These were all great young pitchers," said Hall-of-Famer Frank Robinson, who batted against the quartet as one of baseball's superstar hitters in the late 1950s and early 1960s with the Cincinnati Reds.

"If they hadn't gotten hurt, the Cubs probably would have been in several World Series," Robinson said. "And we would have thought of them the same way we think of the Atlanta starters today."

Drott, Drabowsky, Hobbie, and Anderson all started out in their careers as well as any young pitchers could. And before they had a chance to establish themselves, to give the Cubs and their timid management confidence, they got hurt. Timing is everything, and the Cubs' timing was all wrong. The foursome of pitchers came up, just as even more talent was emerging from the usually-moribund Cubs' farm system.

The rotation could have been rounded out by lefthander Dick Ellsworth. They could have been relieved on lesser-light days by southpaws Ron Perranoski and Jim Brewer. They'd be given leads to protect by top young hitters Billy Williams, Ron Santo, and George Altman. Stealing some runs would have been the province of another great young outfielder, Lou Brock. Saving some runs was going to be the responsibility of slick-fielding second baseman Kenny Hubbs. And it all could have been managed by Bob Scheffing.

The talent flow into Wrigley Field was as good as any team in baseball at the end of the 1950s, going into the Kennedy 1960s. Not even the vaunted Dodgers could boast of so many good-looking young pitchers and hitters in a four- or five-year period at that time.

But the kids never coalesced as a potential National League powerhouse, fulfilling Frank Robinson's projection as Fall Classic material. They never got a chance to play together, a cohesive, healthy unit establishing a new winning tradition at Wrigley Field and shaking off the cobwebs that had encrusted the front office.

They were the Lost Contender, a team that should have been, but wasn't. And when the gaggle of kids never meshed, never avoided the jinxes of injuries, mismanagement and tragedy, the Cubs lost one of their three golden opportunities to break the million-to-one streak when it was, maybe, 50 to 1.

"I always thought we had a contender, even if it didn't end up that way," catcher Dick Bertell said. "We had a good lineup and those good young pitchers coming up."

The passage of decades dims the story of the Lost Contender. Other Cubs teams have forged ahead in the consciousness of fans. Most famous was the 1969 Cubs, which had some of their roots in the Lost Contender, the most prominent second-place team in modern-day baseball. Most frustrating was the 1984 Cubs, just three innings and a couple of infield catastrophes away from a World Series berth against the Tigers.

But perhaps most tantalizing about what might have been were the enthusiastic baseball youngsters that dotted the roster four-plus decades ago. Leading the way was the four pitchers, three of them original Cubs property, who flamed out much too early after providing a glimmer of hope that the tandem of GM John Holland and manager Bob Scheffing would develop a winner at Wrigley Field. The failure of the quartet of pitchers to dodge the injury jinx and develop into some of the NL's best triggered a chain reaction of events, some of them truly wacky, that cemented the Cubs' position as the million-to-one team, even having an effect, several times removed, on the flow of team events at the turn of the millennium.

The testimony of Frank Robinson says a lot about the potential impact of the pitching foursome. "That's big praise from Robinson," said Hobbie. "I tried to get him out so much, but I couldn't." An old-fashioned competitor who gave no quarter on the field, Robinson was an expert on what made up a capable foe for his bundle of motivation at the plate. The Cubs' quartet was more than capable before the pain and the mishandling by team executives and physicians derailed their date with stardom.

"We were all young, we had good stuff and were getting people out, said Anderson.

"We felt our best years were in front of us. We felt that pitching every fourth day, we had something good going in."

They not only impressed foes like Robinson, but also teammates who grew confident at the crackle of their fastballs and the hooks on their breaking pitches.

"The pitchers were all outstanding. They all threw hard," said Jerry Kindall, then a young Cubs infielder, now a senior advisor to USA Baseball, the governing body of the U.S. Olympic baseball team in Tucson, Arizona.

What happened to Drott, Drabowsky, Hobbie, and Anderson is not unusual in the bigger scheme of things in baseball. Pitching injuries, 1959 or 1999, in spite of the advances in sports medicine and conditioning, are as much a part of the game as scratching and spitting. The art of throwing a baseball is the proverbial unnatural act. Mortality rates are high, thus teams stock their amateur drafts with pitching picks every June expecting a goodly number of kids to break down.

"It seems every organization has guys who have arm problems or other injuries," said Drabowsky. "Sometimes it runs in spurts."

And often the injury plague hits the teams that can ill afford to withstand it. Pitching-challenged most seasons since the 1945 pennant, the Cubs just couldn't get a break with their young hurlers' health. That's in contrast with the Dodgers of Koufax and Drysdale, who stayed fit long enough to garner three World Series berths in the 1960s. How about the Braves of recent vintage, whose pitchers have worked through injuries to make Atlanta a perennial (albeit not-too-successful) Fall Classic participant.

What might have been still is a part of the collective memories of three men in their 60s. Drabowsky is the pitching coach of the Baltimore

Orioles' Class A farm club in Salisbury, Maryland. Hobbie is retired, living on a downstate Illinois farm not far from St. Louis. And Anderson has long been in business in Tulsa, Oklahoma, his latest incarnation working for a firm making insulation for the plastics industry.

At 49, Drott, suffering from cancer, died too young on August 16, 1985. Oddly enough, he was the pitcher with the most outstanding stuff, and he buckled the earliest.

There's a sense of bitterness and puzzlement over what went wrong and how the Cubs treated them when they weren't fit to pitch. A combination of medical misdiagnosis, old-fashioned macho baseball attitudes that proclaimed you "don't make the club in the [whirlpool] tub," and impatience by Cubs management ended their trip upward long before they even flirted with age 30.

The Gold Dust Twins

Drabowsky was the first to make it up, in 1956. Drott followed at the start of the 1957 season, while Hobbie and Anderson made their major-league debuts later in '57. Oddly enough, all were corraled by the Cubs organization during the tenure of discredited personnel chief Wid Matthews.

Drabowsky signed for a $50,000 bonus out of Connecticut's Trinity College as a 20-year-old in '56, making it up to the Cubs late in the same season. Then Drott joined him in the rotation in 1957. They quickly earned the nickname "The Gold Dust Twins," the dual pillars of hope on a 62-92 last-place team.

Drott, a Cincinnati native, attended the same Western Hills High School that produced Pete Rose and future Cubs managers Jim Frey and Don Zimmer. Nicknamed "Hummer" for his great stuff, he came into the Cubs' organization in 1954. Pitching for Bob Scheffing at Los Angeles in 1956, he was the Pacific Coast League strikeout champ with 184 whiffs in 197 innings.

He drew all the focus to his gifted right arm when he set a Cubs' single-game record with 15 strikeouts against the powerful Milwaukee Braves on May 26, 1957 at Wrigley Field as 32,127 watched spellbound. Drott got Henry Aaron looking three separate times. The crowd booed Bob Scheffing when he went to the mound twice in the ninth inning as the Braves rallied, but Drott stayed in to finish the 7-5 victory. In another game, he whiffed 14 Giants. For the prodigious loser Cubs, Drott finished

'57 with a 15-11 record, 3.58 ERA, and 170 strikeouts in 229 innings. His only weakness was Nolan Ryan-style wildness—129 walks.

Immediately, he emerged as a man evoking respect from opponents, who had to resort to creative ways to throw Drott off his game. Hanging out with Drabowsky one evening before the pair were to pitch a double-header the next day, the pair were being plied with drinks sent over by a mysterious benefactor. He turned out to be Fred Hutchinson, manager of the St. Louis Cardinals, the foe the pair were going to face. Hutchinson had good reason to try to infuse Drott with a hangover.

"Drott had a killer curve," said Jerry Kindall. "The first time Willie Mays ever faced Drott, he sat down in the batter's box to avoid a fastball he expected. Instead, it broke over the plate, a curveball for a strike. I was playing shortstop and I heard Willie say, 'Oooh, that was such a good curve, I'll never hit it out.' Well, he did homer on the next curve. But that pitch got the batters talking."

He showed no fear of Mays. In another early spring-training duel with the Giants superstar in 1957, Mays kept looking down to see the sign catcher Cal Neeman flashed at Drott. Pacing in the dugout, manager Scheffing wanted Drott to knock Mays down to stop the sign-stealing. Drott was mentally in tune, whistling the next pitch by the buttons of Mays' shirt.

"I never thought the kid would have the nerve to dust off Mays," Scheffing said soon afterward. "After that I knew he could take care of himself. I decided then and there he'd have to pitch himself *off* my ballclub."

Veteran pitchers praised Drott to the heavens. "He's the best young pitcher in the league," said the Phillies' Robin Roberts. "In fact, he's as good as any pitcher I've seen at his age. I don't see how he can possibly miss being one of the really great pitchers in baseball."

He did, the first victim of a four-decade-long injury jinx to pitchers that reached out to grab Kerry Wood as its latest casualty in 1999. Drott first experienced control problems in a sophomore-jinx manner with a 7-11 record, a 5.44 ERA, and 99 walks allowed in 167 innings. But he still showed his pure stuff with 156 strikeouts.

Then Drott hurt his elbow. He appeared in only eight big-league games in 1959. His only victory was a shutout. The sands of the hourglass were starting to run out in John Holland's mental schedule for Drott.

Drott tried to come back in 1960, but was used sporadically. One Cubs teammate, quoted anonymously by Jack Kuenster of the *Daily News* on July 19, 1960, said: "His arm is OK, and he's throwing as good as ever. But, how's he gonna get confidence when they don't use him in the starting rotation, and stick with him? Why don't they stick with him? We're not going anywhere."

A freak injury soon added to Drott's woes. In the million-to-one era, the nature of the mishap made perfect sense.

"I was rooming with Dick," said Glen Hobbie. "In 1960, he was just starting to throw the ball well. One night on the road, we went back to our hotel room. The maid had just sprayed the room with something. Dick sneezed and pulled a muscle [in his rib cage]. We didn't know when he could start again."

Drott finished 1960 at 0-6. And if he felt he couldn't go any lower, he had to hear some kids in the sparsely-populated Wrigley Field stands chanting, "Who hasn't won a game since '58? Drott...Drott...Drott."

In 1961, Drott mainly pitched out of the bullpen, racking up 98 innings. Batters didn't hit him hard; he allowed just 75 hits. But the ol' hummer and curve weren't quite the same; he fanned just 48 while walking 51. The Cubs let him go to the expansion Houston Colt .45s in 1962. He finished his big-league career with anything but a flourish, a 2-12 record in 1963, the promise of '57 long-gone at the ripe old age of 27. Drott, who kept his home in the Chicago area, went to work coaching sports for the Chicago Park District.

In 1963, Drabowsky still had some momentum going in his career. He was in baseball purgatory with the hapless Kansas City Athletics, wondering where all the promise had gone. It had evaporated one afternoon in 1958, after he had teamed with Drott to provide so much anticipation in Cubdom.

Drabowsky, born on Ozanna, Poland, showed his potential with three complete games in his late-season 1956 callup, going 2-4, but allowing just 37 hits in 51 innings. He started slowly in 1957, but came on in the second half to finish 13-15 with a 3.53 ERA and 170 strikeouts in 239 2/3 innings.

"That kid's the best young pitcher since Dizzy Dean joined the Cardinals," Reds broadcaster Waite Hoyt said at the time, rating him ahead of Drott. "Moe's fastball isn't as good as Dean's, but his curve is unequaled."

And Drabowsky became the club's leading character and prankster.

An economics major at Trinity College, he worked as a stockbroker in the off-season. He discovered that Wrigley Field's bullpen phone had an outside line. He called up a fellow stockbroker to get market updates during a game while Glen Hobbie pitched. The visiting team began to bomb Hobbie, and Bob Scheffing tried to call the bullpen to get a reliever ready. The line was busy. Scheffing thought he misdialed, so he tried again. Busy again while Moe chatted away. Finally Scheffing had to signal with towels for a new pitcher.

The manager had no problems with Drabowsky's fun-loving stance. In the spring of 1958, Scheffing predicted he'd win 20 games. Drabowsky allowed Stan Musial's 3,000th hit on May 13, 1958 at Wrigley Field, but then continued his 1957 momentum. He pitched a one-hit shoutout against the Pirates a month later.

Another appearance against the Pirates on July 11, 1958 later proved to be Drabowsky's undoing with the Cubs.

"Bob Skinner was batting, and I had an 0-and-2 count on him," Drabowsky recalled. "I wanted to throw a fastball by him, getting a little something extra on it. I felt something pop in it. I tore the muscle capsule of the elbow. I had no idea what the cause was."

No rehab program, no special medical treatment was in store for Cub pitchers. Sports medicine as such didn't exist. To be sure, medicine in general in 1958 had progressed beyond the witch-doctor stage, but the Cubs were not cutting-edge, in keeping with the personality of their owner and general manager.

Drabowsky decided to rest the elbow, which practically locked up, to see what would happen. "A few days later, I had 5 to 8 degrees more extension," he said. "In a week's time, it was straightened out. The Braves were coming in, and I told Scheffing that my arm was straight and I felt no pain. I pitched [on July 19, 1958]. First inning, bam, after several pitches, I was back to where I was.

"When you're young and strong, you go out there and think you're pretty much invincible. I don't think we babied ourselves until we hurt it the second time."

Lifted after just a third of an inning, his elbow throbbing, Drabowsky laid off pitching until September. He won only one more game in '58 after the original injury, finishing 9-11 with a 4.51 ERA. Five months later, he reported that his elbow had healed over the 1958-59 off-season. Although Cubs pitching coach Freddie Fitzsimmons generally drew raves about handling younger pitchers, the proper techniques and technology of teaching proper mechanics lay in the future.

"You didn't have VCR's and didn't have a frame-by-frame ability, forward and backward, to analyze your delivery," Drabowsky said, admitting he had poor mechanics that led to the injury. "We had films, but we had no way to break it down to your release point on films. Only after I became a pitching coach and I saw old 16 mm films of myself did I see I had bad mechanics. I didn't know anything about mechanics other than working pitches in and out."

Without the proper knowledge of mechanics in the first place, Drabowsky only made matters worse in 1959.

"I made sure I didn't hurt it a third time," he said of the elbow. "I started favoring it and began overcompensating in other areas. My shoulder wasn't right."

Most pitchers tried to work through injuries, partially out of macho pride, partially due to job insecurity in an era of minor leagues going down to Class D level, and partially due to the fear of the surgeon's knife. An arm operation often was career-ending. Surgeries were major productions, traumatic to the entire muscle-and-tendon area afflicted. The less-invasive arthroscopic surgery was still on the drawing board. "I didn't want it cut on," Drabowsky said.

Drabowsky was 5-10 with a 4.13 ERA in 1959, making only 23 starts and seeing some relief service. "The Cubs did stick with me, hoping I'd get better," he said. But Holland soon itched to pull a quick hook.

"I was getting healthy in 1960, but I had lost so much time, my development had ceased for all practical purposes," said Drabowsky. New manager Lou Boudreau reduced him to mop-up duties. He had a 6.44 ERA, allowing 71 hits in 50 innings. Holland even demoted him for a while to Triple-A Houston. Eventually, he was traded at the end of spring training to the Braves, and bounced around for a few years until he regained effectiveness as a reliever, striking out six in a row and 11 overall in a relief stint for the Orioles in Game 1 of the 1966 World Series. Drabowsky almost came full circle, finishing his career with the White Sox in 1972 at 37.

"Part of the Program"

With the injuries and ineffectiveness of Drott and Drabowsky, Holland felt he had to trade for pitching early in 1960. He dealt sparkplug second baseman Tony Taylor to the Phillies for hard-throwing right-hander Don Cardwell on May 13, 1960.

Two days later, Cardwell amazed baseball by no-hitting the Cardinals in his Cubs debut in the second game of a doubleheader at Wrigley Field, the first man to ever toss a hitless gem in his first start after being traded to a new team. Normally a man of few words in his rare broadcast interviews, a happy Holland told Jack Brickhouse live on WGN-TV a few minutes after the no-hitter that the fastball-tossing Cardwell would be "part of our program, with [Glen]Hobbie and [Bob] Anderson." No mention of Drott and Drabowsky. "The what have you done for me lately attitude" prevailed. The former Gold Dust Twins still hadn't seen their 25th birthdays.

While Drott and Drabowsky broke down early in their careers, Hobbie proved to be the most durable. He lasted with the Cubs all the way through 1964.

A classic strapping country-boy pitcher, the 6-foot-3, 195-pound Hobbie grew up in Witt, Illinois, between Springfield and St. Louis. The only member of the quartet of promising pitchers not originally signed by the Cubs, Hobbie started his pro career in 1955 with Charleston, West Virginia, briefly pitched in the White Sox organization, and was purchased by the Cubs for $85,000 while pitching for Double-A Memphis in 1957. Longtime Wrigley honcho Pants Rowland saw him pitch in a doubleheader, starting in the first game and relieving in the nitecap. His rubber-arm status impressed Rowland, the Cubs signed him, and Hobbie became a busy man the next three seasons with the Cubs.

Hobbie started and relieved for the 1958 Cubs, appearing in 55 games, including 16 starts to fill in when Drott and Drabowsky had their troubles. He impressed with a 10-6 record. He was promoted to the starting rotation in 1959, blossoming with a 16-13 record, three shutouts, and 3.69 ERA. The Cubs couldn't get enough of a good thing, though. Hobbie started 33 games and relieved in 13 more, his hard sinker perfectly suited for Wrigley Field. "They didn't have radar guns like they had now, but I think I threw between 90 and 95 mph," he said.

The righthander didn't do badly for himself, all things considered, for the horrible 60-94 Cubs of 1960. Hobbie led the league in defeats with 20, but also won 16 games, four of which were shutouts. He made 36 starts and 10 relief appearances, going 2-3 with one save.

"I actually thought I pitched better baseball in 1960 than the year before," Hobbie said. "I had all the pitches working—fastball, curve, changeup.

"I really thought it was a matter of time before I became the best right-handed starter in the league."

But maybe the 26 complete games twinned with the relief outings between starts and inattention to mechanics were taking a subtle toll.

"They overworked a lot of these pitchers," catcher Dick Bertell said.

Hobbie's fortunes nosedived early in 1961. He began experiencing lower-back pain, above his right hip. "I couldn't follow through," he said. "I was pitching straight up. Every game it got worse and worse. I told the team I was having problems."

On a West Coast trip, Hobbie visited Dr. Robert Kerlan, the Dodgers' team physician and a sports-medicine pioneer. "He told me not to pick up my year-old son [Glen], that it could be a serious problem," he said of the back. The implication was that Hobbie should rest his back, but that wasn't Kerlan's decision to make.

Finally Hobbie saw the Cubs' physician. "He stuck a big needle in my back with cortisone and told me to go back out to pitch," he said. "But the cortisone didn't last the whole game. I changed my delivery to compensate for the back pain. My normal delivery was to drive low off the mound to throw the sinker. It helped me; I loved to pitch in Wrigley Field. I ended up hurting my shoulder, and it hurt like a toothache.

"After the first few years I had in Chicago, you'd figure they'd be concerned," said Hobbie. "But they thought of me like a piece of meat. Today, they would have had enough money invested in me to have not taken those kind of chances. If I'd have been on the disabled list for 15 days, I'd have been fine. But then, the credo was to pitch. You felt you were going to lose your spot."

Hobbie was never the same after his back injury. He finished 1961 7-13 with a 4.26 ERA, then declined further to 5-14 with a 5.22 ERA, dividing his time between the rotation and the bullpen for the 103-loss Cubs of 1962. By 1963, he was merely the fourth or fifth starter, going 6-10 in 24 starts (7-10 overall).

Eventually, Holland traded Hobbie to the Cardinals for former Braves ace Lew Burdette on June 2, 1964. Hobbie actually played an unusual role in the disastrous Lou Brock-for-Ernie Broglio deal 13 days later. Hobbie pitched well in his first two Cardinal starts, convincing the Redbirds they had an extra starter to spare, in this case Broglio. Had Hobbie flopped, the Cardinals might have pulled Broglio off the table, Brock might have stayed a Cub, and two teams' histories would have been different.

The Cards landed Brock, and then Hobbie's career flickered out at 28. He pitched poorly in mid-summer, his '64 major-league line 1-5 with a 5.65 ERA. He was demoted to Triple-A Jacksonville late in the summer, missing out on the Cardinals' near-miracle pennant rally at the end of September. He never pitched again in the majors.

Hobbie had the privilege of pitching for the two NL clubs closest to his downstate Illinois home. Bob Anderson was even luckier. Growing up a Cubs fan in Hammond, Indiana, less than 25 miles from the Loop, he was thrilled when his childhood heroes signed him at 18 out of Hammond High School in 1954. He pitched in Cedar Rapids and Des Moines in 1954 and 1955, then attracted Bob Scheffing's attention with a 12-4 record and 2.65 ERA in 70 games as a reliever in 1956 at Los Angeles. More minor-league seasoning in 1957 and 1958 followed, sandwiched around a brief callup to the Cubs.

Anderson stuck with the Cubs in the middle of 1958, going 3-3 while shuttling between the rotation and bullpen. Scheffing then inserted him full-time in the rotation in 1959. He pitched competitively, falling below .500 only in his final start to finish 12-13 with a 4.14 ERA.

Anderson, of course, loved pitching at home. For many games he'd hop the South Shore electric commuter train in Hammond, travel to the end of the line in downtown Chicago, then switch to the "L" for the rest of the trip to Wrigley Field. And he found his share of fun. He was the pitcher on the mound who triggered the wacky incident in which two balls were inadvertantly put into play in a game against the Cardinals on June 30, 1959 at Wrigley Field. Umpire Vic Delmore absent-mindedly handed Anderson a new baseball while the actual, live ball had gotten behind the plate. Amid an argument at homeplate, Anderson heaved the ball toward second base, just before the real ball was thrown there.

"Bob was something," Jerry Kindall said. "He could eat. We'd go out to eat dinner, and he'd have three milkshakes at one sitting."

Anderson first flirted with physical problems after 1959. "I had an elbow problem and I got cortisone shots," he said. The clock then advanced to 1961, in the middle of the chaos of the College of Coaches regime. Top Cubs reliever Don Elston had arm problems, and starter Anderson was asked to switch to the bullpen to fill in.

"They came to me and asked if I would take over relief duties," Anderson said. "I wanted to pitch, sure. But in those days if they asked you to do something, it was like telling you. The worst decision I made was to pitch in relief.

"I'd pitch four or five days in a row, have a day off, and then another four or five days in a row."

Anderson's downfall came during the August 25 to 27, 1961 series in Pittsburgh.

"I pitched three innings one night, then four innings for the win the next night and three innings for a save the third night. The last guy I faced was Roberto Clemente. It was a pitch that didn't need to have thrown.

"I had a 1-and-2 count, and threw a pitch just below the waist. Roberto dropped his bat, thinking he was called out. The whole ball was over the white of the plate. The ump missed it. The catcher walked away, I was walking off the mound, and Roberto was walking off.

"I had to throw another pitch. It was a fastball on the inside of the plate. I jammed him and got Roberto out. I felt something in my shoulder, a sensation, not pain. I think the handwriting was on the wall."

After an off day in Chicago, Anderson warmed up for the game in the bullpen. "When I tried to put something extra on it, it felt like someone jabbed a hot poker in my shoulder," he said. "After three innings, I asked to be taken out of the game. It was a few weeks again before I pitched. When I did get into a few games, I did absolutely lousy. It hurt, and I kind of slung the ball instead of throwing it with a snap to it. I got a few guys out because they weren't used to seeing me throw that slow."

Like most pitchers of the day, Anderson dreaded visiting a doctor due to the fear of major surgery and job security. But he did ask to see a physician. Management told him a visit wasn't needed. "They implied I was just shirking it, that there was nothing wrong with me," he said. "That was the attitude management had."

From that point forward, Anderson felt a "tug" in his shoulder every time he pitched. "After a time, the pain went away, but the life in my fastball didn't' come back," he said. "I was very ineffective. I had a feeling that what was in there nobody could really help me with."

Anderson finished 1961 with a 7-10 record and 4.26 ERA. Still chucking in the bullpen, he was 2-7 with a 5.02 ERA in 1962. He was traded to the Tigers for infielder Steve Boros before the 1963 season, going 3-1 with a 3.30 ERA, mostly in relief. But, barely 28, he was finished.

Anderson went into business. He didn't need his shoulder to sell products for Inland Steel in Tulsa. But one day in the early 1990s, he saw an orthopedic physician after his son, David, broke his leg. Anderson wanted his left shoulder looked at after hurting it on a golf swing. Then he mentioned the old right-shoulder injury from his pitching days. The doctor pushed at the area, driving Anderson to the floor.

"It was my rotator cuff," he said. "That's what I had hurt in 1961. I don't know if it hit them that they were handling people wrong, that pitchers needed some rest. Look at the way Paul Richards ran his pitching staffs; he only let them throw a certain number of pitches. With the Cubs, only when things were going bad would they take you out of there. You'd throw a lot of pitches, you were still out there."

He Didn't Need a Relief Manager

The injuries to Drott, Drabowsky, Hobbie, and Anderson robbed the Cubs of a potentially solid rotation just as home-grown young hitters such as Billy Williams, Ron Santo, and George Altman were coming up on the cusp of the 1960s, followed in short order by Lou Brock and Kenny Hubbs. And their unavailability to vault a slugging Cubs team into contention in 1958 and 1959 indirectly cost the Cubs the services of Bob Scheffing, probably the best manager of the second-division era.

A Cubs catcher in the 1940s, Scheffing was named "Grumpy" for his disposition. But he soon developed a reputation as a good handler of young players. When Scheffing and John Holland were promoted from Los Angeles in 1956, they enjoyed a honeymoon period despite the Cubs' 62-92 record the next season.

Holland swung some good trades for veteran hitters to supplement one-man-gang Ernie Banks. By early in the 1958 season, first baseman Dale Long, outfielders Bobby Thomson and Lee Walls, and third baseman Alvin Dark joined Banks and left fielder Moose Moryn to give the Cubs a crowd-pleasing, albeit one-dimensional corps of hitters who set a team record with 182 homers.

The Cubs began to shed their sad-sack image. And that good feeling filtered down to the minor leagues.

"Bob Scheffing pumped some life into the team," second baseman Jerry Kindall said of his 1957 service under Scheffing prior to going back to the minors. "I enjoyed playing for Bob. In 1959, at Ft. Worth, we were following the parent club. I was anxious to get back to Chicago because the team was doing well. We as players all felt confident in Bob. A winning spirit had developed."

"He was low-key, but still a very good communicator with his players," said Jim Marshall, a Scheffing successor many-times-removed, but in 1959 a part-time Cubs first baseman. "The team had a good attitude."

Scheffing also was a straight shooter with the beat writers covering the Cubs.

"Scheffing was very honest," said Jack Kuenster, then of the *Chicago Daily News*. "He said, 'I'll never lie to you.' Any guy who played for him will back that up."

But Scheffing had to mix and match in his starting rotation as Drott and Drabowsky came up lame in 1958. Joining the Gold Dust Twins as starters were Hobbie, Anderson, Taylor "T-Bone" Phillips, Dave Hillman, Johnny Briggs, Marcelino Solis, Jim Brosnan, Gene Fodge, John Buzhardt, and 18-year-old Dick Ellsworth. He was helped by the first (and, if the truth be known, one of the very few) legitimate effective lefty-right bullpen combos in Cubs history—righthander Don "Everday" Elston and southpaw Bill Henry. The duo would go on to repeat their stellar work in 1959, leading baseball writer Jerry Holtzman to successfully campaign for the introduction of the save as an official statistic.

In spite of the Elston-Henry bullpen duo, shaky overall pitching made worse by stone-fingered defense from the slow-footed sluggers, the Cubs couldn't build on a 46-42, third-place record in late July, falling to 72-82 in fifth by season's end. Clearly, continued health and improvement by Drott and Drabowsky might have kept the Cubs safely over .500, if not continuing marginally in the pennant race against the arch-rival Braves.

By all measures, Scheffing had the Cubs on the move as a franchise despite the late-season fade. Perhaps Phil Wrigley expected a continued linear trend moving up on the winning charts. Scheffing still had pitching inconsistency and the after-effects of Drott and Drabowsky's injuries with which to contend in 1959. And now he had a new problem, similar to one faced by Jim Riggleman, another Scheffing successor-many-times-removed, 40 years later: Aging veterans often don't repeat good years.

The production of Moryn, Walls, Thomson, and Long fell sharply. Banks went on to a stupendous season by 1959 standards—45 homers and 143 RBI—to capture his second straight NL Most Valuable Player Award. But no other Cub had more than 14 homers. George Altman provided some punch and speed as an outfield rookie, but he suffered through some of the usual first-year troubles. Scheffing, an expert on juggling his pitchers by now, had to do the same with his lineup, instituting platooning at different positions.

"Bob was trying to platoon, to create as much offense as he could that year," said Jim Marshall, who in '59 split time with Long at first base.

In spite of the productivity problems springing up all over, Scheffing had the Cubs playing at a 50-48 clip near the end of July. But a seven-game losing streak dropped the Cubs under .500 for the rest of the season, brought to a head some long-festering clubhouse problems and ended the Holland/Scheffing honeymoon. The really strange days of Cubs history were about to commence.

As the Cubs slid out of contention in August 1959, several of the slumping players started to grouse about being benched. First Dale Long complained. Then roommate Moose Moryn, also suffering through his worst Cubs season— .233 in 303 at-bats —spoke up before the August 25, 1959 game at Crosley Field in Cincinnati. The Moose's ire, vented in an interview with Jack Kuenster and published two days later in the *Daily News*, was directed at GM Holland, not Scheffing. He accused Holland of dictating the lineups to his manager.

"He's the guy who runs the club, not Scheffing," Moryn said.

Kuenster warned Moryn that his comments were bad for his job security. Moryn plowed ahead, anyway.

"I don't care," he said. "The way they've been using me, I'm not much good to them anyway.

"I don't think Wrigley knows what's going on. Maybe this is one way he'll find out."

Moryn also lashed into Holland for his poker-playing with players on the back of team chartered flights and alleged trips to Chicago-area race tracks on off-days in Chicago.

Holland denied he dictated lineups. Meanwhile, Wrigley cast a jaundiced eye at the poker games, although he admitted he used to play gin rummy with ex-manager and catcher Gabby Hartnett.

"That's too much," Wrigley said of the poker pots running to almost $200, "but most of the players can afford it better than Holland. The GM explained to Wrigley that he played poker "because he felt he got close to the players that way." Meanwhile, the White Sox prohibited poker games in their traveling party to prevent the bad feelings from losers being carried over onto the field.

Moryn promised Kuenster he'd really let loose when and if he was traded. Holland dealt him to the Cardinals on June 15, 1960—exactly one month after the Moose made his famous shoetop catch to end Don Cardwell's no-hitter against the Cardinals at Wrigley Field. During the Cubs' first trip into St. Louis after the deal, on July 16, 1960, the Moose said the only way the front office would change would be under new ownership.

"And if Holland goes, I'll send him flowers," he said.

He posed a question, never sufficiently answered through the decades: "Why was Scheffing railroaded after bringing the club to a fifth place finish? Why couldn't he play the guys he wanted to in 1959?"

Many in baseball were similarly puzzled the first day after the '59 season ended—Monday, September 28. Despite the roster holes and poor performances, Scheffing brought to the Cubs in to a 74-80 finish, fated to be their best record between 1952 and 1963. Almost all pundits and insiders in the game praised Scheffing for a job well done. The *Chicago Tribune* said the Cubs had shown "steady but not spectacular improvement under Scheffing." Interestingly, "steady but not spectacular" was Andy MacPhail's stated philosophy, almost word for word, to uplift the Cubs 35 years later.

"I figured I'd get both a new contract and a raise," Scheffing later recalled. But when he met Wrigley, he was informed that he, pitching coach Freddie Fitzsimmons, hitting coach Rogers Hornsby, and coach George Myatt were being cashiered.

Wrigley told Scheffing he was recycling Cubs war horse Charlie Grimm "in an effort to loosen up the club because it was too tense." That apparently made reference to the Long-Moryn dissension of a month earlier.

Wrigley obviously didn't ask his players if they were tense.

"I thought Bob did a super job," Glen Hobbie said. "I was really, really disappointed when he was fired."

Tribune sports columnist Dave Condon, who usually stayed away from hard-hitting columns, labeled Scheffing a "scapegoat."

The owner, as usual, made the wrong move with the wrong people. And, not possessing the networking skills in the game, he called upon his pool of Cubs lifers, in this case Grimm, 63, for his third term as manager. Grimm had served with Holland and Pants Rowland, 81, as a part of a three-headed group of team vice presidents since the fall of 1956, his own managerial achievements of pennants in 1932, 1935, and 1945 already belonging to a bygone era.

"Every time we call on Grimm, the Cubs win a pennant," was Wrigley's rationale in the press conference. "I always thought we should have relief managers, just like relief pitchers," adding that managers were expendable.

Showing his lack of understanding of his personnel, Wrigley said Grimm was better able to handle young players. The contrarian in him struck again. Scheffing, 15 years younger than Grimm, had gained notoriety all over the game as a good handler of young players.

"Bob is a sincere, conscientious worker," Wrigley said. "We have the same high regard for him as on the day he joined our club. We feel he is a valuable asset to our organization."

If so, why the move, which made little sense for baseball reasons, a recurring theme in the million-to-one era? A common theory held that Wrigley desired to stir up some publicity for the Cubs to compete with the pennant-winning White Sox, who had virtually taken over the town from mid-summer on. Even during their worst years, the Cubs often enjoyed a publicity advantage compared to the Sox. Playing all day games at home, newspapers could more easily lay out nice packages of stories and photos without the deadline dash of night games. Dave Condon later remembered how he had hours after Sam Jones' May 12, 1955 Cubs no-hitter to track down Jim "Hippo" Vaughn, the last Cub prior to Jones to toss a no-no, back in 1919. He would not have had that luxury if the no-hitter had been played at night. In the 1970s, Bill Veeck complained about imbalanced coverage, even measuring column inches. Yet even today, with broadcast outlets now the dominant way fans receive their sports news, the Cubs' predominantly daytime schedule gives them an advantage in coverage against the Sox.

But in 1959, the newspapers were chock full of Sox stories. Future Pulitzer Prize winner Lois Wille even penned a series of features on Sox families at home in the *Daily News*. The pages were loaded with extra coverage and player profiles. For the first time under Wrigley's ownership watch, the Cubs were losing the publicity battle, and looked bad compared to the Sox achievements.

"Wrigley denies it emphatically, but one fact is most obvious in the removal of Scheffing," Condon wrote on September 29, 1959. "Bob has been made the sacrificial lamb for a Cub organization that finds, now that the White Sox have won a pennant, its fans no longer will stand for excuses and alibis and poor baseball."

Wrigley obviously was irritated by the fans' mass letter-writing assault on him in the *Daily News* at the end of July 1959. But believing that managers were expendable and seeing how GM Holland kowtowed to him, Scheffing got the gate. Moryn's comments to Kuenster also hinted at behind-the-scenes conflicts between Holland and Scheffing, and Scheffing would only lose those disputes under Wrigley's ownership. Obviously, Holland did not fight for Scheffing, his partner since their Los Angeles Angels days in 1959, a fact *Tribune* baseball writer Ed Prell would go on to note during the 1959 winter meetings.

One other factor could have been present. In Peter Golenback's *Wrigleyville*, Don Elston remembered how Scheffing's wife, Mary, had made some negative comments that irritated Wrigley prior to the 1959 season. If that was the case, it did not help her husband when he became a victim of circumstances and an eccentric owner.

Scheffing was not out of luck by any means. He became manager of the Detroit Tigers. Born too soon to benefit from baseball's wild card, Scheffing piloted the Tigers to a 101-win season in 1961, good enough in most years for a near-runaway pennant win, but in '61 only a very respectable runner-up finish to the 109-victory New York Yankees of home-run kings Roger Maris and Mickey Mantle. He went on to serve as New York Mets general manager. Scheffing died at 72 in 1985.

His post-Cubs life immersed him in a more successful atmosphere than he left behind in Chicago. All the positive momentum and team attitude built up from 1957 to 1959 began to dissipate with his firing. The managerial chaos Wrigley wrought with his firing would soon engulf the Cubs. But, first, Holland made the first in a long series of bad trades.

No team ever could have enough pitching, particularly the Cubs. Yet Holland, like Jim Frey three decades later, thirsted for power in Wrigley Field. He had short-term success with imported sluggers in 1958. Now he went to the trading marts to find another long-ball threat. The slumps of the veterans led opposing pitchers to issue 20 intentional walks to Ernie Banks during the 1959 season. Holland wanted a slugger, any slugger, to protect Mr. Cub in the batting order. His chronic impatience also showed, not believing any existing Cubs like George Altman or Lee Walls could provide that protection.

Giving the League Left-handed Relief

Good left-handed pitchers don't grow on trees. Holland ignored that axiom by dealing Bill Henry, Walls, and promising young outfielder Lou Jackson to the Cincinnati Reds for Frank Thomas, no relation to the White Sox first baseman.

Thomas, an outfielder-first baseman-third baseman whose main position was swinging the bat, had belted 160 homers for the Pirates from 1953 to 1958. But he had slumped to 12 homers and .225 in '59 in Cincy, his swing apparently hampered by a nerve condition in his right thumb. Holland drooled at the thought of a revival of Thomas' 1958 campaign, in which he belted 35 homers in spacious Forbes Field.

At the same time, Holland ripped open his bullpen. Henry had been a workhorse for Scheffing, hurling 134 innings, giving up just 111 hits and 26 walks to go along with 115 strikeouts. Henry had a 2.68 ERA with 12 saves. Along with another ex-Cub, Jim Brosnan (10-4, 3.04 ERA, 16 saves), Henry would turn into a mainstay of the pennant-winning Reds bullpen in 1961 with a 2.19 ERA and 16 saves.

"I was surprised they traded me," Henry later said. "I had heard that Casey Stengel had wanted me for the Yankees, but the Cubs first said there was no way they were going to trade me. I came up with a pretty good changeup (with the Reds). And the teams were a little better than in Chicago."

Holland had no faith that Walls, still just 26, who had hit .304 with 24 homers in 1958, would revive after a dropoff to eight homers and .257 in '59. Nor did he see the wisdom of further developing Jackson, a speedy outfielder who led the Eastern League in hitting with .338 in 1959.

Fans wrote in to the (italics) Daily News (end italics) with more dissent against the Cubs. "I think the Cubs got the worst of the Thomas deal," said Edward Gyurina of Kenosha, Wis. "They gave up a top relief pitcher in Bill Henry and a good rookie in Lou Jackson for a player who I think is over the hill (Thomas). Penned Raymond P. Fitzpatrick of River Forest, Ill.: "I think the Cubs gave away one of the best relief pitchers in the game for a guy who hit below .250 last year."

Holland compounded the error of giving up precious left-handed pitching near the end of the following spring training in 1960. The GM would make, in the words of Ron Santo, "an unnecessary trade" that would further deplete Cubs pitching in years to come.

Santo himself inadvertantly triggered the deal. On the fast track upward after just one minor-league season. a productive one (87 RBI's, .327) at Double-A San Antonio in 1959, Santo was practically promised the Cubs' third-base job by Grimm and Holland coming out of spring training. But he was unexpectedly called into Grimm's office one morning, informed by the manager and Holland that he was being optioned to Triple-A Houston. Holland had to calm down a disconsolate Santo, and even sweetened his contract to cushion the blow.

He did not look at his own roster to try to find a third baseman. After all, Thomas had played some third, Holland never really cared for a slick-gloved roster as the makeup of the 1958 team indicated, and Thomas was only being added to a crowded left-field and first-base situation. But the GM instead took inspiration from Wid Matthews and called up the Dodgers. Veteran utilityman Don Zimmer was available, having nowhere to go in the Los Angeles infield behind starters Junior Gilliam at third, Maury Wills at shortstop and Charlie Neal at second. The pitching-conscious Dodgers knew an easy mark—and they knew who they wanted. So on April 8, 1960, Holland dispatched his top left-handed pitching prospect, Ron Perranoski—Santo's San Antonio roommate—along with infielder Johnny Goryl and minor-league outfielder Lee Handley for Zimmer.

The end result? Perranoski was safely in the Dodgers' winning clutches. Meanwhile, Santo's demotion did not last long. He was called up to the Cubs June 26, 1960. He did not vacate the third-base job for the next 13 1/2 years. The Cubs did not need Don Zimmer, but they sure could have used Perranoski.

The deal fulfilled the prophecy of Dallas-Ft. Worth manager Lou Klein when Perranoski was called up from San Antonio to help bolster the Cubs' Triple-A team in the 1959 playoffs. The taciturn Klein, a lifelong Wrigley loyalist, would make one of the most outrageous statements ever uttered in modern baseball.

"I won one game in the playoffs, and then we got knocked out," said Perranoski, now special assistant to San Francisco Giants GM Brian Sabean. "After the playoffs, Klein called me into his office. He said, 'Ron, next year, you have a good year, make a name for yourself, and maybe we can trade you and get something for you.' I was shocked. I had a pretty good year. I couldn't believe it."

Neither could old hands around the Cubs or others to which Klein's comments were repeated 40 years later. "See what kind of assholes we had in the organization," huffed Billy Williams, another Perranoski teammate in San Antonio in 1959, when informed of the statement before one 1999 Wrigley Field game.

"Lou was a very abrasive guy, a very intense guy," remembered Jerry Kindall, who also played for Klein. "Lou sometimes said things that were ill-advised. But in spite of that abrasiveness and having some guys mad at him a lot of the time, he knew baseball."

He also must have known his front-office boss in Chicago. Klein apparently was tuned into Holland's modus operandi of habitually trading young players for veterans, of always believing the Cubs could get better value from other team's players instead of grooming their own home-grown talent.

Perranoski was the epitome of the latter. The Cubs had been lucky to land him in the first place out of Michigan State University in 1958. The White Sox had originally been on his trail, but cooled on him as he graduated college. Ohio-based Cubs scout John Streza liked him and signed the lefthander for $21,000, a respectable bonus for the time, ahead of overtures from the Washington Senators and Philadelphia Phillies.

After a rocky start in the lower minor leagues in 1958, Perranoski blossomed at San Antonio the following season. He was 11-10 with a 3.12 ERA in 37 games. His 139 strikeouts were one short of leading the Texas League. Perranoski, San Antonio teammate Jim Brewer and 19-year-old Dick Ellsworth gave the Cubs a trio of top southpaw pitching prospects.

Of course, the pitching-conscious Dodgers would pluck Perranoski, then re-unite him with the underperforming Brewer four years later. Migrating to a club expert on developing hurlers, Perranoski learned not only from the Dodgers' coaches, but also from the mere presence of pitching giants like Sandy Koufax, whom he befriended, and Don Drysdale. He was converted to bullpen duty in 1960.

Promoted to the parent club in 1961, Perranoski was 7-5 with a 2.61 ERA. By 1963, he was baseball's best left-handed reliever with a 16-3 record, 1.67 ERA and 21 saves, anchoring the bullpen for three World Series clubs. He continued to be effective for the Minnesota Twins, for whom he helped win AL West divisional titles in 1969 and 1970 with a total of 65 saves. Perranoski finished his big-league career with a 2.79 ERA and 179 saves. He later served as pitching coach for some fine Dodgers staffs in the 1980s.

Maybe Perranoski wouldn't have developed in the same manner as a Cub. By the time he was traded at the end of spring training 1960, the Cubs were fast creating a near-comical on-field and front-office atmosphere that would hamper the development of a slew of good prospects. It's a miracle Ron Santo and Billy Williams survived the ordeal to become Hall of Fame-calibre players, with Williams actually getting the nod for Cooperstown enshrinement.

Perranoski would go on to see some finely-tuned spring-training camps at Dodgertown in Vero Beach, Florida. The camps were a 180-degree turn from the languid operation that old warhorse Grimm ran in 1960 in Mesa, and many Cubs camps to come.

Grimm brought in 1930-era Cubs teammate Charlie Root as pitching coach. He ran a lax camp, simply throwing the balls and bats out there to let the players play. There was little emphasis on fundamentals.

"The game had passed Charlie Grimm by in 1960," Glen Hobbie said. "We didn't work on anything. We just went out there and played. It was a wasted spring training."

Later on one Cub, quoted anonymously by Jack Kuenster in the *Daily News*, said the young pitchers did not learn anything new in camp in Mesa. No pitcher worked more than five innings in the spring.

Cholly Not So Jolly

The lack of fundamentals instruction and proper workouts had an immediate effect. The 1960 Cubs stumbled badly out of the gate as Grimm, suffering from a foot ailment, walked the streets at night frustrated. On May 4, with the Cubs at 6-11, Phil Wrigley relieved him. Again, he could not plug into the baseball network, so he looked inward. His choice was at once bizarre and potentially great—Lou Boudreau.

Jack Brickhouse was astonished when Wrigley proposed a trade—Grimm for Boudreau, then in his third season as WGN-Radio color analyst. No owner had ever traded a manager for a broadcaster before. But the contrarian was true to his reputation. At least in this respect, he tapped the best-qualified baseball man on site at Wrigley Field. And WGN was not getting a neophyte behind the mike. Grimm, colorful off the field and a top baseball storyteller, had worked in radio in the 1930s.

Boudreau at last fulfilled his dream of an on-field job with the Cubs. Overcoming some initial family misgivings and the sagging team fortunes, he jumped at the job. The Cubs, at least outwardly, had the veneer of a winner, Boudreau's reputation as a 30-year-old player/manager and AL MVP of the 1948 world champion Cleveland Indians still fresh on everybody's minds. Later, in the 1950s, Boudreau had managed lesser clubs in Boston and Kansas City.

Unfortunately, the Cubs were too far gone, physically and emotionally. The Boudreau appointment did not help at all. Cubs pitching remained in a shambles, forcing Holland to trade a key lineup contributor, second baseman Tony Taylor, to the Phillies for pitcher Don Cardwell on

May 13, 1960. Two days later, Cardwell hurled his famed no-hitter at Wrigley Field. But he was fated to stay a Cub only two and one-half seasons, while Taylor, the Cubs' first Cuban player, became a sparkplug-type big leaguer for the next 14 seasons.

"I thought I'd be here all my life," Taylor said of the Cubs. "I almost quit," he said. "I almost went back to Cuba."

Ernie Banks and Taylor chum Frank de Lama talked him out of it, and the rest was history. Before he got the rest of his career in gear, he exacted his revenge on the Cubs the old-fashioned way, with a shower of basehits later in 1960.

"My first game against the Cubs, I wanted to show they traded the wrong guy," Taylor said. "I played great. For three games it was unbelievable."

That only added to the misery that Boudreau could not alleviate. The Cubs continued to wallow in last place. And as the hot summer wore on and players shuttled in and out of the lineup, team morale plummeted, making the gripes of Moryn a year earlier seem like a whisper.

Once again it was young muckraker Jack Kuenster serving as a conduit in the *Daily News*. Three days after Moryn's post-mortem blast at Holland in St. Louis, a chorus of Cubs bent Kuenster's ear in Cincinnati. He quoted them anonymously in a July 19, 1960 story.

First nameless player quoted said the majority of Cubs had lost faith in Boudreau after only two and one-half months on the job. He added the Cubs needed a "guy like Leo Durocher." Perhaps he planted a seed in Phil Wrigley's mind. Another said the Cubs had "lost faith in themselves."

A player backed up Moryn's analysis of control-freak Holland, claiming the GM "is still calling the shots." Dissenters like Moryn, Long, Earl Averill and Cal Neeman were traded away, noted another.

One Cub said there was an "uncertainty and tenseness" among players who did not know whether they were in the lineup from one day to another. A teammate, whom Kuenster described as being "bounced in and out of the lineup," told Boudreau to "play me or trade me."

That player could have been Frank Thomas, who suddenly found himself a platoon player in left field, starting only against lefthanders despite ranking second to Ernie Banks in homers on the club. Four decades later, Thomas said Boudreau said the platoon idea came from "the front office, then he said it was his doing."

Hearing Thomas' complaints, both Holland and Boudreau asked Thomas to breakfast one morning on the road. Thomas, then 31, was told the

Cubs wanted him to work with their younger players. Within a few weeks, Holland cut Thomas, who was making around $30,000 at the time, two additional checks. "He gave me those checks to appease me," Thomas said. The following off-season, Holland cut Thomas' salary by $8,000. "He said he was going to get back the money he gave me," Thomas said, still wondering after the passage of decades why his 21-homer production in 1960 didn't merit more playing time on a team still short of power other than Ernie Banks.

Before Holland dipped into the treasury in an attempt to buy off Thomas, he had ordered traveling secretary/public relations man Don Biebel to put the best possible spin control on Kuenster's story. A press release was issued to the traveling writers on July 21, 1960 as they boarded the team bus heading for another game at Crosley Field.

"As a result of the article that appeared in the *Chicago Daily News* of July 19, the Chicago Cubs players and coaches voluntarily held a meeting and issued the following statement:

'The Chicago Cubs unanimously agree they are 100 percent behind manager Lou Boudreau. The statement attributed to various Cub players in no way reflects the general attitude of the team.

'We all agree that the blame for our recent poor showing should be laid at our feet and not at Boudreau's.

'We, the players and coaches, consider this a closed issue.'"

It wasn't. Player-coach Elvin Tappe, who had Wrigley's ear, spit at Kuenster's feet as he boarded a team bus. Jack Brickhouse, who was closer to management than most broadcasters in his dual role as manager of WGN Sports for both TV and radio, denounced Kuenster's article on a Cubs telecast.

The '60 Cubs then limped to the finish line, 60-94 overall and 54-83 under Boudreau. The only diversion the rest of the season after the controversy in Cincinnati was Billy Martin's anti-social personality sticking its fist squarely into the million-to-one streak. The maladjusted infielder, then winding his career down with the Reds, cold-cocked Jim Brewer for little apparent reason on the mound on August 4, 1960 at Wrigley Field. Welcome to the majors, Jim. The rookie suffered a fractured cheekbone and underwent three operations in the next few months. Brewer and the Cubs sued Martin for $1 million. Brewer never developed as a Cub, and Martin's punch sure didn't help.

After the season, Boudreau asked Wrigley for a two-year contract. That might have been the equivalent of asking the old man to chew

Beechnut. Boudreau was summarily rejected, but had the cushion of his old job at WGN waiting for him. The loser was Wrigley, who was plum out of ideas and job candidates. What to do, who do I talk to?

A College, But No Sheepskins

The wheels began spinning in the contrarian's head. Managers are expendable; maybe they're also obsolete. Why even hire a manager? You'd have to fire him.

The College of Coaches was born.

Or, in early 1960s catcher Dick Bertell's words, "The College of Complexes."

Or, in sportscaster Chet Coppock's words, "The dumbest single coaching situation in history of modern sports."

Wrigley sprung a Christmas present like none other on Cubs fans on December 20, 1960, amid an early-winter blizzard and cold snap that made for even lower morale in Chicago. After consultations with loyalist Elvin Tappe about a way to standardize instruction throughout the Cubs organization, Wrigley went to the outer limits to unveil a scheme in which eight coaches would rotate throughout the Cubs system, from Class D up to Wrigley Field. The original scheme did not provide for any kind of manager until all the coaches, who would average $15,000 pay each, would be selected. And they would be fed baseball information from a new-fangled IBM computer system.

"We're getting together our army before picking the general," Wrigley said. "We're going after good men. We've decided they are the heart of a ball club. They'll be on a sort of civil service basis. Instead of going fishing or hunting after the season ends, they'll be in the office tabulating and working on a scientific system which we hope will be reflected in winning teams."

In their 1961 media guide, the Cubs further tried to explain the College of Coaches concept—and why the team believed it could function without a manager.

"The custom of having a manager has been followed for 90 years in baseball—that is, ever since the professional game started in 1871.

"The manager set-up has meant constant turnover both in personnel and style of play. In the last 14 years in the two major leagues, 103 changes of managers have been made. And each new manager generally meant a new style of play and a new set of coaches who, for the most part, were special friends of the manager.

"The core of the new Cubs program is a standard system of play, administered by a stable, good-sized group of coaches. The coaches are selected on the basis of merit, knowledge of the game, and ability to teach, rather than personal favoritism."

Rotating the coaches throughout the minor-league system seemed designed to increase the familiarity of player to coach, and vice versa.

"He will not come to the major league club as a stranger in strange surroundings," the media guide said of minor-league callups to the Cubs. "When he arrives on the Cubs roster, he will know personally—and be known by—the coaches who have worked with him on his way up."

In theory, an expanded coaching staff and standardized instruction sounded like a good idea. Amid a goodly amount of media satire of Wrigley's plan, *Chicago Tribune* columnist David Condon wrote, "The forecast is that rather than spoiling the broth with too many coaches, Wrigley has made a move that will pay dividends to the long suffering Cub fans."

The coaches themselves had excellent baseball pedigrees, and not all of them were inbred Cubs lifers. In addition to Elvin Tappe and Charlie Grimm, pitching coaches Vedie Himsl and Fred Martin were added from the Cubs organization. So were ex-catcher Verlon "Rube" Walker and Lou Klein. The pitching brain trust supposedly was boosted further by Goldie Holt, who had been roving pitching instructor in the Dodgers' farm system. Ex-Cubs Bobby Adams and Ripper Collins came on board. Former Kansas City Athletics manager Harry Craft was added to the mix, which expanded to 10 coaches early in the 1961 season.

"The individuals in the College of Coaches were good ones," said Jerry Kindall, who fought for an infield job in the 1961 season. "They were lifetime baseball men. These were such terrific baseball men. But all of them had a little different approach. I have a way of coaching now that's different than other coaches. No one's the same."

The premise of a standardized method of instruction fell by the wayside due to the different personalities and the lack of strong leadership and coordination in the front office. John Holland wasn't going to lead the charge, and neither was the bookish Gene Lawing, a no-nonsense fellow in charge of the farm system and scouting staff. Perhaps they didn't understand it themselves. When Wrigley announced the coaching system, Holland conceded the Cubs were "trying something new which is probably very difficult to explain."

No additional front-office personnel were added to coordinate the greatly expanded coaching staff. Astute baseball types said the coaching system could have worked if it was confined to the minor leagues, where instruction was most needed, instead of rotating the coaching corps up to the big leagues and back again. Each minor-league team of the era always needed more instructional help; their managers typically did not have any full-time, traveling coaches helping them in the manner of recent decades.

Without careful coordination, the instructional system ran amok. In impressing his own philosophy on players, each coach added to mounting confusion in the organization as the '61 season got underway. Always insecure about their jobs unless they were superstars, the players' morale plummeted. The instability couldn't have come at a worse time for the development of the organization. The average age of the Cubs going into the 1961 season was 25.1. The players needed consistency of instruction, and plenty of it. They got none of the former, negating any quantitative benefits from the latter.

"It was a mystery to players," Kindall said. "There was a feeling of skepticism and wonder. Most were willing to give the College of Coaches a chance, but it didn't work. The 1961 season was turmoil all year."

Somehow, some way, prime young players such as Billy Williams and Ron Santo fought their way through the psychological minefield of the College of Coaches. Williams, whose natural swing couldn't be hurt by anyone, won the Rookie of the Year award with his 25-homer, 86-RBI production. The 21-year-old Santo had 23 homers, 32 doubles, 83 RBI, and a .284 average. But veteran infielder Don Zimmer, who had taken Santo under his wing the previous season, was upset at the different coaching styles to which Santo was exposed. Zimmer criticized the College's potential for confusing Santo on Lou Boudreau's pre-game radio show one day late in the '61 season. His reward from Wrigley and Holland was banishment to the original New York Mets via the expansion draft after the season.

Despite the presence of capable coaches Martin and Himsl, pitching instruction lagged amid the turmoil. Another tone of generally substandard help for hurlers was set for the million-to-one era.

"You really couldn't get any help from the coaches," said righthander Bob Anderson, who was converted to the bullpen with disastrous results in 1961. "I wanted to develop a slider, and I had to ask another player. You couldn't ask anyone for help. I don't think you had any coaches there who were knowledgeable about pitchers, or knew how important it was to handle people. The Cubs just didn't know how to handle pitchers."

Making the situation even worse was the rotating system of "head coaches," the *faux* managers. The idea of a permanent manager was shelved. Holland announced just before the '61 season that Himsl would open as head coach. After 11 games, Craft replaced him as Himsl went to Double-A San Antonio. Himsl returned two weeks later. The baton then was passed among Craft, Tappe, and Lou Klein for the rest of the season, the lineups changing depending on which man was annointed head coach that week. Ernie Banks, hobbled by an injured knee, moved from short-stop to left field to first base and back to shortstop.

"For a four-game series in Pittsburgh [August 25-27, 1961], I went 11-for-16, and caught 18 innings in a doubleheader on Sunday," Dick Bertell remembered. "Tappe was the head coach. Then we go back to Chicago, and Lou Klein takes over. I sat for a week. What did I do, hit my way out of the lineup?"

Ballplayers respond to strong leadership, as Lou Brock noted. He had been on the fast track since he signed with the Cubs for $30,000 out of Southern University in 1960. "John Holland is high on Louis Clark Brock, who will make his pro debut this season in the Cubs' farm system," the *Chicago Tribune*'s Ed Prell wrote on April 2, 1961. Other organization men raved about him. "Joe Macko was his [minor-league] manager, and he told me this kid was going to be phenomenal," Dick Bertell recalled. Called up during the last month of '61 from Class C St. Cloud, Brock must have wondered if the majors were all they were cracked up to be at the sight of the coaching traffic jam.

"Players are great followers of rules and regulations of one manager," Brock said three decades later. "When you have 14 coaches, who do you follow?"

Brock and his teammates also picked up on behind-the-scenes politick-ing among the coaches. Obviously believing the College was a wacky idea that was doomed, several of the coaches began jockeying to become the per-manent manager whenever that position would be re-instituted. Tappe, having bent Wrigley's ear, was foremost in that backstage maneuvering. One way to get Ron Santo agitated today is to bring up the coaches' politicking.

"All were competing for the job of head coach," Brock said.

Outsiders had the same idea. When he announced the College of Coaches in 1960, Phil Wrigley complained about the lack of applications for the coaching jobs.

"Most everyone who contacts us wants to be a manager," the owner said. "A fellow who is with the Detroit Tigers in a minor capacity called today. I asked him if he was interested in coaching. He said he wanted to be a manager."

Imagine the coaches-who-would-be-managers sniping and backbiting at each other away from earshot of the newspaper beat reporters. The undercurrent only resumed after the Cubs assembled in Mesa for spring training in 1962, hopeful but not all-that-confident of improving on their 64-90 finish in '61. On March 7, 1962, such opinions came within range of the *Chicago Tribune*'s Richard Dozer.

"This is the easiest spring training I've seen in 10 years. This club isn't being worked hard enough," one coach said anonymously to Dozer. The pitchers were getting plenty of running, but the coach—who may have been the newly-added Charlie Metro—insisted that the fitness levels of most of the players were substandard.

Adding to the confusion in the spring of '62 was the presence of Dale Ranson, track coach of the University of North Carolina, who had been recruited by the Cubs to teach his running techniques.

"I was never so unready for a season in my life," Glen Hobbie recalled. "We were getting ready to run track, not play baseball."

College Flunks Out with Brock

Brock would have given Ranson's best Tar Heel trackmen a run for their money. With his 3.6 time to first base, second to the Reds' Vada Pinson in the NL in 1962, he didn't need help in improving his speed. The system simply was not able to get Brock ready to play in the majors, period.

Brock, possessed of the exquisite combination of speed and power, had trouble against left-handed pitchers. In the outfield, he could barely pick up a ball that hit the ground near him. Looking up in the sun, he was lost. He had played mostly night games in St. Cloud, and nobody in camp taught him how to flip his sunglasses down. That would cost him dearly playing the tortuous sun field in right field at Wrigley Field.

The College of Coaches' mere presence may have eventually cost the Cubs Brock's development, period. John Holland had taken a huge risk by calling up Brock after just one season. Then to not have a well-developed, stable system in place to groom the future Hall-of-Famer only compounded the problem.

"I probably came along at the wrong time in the Cubs organization," Brock said. "I was a shooting star in the Cubs organization. To shoot from Class C to the majors in one year had to do with the lack of talent in the organization. I didn't start to learn to play the game until I got there. And when you're learning like that, you're going to tee off somebody."

The Cubs were unable to settle in their minds on what type of player Brock should become. "I was a [power] hitter who could run," he said. "There already were big hitters in the middle of the Cubs' lineup. They had me lead off, but I didn't swing like a leadoff hitter. I had no experience hitting like that."

One coach would try to develop the power swing of Brock, who possessed a lean but powerful body. Another wanted him to try to drag bunt, building up leadoff-man skills. Billy Williams, already established as a hitter, was pained to watch the confusion mounting in Brock.

One coach seemed to get through to Brock, logging most of the center-field time in 1962. He was Charlie Metro, an émigré from the Detroit Tigers' organization who had replaced Craft in the College of Coaches for 1962. Metro followed Tappe and Klein as head coach in '62, taking over for the entire second half of the season.

"If Charlie Metro had been the manger, not just one of the rotating coaches, I would have responded to him," Brock said. "He was a perfectionist. We got along and he started to work with me to hit like a leadoff hitter."

Problem was, Brock seemingly was a majority of one among Cubs players getting along with Metro. A martinet type, he quickly angered the roster of the sagging team with ridiculous rules. Angered at an apparently lack of intense preparation for a game, he banned shaving before and after games in the clubhouse. Players tried to get Metro removed as head coach without success.

But the controversy did not stop second baseman Kenny Hubbs from giving the Cubs their second straight NL Rookie of the Year in 1962. Although Hubbs had some holes in his swing in his .260 season, he astounded baseball with his defensive brilliance at second base, going 78 games without an error to set a major-league record. Now the Cubs had a lineup of Hubbs, George Altman, Santo, Williams, Banks, and Brock. The latter three would make the Hall of Fame—and the Cubs had a record-worst 59-103 record, finishing behind the expansion Houston Colt .45s.

Horrific pitching (a team ERA of 4.54) told almost the entire story. Wrigley did not officially abandon the rotating coaches' system. Here's what the Cubs' 1963 media guide had to say: "Even in an age of orbiting space vehicles, computers, television and countless modern marvels of recent years, anybody who wants to change anything in baseball—even the style of the uniform, much less the application of modern management techniques and tools—is considered to be 'unrealistic.' Anything new in baseball therefore is generally the object of sarcastic comments from the sideline snipers. The degree of their good faith and knowledge is indicated by the outworn hilarity about the 'eight coaches'...So, for the benefit of the comedians, the Cubs have 12 coaches, not eight, or 10." Sarcastic in its own right, the media guide's explanation was the team had continually expanded the pool of coaches, and that 12 may not be enough to instruct 125 minor-leaguers.

Beneath the bluster, Wrigley quietly turned over the reins to Bob Kennedy in the off-season of 1962-63. He was still called "head coach," but he was manager in all but name only. Fred Martin was named pitching coach.

"We have had several head coaches for the Cubs and we learned that, despite our grand plan, each of the head coaches had his own individual ideas," Wrigley said. "The aim of standardization of play was not achieved because of the various personalities. We learned that the players didn't know where to turn. Each coach had a different idea. I guess it was something like the Irish policeman who said, 'It's not that I bait you because I hate you, but just to show my authority.'"

Wrigley, though, couldn't go through a season without a bizarre move.

On January 10, 1963, he named a retired Air Force colonel, Robert Whitlow, as baseball's first "athletic director." Whitlow had been friendly with Wrigley (Bud) Offield, Phil Wrigley's nephew and advertising director of the Wrigley Gum Co. When he called on Offield at the Wrigley Building in the fall of 1962, he struck up a friendship with Phil Wrigley, who had another light bulb go off in his head. Once again, instead of boosting his organization through a conventional baseball structure, the owner went against the flow.

The original plan was for Whitlow to be a kind of "centralized director," outranking John Holland. Fortunately, Whitlow had little impact on the Cubs other than erecting the "Whitlow Wall," a screen above the Wrigley Field center-field fence that hurt batters who belted pitches 410 feet. Instead of a well-deserved homer, the hitters had to settle for a double or hustle out a triple. He tried to lead Cubs players in calisthenics during spring training, and once almost got into a fight with a Cubs coach in Philadelphia. Whitlow departed rather quietly, tendering his resignation on January 7, 1965, believing he wasn't earning his $25,000 salary. "Baseball was simply not ready for an athletic director," Wrigley said. The game still isn't ready, a generation-plus later.

The Best Pitching in Baseball

Even with Whitlow's presence and the bad memories of the College of Coaches, the Cubs got a second chance at building on their crop of young players in 1963, the failure of the Drott-Drabowsky-Hobbie-Anderson foursome receding into the past. Only Hobbie remained a Cub, as a fourth or fifth starter, at this point. Santo and Williams continued their upward progress as impact hitters. Hubbs and Brock were inconsistent, but Kennedy stuck with them as regulars. Banks suffered through injury and illness, and, as a result, the Cubs hitting sputtered frequently.

But fueling a big upsurge in the standings to contender status in midsummer was a dramatically improved pitching staff. Holland finally got the better of a deal with Bing Devine just after the 1962 season, trading George Altman and Don Cardwell in exchange for starting pitcher Larry Jackson and reliever Lindy McDaniel. Jackson pitched effectively in 1963 with a 2.56 ERA, starting out 14-11 before a series of tough-luck losses dropped him to 14-18. McDaniel emerged as the franchise's second-ever heavy-duty stopper after Don Elston with a 13-7 record and 22 saves.

Altman, who had slugged 49 homers and hit more than .300 in 1961-62, slumped badly as a Cardinal. An aging Branch Rickey, then St. Louis owner Gussie Busch's special consultant, wrongly directed Altman to change to a pull hitter to take advantage of old Busch Stadium's short right-field dimensions. However, if the Cubs' pitching hadn't suffered from an epidemic of injuries and ineffectiveness over the previous five seasons, perhaps Altman could have stayed in Chicago and Brock might have developed in center field, away from the glare of the sun in right.

"I was ready to play center field and all of a sudden I had to learn to play right field," Brock said. "I guess they felt a guy like Billy Cowan [regular center fielder in 1964] was coming up and they wanted to make room for him."

But the pitchers overcame Brock's fumbles and foibles in right field. Biggest improvement in 1963 was by lefty Dick Ellsworth, another player prematurely promoted by Holland at age 20 in 1960. Ellsworth had struggled most of his first three seasons, a virtual batting-practice hurler at 9-20 during the College of Coaches chaos in 1962. But he mastered a slider and got control of his sinker in 1963.

"If you play on grass, it doesn't matter whether the fences are 300- or 500-feet deep," Ellsworth said. "If you keep the ball on the ground, you'll win the majority of your games."

That philosophy helped the majority of Cubs pitchers in 1963, according to Dick Bertell, by then the No. 1 catcher.

"The whole secret that year was keeping the ball down," he said. "You could not drive a groundball through that infield with the high grass. If you put a groundball two inches into the grass, you could not see it. Ernie Banks had 22 putouts at first in one game. I took a lot of joy catching those games."

But Ellsworth stood out among the hurlers. Still just 23, he was one of the more dominant pitchers in baseball for that season, going 22-10 with a 2.11 ERA. No Cubs starter in the million-to-one era has ever had a season ERA as low as Ellsworth's. Greg Maddux came the closest with 2.18 in his first Cy Young Award season in 1992, but that's another story.

"I don't think a day went by in Wrigley Field that I and at least four other pitchers, along with the catcher and Ron Santo, sat in the clubhouse for an hour after the game, and critiqued what happened," said Ellsworth, now a real-estate executive in his native Fresno, California. "And on the road, the pitchers were together—we sat in the lobby together and always had dinner together. On off days, we'd charter fishing boats.

"It was invaluable to me, having come off a bad, losing season. My mind was wide open. Everyone was sincere in helping each other. I sense there isn't that togetherness today. The last thing in the world we talked about was salaries.

"Fred Martin constantly talked about how important it was to change speeds and have a good changeup. Bob Kennedy demonstrated he was going to be a players' manager. We knew he was going to be there all year after all the problems with the rotating coaches. He was a competitor, thought pitching was important, and I think he elevated the pitching staff's self-esteem."

On July 30, 1963, the Cubs had allowed the fewest runs (337) of any major-league team up to that point of the season, below that of the traditional pitching-rich White Sox (348) and Dodgers (371). Chicago also paced the NL in ERA with 2.88 and tied the Pirates for fewest walks (257). The Cubs ended up second to the Dodgers in ERA at season's end at 3.08, lowest of the million-to-one era, putting to the lie yet another ol' chestnut—the inability to have effective pitching in cozy Wrigley Field. An August slump prevented the Cubs from climbing out of the second division, but the 82-80 finish was a 23-game improvement over 1962. The above-.500 record would turn out to be the only plus-side finish between 1946 and 1967.

Clearly, the Cubs seemed on the move toward legitimate upper-echelon status. But this group of players started on the slippery slope to status as The Lost Contender in the off-season of 1963-64.

In a little-known deal on December 13, 1963, John Holland dealt lefty reliever Jim Brewer and backup catcher Cuno Barragan to the Dodgers for pitcher Dick Scott. Brewer had struggled over the past four seasons, the assorted coaches unable to soften up his game as he worked mainly in relief.

"Throwing on the side and watching Jim, I don't think I ever saw better stuff. He looked fabulous with a sharp, breaking curve," Bob Anderson recalled. "But on the mound, there was a transformation. One game he came in, the first pitch to Orlando Cepeda ended up in the upper bleachers. Jim dropped his shoulders. It affected him."

"He had an outstanding curve," said Ron Perranoski, like Brewer a homegrown Cub, but by 1963 the NL's best reliever. "His fastball was pretty straight for a lefthander."

Brewer had to leave the Cubs to get his career in gear.

"Warren Spahn in Milwaukee taught him the screwball," Perranoski said of one game in 1964 when both he and Brewer were Dodgers. "We were talking in the bullpen, and Warren showed him the grip on screwball. It took him a while, it was a difficult grip. He really didn't pitch much with the Dodgers until I left."

Brewer took over superbly for Perranoski, who had moved on to the Minnesota Twins. From 1968 to 1974, the hard-to-hit screwballer had ERA's of 1.26, 1.89, 2.49 and 2.54, saving 20 or more games four times. Once again, the Cubs produced a good pitcher—for another team—and the pitching-rich Dodgers would not finish raping the Cubs for mound talent.

Brewer would come back to haunt the Cubs much later. More immediately, the franchise was emotionally weighed down when one of the biggest tragedies in modern baseball took place on February 13, 1964.

Having proudly taken up flying the previous year, Kenny Hubbs and friend Dennis Doyle took off on a flight to California from Provo, Utah in marginal weather on that winter day. Minutes later, the small plane crashed into a lake, killing Hubbs and Doyle. Baseball had lost an upstanding young player who was the defensive equal of Ryne Sandberg. Just 22, Hubbs had the promise of being a fixture at second base for a decade to come. The Cubs had lost good young talent through the conscious actions of men, but now cruel fate intervened.

As if the Cubs were cursed, the team suffered another grievous loss 13 months after Hubbs' death when WGN-Radio play-by-play announcer Jack Quinlan, a rising superstar in the business, was killed when his convertible crashed into the back of a truck during spring training in Arizona.

Back in 1964, as the Cubs tried to get over the shock of Hubbs' death, the likes of rookie Jimmy Stewart and veteran Joey Amalfitano were tried at second base. But the Cubs still had Williams, Santo, a Banks poised for a comeback year, and Brock, logically ready to improve after a .258 campaign in 1963.

The Worst Trade in Baseball History?

But while the big three of sluggers got off to good starts—Williams was positively torrid at .400 going into June—Brock struggled again. John Holland's impatience began to bubble to the surface again. Never mind that Brock had to do much of his learning on the job in the major leagues. Never mind that as June began, Brock began to hit well and steal bases. Too bad he didn't steal more as a Cub, a fact Bob Kennedy regretted decades later.

"One thing I didn't do that I probably should have done was turn him loose on the bases," Kennedy said. "I wanted to control it at the time because of [Ernie] Banks, [Billy] Williams and [Ron] Santo hitting behind him."

As May 1964 ebbed and the Cubs, who had slumped early, climbed toward the .500 mark, Holland got his itchy finger to trade with the Cardinals again. Somehow, he believed one more veteran starting pitcher added to the Big Three of Dick Ellsworth, Larry Jackson, and Bob Buhl could vault the Cubs into contention. Old buddy Bing Devine had long been interested in Brock for the Cardinals. Trade overtures were first reported by Richard Dozer in the May 26, 1964 *Chicago Tribune*. Holland first asked for rising lefty Ray Sadecki, but St. Louis GM Devine turned him down.

More talks ensued as Brock's average climbed to .251. He slugged a two-run homer in the seventh inning of the Cubs' 4-1 victory over the Pirates at Wrigley Field on June 14, 1964. Out in Los Angeles, Devine was getting desperate with the June 15 trade deadline looming. His Cardinals had experience a total offensive meltdown, but had an extra starting pitcher to spare to snare a hitter. He offered Holland veteran Ernie Broglio, who had been 18-8 in 1963, on a list of three pitchers available. Finally, Holland bit, and the deal was announced on June 15. Brock got the news via phone from Holland while signing autographs at "Cub Day" at the Wieboldt's department store in downtown Chicago.

The trade, of course, backfired as none other has in Cubs history. Brock hit .348 the rest of the year to help the Cardinals win the World Series, playing 15 more seasons, stealing a total of 938 bases, and collecting 3,023 hits, earning an express trip to the Hall of Fame.

Broglio broke down, his fastball just a rumor in the view of Lindy McDaniel as he struggled through his first two months as a Cub. On August 23, 1964, Broglio woke up in his hotel room in New York to find his right elbow swollen to the size of a cantaloupe. He underwent surgery two months later to repair a frayed ulnar collateral ligament. Broglio seemed to be on the comeback trail in spring training 1966, but lost his control in the regular season and was released July 5, 1966, his big-league career over.

Meanwhile, Holland's designated replacement for Brock in right field, rookie Billy Ott, bombed out quickly, going 7-for-39 before disappearing from the majors forever. The Cubs never enjoyed another day-in, day-out right fielder until Jose Cardenal in 1972.

The Brock-Broglio deal is full of strange angles and conflicting stories. Broglio said he was administered 21 shots in his arm for tendinitis in 1962; why didn't Holland pick up on this? He also "did not endear himself with club brass while sidelined for two weeks by a minor ailment" in May 1964, wrote Jack Herman in the *St. Louis Globe-Democrat*. That "ailment" was described in the *Chicago Daily News* as a "groin injury." While coming through Wrigley Field on a road trip on June 2, 1964, Broglio's groin injury was treated by the Cubs' team physician.

Whether the Cubs were trying to shuffle Brock out of town is up for debate. With the Chicago National League Ballclub, there always was the possibility of non-baseball reasons for dispatching players elsewhere. Bob Kennedy told *Chicago's American* columnist Bill Gleason at the time that he had two players, Billy Williams and Lou Brock, and had to get rid of one of them. Williams was headed for the starting left-field berth on the NL All-Star team with his .400 start in '64, so by that unusual logic, Brock had to go.

Cubs players polled in later decades said they were aghast that Holland would trade a player like Brock on the verge of stardom. But on June 15, 1964, the Cubs, like Chicago media, seemed overjoyed to land Broglio. Kennedy was quoted then as endorsing the trade, echoing the company line, and the *Chicago Tribune's* Richard Dozer, always plugged in to inside information on his beat, wrote on June 16, 1964 that Kennedy had been irritated by Brock's sometimes fundamentally unsound play in the outfield and on the bases. Yet 35 years later, Kennedy said he and his coaching staff were opposed to the deal, believing Brock just needed a little more patience, and had tried to dissuade Holland from pulling the trigger.

On June 15, 1964, Kennedy was playing golf with Williams and Ron Santo at a tournament in north suburban Wheeling. Williams and Santo said Kennedy, informed of the trade in a call to the golf-course clubhouse, looked crestfallen when he came back out onto the course. But Kennedy said in 1999 that he had never played golf with Billy Williams, and was on a South Side golf course, trying to duck Holland, at midday June 15. Santo became agitated when he learned that Kennedy denied he played golf with him and Williams on the Brock trade day.

The parties involved seemed to want to distance themselves from involvement in the infamous deal. There was something more to this story that begs to be told, but has been lost in the passage of time and deaths of many of the people involved.

The disastrous impact of the Brock trade was felt beginning six weeks later. Brock went 7-for-16 and ran wild on the bases in his return to Chicago July 28-30, 1964. The Cubs, puttering around the .500 mark, were swept three straight by the Cardinals and never saw the break-even point the rest of 1964.

Meanwhile, other wheels were falling off Holland's hoped-for contender. The pitching, so magnificent in 1963, had done a nearly 180-degree turn. Only Larry Jackson, who would finish 24-11, was pitching superbly in the second half. The bullpen was a disaster.

Dick Ellsworth started out 10-6 in 1964. He finished 14-18.

"I was disappointed I couldn't put together a full year of quality pitching," he said. "The slider caused tendinitis. When I quit throwing the slider, the problems went away. I'd get off to good starts, then it would hurt. But you kept on pitching—you didn't go on the disabled list. You weren't guaranteed anything then."

Except more woes by continuing to pitch with tendinitis. Ellsworth's promising Cubs career began to cave in. He began 1965 with a 12-6 record, then collapsed to finish that season 14-15. He'd like to forget 1966, the Cubs' first year under Leo Durocher: 8-22 with a whopping 321 hits allowed in 269 innings. By age 26, the lefthander had become the only Cubs pitcher to lose 20 twice in his career. Ellsworth was traded to the Phillies for Ray Culp, then moved on to Boston for the 1968 season. Strangely enough, he was 16-7 overall, pitching in Fenway Park, a graveyard for southpaws.

After the 1964 season, Holland demoted pitching coach Fred Martin to roving pitching instructor in the minor leagues. Martin supposedly had a few conflicts with veterans, but Cubs business maven Salty Saltwell believes Holland did not like Martin's wife for some reason and banished him from the major-league team. The Cubs' loss was the farm system's gain, though. Martin helped develop a slew of homegrown pitchers who eventually made it to the majors. He was best-known for teaching his pet pitch, the split-fingered fastball, to Bruce Sutter down on the farm. The rest was history.

By 1965, life with the Cubs got stranger. Kennedy had Billy Williams open the '65 season in center field. Earlier, Santo, by now a Gold Glove third baseman, had volunteered to play shortstop, but Kennedy did not take him up on the offer with the arrival of the immortal Roberto Peña.

The Cubs entered a dark two-year period, winning just 72 and 59 games, respectively, in 1965 and 1966. Leo Durocher arrived in the latter year to spark a revival. But what might have been starting in 1957 had a domino effect on Cubs history, and arguably impacted on modern-day events.

If Dick Drott and Moe Drabowsky didn't get hurt, then maybe Bob Scheffing wouldn't have been fired. Maybe Perranoski and Brewer stay Cubs and plug up the bullpen holes. If Hobbie and Anderson stayed healthy, the Cubs wouldn't have had to trade away good ballplayers like Tony Taylor and George Altman to get pitchers. If Scheffing stays, the College of Coaches isn't concocted. With one manager, maybe Brock doesn't get confused and develops in Chicago. And maybe he's the missing ingredient to have finally gotten the Cubs over the hump in the Durocher era.

"I thought the Cubs would have won [in the late 1960s] if they had a leadoff man with my numbers," Brock said.

Ol' Chet Chestnut's voice is heard from 1974: "'If' is not a word." But "if" starts with a giant capital "I" in Cubs history when The Lost Contender is considered.

What happened in 1957 and 1964 does have an effect on the turn of the millennium. Events are not exactly linear. But in baseball, no matter which way you cut it, past is prologue.

Chapter 4

DANDELION WINE:
Wrigley's Farm and Scouting Systems

THE CUBS LAGGED far behind the St. Louis Cardinals, Brooklyn Dodgers, and New York Yankees in developing capable scouting staffs and a productive farm system, and through the decades never really caught up.

It's that simple. Much of the woe of the million-to-one era was created by inconsistent scouting and substandard minor-league instruction and facilities. Owner Phil Wrigley, not knowledgeable about the nuances of the game and unable to network himself among its executives, never properly funded a player development system comparable to the top producers in the game.

How bad was it? Between the 1965 callup of shortstop Don Kessinger and the 1985 promotion of shortstop Shawon Dunston, no non-pitching product of the Cubs' farm system became a day-in, day-out regular on the major-league team. No farm product had such an impact and personal talent profile to just seize a job without being traded away or fizzling out.

Frequently in the *Chicago Daily News*, then the *Chicago Sun-Times*, Ray Sons summed up the scouting and farm system dilemma. He compared it to a gardener sowing weeds instead of roses. The Cubs were cultivating "dandelions" in the minors.

Whatever baseball orientation Wrigley possessed was geared toward the antediluvian baseball system of purchasing talent from independent minor-league teams. He displayed that mindset when revealing his College of Coaches scheme late in 1960.

"Commissioner [Kenesaw] Landis fought the farm system because he said it would kill the flow of free talent," Wrigley told the *Chicago Tribune*'s Ed Prell. "Because of this, minor league operators had a chance to find, develop and sell talent. But now, the minors are controlled by the majors.

"Here's an example of what that now means: We'll say the Cubs are short of a first baseman and that to get one from the high minors we must outbid other clubs to land him, if indeed he is available.

"Now there is no longer the free flow of talent, so we must develop our players of tomorrow. This is where our enlarged coaching staff will be important. We'll rotate three or four of these coaches among our minor league teams, keeping in mind the positions which are most critical for the Cubs. Eventually, we hope to have players ready to step up to the Cubs when they are needed.

"You might say we're tailoring our system after that of the New York Yankees, who usually can tap their farm clubs for players who are ready for the majors."

But Wrigley was off-base in his analysis. By trying exotic, never-duplicated schemes like the College of Coaches, he was getting as far away from the Yankees or Dodgers model as possible. Instead, he needed to hire both quantity and quality in scouts. He needed to provide them with dynamic leadership and consistently large enough funding to sign players. And then he needed to field a competent corps of minor-league managers and instructors working in adequate facilities in both spring training and in the minors.

Nothing of the sort occurred on Wrigley's watch, at least not consistently. The Cubs' player development system had bursts of productivity, even brilliance, but too often lapsed back into mediocrity. The team was never able to continually stock the major-league roster with homegrown talent. And those promising players making it up to Wrigley Field often were mishandled by the managers and coaches before being traded away by an impatient general manager, John Holland.

Holland's predecessor, Wid Matthews, actually had boosted the laggard scouting staff and minor-league instruction in the mid-1950s from the low levels to which they had plunged under 1940s GM Jim Gallagher. The Cubs always had a few individual top-flight scouts like Jack Doyle, Tony Lucadello, and Ralph Di Lullo. Under Matthews, they garnered a few more like Gene Handley and John "Buck" O'Neil. In fact, Handley's and O'Neil's records were as good as anyone's in the game.

A former infielder with the Philadelphia Athletics, Handley, still on the job with the Cubs at 84 in 1999, joined the organization as a Class C-level manager in 1954. He shifted to scouting the following season. In the ensuing decades, based in the Los Angeles area, he snared the likes of the late Kenny Hubbs, Dick Ellsworth, Mike Krukow, Mike Harkey, and Bill

Bonham. As an area supervisor, he backed up other scouts' finds such as Greg Maddux and Damon Berryhill. Other Handley scouting reports would be instrumental in Cubs trades for Bill Madlock and Bill Buckner.

O'Neil, a longtime first baseman and manager with the Negro League Kansas City Monarchs, was the first Cubs' scout to actively recruit African-American talent. Vedie Himsl, another good scout who later would be the first "head coach" in the College of Coaches, had been instrumental in signing Ernie Banks. Now O'Neil, working out of Kansas City, became a celebrity on his scouting rounds at African-American colleges and high schools in the Deep South. Banks had played for O'Neil on the Monarchs, as had 1955 Cubs signees George Altman and Lou Johnson. Eventually, O'Neil's finds would include Lou Brock, Joe Carter, Lee Smith, and Oscar Gamble. O'Neil became the first African-American coach in the majors with the Cubs in 1962, but never got near a big-league managing job. No regrets, he said; he reasoned that the scouting and coaching work he did for the Cubs was just as important to the organization as a manager's job.

Handley, O'Neil, and other scouts got an improved talent flow going into the organization by the time Holland took over in 1956. But there were still inherent flaws in the player development scheme.

The biggest problem as Matthews yielded the GM role to John Holland was leadership. In this case, it was Gene Lawing, director of what Wrigley called "player development and procurement." Adorned with thick coke-bottle glasses, Lawing, who first joined the Cubs organization in 1946, held forth in his job for nearly two decades, until the early 1970s. A master of paperwork and rules and regulations he was; a back-slapper and motivator he was not.

"When we would get together and talk, he was kind of quiet guy, never committing himself," recalled Phil Cavarretta of his conversations with Lawing when Cavvy was manager in the early 1950s. "He would disagree with you a lot. I said, 'Gene, let's try to get together with something we agree on.' He says, 'Let me think about it.'

"He was honest as the day was long," Handley said. "He was a book man, an office man. He was not one who you'd say was the most personable individual, to go around and pat people on the back."

Lawing was a typical Phil Wrigley employee, entrenched in the job and protected by his loyalty to the organization. Like Holland, he was not going to push the owner to boost the baseball budget. The results of his managerial inertia showed over the decades.

In 1976, when Bob Kennedy took over as general manager, he noted that the Dodgers, everyone's role model for player development, possessed five to six times as many scouts as the Cubs. They also had a winning tradition and pursestrings that could open at opportune times. Such was the handicap under which the likes of Handley and O'Neil operated in the decade prior to the start of the amateur draft in 1965.

Actually, the Cubs often operated at a scouting staffing level not much under the present day's complement. The 1961 team media guide listed 16 scouts plus sectional supervisors Roy "Hardrock" Johnson and H.D. "Rube" Wilson.

"We weren't understaffed," said Handley, "but other teams had more leeway and gave more money to prospects. It was dog-eat-dog. The organizations that spent money on prospects, like the Dodgers and Yankees, got the best players.

"The Dodgers, if they wanted a player, they did everything possible to get that player. They had more money to spend. At one time, they used the cliché to players, 'Listen to everyone else, then come back to us and we'll give you more money.'"

O'Neil had to outwork his competition, with some creative salesmanship.

"I would not only take the kid to dinner, but I also would go to church with him," he said. "If the Yankees were after a kid and I was after him, I'd tell him if you go with the Yankees, you'd be in the minor leagues five to six years. If you're with the Cubs, they'd get up to the major leagues faster. They weren't a winning team, and they needed help."

Handley refused to knock top management for not arming him with more cash.

"I can't criticize Mr. Wrigley," he said. "He was a businessman, and the Cubs weren't his primary business. From his experience in the gum business, it was pretty hard to figure giving a young player who never did anything so much money. He wasn't interesting in throwing away money for something that was intangible [a young prospect's potential]. But everything he did was on the up-and-up. There wasn't anything under the table like some other organizations.

"He was a fine person to work for. His word was gold. If you were a good scout, you had a position for as long as you had anything to say about it."

Too Many "Yes-Men" Scouts
Unfortunately, a surfeit of mediocrity crept into the scouting ranks,

and management did not move out the non-producers. Handley, O'Neil, Himsl, and others did their jobs well, but a number of their comrades stayed in place because they were "yes men."

"Many of the scouts wanted to please John Holland," said Blake Cullen, the Cubs' traveling secretary who had expanded his role to *de facto* assistant GM in the early 1970s. "Everybody had to be loyal to the organization. John could be intimidating in person. He could get irritated and mean. You'd be afraid of telling him, 'You're full of shit.' We didn't have too many guys being contrary to him. In evaluating talent, I don't think you can have 15 guys sitting around, all agreeing with top management."

Cullen believed Rube Wilson was one exception to the "yes man" corps.

"One day we were discussing the trade of Fergie Jenkins for Bill Madlock," he said. "Rube got up and did something corny. He said you can have every penny and every paycheck he had, that if Madlock wasn't the best [young] hitter available, he'd work for free. If I had become the GM [succeeding Holland in 1975], I'd have made Rube my overall chief scout."

Without much dissent and debate in the front office, the Cubs continued a trend that had begun in the 1930s with the passing up of Joe Di Maggio and Lou Boudreau. For the price of a few truckloads of Wrigley gum, the team lost out on some notables who were there for the taking. A mossified executive like Lawing was always present to say no at just the wrong time.

Newark Star Ledger columnist Jerry Izenberg related one story upon the death of former scout Ralph Di Lullo in 1999. One day around 1954 or 1955, the New Jersey-based Di Lullo watched a hard-throwing University of Cincinnati lefty out of Brooklyn blow down hitters. He ran to the phone to call Chicago, reporting he had just witnessed the best pitching prospect he had ever seen. But the Wrigley loyalist on the other end of the line turned down the Di Lullo request to pony up some healthy bonus money for Sandy Koufax. The Dodgers then swooped down on the southpaw, signing him for a reasonable $17,000. The rules of the day required that any player signing for more than $4,000 had to stay on the major-league roster for two seasons. Koufax' development was thus retarded, but the wait was worth it for Koufax to develop control and punch an express ticket to the Hall of Fame.

The clock moved forward a decade and the location shifted 3,000 miles west to Los Angeles' San Fernando Valley. Always with a good eye for pitchers, Gene Handley had worked himself into an insider's position with a high school star named Larry Dierker. Handley believed, and his Chicago bosses concurred, that Dierker was worth a $35,000 signing bonus. Suddenly, Paul Richards' Houston Colt .45's scouts barged in with a $50,000 offer. Handley had gotten $40,000 for Dick Ellsworth and $35,000 for Kenny Hubbs. But 1060 W. Addison wasn't going to go much beyond these figures for Dierker, leaving the 1962 expansion team to outbid the established Cubs for Dierker. Now the Astros' folksy manager, his career was shortened by injuries, but not before he won 20 games for the Colt .45s-turned-Astros in 1969, and had seasons of 16 and 15 wins soon after.

In the same era, the Cubs lived to regret huge bonuses they did shell out. During 1956, GM Wid Matthews was determined to sign two of the best college players in the country. He gave $50,000 to pitcher Moe Drabowsky out of Trinity College in Connecticut, and for a while, until Drabowsky got hurt, the money looked well-spent. Matthews and Vedie Himsl went to Minneapolis to sign Jerry Kindall, star infielder for the national champion University of Minnesota baseball team. Kindall also received $50,000 ($32,000 for signing plus a $6,000 salary for the next three years). Any bonuses above $4,000 required the player to be placed on the major-league roster, hence the term "bonus babies"—well-paid but green players advanced prematurely to the majors. Kindall stayed with the Cubs the rest of 1956 and all of 1957, but did not hit consistently at any level of the organization.

Even more dollars were splurged on two failures under GM John Holland. Just 17 in 1960, 17-year-old left-handed hitting outfielder Danny Murphy of Danvers, Massachusetts, was granted a then-record $130,000 bonus by the Cubs. Scouts had salivated over Murphy's power potential. "The day Danny signed, they were lined up from Danny's house to the motel across the street," recalled former Cub Lenny Merullo, who signed Murphy, coming out on top of a series of sealed envelopes with bids from 10 teams. Murphy was immediately brought up to the Cubs for a 31-game trial in '60, hitting just .120 and causing resentment among some veterans. Murphy had huge holes in his swing, and was traded during spring training 1963 to the Astros for catcher Merritt Ranew. He was converted to pitching back down in the minors and re-surfaced as a White Sox reliever in 1969-70.

Holland and Lawing tapped the Wrigley treasury for more money. Soon after Murphy signed, the execs gave a $70,000 bonus to slugging first baseman prospect Mack Kuykendall. But Kuykendall never got a whiff of the majors, his bat allergic to curveballs and first base occupied in Wrigley Field by one Ernie Banks.

Soon Wrigley got tired of throwing bonus money away on bustouts. He was further aggravated when Lawing told Wrigley he had to release 42 players during spring training 1962. Another strange Wrigley dictum then followed: the scouts could not sign *any* new players that season.

"You could go out and scout, but you could not stay overnight," said Bill Capps. "You had to come home the same day. You take one year where you didn't sign people, it hurts you three-to-four years down the line."

For the entire calendar year of 1962, the Cubs signed only six new players; none received more than $8,000 to sign. Wrigley soon lifted his signing ban, but not before Capps was proved right about the domino effect on minor-league talent. Braves manager Bobby Cox, an infielder in his playing days, recalled signing with the Cubs' Triple-A team in Salt Lake City in 1965 after service in the Dodgers' farm system. Cox said Salt Lake was so bereft of talent that management had to scrape and scrounge all over the minors just to fill out the roster.

Striking Out in the Draft

Another seminal event took place in 1965 with the start of the June amateur draft and a smaller January draft for players who graduated at mid-year. Both drafts were instituted in an effort to hold down bonuses that had inflated to $205,000 with the Angels' signing of outfielder Rick Reichardt. The Cubs had allowed their scouting ranks to decline in numbers after 1961, but increased them again to provide the geographical coverage the draft required. No longer could scouts develop special relationships with players and lock them up in a free-for-all signing field.

The talent procurers who landed Ernie Banks, Billy Williams, Ron Santo, Lou Brock, George Altman, Kenny Hubbs, Ron Perranoski, Jim Brewer, Dick Ellsworth, Dick Drott, Moe Drabowsky, Bob Anderson, and Don Kessinger [signed in 1964] no longer had the latitude, their evaulations reduced to reports sent to Wrigley Field. They could not spend years building up relationships with prospects on whom they had zeroed in. The draft was set up as a great equalizer. Although the front office often had kept the reins on signing bonuses, the scouts still had the opportunity to reel in some good players. But after the end of every-man-for-himself talent procurement, the power to choose players now passed into the office-bound Wrigley lifers would now select the talent off the scouts' one-dimensional reports. As late as 1981, Vedie Himsl, who handled most of the drafting in the final decade of Wrigley family ownership, conducted the draft by himself in his Wrigley Field office, hooked up by a balky intercom to four area scouts. Meanwhile, the White Sox brought their entire scouting staff in as a group effort in '81.

"One mistake we'd make in the draft is to change the focus every few years," Blake Cullen said. "One year we'd take a lot of junior-college or college players. Then we'd shift to another category [instead of taking the best-available athlete]."

A modern draft, requiring flexibility, creativity, and preparation, did not mix with the Cubs' creaky style. In that respect, the Cubs mirrored their Wrigley Field tenants, the Chicago Bears, whose old-fashioned front office mishandled scores of NFL drafts for years until Jim Finks began modernizing the process in 1975 with Walter Payton's selection.

During the draft era, the Cubs' decent flow of talent that marked the late 1950s and early 1960s dried up, with the most spectacular failure taking place at the beginning, in 1965.

Dallas-based Cubs scout Bill Capps was distressed when the Cubs picked 17-year-old right-handed pitcher Rick James of Florence, Alabama, No. 1 in the first draft. He had begged the front office to take a strong young catcher out of tiny Binger, Oklahoma, whose hands were big enough to hold a bushelful of baseballs. Once again, the Cubs had a Hall-of-Fame player in their own hands and let him slip away.

"I got real close to Johnny Bench," Capps said. "I thought we were going to take him. I recommended we take him No. 1. But we didn't, and the Reds took him in the [second] round. He was disappointed when the Cubs didn't pick him—a limited number of people had gotten close to him. I saved the draft list because I had Johnny Bench at the top."

Apparently, the Cubs cooled on Bench when the team's crosschecker scout saw Bench play the day after the catcher's senior prom. After the late night, Bench did not offer up a vintage game for the scout, who downgraded the team's evaluation and refused to come back to watch Bench play another game. Then-Cubs official Blake Cullen recalled that there was another train of thought that Bench, valedictorian of a high school graduating class of 22 in 1965, was "more of a football player with a bad knee; they were afraid he was a football player with limited potential."

Cynics can state that every team, including the Reds—who selected outfielder Bernie Carbo in the first round—passed up Bench. But the

Cubs compounded their error by again ignoring Bench in the second round, instead taking Los Angeles junior college catcher-outfielder Ken Rudolph, who was recommended by Gene Handley. The Reds snapped up Bench in the second round for less than $8,000. Bench made it to the majors at the end of the 1967 season, his Hall-of-Fame career stretching until 1983. James appeared in three big-league games in 1967, never to be heard from again. Stuck behind Randy Hundley, Rudolph never was more than a rarely-used backup catcher for the Cubs from 1969 to 1973.

Misevaluations and acquiring players based on their modest signing demands became the benchmark of the Cubs. Sometimes it appeared the Wrigley Field execs were simply flying blind. In the January 1968 draft, the Cubs, described as "poorly-prepared" by *Baseball America*'s book recapping the first 25 years of the draft, picked left-hander Dave Baldwin out of Manatee Junior College in Florida. One hitch: Baldwin had been signed two months previously by the Tigers.

"It's truly puzzling," Vedie Himsl said at the time. "Baldwin's name wasn't among the ineligibles so we assumed he was available. Oddly enough, the Tigers selectors sat at the table next to ours and said nothing when we made our first call."

The Baldwin pick was, of course, voided. Compounding the faux pas, Himsl picked two other college pitchers, N.D. Bingham and Thomas Palmer, who also were ineligible for the '68 winter draft.

Ignoring other obvious needs like pitching and outfield depth, the Cubs erred on two No. 1 June picks in the same era. In 1967, drafting second after their 103-defeat big-league season in 1966, the team selected high school shortstop Terry Hughes out of Spartanburg, South Carolina. Problem was, the Cubs already had 25-year-old up-and-coming Don Kessinger at shortstop. The Cubs passed up players like Don Baylor, Vida Blue, Ted Simmons, Richie Zisk, John Mayberry, and Jon Matlack to take Hughes.

"Every organization I was with, I had to play behind an established star," said Hughes, now a junior-high football coach in Spartanburg. "I didn't have the opportunity." Hughes, who signed for $50,000, seemed a legitimate prospect in the wrong organization. Red Sox scout Mace Brown, who had served up Gabby Hartnett's "Homer in the Gloamin'" in 1938, said he "wanted to sign Hughes more than any boy I've ever seen. He's got all the equipment." Meanwhile, John Holland waxed eloquently: "This boy has no faults. He could step into the field right now and hold his own with the glove."

Two years later, in 1969, while Hughes was stuck in the minors be-hind Kessinger, now an All-Star shortstop, the Cubs selected another shortstop No. 1—Roger Metzger out of St. Edward's University. Hughes eventually played in just 54 big-league games with three teams, none at shortstop. Metzger was traded in 1970 for Joe Pepitone while Kessinger held forth for another five seasons.

Infielders Hughes, Metzger, and Matt Alexander, along with outfield-ers Oscar Gamble, Bill North, Jimmy Lee McMath, "Tarzan Joe" Wallis, and Scot Thompson, were among a minority of truly athletic Cubs ac-quired in the draft process. Believing the stereotype about Wrigley Field being a playground for power hitters, John Holland and Co. began focus-ing on heavy-legged, one-dimensional strongmen who they projected would conquer the Wrigley Field walls. But they ended up coming to the Friendly Confines only if they bought a ticket. "Prospects" like Brian Rosinski, Karl Pagel, Jerry Tabb, Ed Putman, Ralph Rickey, and Pat Bourque littered the farm system. Bourque, a former linebacker at Holy Cross, somehow managed to hit six homers in a short span as the regu-lar Cubs first baseman in June 1973, but found his way back to the bench when pitchers discovered the holes in his swing the second time around the league.

"You had to have some speed in there, and they didn't have any speed," said Bill North, who could run rings around most of his minor-league teammates in 1970-71.

The Cubs' lack of well-rounded talent was noticeable to opponents, including former farm product Ron Perranoski, who was a Dodgers minor-league pitching coach in the mid-1970s and who shook his head at the sight of Cubs talent in the fall instructional league.

"At that time, they really did not go out and sign athletic-type people, with good bodies," said Perranoski.

"They weren't very tall, weren't very lean, weren't very fast. They weren't athletic."

The philosophical bent toward the one-dimensional, would-be big bopper was twinned with the eye toward the lock on the Wrigley pock-etbook. The Cubs obviously took some players higher than they should have been picked due to easy signability.

Coming out of high school in Pennsylvania in 1974, Scot Thompson had confidence in himself, but didn't believe he'd be the No. 7 pick in the country. But that's where the Cubs selected him for a $40,000 signing fee. "Teams that had talked to me drafted after me," Thompson said. "My bonus was $10,000 or $20,000 below where we thought we should be. But I wanted to play."

The Cubs' talent evaluation process declined even further in 1975 when the Major League Scouting Bureau began. Feeding generic reports to all teams, who paid $115,000 apiece to join, the scouting bureau enabled penny-pinching teams to save on the cost of scouts. The Cubs were more than happy to oblige, cutting their own scouting staff down to nine, including stalwarts Gene Handley, Buck O'Neil, and Bill Capps.

Bob Kennedy took over from Salty Saltwell as GM in the fall of 1976, remarking how the role-model Dodgers had five to six times as many scouts. He somehow persuaded Bill Wrigley, taking a more active role in the Cubs as his father, Phil Wrigley, aged, to sign off on an increased scouting budget. By 1979, 22 scouts were listed in the Cubs' media guide, some of them aged veterans that Kennedy had brought back from baseball's retirement home. The scouting staff didn't possess a lot of fresh, energetic blood.

"We hired several scouts who had been retired or let go by other organizations," Kennedy said. "The older the better. You don't lose your brains when you get older and it's a little tougher to get around."

Baseball 101 Not Taught by Cubs

But no matter who scouted them, Cubs minor leaguers of the postwar Wrigley family ownership era could depend on one thing—they were virtually on their own in learning fundamentals and getting positive feedback from Chicago.

While the scouts had done a good job prior to the early 1960s, the quality of instruction in the minors remained consistently poor starting from the Jim Gallagher GM days of the 1940s. Successor Wid Matthews tried to improve instruction, but ran into the usual Wrigley budget limitations and lack of support. While the Dodgers drilled the concept of fundamentals to their minor leaguers morning, noon, and night, the Cubs lagged far behind in quality of instruction, whether it was the 1950s or 1970s.

Each Cubs minor-league team had a manager, who was supposed to do everything except drive the bus. Most baseball organizations of the day did not provide one to three coaches for each minor-league team in the manner of modern-day farm systems. Yet the best-run organizations, like the Dodgers, offered regular, organized instruction from a variety of roving coaches. Other than the College of Coaches era, the Cubs never fielded more than two roving coaches—one for pitching, the other to handle hitting and defense. Cubs minor leaguers might not see the rover come to town for several months.

The 1958 Cubs media guide crowed that minor leaguers received "guidance and training by experienced managers specially selected because they like to work with youngsters. Cubs farm system managers include such top-notchers as Lou Klein, Tommy Heath, Ray Mueller, and Hershel Martin." The propaganda piece also bragged about a "skilled instructional staff," citing the presence of Rogers Hornsby as the hitting coach. Left out, of course, was Hornsby's utter inability to relate to his fellow man. One day in 1959, Hornsby verbally picked out Billy Williams and Ron Santo as surefire major-leaguers, while dismissing all the other minor leaguers as failures. Hornsby was the last individual in baseball who should have been working with young players. The quality of instruction in the minors reflected such poor personnel decisions.

"It was not first-rate," George Altman said of instruction in his minor-league days in Burlington, Iowa and Pueblo, Colorado, in 1956 and 1958, respectively. "We were kind of weak in certain areas of fundamentals. I was never taught to slide correctly, and I got hurt as a result."

"I played for Bobby Winkles at Arizona State," recalled ex-pitcher Sterling Slaughter, a 1963 signee. "I had been very strong on fundamentals going into the minors. The thing that amazed me is how little knowledge players had of fundamentals. They didn't know how to back up third base. The whole three months I pitched for Amarillo [1963], no one [roving instructors] came down. And we didn't have any meetings."

"They were far behind other farm systems, in the bottom third as far as cultivating players," Bill North said.

Little had changed through the decades. Farm director Gene Lawing, who died in 1972, was succeeded by Whitey Lockman. The ex-first baseman served almost two years as Cubs manager (1972-74) in between two stints as player-development chief—yet another example of Phil Wrigley recycling his own loyalists from top to bottom in the organization. Lockman did not upgrade the minor-league operation or the lines of communication with players. Lockman, now a scout for the Florida Marlins, declined to comment for this book.

"I got no feedback from Whitey Lockman," Thompson said of his 1974-76 farm-system days under the ex-Giants first baseman. "Nothing negative, nothing positive. In fact, I can't think of a time when I sat down with any of the top executives [his first three seasons]. Finally, Bob Kennedy did talk to me when he took over."

And although Kennedy beefed up the scouting staff, at least in numbers, in 1977-78, he left managers to continue their jack-of-all-trades acts. The Cubs did not hire pitching coaches for each team until Tribune Co. and Dallas Green took over late in 1981. Hitting coaches for each farm club were even further off in the future, added under the Andy MacPhail-Ed Lynch regime in 1995.

"Truthfully, I didn't think a pitching coach and hitting coach with each team was a good idea," explained Kennedy, who earlier in the 1970s had run the often-productive Cardinals farm system. "Sometimes you could get too much instruction. The roving coaches could help the kids, and the minor-league managers are pretty astute people."

But whoever was in charge did not provide enough help for the kids.

"Hitting instruction was almost non-existent until I got to the major leagues," Scot Thompson said. "I started out 0-for-32 in rookie ball [in Bradenton, Florida, in 1974]. "All I wanted was extra hitting, and I couldn't get it. There was no extra time. The manager was Jack Mull. He was terrible, and he had no business working with kids. I had to teach myself how to put the ball in play."

"When I first signed, Lou Klein tried to help me," Terry Hughes said of the longtime Wrigley-era coach. "After that, I never saw a whole of instruction. I never got any encouragement. If you needed help, you were in a slump, if the manager couldn't help you, you didn't get any extra instruction. If you're 18 years old and never been in a hitting slump before, you need some help. The way it was, if you didn't get the job done, you just had to struggle the best way you could."

"Players were left to their own devices," said ex-outfielder/first baseman Pete LaCock, the Cubs' No. 1 winter draft choice in January 1970, who thrived in the minors before he came up to the majors to stay in 1974. "They had to learn themselves. The farm system was understaffed compared to other organizations. I knew I'd get better coaching when I went to winter ball. The players had to help each other. If you didn't have talent, you just didn't make it. The managers were so busy doing reports, doing interviews, they didn't have time to really coach."

The Cubs farmhands could not progress as a result of work done in spring training, when a large amount of instruction was conducted.

"I spent six spring trainings in Mesa," recalled Jerry Kindall. "The instruction wasn't good. I had come from a college program at Minnesota under Dick Siebert, and he had been a great instructor."

A major problem was poor facilities. In the 1950s and early 1960s, Cubs farmhands stayed in spartan barracks underneath the stands at Rendezvous Park in Mesa, Arizona. They trained and played on a rocky field at nearby Mesa High School. "We called it 'Jackrabbit Field.' It was limited," said former catcher John Felske, who later managed the Philadelphia Phillies before starting a Chicago-based franchise quick oil-change business called Oil X-Change.

The Cubs major leaguers hardly had it better.

"When I was in Scottsdale as a Cubs coach [1967-71], we had one field—the stadium—and one batting tunnel," said then-first base coach Joey Amalfitano. "And we had spring training once in Long Beach, California [on the same field where Amalfitano had played high school baseball]. It was a disaster. We had to get off the field by a certain hour because the university had to use it. The dampness in the morning in Southern California made the field wet when we first started."

Meanwhile, the Dodgers could easily accommodate both their major- and minor-league players at their sprawling Dodgertown complex in Vero Beach, Florida. Ex-Cubs reliever Phil Regan remembered how the Los Angeles pitchers, with their own field on which to work out, could get their spring-training work done in less than two hours. In Scottsdale in the late 1960s, the Cubs pitchers, including Regan, had to stand around waiting for field time, crammed into one and a half diamonds. The minor leaguers were left with whatever scraps remained.

If Dizzy Dean felt he was going from hamburger to steak when he was traded from the penny-pinching Cardinals to the still-prosperous Cubs in 1938, imagine how pitcher Jeff Albert felt going from the mighty Dodgers organization to the lowly Cubs as part of the Bill Buckner trade in 1977. Righthander Albert, a 21st-round pick out of C.W. Post College in 1976, remembered how the Dodgers farmhands enjoyed new uniforms, "instead of getting hand-me-downs from the big club" with the Cubs, and new baseballs instead of used. "I remember with Midland, they had to take somebody's name off an old Cubs uniform," said Albert, who now is in the new-car business in Skokie, Illinois.

In 1966, Phil Wrigley and John Holland had bandied about the idea of a separate Cubs spring-training facility in Escondido, California, a San Diego suburb. The team had temporarily moved from its longtime home in Mesa because Wrigley had been angered at one of the locals "calling him a cheap SOB," Blake Cullen said.

"The plan was to go to Long Beach to train for one year, then have a facility like Dodgertown in Escondido," Cullen added. "Mr. Wrigley flew out to California, and we all had dinner with John Holland and Leo Durocher. Mr. Wrigley was going on and on and said we should move to Escondido. Leo was not happy with that. Leo insisted we should have spring training in Arizona; that's where the teams were. Leo was old-school. There wasn't nearly the space to build something in Arizona."

Elvin Tappe's Good Book

Not everything was totally negative in Cubs player development. At least one Cub official took initiative in trying to codify fundamentals throughout the organization. Although coach Elvin Tappe was slavish in his loyalty to Phil Wrigley and politicked for the eventual manager's job while a member of the College of Coaches, he was devoted to trying to teach the minor leaguers. He authored a simple, typewritten bound book called the "Chicago Cubs System of Play," made available to players. Jerry Kindall kept his copy and provided it for perusal for this book.

Tappe obviously was a majority of one in authoring the book. Wrigley and John Holland didn't spend any money in making it look professional as a typeset product. The work appears to have been written up on a manual typewriter, then placed into a brown binder. Some letters are partially faded due to a keystroke not hitting home and true. Kindall's copy looks like an original. Diagrams of defensive plays appear to be hand-drawn with a ruler, like a kind of baseball draftsman. But with the gross underdevelopment of teaching in both spring training and the minor leagues in the era, the "System of Play" was better than nothing.

"I came from a college program [Minnesota] under Dick Siebert, who had been a great instructor," Kindall said. "I spend six spring trainings in Mesa, and the instruction wasn't good. So Elvin Tappe should be given credit for writing this manual, trying to get some consistency throughout the organization. Some of the older players scorned it, and some of the coaches didn't use it consistently. You needed someone in power to implement this so everyone used it."

"It was a lot of mundane things, but it was an effort to show they were trying to do something with instruction," former pitcher Bob Anderson said.

Tappe started out with a general outline of awareness of situations as a hitter and baserunner, instructing the coach to assemble his players on the bench, then the batter's circle, batter's box, and each of the bases. The instructions are basic and common-sense.

In the same section, Tappe covers hitting. The basic tenet: "Never attempt to change the stance or style of a young player until you have seen him hit a number of times and you are solidly convinced he needs help." Such advice obviously was not followed by the College of Coaches when they dealt with Lou Brock in 1961-62. Other directives that weren't followed to the letter in the instruction-poor Cubs organization: "Give each player as much personal attention as possible." "A drill to encourage hitting to all fields is recommended." "Psychology plays a prominent part in hitting. Encourage players to believe in themselves and their ability to develop into successful hitters and useful men in the batting order."

A section on bunting followed. Tappe included only three numerical points on stealing bases, an obviously neglected part of the Cubs organization in this era. But he did include a two-page section on baserunning, traditionally a weak fundamantal among many young players. His reminders: "Where is the ball? How many are there out? Look for a possible sign. Don't talk to the opposing infielders. Players should always run with their heads up. Always tag up on all foul flies. Touch all bases. Run using arms as pistons in front of the body. Always run on toes, not flat-footed."

Another 12-point entire page was given to the proper techniques of sliding. The late Richie Ashburn said in 1997 that sliding ended up a neglected fundamental in late-20th century baseball.

The most comprehensive parts of the manual are the 18 hand-drawn diagrams of defensive positioning covering the gamut of situations: a single with nobody on base, a man on first with an extra-base hit creating a possible play at the plate, a runner at second representing the tying run with a single to left field, bases-loaded situations, flyballs and pop flies, and bunts.

Another large section covered pitching. The style of the times was reflected in Tappe's admonition to focus on the fastball, curve, and changeup. "Discourage use of knuckleball, slider, forkball until pitcher can control the first three pitches." Tappe also advocated that pitchers work from the stretch position "at least 50 percent of time in practice." He also tried to instill a mindset often ignored by pitchers who were out of position to field their position: "Pitcher should expect every ball to be hit right back at him" and "Break toward first base on ALL balls hit to the first base side regardless of if they are fair or foul, line drive or on the ground." On plays at first base: "Catch the ball with both hands when possible."

Other pitching advice seems quaint and antique: "All pitchers should have at least three long sleeve sweat shirts, at least 50 percent wool. Keep throwing arm covered when pitching." And: "Pitcher should walk to and from mound in a businesslike manner—don't drag back and forth—enjoy your work."

Still another piece of advice was ignored by a slew of Cubs managers: "Relief men with good arms can pitch an inning or two, two or three days in a row. If they are used three or more innings in a game they should be given a day's rest." Also: "Don't work a good prospect out of turn."

Tappe continued on with four pages' worth of catcher's fundamentals. Eight pages of infielder's advice and two pages on outfielder's preceded the wrapup on how to analyze films. For hitters, Tappe said to look at feet first, then arms and hands, and finally the head in breaking down the mechanics of a swing. He was basic in pitching: "If you land on your heel you are overstriding" and "Do you cross over or throw across your body? This habit will tend to make you a bad fielder and a wild pitcher." He left out setting up the pitcher for career-threatening injuries. Finally: "Do you keep your eyes set on the target or is your head always in motion before throwing the ball?"

A few of the manuals survived into the 1980s in the Cubs' front office files. But the book became a relic. Why it was never made a bible of instruction, and greatly expanded upon, by John Holland and Gene Lawing remains a mystery.

Bad timing reared its ugly head again for the Cubs. Tappe authored his manual just prior to the institution of the College of Coaches system, of which he was a part. When the rotating coaches began pulling in opposite directions and offering conflicting advice, the impact of the manual was lost. The coaches impacted negatively on the kids down below as much as on the big leaguers in Wrigley Field.

Catcher John Felske was trying his best to adjust to the semi-tropical climate at Class D Palatka, Florida, in 1962. The players dodged snakes by the outfield fence as manager Hal Jeffcoat quit midway through the season to go into business, replaced by Ripper Collins. On top of all of that, the waves of coaches confused the kids.

"All of the coaches wanted to help everyone on the team," Felske said. "The problem was that they were there only a limited amount of time. Then you'd have another coach coming in a few weeks later, telling you different things compared to before. One coach had his theory, then the next one had a different theory. If you didn't listen to the next guy, he'd get upset that you're not doing it. You're trying one thing, a new guy comes in, and you're confused."

Fortunately for the kids, the College of Coaches was soon abandoned. And although the Cubs did not beef up minor-league instruction in more conventional ways, there were a handful of good coaches and managers who helped the confused kids along.

Despite his brusque personality, Lou Klein was cited as helpful by several players. So was South Carolinian Walt Dixon, who managed a number of teams in the lower minors in the 1960s and 1970s and somehow got along with the outspoken Billy North, an African-American from Seattle, and La Cock, the would-be hippie/yoga practitioner from Hollywood.

"Walt Dixon was a good manager, as country as watermelon stew, but a nice man," said North. "Walt tried his best to help the kids," La Cock said.

They Should Have Cloned Freddie Martin

The one shining talent was roving pitching coach Freddie Martin. His work was largely responsible for helping the majority of big-leaguers who did make it up to the Cubs. For a team that was perennially pitching-challenged, the Cubs had a nice pipeline of good-looking young hurlers coming up starting in 1965 with Ken Holtzman, no small thanks to Martin's instruction. Holtzman was followed by the likes of Rich Nye, Joe Niekro, Bill Stoneman, Gary Ross, Jim Colborn, Joe Decker, Dave Lemonds, Larry Gura, Burt Hooton, Rick Reuschel, Bill Bonham, Ray Burris, Buddy Schultz, Bruce Sutter, Mike Krukow, Donnie Moore, and Dennis Lamp. All the pitchers eventually enjoyed some productive time at the big-league level, more often than not with another team.

But Martin had done his part. The Cubs lost out at the major-league level when John Holland, who did not like Martin's supposedly domineering wife, banished him to the bushes after the 1964 season. Former Cubs media-relations director Chuck Shriver remembered scuttlebutt about Martin coming back to the majors around 1970, but Holland quashed that quickly. Fortunately, the Wrigley code of loyalty—don't diss the organization, you'll have a lifetime job—finally benefited the minor leaguers. Martin did not complain about his enforced and continued demotion to the minors, and went about his business teaching young pitchers. He thus was kept on the job.

A longtime pitcher in the Cardinals' organization, Martin had joined the Cubs to manage Class C St. Cloud in 1960 before assuming pitching-coach duties in the College of Coaches. He was best known for teaching Sutter the famed split-fingered fastball in 1973. Martin also tried to give his other young charges the technique of that "drop" pitch, but none mastered it as well as Sutter. Despite his love of the splitter, he was no one-note Joe.

"He was like an uncle, giving us emotional support," said Colborn, a 1967 signee out of Whittier College who now is the Seattle Mariners' Pacific Rim scouting coordinator. "I remember him showing us the split-finger. He talked to us about pitch selection."

"Freddie Martin showed me something the very first day I reported in 1966 at Caldwell [ID]," said Stoneman, now Anaheim Angels general manager. "The very first time I threw in the bullpen, he showed me a little technique that had to do with footwork and the start of my delivery. Now that I look at it, it was so simple and obvious. Had he not showed me that, I would not have had the career I had."

"The thing that was impressive about Freddie Martin was the first time he saw me, he said, 'You do everything wrong,'" said Archie Reynolds, a 38th (and final)-round pick in 1966, who now sells mobile homes in his native Tyler, Texas. "I just had to change my arm action. Freddie Martin was somebody you could sit down and talk to. He'd tell you the positives. He was pretty consistent with you, and made everyone feel they had something to look forward to."

Martin could only do so much. As a roving instructor, he couldn't be everyone at once. Colborn remembered how he, Gura, Decker, and Reynolds had to learn from veterans like Bob Tiefenauer and Ron Piche at Triple-A Tacoma in 1969. "They were serving as player-coaches," Colborn said.

Martin's own prodding of pitchers sometimes was countermanded by Gene Lawing's meddling, and motivation was not Lawing's strong suit.

Reynolds ran off seven straight wins in Double-A in 1968. He was told by Lawing that he would be called up to the Cubs if he pitched well in his next start. But at the same time, Reynolds was trying to pitch through rotator-cuff problems.

Gary Ross was called up instead. Reynolds asked Lawing why. "He said, 'Win seven more in a row,'" Reynolds recalled. After a game in Little Rock, Reynolds met Lawing again, and told him his arm was "killing" him. Lawing's response, cleaned up, was that Reynolds did not have the intestinal fortitude to pitch with pain. "We almost had a problem at the hotel," Reynolds said.

That wasn't the first time Lawing did not believe one of his minor-league pitchers was hurting. In 1964, hard-throwing Sterling Slaughter had shut out the powerful Milwaukee Braves on one hit after just one year in the minors. He went back down to the minors for 1965. "Every time Freddie Martin came around to see me, he said the organization had high hopes for me," he said.

But not high enough to believe Slaughter when he said his shoulder hurt.

"The more I tried to pitch, the worse it got. My 96 MPH fastball disappeared," he said. Les Peden, manager of Triple-A Tacoma, told Slaughter to tape saran wrap on his shoulder with hot compresses. "They thought I was jaking it," he said.

The next year, he was demoted to Double-A Dallas-Ft. Worth with the continued ache in his shoulder. Slaughter got manager Joe Macko to call Chicago for direction. "They just blew me off; they again told me I was jaking it," Slaughter said. "They never, ever sent me to a doctor. I never got to see Dr. Jacob Suker (Cubs team physician). You'd think that with the best pitching prospect they had, they'd believe me." Cubs trainer Al "Doc" Schueneman told Slaughter he was out of shape. Finally, in 1968, with the pain lingering, Slaughter quit baseball. He saw a physician on his own coin. The diagnosis: a rotator cuff tear. Slaughter rejected surgery, knowing he could live an everyday life with the rotator tear. He's happy in the real estate business today in Gilbert, Arizona.

The young pitchers, along with some regular players, also risked damage to their psyches playing in the Cubs' organization in the 1960s. John Holland and Gene Lawing promoted players when they were either too young or did not have enough minor-league experience under their belts.

Management even boasted that Cubs would get to the majors quickly. "The player with ability won't get lost in the shuffle," the 1958 team media guide stated. "He can be sure of moving up to the major league club as quickly as his development warrants." The emphasis seemed to be on the word "quickly."

The most outrageous rush job was Lou Brock, brought up after just one summer in Class C ball in 1961. Brock did his learning on the job in the majors, and was finally ready to play in The Show at the point he was traded in 1964. Dick Ellsworth came up at 20 in 1960, after pitching in one big-league game at 18, and was cuffed around for much of his first three seasons. Kenny Hubbs was lucky to come up at 20 and win the NL Rookie of the Year Award. Ken Holtzman was summoned at 19 after just three months of low minor-league experience. Oscar Gamble, also 19, was just about 14 months out of high school when he was promoted and thrown into center field in the middle of the pennant race in the last week of August 1969. Bill Bonham had just 26 games of minor-league experience before he was called up to the Cubs in 1971. Ray Burris pitched one year in Double-A before making the Cubs' Opening Day roster in 1973. And although they were college graduates, Joe Niekro, Rich Nye and Bill Stoneman all were promoted to Chicago after a year or less of minor-league service, most of it below Triple-A.

Oddly enough, two-plus years of low- to middle minor-league experience in which he had already mastered the split-fingered fastball should have qualified Bruce Sutter for promotion to the Cubs in spring training 1975. "I wrote down his name," Blake Cullen recalled. "They were going to send him out [to the minors]. I told Jim Marshall and Whitey Lockman that Sutter was ready, the batters were missing the ball by 10 feet. But Lockman disagreed, and Sutter was sent down." He was not called up to the Cubs until early in the 1976 season.

Once Sutter and the other home-grown pitchers were promoted to Chicago, the pitchers could not even rely on an occasional Freddie Martin visit for help. The Cubs couldn't get enough of rotating coaches; they ended up with a revolving door of big-league pitching coaches with the same negative effect as the College of Coaches. Virtually every year offered up a new coach and different ideas, with the end result being confused players.

Martin was succeeded as pitching coach in 1965 by Mel Harder. He yielded to Freddie Fitzsimmons in 1966 under Leo Durocher. Former Dodgers pitching coach Joe Becker took over in 1967 and served nearly four years. But Becker was not a pitching technician; he merely ran his pitchers until their tongues were hanging out. Most Cubs recalled that Becker was not able to teach them new pitches, and in fact joined Durocher in an epidemic of negative feedback.

"He was a tough guy, who made you compete in a tough way," Jim

Colborn said of Becker. "Technically, I didn't see anything new. He was conservative. I gave up a hit on a slider to Cookie Rojas. He said, 'Stick that pitch up your ass and never throw it again.' I won 20 games with the Brewers and the last pitch of my no-hitter [May 14, 1977 with the Royals] was a slider. That style of coaching was second-guessing. It wasn't planning and percentages."

The merry-go-round continued after Becker suffered a heart attack and retired in 1970. Mel Wright was pitching coach in 1971, followed by Larry Jansen in 1972-73. Hank Aguirre succeeded Jansen in 1974. Marv Grissom took over under Jim Marshall for 1975-76, then Barney Schultz was Herman Franks' pitching coach in 1977. Mike Roarke had an uncommonly long stay of three years from 1978-80 before Les Moss served as the last pitching coach of the Wrigley family era in 1981.

Ray Burris recalled that he played 15 years for 15 different pitching coaches.

"It takes time when dealing with young people to get your (instructional) system in place," said Burris. "Bill Bonham could have been like a Randy Johnson, if he had just had a consistent pitching coach working with him over a long period of time."

Wrong Names, Right Quotes, Bad News

Once the young players faced the chaotic conditions in Wrigley Field, the media publicized their plight. But rarely did Chicago newspapers really expose the rot of the organization at its core. Coverage was so focused on the histrionics of the big-league club that rarely was the stark reality of Cubs minor-league life examined on the spot. That changed on July 11, 1976 in the *Chicago Tribune*.

Writer Al Solomon, who had maintained his seat in the right-field bleachers and his passion for the Cubs while a news columnist for the *Tribune*'s suburban supplement, had embarked on a short free-lance career earlier in 1976. He journeyed down to Texas to write about the Cubs' Double-A team in Midland. The *Tribune* agreed to purchase the article.

"What I found was a lot of people were really unhappy with organization," said Solomon, in his latest incarnation author of the "famous American drives" series in the *Chicago Tribune*'s Sunday travel section. "That surprised me, because I thought young players would be more enthused about just being pro baseball players and looking ahead. I found there was a team where players felt there was no commitment by the big-league club to their progress."

Solomon got right-handed pitcher Jay Temple to talk on the record.

"The main thing is that they don't stress fundamentals in this organization," Temple told Solomon. "For instance, there's so many times when a situation might require bunting a guy to second base or hitting to right field behind the runner, cutoffs and relays and things like that, things that win ball games.

"They don't teach you, they don't work with you. In this organization, they give you the ball and say, 'Here, go out and play.'"

Temple said Ernie Banks, shuffled into a roving hitting coach's job in the mid-1970s amid Mr. Cub's informal lifetime employment pact with the Wrigley family, rarely fulfilled his duties with the Midland Cubs. "Ernie doesn't come around," Temple said. "I don't know what Ernie does. As a matter of fact, he met us for one day in Lafayette [LA]. The next day he was gone. It's things like that."

Temple also said that Scot Thompson, then the Midland first baseman, was not able to learn the fundamentals of playing the position. A generation later, Thompson confirmed that analysis.

"I was struggling at first because of [Midland manager] Denny Sommers," he said. "He was a tough guy, a former catcher, who wanted me to play first base like a catcher. Then, the following spring training [1977], Charlie Grimm worked with me after asking me, 'What are you doing?'"

Solomon's story caused a stir in Chicago, but for the wrong reasons. In interviewing Temple, he had gotten the pitcher mixed up with another Midland hurler, Wayne Doland, a former Cubs' No. 1 draft pick. Doland wore uniform No. 15; Temple No. 16. Solomon confused the two. All the quotes were attributed to Doland and a photo of Temple in the *Tribune* was identified as Doland.

"He got the story right," Solomon said of Temple, "and I got the story wrong."

Solomon's own career was threatened due to the serious faux pas. Eventually he recovered, and made it back to Chicago with the *Tribune* as a baseball beat writer in the late 1980s and early 1990s. Temple's baseball career also was in jeopardy when an enraged farm director, Whitey Lockman, came down from Chicago to sort things out. Temple was given his release, and he gravitated into the Phillies' farm system. Neither Temple nor Doland ever made the majors.

Lockman denied the organization had severe problems—until Bob Kennedy fired him after the 1976 season, replacing Lockman first with John Cox, then with former White Sox farm director C.V. Davis.

"It doesn't look good, and I'd tell you that even if I was still with the club," Lockman told *Chicago Tribune*'s Rick Talley on January 26, 1977. "The major-league team needs everything, and to be honest, it just isn't there in the minors at this time."

The situation remained unchanged for years, well into the Tribune Co. regime that succeeded the Wrigley family. Oddly enough, the Cubs had their greatest success in producing quality everyday players in the last two drafts conducted under the Wrigleys in 1981. In January, Vedie Himsl took outfielder Billy Hatcher No. 6. Hatcher eventually starred for the Astros and several other teams. In June, Himsl landed Joe Carter No. 1 and Darrin Jackson No. 2. Carter was begrudgingly traded to the Cleveland Indians for Rick Sutcliffe in 1984, going on to a star slugging career throughout the majors. Jackson became a fine outfielder, elsewhere, after being traded along with Calvin Schiraldi to the Padres for Luis Salazar and Marvell Wynne late in the 1989 season.

A few regular players here and there and a string of pitchers who found their greatest success elsewhere. That was the sum total of Cubs scouting and player development, particularly in the amateur draft era. The dandelions alone sprouting throughout the minor-league system must have contributed about 100,000 to one toward the million-to-one era.

Chapter 5

RACE AND THE CUBS

THE SCENE IN Wrigley Field's Stadium Club on November 1, 1999 could not have taken place 20 years previously. Period.

Here was Don Baylor, banker-like in his suit, the centerpiece of his first press conference as Cubs manager. The questions peppered Baylor: What were his philosophies as a manager, how would he instill discipline in a clubhouse sorely needing it, whether he would order the slow-moving Cubs to steal more bases. All the requisite baseball issues.

Then, almost as an aside on the back nine of the press conference, someone asked Baylor his reaction to becoming the first African-American to manage the Cubs. Quick on his feet, Baylor responded that was the first time he had thought of himself that way, but that he was honored, and then made a quick transition back to the issues of winning at Wrigley Field.

Off to the side, proud and beaming, was Baylor's wife, Becky. This day was a triumphant return to Chicago. Becky Baylor had lived in the Second City previously when she worked as a United Airlines flight attendant. She was enthusiastically welcomed by the assembled media and Cubs officials, and was an immediate hit. In the weeks to come, Becky Baylor would serve as an ex-officio assistant to her husband, helping book phone interviews for the manager at his San Diego-area home as inquiring media asked about who'd be named to his coaching staff and his opinions on a variety of subjects.

This was progress, in modest increments. Twenty years ago, Don Baylor's appointment as Cubs manager would have set off radio net-alert bulletins and a whole string of bells and whistles. But few had to worry about their quiet being disturbed, because then-Cubs owner Bill Wrigley likely would not have appointed an African-American manager.

Move the time frame back five or 10 more years. Don Baylor, an intense

112

competitor in his playing days, would not have lasted long as a Cub had he somehow made his way onto the roster amid considerable management bumbling. He would have been too emotional and perhaps even outspoken for an African-American, violating the organization protocols of the era. And the sight of Becky Baylor would have been like waving a red cape in front of a bull. See, Becky is white. None at the press conference looked askance at her in 1999. But in 1969 or 1974, an interracial marriage or relationship warranted capital punishment in the eyes of old-school Cubs management. The Baylors would have been dispatched to some other outpost in baseball.

Frustrated Cubs fans worldwide should be thankful that the concept of color-blindness was applied in Baylor's hiring and his personal life. Race relations overall are far from perfect as a new millennium begins. Whether they ever will be truly enlightened is a subject for generations to come in the "Star Trek" era a couple of hundred years down the line, if even then.

In the little world of the Cubs, though, the virtual non-issue of Baylor's color shows how far the organization has come in eliminating race, color, and creed from deciding who plays and works for the team, and how they must behave on the field, in the clubhouse, and in their personal time.

Race played an unfortunate factor in the Cubs' evolution into the million-to-one team. They were far from a majority of one in putting a long list of qualifiers on conditions for African-Americans, and later Hispanics, donning and remaining in Cubs uniforms. Most of Major League Baseball moved haltingly into the era of integration and globalization after Jackie Robinson shook the world by busting the color line in 1947 for the Brooklyn Dodgers. But few teams would develop the pre-eminence of losing as did the Cubs during the same period. Not fully tapping into such a bountiful pool of talent only condemned the team to more futility.

The Cubs were by no means the last National League team to integrate in the 1950s. Ernie Banks and Gene Baker became the first African-American Cubs during the last month of the 1953 season. At that point, the rosters of the St. Louis Cardinals, Cincinnati Reds, Pittsburgh Pirates, and Philadelphia Phillies remained lily-white.

But the Cubs could have integrated even earlier, close behind the New York Giants and Boston Braves. Banks was signed fresh off the Negro League Kansas City Monarchs roster directly to the Cubs. But Baker, first African-American signed into the Cubs' organization on March 8, 1950, had been virtually frozen at the Triple-A Los Angeles Angels for the better part of four seasons. He was summoned to Wrigley Field only in tandem with Banks, largely to be his roommate.

In the years that followed Banks' and Baker's debuts, the pace of signing African-American players picked up under the administration of GM Wid Matthews. But further progress was not forthcoming when John Holland, who had spent his formative years in segregated Oklahoma, took over the GM reins in 1956. If anything, the Cubs backslid somewhat, with all kinds of unwritten rules about the makeup of the select group of African-Americans in the organizations. Meanwhile, as teams like the Pirates, Giants, and Dodgers began to make forays into talent-rich Latin America, the Cubs largely sat on the sidelines, a decision that has hurt them up to the present day.

The Cubs' attitude toward integration was commented upon bitterly by columnist Mike Royko, the Babe Ruth of Chicago journalism, in what turned out to be his last piece prior to his death in 1997. He held owner Phil Wrigley and his baseball management responsible for the decades of mediocrity as a result of their racial attitudes.

Published on March 21, 1997 in the *Chicago Tribune* under the headline, "It was Wrigley, not some goat, who cursed the Cubs," Royko castigated Wrigley for not swooping in on Negro League talent right after Robinson broke the color line, thanks to visionary Dodgers boss Branch Rickey.

"Had Wrigley followed Rickey's lead, he could instantly have had a competitive team," Royko wrote. "And depending on how many black players he could have tolerated, maybe a great team.

"By the time Cubs management got over their racial fears, the black league was getting ready to fold. Fewer players were available and better teams competed for them. Other sports, college and pro, began going after black athletes."

The last words Royko ever wrote: "I do know that if they [Tribune Co.] thought a three-legged creature from another planet could hit homer runs or throw a 95 MPH fastball, they'd sign it. And we'd cheer."

Maybe. But truth often is stranger than fiction in Cubs annals. The supposedly true-blue, loyal Cubs fans, starving for a winner, played a small role in management's hesitancy to deploy large numbers of African Americans as late as the 1960s.

But at the dawn of the 1950s, the prevailing sentiment of increasingly frustrated Cubs fans was pro-integration. Fans and media peppered Phil Wrigley with inquiries over why the Cubs did not field an African-American player.

Wrigley replied that the first black Cub should be a star-calibre player. He was under little economic pressure to integrate the Cubs. One of the most segregated cities in the country, Chicago featured very few African Americans living on the North Side in the 1950s. Unlike the White Sox at old Comiskey Park, the Cubs did not depend on black fans for a portion of their gate.

Wrigley himself was not outwardly racist. He simply was a product of his time in his attitudes toward race, believing in slow progress with a ton of qualifiers attached. Conservative in his attitude toward his employees' behavior, he no doubt fell victim to stereotypes about African Americans' personalities and "place" in society.

Gene Baker's Long Wait

So the owner was not going to push Wid Matthews to promote shortstop Baker, a Davenport, Iowa native who watched helplessly as Roy Smalley and a gaggle of former Dodgers lesser-lights Matthews had imported struggled in the middle infield for the Cubs.

Baker, who died in 1999, six years earlier recalled his mounting frustration at being stuck in Los Angeles.

"I started getting edgy in '51," he said on the 40th anniversary of his promotion to the majors. But in those days, you didn't ask. I was getting impatient, and it got me down. I saw other players from other teams going up."

Cubs mainstays wondered why the Cubs did not integrate sooner.

"Looking at it now, why would we take all these second-line [ex-Dodgers] players to start on our ballclub?" former slugger Hank Sauer, the NL's Most Valuable Player in 1952, said. "Why wouldn't you have taken a guy like Baker over them? But I didn't pay attention to the minors at the time, so I really didn't know what Gene was doing."

Simple math was the reason. Players had to have roommates on the road. Segregation continued in the supposedly integrated major leagues. No black-white roommate tandems existed anywhere in the early 1950s. Baker was the only African-American in the organization until outfielder Solly Drake was signed early in 1953. Drake was not ready.

"They wanted to bring up two players at a time, so they could be roommates," was the recollection of Neil Gazel, who covered the Cubs for the *Chicago Daily News* at the time. "If it wasn't for the roommate routine, they might have brought Gene up."

Eventually, the Cubs signed Banks and pitcher Bill Dickey from the Monarchs for $10,000 each on September 8, 1953. Wrigley briefly questioned Matthews about signing additional African-American players, but then butted out. Baker was finally called up on September 14, 1953, joining Banks for a workout at Wrigley Field.

Some Cubs weren't all that thrilled, but Sauer welcomed the newcomers.

"They picked two dandy players," he said. "Ernie was a very shy kid, while Gene was more talkative. I tried to help Ernie feel a part of the club. We talked after games. Both of us always were the last out of the clubhouse after games."

As he gradually grew out of his shyness with his 44-homer breakthrough season in 1955, Banks joined Baker in talking up some of the Kansas City Monarchs teammates they left behind.

"We would recommend them and talk up some of the kids we thought could play," Banks said. "That was our commitment to each other. The Japanese call it *wa*: brotherhood, teamwork, togetherness."

Matthews did direct his white scouts to sign outfielders George Altman and Lou Johnson off the Monarchs roster in 1955. Matthews then made an even more crucial decision: offering Monarchs manager Buck O'Neil a scouting job for the Cubs in 1956, knowing that the Negro Leagues were collapsing. He also added to the double-play combo of Baker and Banks. By 1956, the Cubs had five African-Americans with pitcher Sam "Toothpick" Jones, and outfielders Monte Irvin and Solly Drake.

Away from the glamour of the big leagues, O'Neil used his contacts and reputation throughout the South to begin snaring African-American talent for the Cubs. "All of the white guys could sign black ballplayers," O'Neil said. Nevertheless, O'Neil was the only Cubs scout actively recruiting African Americans. In 1962, the *Chicago Tribune* credited him with signing "most of the Negro players in the Cub organization." The one star he did not get was Billy Williams. Scout Ivy Griffin signed Williams out of Whistler, Alabama in 1956. Williams joined a fully-integrated Class D Ponca City, Oklahoma, Cubs farm club that summer.

O'Neil said the Cubs weren't actively looking to stock their organization with as many African-Americans as the Dodgers. But in the racially-charged 1950s, prejudiced pitches were ripe among other scouts.

O'Neil recalled how white scouts tried to steer white prospects away from signing with the more racially progressive teams. "They told them, 'Why would you want to go over there with all those black players?'" O'Neil recalled.

Late in 1956, John Holland succeeded Matthews in the GM's role. Holland, of course, had grown up in Jim Crow-era Oklahoma City, where he and his father had run the local minor-league franchise. While Holland did not bar further integration of the organization, he didn't nurture it, either. Like Wrigley, his racial views were the product of the times and his upbringing. And he would not do anything to cause embarrassment or controversy for Wrigley.

Holland's attitude was subtle, latent. For instance, he could be gracious to the families of his small core of African-Americans. Shirley Williams, married to Billy Williams for 40 years now, recalls that Holland was nice to her. But behind closed doors, the tenor of his conversations was likely different.

"The front office was pretty prejudiced," 1960s Cubs media-relations director Chuck Shriver said. "They were out of that 1930s and 1940s mold. They were careful which black players they selected. Our scouting staff tended to be the old-boys school, older guys, very few who had played major-league baseball. A lot of old Southerners who had played in the minors down there. They thought along John's lines.

"Buck was an excellent scout. He'd talk about certain players, and the front office didn't even want to take a look at them."

Holland's behind-the-scenes prejudices did not extend just to blacks.

"He kept making comments about our 'Italian third baseman,'" Shriver said of Holland's references to Ron Santo. "He wasn't enamored of Jewish players, either. Kenny Holtzman proved to be such a good pitcher, John couldn't say no to that."

But players of Italian and Jewish ancestry hardly constituted the same kind of talent pool as African-Americans—or Hispanics. The Cubs also lagged behind in scouting the Caribbean, by Holland's choice. His suspicions about Latin players and scouts also put the Cubs far behind the times, and the organization has not quite caught up even today.

The Cubs' first Latin non-pitcher was Cuban second baseman Tony Taylor, drafted from the San Francisco Giants' organization in 1958. The next starter, briefly, was Dominican shortstop Roberto Peña, obtained from the Pittsburgh Pirates, in 1965. Panamanian center fielder Adolfo

Phillips' star briefly shone after coming over from the Philadelphia Phillies in 1966. Veteran Juan Pizarro, a Puerto Rican, was briefly a member of the starting rotation during his 1970-73 Cubs days. A few other Latins were bit-part players until Cuban Jose Cardenal came over from the Milwaukee Brewers in a trade in 1972. Cardenal began the first influx of starting Latin players that included Jerry Morales, Manny Trillo, and Ivan DeJesus.

But the Cubs did not produce their own Latin player until Puerto Rican shortstop Davey Rosello made his big-league debut at the end of the 1972 season. Rosello was slotted as Don Kessinger's replacement as early as September 1975, but was eventually found wanting. "He just played hard enough to keep you in fifth place," Blake Cullen remembered telling the top brass.

Whatever south-of-the-border scouting effort existed was superficial. The Cubs listed one Caribbean-based scout, Ted Norbert in Santurce, Puerto Rico, in 1958. But no Latin scouts were listed again until Jose G. Santiago, based in Rio Piedras, Puerto Rico, suddenly appeared in the media guide in 1967. Santiago stayed on board well into the 1970s with little impact.

"I never saw Jose Santiago," Shriver said. "He might have been there. If he existed, I never met him.

"John was mistrustful of Latin scouts. The feeling was that Latin scouts would say anything about a player to get him signed. This was another example of just being behind the times, in the 1960s operating like it was the 1940s."

Blake Cullen said he would have hired Pizarro and Cardenal as his Caribbean scouts if he had been named general manager in 1975. But virtually the same attitude toward Latin scouting prevailed while Salty Saltwell, hired instead of Cullen, and Saltwell successor Bob Kennedy worked as GM. The Cubs listed two Puerto Rican-based scouts—Ruben Gomez and Pedrin Zorrilla—by 1979, but Kennedy did not believe Latin scouting was a big part of the game at the time. Ex-slugger Carmelo Martinez—now a Cubs' rookie-league manager—recalled that Zorrilla, who signed him in 1978, worked full-time as general manager of the famed Santurce Crabbers team. The Latin scouting effort was hardly more than an afterthought.

Kennedy was wrong in his view of the impact of Latin players, if the more progressive teams' efforts and end results were considered. Since the late 1950s, the San Francisco Giants and Pittsburgh Pirates had staked out the Latin talent market. The Los Angeles Dodgers joined a little later and zoomed to leadership in the Dominican Republic. The Pirates' Howie Haak became the most prominent procurer of Latin talent in the 1960's. These teams' efforts paid off handsomely. The Giants landed Orlando Cepeda, Juan Marichal and all three Alou brothers—Felipe, Matty and Jesus, among others.

The Pirates? By 1970, they could have stocked two teams with talented players of color, making up for lost time when, strangely, the team was slow to integrate under Jackie Robinson patron Branch Rickey in the early 1950s. One day, September 1, 1971, the Pirates finally fielded a team with an all-minority lineup. For the first time in history, an entire batting order and the staring pitcher consisted of black and Latin players. Media and fans made a big deal of the event, but Pirates players and management hardly batted an eye.

"They made a big deal of starting nine black and Latin ballplayers," said ex-outfielder Gene Clines, a 1970s African-American Pirate who later played and coached for the Cubs. "If you could play baseball, the Pirates wanted you. [Manager] Danny Murtaugh said he never looked at having nine black ballplayers. He looked at putting the nine best players on the field that day.

"If you came to a Pirates' spring training camp in the 1970s and you saw as many blacks and Latins as we had, it would scare you half to death. They'd sign them in abundance, and there was always competition. In 1970, we had Bill Mazeroski as the veteran second baseman, and coming up behind him was Dave Cash, Rennie Stennett, and Willie Randolph. When I came up, they had to trade Matty Alou to make room for me. They brought up Mitchell Page, Tony Armas, Angel Mangual, and John Jeter, and they had no room for them. The talent just kept coming and coming. They put a lot of resources into signing these players."

In contrast, the Cubs always kept a careful eye on how many men of color were on the roster, how they behaved, and what the fans thought.

The number of African-Americans on the Cubs roster had declined to just Ernie Banks for most of 1957 and 1958, the first two seasons under Holland. George Altman became a semi-regular in 1959. Then, Billy Williams, Lou Brock, and Andre Rodgers, the latter a product of Nassau, the Bahamas, all arrived in 1960 and 1961. Coming out of spring training in 1962, the Cubs started five blacks in the lineup—Banks at first, Rodgers at short, Williams in left, Brock in center, and Altman in right.

Perhaps realizing that a black coach might be useful in working with these players, Holland elevated O'Neil to the Cubs' coaching staff on May 30, 1962. In the entire controversial world of race and baseball, the Cubs, of all teams, ended up as the first to field a black coach. O'Neil merely was keeping the uniform on during games. He had worked with players as an ex-officio coach before games and during spring training.

"The umpires ran me off the bench because I was in civilian clothes," O'Neil said. "I had to go into the stands. So to be on the bench, I had to be in uniform."

O'Neil was a coach with the big-league club relatively briefly — only as long as the Cubs had a quintet of black starters. Altman was traded to St. Louis after the season, moving Brock to right. But midway through 1963, the switch-hitting Ellis Burton took over in center, bringing the Cubs' complement back to five starters. Holland also traded Lou Johnson, a 1960 spring training sensation, and another O'Neil signee, speedy outfielder Lou Jackson (who had won the Eastern League batting title in 1959), for white players. Brock was traded in 1964 for the white Ernie Broglio.

Did the Fans Want to Win?

The large number of African-American regulars was not going to last for long under Holland.

"I got all these players, but they weren't playing them at the same time," O'Neil recalled. "I told Mr. Holland we'd have a better ballclub if we played the blacks. Then he showed me a basket of letters from fans saying, 'What are you trying to do, make the Cubs into the Kansas City Monarchs?' We weren't appealing to black fans anyway, playing on the North Side of Chicago."

The reaction of these supposedly loyal Cubs fans had made Holland—always eyeing Phil Wrigley's reaction—even edgier. A few fans, the typical lunatic fringe, also greeted Billy Williams, a quiet, non-controversial man through most of his baseball playing days, with letters peppered with "nigger" and other epithets during his break-in seasons at Wrigley Field.

Blacks could play for the Cubs, but have no voice in leadership. When O'Neil was appointed coach in 1962, Holland took great pains to make sure he would not be a part of the "head coaching" rotation of Elvin Tappe, Lou Klein, and Charlie Metro to manage the team.

"They missed the boat on not allowing Buck to be a part of that," Altman said, remembering O'Neil's many years of managing experience with the Negro League Kansas City Monarchs. "He had that booming voice and commanded players' respect."

An African-American could not serve as Cubs' player representative in the early 1960s.

"We had a meeting to elect a player rep," Altman recalled. "They were trying to get Ernie [Banks] to run. He didn't. I decided to run, and I thought I had some pretty good votes. Suddenly someone came down and they said they wanted Bob Will [a white outfielder] to be the player rep. That was that."

Erring on the side of caution, Holland demanded his African-American players be out of a narrow, conservative mold in their personalities and personal lives.

"The three most prominent black players we had—Ernie Banks, Billy Williams, and Fergie Jenkins—had low-key or happy-go-lucky personalities. Fergie was Canadian. He was good in the Cubs' organization starting out because he was a black player who didn't know he was black. George Altman was laid-back and not tempermental. There were no 'angry young men' types."

The model African-American Cub, of course, was Banks. Famed for his "Let's play two" proclamations and in the wake of his astounding 1950s slugging feats, he became Phil Wrigley's favorite player. The owner cited Banks as a "team player" in an advertisement defending an under-fire Leo Durocher in 1971. Banks never took any bait to criticize the way things were being done. On the very first day of spring training, February 27, 1961, as the chaos of the College of Coaches began, Mr. Cub said: "With or without a manager, it's a good day for baseball."

But it would have been unfair to expect Banks to be stamped out of a firebrand, civil-rights activist mold. Only the boldest African-Americans of the time protested the injustices filling their lives. And in the conservative world of Major League Baseball, where change proceeds at a glacial pace, protest and dissent was beyond the thinking of the majority of players, black or white.

"Very few black players were from the North, hardly any from the Northwest, like I was," said Seattle native Bill North. "Most of the black players were from the South, and they felt they were in the land of milk and honey in the majors, or they felt intimidated by it."

Altman confirmed that the unspoken, but perceptible, atmosphere of "go along to get along" for blacks was entrenched at Wrigley Field.

"It was not a comfortable environment," he said. "Once you spoke out a little, you were gone. It was not an edict, but it was known what the Cubs type of player was like. They did not want anyone to stir the *wa*. I don't think personally that John Holland was a racist. He was a company man and followed the line of top management."

The Cubs' attitude on race was in stark contrast to that of the arch-rival St. Louis Cardinals, operating in a city where Jim Crow laws lasted into the 1950s. Owner Gussie Busch vocally wondered why the team wasn't integrated when he took over in 1953. Nearly a decade later, GM Bing Devine, Holland's frequent trading partner, lent the weight of the Cardinals and the team lawyer to enable star first baseman Bill White to close on a house in a predominately white suburban neighborhood. No one could imagine Wrigley or Holland breaking down the redlining barriers with team attorneys. Wrigley did lend money to Altman from the Wrigley Building bank when the outfielder bought a home in Chatham, a middle-class all-black neighborhood on Chicago's Far South Side. Altman likely would have been a pariah with the organization had he tried to move out of the segregated areas. All prominent Cubs black players were hemmed in on the South Side in the 1950s and 1960s.

Any assaults on injustices had to be done out of the public eye, without causing a stir and aggravation for Cubs management. Billy Williams was angered when the restaurant in the team's Houston hotel in 1962 at first refused to serve African-Americans in the Jim Crow tradition of the day. Williams had to do some quiet jawboning behind the scenes to get the eatery desegregated.

Segregation still held forth, though, within the organization. Reliever Lindy McDaniel, a white Oklahoman, wanted to room on the road with Banks when he came over from the Cardinals in 1963. Banks was agreeable. But management nixed the idea. Then, in 1964, dark-skinned Native American Sterling Slaughter was assigned black outfielder Ellis Burton as a roommate. Some on the team thought Slaughter was black. But Bob Smith, the *Chicago Daily News* beat writer, knew better. He was prepared to write a story on the first integration of roommates on the Cubs. Don Biebel, the team's traveling secretary and media relations director, practically begged him to hold off. Soon Burton was demoted to the minors. Slaughter found himself the odd man out, and roomed by himself.

Exile the Price of Dissent

The controversies of the outside world largely avoided the Cubs until the spring of 1968. Finally, the Cubs had an "angry young man" on their hands.

You wouldn't have expected Lou Johnson to stir up trouble. The Cubs had re-acquired Johnson, nicknamed "Sweet Lou" for his disposition, during the 1967 winter meetings in Mexico City in a trade with the Dodgers. John Holland had originally dealt original Cubs signee Johnson away in 1961, and he wandered throughout the minors before finally surfacing with Los Angeles as a replacement for the injured Tommie Davis in 1965. Johnson helped the Dodgers win two pennants and one World Series with his clutch hitting. He said he was happy to return to the Cubs, while Leo Durocher was thrilled to obtain a regular right fielder after shuttling players in and out of that position in 1967.

But when Dr. Martin Luther King, Jr., was assassinated on April 4, 1968, Johnson wanted baseball to call all the games off as the season began. Around the clubhouse, he no longer was "Sweet Lou."

"Lou tried to petition the black players in the clubhouse to boycott the games," Chuck Shriver said. "They wouldn't do it, and he was absolutely beside himself. Lou also didn't get along with Randy Hundley. It had nothing to do with Randy [who got along with all players], except he had this thick Southern accent, being from Virginia. It drove Lou nuts." Johnson even refused to get on an elevator with Hundley in the wake of the King assassination.

Johnson had led the Cubs in run production in spring training 1968. But after he stirred the cauldron in early April, he was a marked man. When he hit just .244 with erratic defensive play over the first two and one-half months, and a 48-inning Cubs scoreless drought left management grasping for straws, Johnson was traded June 27, 1968 to the Cleveland Indians for the more behaviorally-friendly Willie Smith. But now the Cubs had a hole in right field they did not fill full-time until Jose Cardenal's arrival in 1972.

Another "angry young man" arrived at the end of 1971. Bill North, a 12th-round draft choice out of Central Washington University in 1969, had flashed uncommon speed for a Cubs prospect of the times with 47 steals, leading the Texas League with 91 runs scored, at San Antonio in 1971. He seemed the long-term answer in center—if he could calm down.

Pete LaCock recalled playing right field in San Antonio one day in 1971. North was in center. "He'd come flying by and catch balls from center that should have been mine," LaCock said. "I told him if I'm standing under the ball, he couldn't do that. I told Bill if he did that again, I'd punch his lights out. He did, and I jumped on him in the dugout." The two eventually would become friends.

Years later, North was involved in the clubhouse tussles of the brawling, but winning, Oakland Athletics. But he couldn't keep up the combative personality as a Cub of color. Neither could he protest his handling too loudly.

North would have been a good bet to handle center and bat leadoff for the Cubs in 1972, but John Holland had traded Ken Holtzman to the A's for center fielder Rick Monday. There was no regular's position for North in the Cubs' outfield.

After a hot spring training, his '72 debut was delayed by a two-week players' strike. When the season resumed, North asked Leo Durocher about his playing time. Durocher told North he'd break him in slowly. He also advised North to get an apartment, that he'd be staying with the big club. "I was a little excited," North said, looking forward to his father and relatives coming to St. Louis during the team's first trip in town to watch him play. But, instead, North was optioned down to Triple-A while in St. Louis.

Hurt, North threatened to quit and go into teaching. Holland warned him he was ruining his career. North went down to the minors, was recalled to Chicago for 10 days, then was sent down a second time. "They told me if I didn't go to the minor leagues, I'd be suspended for the rest of my life," North said. "They had lied to me and told me to get an apartment, that I'd be staying. I had been raised principled."

North may have been a bit immature in handling his demotions to the minors. But his outspoken nature made Holland nervous. "Mr. Holland sent me to a psychiatrist in Arizona; he said he wanted me to be ready for the big city," said North, puzzled because Seattle was not exactly small. "I was from the Northwest and relatively smart, and that threatened the Cubs. Ability wasn't the only criteria for playing with the Cubs."

Placidity was another criteria. Holland couldn't wait to rush his speedy but loud prospect out of town. The A's Charlie Finley, who had seen North's dash and verve, was ready to pick him off. Finley traded aging reliever Bob Locker for North on November 21, 1972 as part of the busy 1970s shuttle of players between the Cubs and A's. Of course, Finley got the better of the deal in the long run. He got Locker back after the 1973 season in exchange for reliever Horacio Pina, then dealt Locker again to the Cubs on October 23, 1974 as part of the Billy Williams deal. In the meantime, North was playing havoc with American League catchers and pitchers as he picked up world championship rings in 1973 and 1974. He stole 53 bases in 1973, led the AL with 54 thefts in 1974, and had a career-high 75 in 1976, also pacing the AL. For 10-year career, North stole 395 bases.

The Cubs were scarcely in a position to give up speed. They couldn't surrender an up-and-coming power hitter, either. But that's exactly what GM Salty Saltwell did on May 17, 1976. Andre Thornton, then 26, was dispatched to the Montreal Expos for two journeymen players: outfielder-first baseman Larry Biittner and pitcher Steve Renko. Thornton had been slumping since the season's start, the Cubs pitching had collapsed totally, and the team needed immediate help.

But that was only the story on the surface. Thornton, a 6-foot-3, 200-pound African-American, seemed a perfect right-handed bopper for Wrigley Field. He had displayed an uncommon blend of Frank Thomas-style power and plate discipline in 1975 when he finally nailed down the Cubs' first-base job. In 120 games, his season having been shortened when Thornton fractured his wrist at the start, he had a team-leading 18 homers, a .293 average, and drew 88 walks. Blake Cullen had been proud that he had helped pluck Thornton from the Braves' organization two years previously in a trade for a burned-out Joe Pepitone.

"Andy and I are going to be at the corners of the infield here for years to come," third baseman Bill Madlock proclaimed early in the 1976 season. But Thornton and the Cubs got off on the wrong foot in spring training that year. He got into a mild feud with Jose Cardenal while criticizing the Cubs' always inadequate spring training facilities. Then, when the season began, Thornton couldn't get his bat on track—and ran afoul of manager Jim Marshall.

"I know Jim Marshall wanted me out of here," Thornton said at the time. "Marshall and I simply couldn't communicate. The only thing is I couldn't understand why. If I couldn't play the position [first base], then maybe I could understand." Early in the season, Thornton was puzzled why Marshall had five different players working out at first, with "the coaches trying to pump them up into being first basemen."

A generation later, Saltwell confirmed Thornton's comments.

"Jim Marshall and him had a conflict of personalities," Saltwell said. "He wasn't playing up to his potential. Marshall felt like he'd like to see us make the move. We needed some pitching, and Biittner was a hard-nosed ballplayer. Thornton had potential, but he had developed a bad attitude."

Marshall, now an Arizona Diamondbacks scout, denied he had feuded with Thornton or asked Saltwell to make the deal as a result.

"I wasn't against him at all," Marshall said. "I felt he was fine. We got in a situation where we could get two players for one. Pete LaCock was there at first base. I was going lefthander/righthander at first base. Personally, Thornton was never a problem."

Whoever and whatever prompted the trade, the problem came a few years later when Thornton moved on to Cleveland and established himself as a first-class power hitter. The end result fulfilled a prophecy by the *Chicago Tribune*'s Richard Dozer the day of the trade: "It was a deal that should get them over an immediate hurdle, but likely will be another of those which have lingered as haunting memories. It could turn out to be a horrible trade...There was a heavy touch of panic in this transaction, and it marked an abrupt departure from the Cubs' advertised trend toward youth. Thornton...seemed their only hope as a 30-home run man of the future."

He soon became the Cleveland Indians' 30-home run man of the present. Between 1977 and 1985, Thornton had six seasons of 22 or more homers, including three campaigns of 32 or more. Meanwhile, late in 1977, the Cubs had to sign the moody Dave Kingman as a free agent to fill the right-handed power void. Ding Dong was gone from Wrigley Field by 1981, when Thornton was in his prime.

The most egregious example of dispatching a dissenting African-American player came early in 1977. The Cubs ran smack dab into the era of rising salaries, opting not to participate—at least for the player they dumped. Over a few dollars, Phil Wrigley, in his last, and one of his most ridiculous acts, ordered the trading of two-time NL batting champ Bill Madlock over a matter of principle that was abrogated as soon as Bobby Murcer arrived in exchange from the San Francisco Giants.

Madlock had earned nickname "Mad Dog" for his intense style, both professionally and personally. The Decatur, Illinois, product could be quick-tempered and foul-mouthed with the best of them. But no one argued that he could hit like a machine, batting .313, .354 and .339 after coming over after the 1973 season in the deal for Fergie Jenkins. In 1976, Madlock, who had spray-hitter power numbers, was asked to muscle up for more homers and RBI, and he complied [15 homers, 84 RBI] without sacrificing much in average. In a memorable display of hitting, he won the batting crown on the last day of the season by going 4-for-4 at Wrigley Field to beat out Ken Griffey, Sr., who had sat out of the starting lineup in Cincinnati to protect a slim lead over Madlock.

After the '76 season, Madlock began publicly campaigning for an enriched contract that would reward him for his hitting feats.

"Coming off two batting titles, I felt I deserved as much as anybody," said Madlock, now Detroit Tigers hitting coach. "But one thing you find out is there's no logic in baseball. Baseball is baseball. You don't get into logic, because you'd make yourself go crazy."

GM Bob Kennedy, just hired, claimed that Madlock wanted a then-substantial $1.5 million for five years. "We can't stay in business paying that kind of money," he said. Madlock claimed the Cubs did not negotiate and could have signed him for "much less." The third baseman attended Ernie Banks' Hall-of-Fame election press conference at Wrigley Field, and the two were compared in personality, unfairly.

"I made a comment that Ernie and Billy [Williams] went through all the stuff they did so I could be paid for what I did," said Madlock. "I was different than Ernie and Billy. I couldn't be an Ernie, I couldn't be a Billy."

Wrigley, 82 and confined to his Lake Geneva estate by now, ordered Madlock traded. Kennedy, who said he had nothing personal against Madlock, had to comply. The Cubs put a February 11, 1977 deal together with the San Francisco Giants for right fielder Bobby Murcer, young third baseman Steve Ontiveros, and a minor-league pitcher. Oddly enough, Kennedy said Ontiveros had come recommended by Buck O'Neil, who must have cringed at the order to deal Madlock.

Madlock called it correctly when he projected that the Cubs would have to grant the same huge contract he asked for to Murcer. "Whatever the Giants sign me for, the Cubs could have had me for less," he said after the trade. "They must want to pay Murcer and not me, but he's a veteran and they won't get him cheap, either."

Backed into a corner to save face on the trade and not anger the commodity they got in return, the Cubs paid Murcer $320,000 per year, more than Madlock had requested. "Murcer had them over a barrel," Madlock said.

The trade did not sit well with most Cubs players and fans. Three weeks later, young pitcher Jeff Albert, who had arrived from the Dodgers as part of the Bill Buckner-for-Rick Monday trade the same winter, remembered the strange initiation he had to Cubs spring training in Scottsdale, Arizona.

"The players were all saying it in the locker room: That Wrigley said he was not going to pay a black man $1 million," Albert said.

Whether Wrigley actually offered up those sentiments is questionable. But dumping Madlock while rewarding Murcer sent out all the wrong messages about prejudice.

The Cubs compounded their error on June 28, 1979. Out of the pennant race, the Giants asked waivers (the trade deadline then was June 15) on Madlock when the NL East-leading Pittsburgh Pirates inquired about his services. The Cubs, below the Pirates in the standings and getting first dibs on waiver moves, could have made a waiver claim on Mad Dog and either acquired him or blocked the trade. They did neither. Madlock went on to help the "We Are Family" Buccos win the 1979 World Series.

"One thing about a team is when they trade somebody, if they bring him back they admit they made a mistake. It's tough to do that," said Madlock, who won two more batting titles, in 1981 and 1983, for the Pirates.

The Cubs had nothing to show for Madlock. Two days earlier, on June 26, 1979, Kennedy dumped off an unhappy Murcer, who had become unpopular with Cubs fans by the middle of 1978, on the Yankees for a minor-league pitcher. The hurler, Paul Semall, never made it with the Cubs.

In '79, the Cubs were lacking some extra speed thanks to yet another deal that followed in the pattern of trading dissenting men of color. The previous December 14, Kennedy traded infielder-outfielder Rodney Scott and outfielder Jerry White, both African-Americans, to the Montreal Expos for outfielder Sam Mejias, a Dominican who had once played in the Cardinals' farm system under Kennedy.

"We lost a little there," Kennedy said of subtracting team speed in the deal.

A flashy player nicknamed "Cool Breeze," Scott had helped make the Cubs into a rare running team with 27 steals (and a .282 average) in 78 games in 1978. White was a defensive demon in center field with some switch-hitting ability. Scott stole 39, 63, and 30 bases for the Expos in 1979-81, while White hit .297 in '79. All Mejias was known for was a strong throwing arm—a favorite Kennedy tool from his own playing days in the 1940s. Mejias hit .182 in 31 Cubs games in '79 and was soon sent packing to the Cincinnati Reds.

What happened?

Scott had dueled verbally over his playing time and getting the green light to run with tobacco-spitting Cubs manager Herman Franks in 1978. Then Scott's agent, Abdul Jalil, flipped off Kennedy with his personal and negotiating style after the season. "Life's too short," World War II Marine aviator veteran Kennedy, a believer in short hair and clean-shaven faces, said of his encounters with the cutting-edge Jalil. White was tossed into the deal for some strange reason. Again, a stinker for the Cubs.

Watch Who You Go Out With...

The long litany of trades was a warning to black players to watch their mouths as Cubs. They also learned they had to be careful about their personal lives. Regarded as a crime just as bad as speaking out was dating or marriage to white women, an eyebrow-raiser in the 1960s in society as a whole, but a particularly severe violation in the nervous, conservative Cubs world. Even a spouse or girlfriend who wasn't lily white was nearly scandalous in the eyes of nervous management.

"John Holland was a person of his time," Chuck Shriver said. "That was a big deal [dating white girls]. John was as much concerned about what the public would say. He wanted to avoid scandal. Someone in the public would raise a hue and cry, and that would get [Phil] Wrigley's attention."

As libertine as Leo Durocher could be in his personal life, he picked up on the Cubs' moral stance early on, and adhered to it when his players were involved.

George Altman found that out in his last full season with the Cubs in 1966.

"My wife was a mixture of [American] Indian-Hispanic from Colorado," Altman said. "I ran into problems with Leo [Durocher] as a result. I think in spring training I was one of the favorite guys until the wives came down. She hadn't been at the ballpark much previously; when she did, they must have thought she was related to Eloise Banks, who was light skinned. When we started out on the West Coast and went to LA, I found myself on the bench that year."

By 1971, when Bill North was first called up to the Cubs, the word was out to be careful around white girls.

"Cleo James and Brock Davis pointed to some girls sitting there,"

129

North said of some ballplayer-hungry females hanging around the Cubs. "They said, 'Don't mess with them.'"

Blake Cullen, then traveling secretary, said all new Cubs were given instructions to "not chat with stewardesses on our charter flights."

But some players couldn't adhere to the Cubs' rules.

"I knew of one kid in instructional league in Arizona," North said. "He had a little white girl living with him. He ended up getting released."

North was circumspect about his own social life. "I was pretty private," he said. "I didn't flaunt my relationships."

Oscar Gamble didn't heed the warnings when he came up in late August 1969, rushed to the majors in another of Holland's premature promotions. The GM only courted trouble by turning a kid loose before he was mature enough to handle the majors. Only 19, a year out of high school in Montgomery, Alabama, and enjoying his first foray into a world-class city like Chicago, top outfield prospect Gamble must have believed he had fallen into the cookie jar.

"Gamble had never been away from home when he signed [in 1968]," Chuck Shriver said. A photo of Gamble looking out from his high-rise apartment, whose address was published, was featured in a newspaper story soon after he was called up. A steady stream of girls showed up at the apartment, and Gamble didn't turn them down. He also enjoyed parties on the road. During the September 12-14, 1969 series at St. Louis, longtime Cubs fan George Wielgus of Morton Grove, Illinois, bumped into Gamble destroying curfew at the team hotel. Wielgus said Gamble entered and left his room via the fire escape after hours.

Both Leo Durocher and John Holland quickly caught wind of Gamble's active social life. They were angered, and Durocher lit into Gamble at a team meeting. "He told Oscar to stay away from a certain girl," North said. Rumors built over the years that Gamble had some kind of a social relationship with a younger Durocher female relative, the apparent cause of The Lip's fury.

Lynne Walker Goldblatt Durocher, the manager's wife at the time, denied that Gamble had social contact with any family members. But she made it clear what Durocher's atttiude would have been if any ballplayer had fraternized with a family member.

"Leo didn't trust any ballplayer around his family," she said. "Leo was of an age were you didn't touch 'nice' girls."

Buck O'Neil had called Gamble "the greatest prospect I've signed since Ernie Banks.""He's going to be around a long time and be a topflight star before he's through," Braves manager Lum Harris said.

But Gamble would be around a long time—elsewhere.

He had been sent to the Arizona Instructional League after the 1969 season. John Holland got word that Gamble again was dating white girls, according to Chuck Shriver. "That was the "straw that broke the camel's back," he said.

Holland and Durocher couldn't wait to railroad Gamble out of town. Both worked together at Wrigley Field the night of November 17, 1969 to trade Gamble and pitcher Dick Selma, who had irritated Durocher, to the Philadelphia Phillies for overripe right fielder Johnny Callison.

Gamble never became the superstar of Lum Harris' predictions. But he had a decent 15-year career, slugging 200 homers, including 31 for the White Sox's "South Side Hitmen" of 1977. He was better than any of the center fielders who followed him in Wrigley Field.

Gamble's exile was the symbol of race relations with the Cubs. The beleagured team needed to be as color blind as possible in uplifting itself from million-to-one status. But to the loyal lieutenants of Phil Wrigley, appearances and decorum meant more than pennants. That alone has to represent 10,000 to one out of the huge odds.

Chapter 6

LEO DUROCHER—
All Hail to Caesar

THE NEWS STRUCK like a bolt out of the blue. Phil Wrigley did something contrarian again, and this time it was really radical. He hired Leo Durocher as manager on October 25, 1965.

Wrigley and Durocher. Ne'er the twain shall meet, socially, philosophically, and, most importantly, morally. On one hand, here was the shy, introverted owner who prized proper behavior and blind loyalty more than ability. On the other hand, there was the brassy, brash, brazen manager who had straddled the gray areas of morality and legality in his personal life, but was best-known for kick-starting three Brooklyn Dodgers and New York Giants pennant winners in the 1940s and 1950s.

But by 1965, 59-year-old Leo Durocher's glory days seemed a part of baseball's past. He had not managed since he left the Giants after the 1955 season. Although he had served as third-base coach of the Los Angeles Dodgers from 1961 to 1964, he seemed more comfortable as a second-line member of Frank Sinatra's "Rat Pack" in both Hollywood and Palm Springs. Perhaps Durocher's highest profile in the early 1960s was hosting a "tryout" for Mr. Ed, the talking horse, at Dodger Stadium on one of the latter's situation comedy entries on CBS-TV.

Leo The Lip somehow dovetailed a desire to win at all costs with his controversial off-the-field associations and crude behavior. "If I was playing third and my mother was rounding the base with the run that was going to beat us, I'd trip her," he once said. "I'd pick her up and brush her off and then I'd say, 'Sorry, Mom, but nobody beats me!'" Such a rascally attitude had its special charms and a place in baseball of the "Gashouse Gang" era of which Durocher was a key part.

As the last third of the 20th century got underway, Durocher was not a hot property as manager. Mindful of his 1947 suspension by then-baseball commissioner Happy Chandler for alleged shady off-the-field asso-

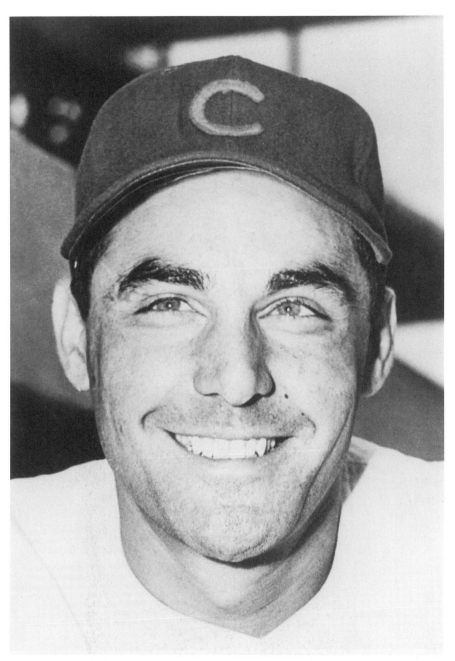

Phil Cavarretta embodied the talent and hustle of the Cubs' last pennant winners. After two and a half years as manager Phil was fired in spring training 1954 for telling Mr. Wrigley the truth about how bad the Cub talent level was.

Shortstop Roy Smalley symbolized the Cubs of the early '50s: flashes of brilliance but otherwise mediocre.

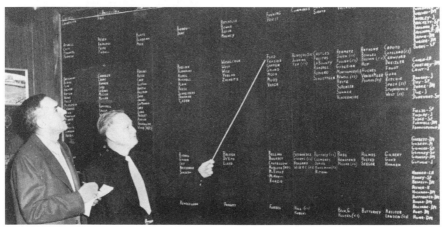

General manager Wid Matthews (right) shows farm director Harrison Wickel a farm system filled with many names and little talent.

When the Cubs finally fielded Black players, they came up with Ernie Banks and Gene Baker.

Gene Baker, first Black player in the Cubs system, came up on Sepetmber 14, 1953 to room with newly signed Ernie Banks.

Hall-of-Famer Billy Williams was one of the few great players to come through the Cubs' farm system in the early 1960s.

The Cubs' College of Coaches meets the press (January 1961). Standing (from left): James (Rip) Collins, Goldie Holt, Verlon Walker, and three-time Cub manager Charlie Grimm. Seated (from left): Elvin Tappe, Harry Craft, owner P.K. Wrigley, and Vedie Himsl.

Col. Robert Whitlow accepts his commission as athletic director of the Cubs from Philip K. Wrigley.

Cub outfielder Lou Brock and coach Charlie Metro. The Brock-for-Broglio trade haunted the Cubs for decades.

Cub executive vice-president John Holland (left) meets with owner P.K. Wrigley (1973). It was time for drastic changes in the Cubs' roster. Again.

Well past his prime, Leo Durocher never won as a Cub despite teams with talent.

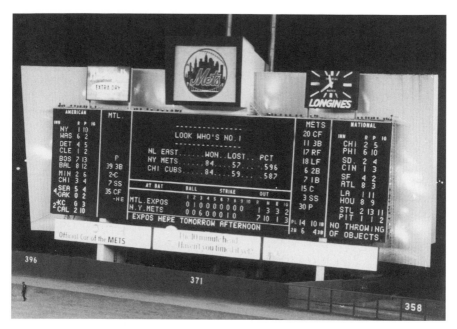

September 10, 1969—so close and yet so far.

Moments of happiness as 1984 brought general manager Dallas Green (left) and manager Jim Frey close to the pennant.

A perennial theme for more than half a century. "Building a New Tradition" was the motto of the Dallas Green regime.

When Dallas Green acquired Ryne Sandberg in 1981, he had the cornerstone for the success that followed.

Gordie Goldsberry, director of Dallas Green's farm system.

Manager of the Cubs' division champion of 1984, Jim Frey replaced Dallas Green as general manager.

George Castle interviews Lee Smith on Opening Day 1987 in the Cubs' dugout—Smith rushed out of town in a hasty trade later that year.

Manager Don Zimmer led the Cubs to the playoffs in 1989.

Mark Grace led the Cubs in longevity and consistent good play in the mid-'80s and '90s.

Sammy Sosa brought fans excitement and a 1998 playoff to the Cubs. Photo credit: David Banks

Kerry Wood's blazing fastball gave Cub fans a glimpse of what a good young pitcher looks like. Photo credit: David Banks

After nearly six years as Cubs general manager, Ed Lynch resigned on July 19, 2000. "We just never clicked. Across the board at one time or another we've had problems in every facet of the game," he noted.

Quiet, conservative, and savvy, Cubs president Andy MacPhail has the Cubs headed toward better days. Assuming Lynch's duties, MacPhail said simply, "I'm going to get it done or it will kill me."

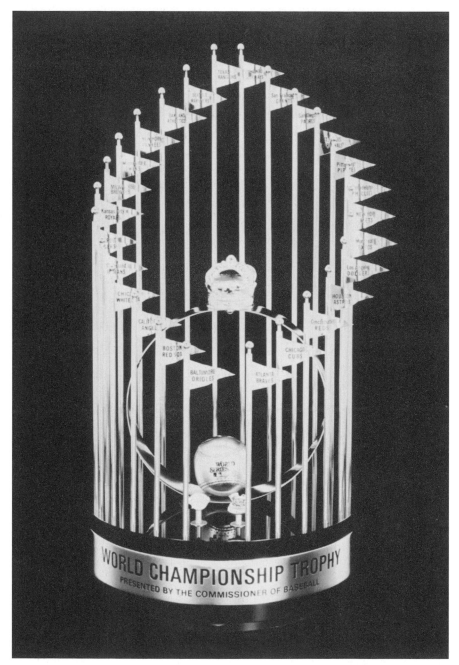

The World Championship Trophy, the holy grail of Cubs fans, didn't even exist when the Cubs last won a World Series in 1908.

ciations, most teams kept a distance from the controversial fellow. Cardinals owner Gussie Busch had a brief flirtation with hiring Durocher in the summer of 1964, with Harry Caray himself brokering the meeting with The Lip at Busch's Grant's Farm estate. But the deal was never completed, and an embattled Cardinals manager Johnny Keane ended up winning the World Series in '64 before bolting for the Yankees.

Durocher spent 1965 as a color commentator on ABC-TV's brief tenure broadcasting the Saturday "Game of the Week." He also hosted a 90-minute sports talk show on Los Angeles' KABC-Radio. Thus he was available when Wrigley came up with another brainstorm: Hire a man who stood for almost everything the owner abhored. At his wit's end on who to run the Cubs, Wrigley made his biggest departure from tradition in an attempt to turn around the backsliding 72-90 team. He mentally swept away Durocher's past, rife with adultery, borderline criminality, and shady associations in deciding to contact the manager.

Wrigley kept his own counsel on courting Durocher, the groundwork being done by John Holland at the 1965 World Series. The move came virtually as a surprise when announced three weeks after the '65 regular season ended.

Annointed at a Wrigley Field press conference, Durocher said "I don't mean I'm going to be a dictator. I never was." But he gave clear notice he would be the dominant half of the Cubs' decision-making duo with general manager John Holland. He couldn't have been any other way in tandem with the low-key, publicity-shy Holland.

"It will be a 50-50 thing," Durocher said when asked who would make the trades. "If I don't like a deal John suggests, it won't be made. And if it's the other way around, it will be out, too." Leo, of course, mentioned his power of veto first.

"I'm going to get the best of any trades," he bragged. "In fact, they'll be one-sided. If some team wants one of our top players, it will have to give up a lot more than we give."

His style of play? "I like to play a wide open game," Durocher said. "The first time I see a safety first player he won't be around long. I want the guys who run 90 feet when they hit the ball and when they pick up the ball I want them to throw it. I like to try things, sometimes against percentages."

Durocher summed up his own personal style: "I'm not coming here to win popularity contests. And I'm not a nice guy. I haven't mellowed. I'm still the same SOB I always was. I should know. I'm the guy I'm talking about."

He fancied himself almost larger than life, especially after running around with the fast crowd in both Hollywood and New York.

"They don't make rules for guys like that," said Lynne Walker Goldblatt Durocher, who married The Lip on June 19, 1969 in Chicago's top gala event of the season. "They make their own rules. I don't know if Leo considered himself a celebrity. He considered himself a good manager. He loved baseball. A 'Damon Runyon' character was the best description for him."

Most of his 1965-66 statements would come back to haunt Durocher, Wrigley, Holland, and the Cubs starting three years later. Like Wrigley a man out of his time, Durocher was indeed a dictator at a time when players no longer ran through walls on command. When WGN-TV sports editor Jack Rosenberg received some rare nice words from Durocher, coach Pete Reiser told him a minute later, "You just got praise from Caesar."

Cantankerous, condescending, contradictory, crude, and cruel, Durocher treated many players as interchangeable pieces of meat. He had no use for the press. He put himself above everyone else, but got away with his style through a near Svengali-like influence on Phil Wrigley, who was grateful Durocher put a spark into the Cubs.

But that spark was like a baseball version of a sugar fix. It didn't last. He and Billy Martin, who revived other teams as manager, were kindred souls. Durocher built up the Cubs, and then he tore them down. He squandered the best opportunity to reach the World Series between 1945 and 1984 with abject mismanaging of the 1969-through-1971 teams. His daring strategy of his first two seasons quickly changed to safety-first baseball, his Cubs reduced to station-to-station status on the basepaths by 1968. He aged rapidly right before the eyes of his players and the increasingly frustrated fans.

"You know, when I first knew Durocher, he was one of the sharpest riverboat gamblers I ever saw in my life," Jack Brickhouse told Rick Talley in the 1989 book *The Cubs of '69*. "You didn't have to tell Leo if a guy had thrown 87 pitches. He knew whether a guy was tired or not. In those days, he was a son of a bitch, but he was a sharp son of a bitch. But by the time he was finished in Chicago, he was just an old son of a bitch."

The only other time I have ever heard Brickhouse—as positive a man as there ever was—as critical about a personality was in comments about a 1960-vintage WGN traffic manager who ordered the destruction of a whole storehouse of vintage kinescopes, newsreels, and first-generation videotapes. "I hope he burns in hell," Brickhouse said of the station honcho three decades later. An individual had to be especially loathsome to earn his enmity.

Durocher earned it, all right, although Brickhouse kept his criticisms off the WGN-TV airwaves. The autocratic manager abused his starting lineup, rotation, and bullpen, refusing to employ backup players and relievers who didn't possess the hot hand. And his handling of a near-bumper crop of good young pitchers produced by an otherwise unproductive Cubs' farm system was atrocious. Stymied emotionally and physically in Chicago, several of these hurlers went on to good careers elsewhere. The Cubs were an aging team of flagging spirit when he finally departed in 1972, and the die was cast for a largely bad decade of Cubs baseball as the after-effect of Durocher's leadership, or lack of the same.

A Honeymoon for Leo

Few such warning signs could be detected as Durocher became the toast of Chicago in the winter of 1965-66, preparing for his first spring training. Cubs players eagerly looked forward to his regime.

"Maybe he can put some fire into us," Billy Williams said of Durocher's appointment.

"I was overwhelmed," Ron Santo said. "It's a great move. He's not used to handling a loser. He must think we're a first division club or he would not have taken the job." Years later Santo would recall Durocher's celebrity status enveloping the Cubs: "He was like Joe Hollywood out there."

Former pitcher Ken Holtzman, a rookie who Durocher placed into the starting rotation in 1966, remembers Durocher's stature on a roster chock full of kids.

"The relationship was one of a father figure to most of us," he said. "Here we were just starting out and he had 40 years of experience in the game."

The honeymoon between Durocher and the Cubs' organization and fans was powerful as 1966 got underway with the team enduring an uncomfortable spring training at temporary quarters in Long Beach, California. "The Cubs are going to shoot from the hip with Leo The Lip," proclaimed Ernie Banks. Durocher was the centerpiece of a supposedly new Cubs era, and the manager prodded GM Holland to stock it with fresh faces. Two trades, on December 2, 1965 and April 21, 1966, rounded out the Durocher team by landing four key young players: pitcher Bill Hands and Randy Hundley (from the Giants in '65) and pitcher Fergie Jenkins and center fielder Adolfo Phillips (from the Phillies in '66). These deals would turn out to be by far the best of Holland's otherwise undistinguished Cubs career.

The energizing force that Durocher supposedly provided was put on display when his opening speech to the team in Long Beach was recorded for posterity on WGN-TV's pre-season Cubs special:

"I don't want to say one word about what was here before I got here. I will run this ballclub the way I see fit. I am the manager of this ballclub and the only one that's going to manage this ballclub. Nobody else, front office or anyone else, will run this ballclub but me.

"Now about the rules on the club. Twelve o'clock you're in your room. Of course, I could put a rule on the club, 'No drinking.' What good is that kind of a rule? But I can't go and check your room. If you want to take a drink, you'll take it on me anyway. I say, like I've always said, 'You can't play this game on ginger snaps.'

"If you want to have a drink, go ahead. It's perfectly all right with me. What I don't want is if during the season we play night ballgames, the game's over at 11:30 and I look at the clock and say, 1:30, boys. 1:30, two hours should be enough time to have a sandwich and a glass of beer, a drink or something and go to bed. I don't want you bellying up to the bar 2:30, 3, 4 o'clock in the morning. At least don't let me catch you. I'm liable to catch you because I've been known to be walking around at that hour myself."

Active nightlife, within certain limits and no embarrassment to the prim and proper Phil Wrigley, was permitted. "Leo allowed the players to drink at the hotel," pitcher Dick Selma remembered. "Normally, the coaches and staff drank at the hotel while the players had to go elsewhere."

Durocher was temporarily hoisted on his petard when the '66 Cubs tied their '62 predecessors for worst record in team history—59-103 — and sank to their lowest-ever finish in the standings, 10th in a 10-team league. When he was hired, The Lip allegedy said, "This is not an eighth-place team."

But even through that dark season that was beset by an endless merry-go-round of ineffective pitchers, the Cubs' younger players displayed progress. The team hustled, just as Durocher had promised. Jenkins was installed in the starting rotation, immediately proving he belonged. The '66 Cubs were probably the most promising 103-defeat team in modern baseball history. And Durocher seemed to be a motivator to his players, touting Adolfo Phillips as possessing Willie Mays ability and playing cards with Ken Holtzman.

Less than a year later, Durocher was lionized in Chicago. The upward trend of the end of '66 picked up warp speed when the Cubs stunned baseball by zooming to the top of the NL standings on two occasions in July 1967, latest the team had been in first place since the pennant season in 1945. In addition to the usual Cubs power, Durocher put his players in motion on the basepaths. In one game against the Mets, right fielder Ted Savage stole home. Moments later, Adolfo Phillips also tried to swipe home, and had his bell rung when he was roughly tagged out. The moves, before and after, were very un-Cublike, and endeared the team to the masses.

Sure enough, huge crowds returned to Wrigley Field on several occasions, including a 40,000 mob that watched the Cubs beat the Reds 3-1 on July 2 and then refused to leave after the game until the Cubs flag above the scoreboard was hoisted atop all other team flags. Inexperienced starting pitching, a thin bullpen, and the second-half onslaught of the "El Birdo" first-place Cardinals, an eventual 101-game winning team, ended the pennant dreams by mid-August.

Still, the end 1967 result of an 87-74 record and third-place finish, best since 1945, so thrilled fans that they mobbed the Cubs at O'Hare Airport, returning from the season finale at Cincinnati. The Cubs had led the NL in runs scored with 702 while cutting the team ERA to a respectable 3.48, with Jenkins recording 20 wins for the first of six consecutive seasons. Even in doubleheaders, an old team headache, the Cubs won six, split 11, and lost just two.

"The Cubs found themselves with a whole gang of guys, all 23 and 24, who could play in '67," said former pitcher Bill Stoneman, a rookie that season. "We all found out we could play. Ron Santo, Billy Williams, and Ernie Banks provided the stability for the young guys."

The dramatic upsurge earned Durocher "manager of the year" honors by United Press International. He finished second for the same award given by the Associated Press.

Durocher's Wisdom—for a Price

Pennant talk for 1968 and beyond was rife. Durocher could do no wrong. That was the public profile. Behind the scenes, trouble had been brewing from almost the day Durocher arrived. The Lion did not change his personality, as promised. But the Cubs were so hungry for a winner that the dark side of Durocher was glossed over at first. He lived up to a persona best summed up by Tom Fitzpatrick in the *Chicago Sun-Times* on September 7, 1969: "Leo must always set himself against the crowd, attempting to bend it to his will. The weak he dismisses with insults and his unsurpassed mastery of the language of the gutter; the less vulnerable with carefully timed and staged displays of truculence."

He was a money grubber without parallel in Chicago sports. Durocher had once been paid $25,000 by the *Saturday Evening Post* to co-write his baseball memoirs with Roger Kahn. Appropriately, they were called "I Come to Kill You." In 1966, the *Post* sent Kahn to write a feature on Durocher's arrival in Chicago. This time, Kahn said Durocher wouldn't be paid for a standard feature article written through Kahn's personal observation and interviews. Durocher responded with a gesture that he was going to zip his lips around Kahn. Undeterred, the future author of *The Boys of Summer* hung around the Cubs for a week, gathering quotes from group interviews with The Lip. Eyeing Kahn all the while, Durocher finally exploded: "You're stealing money right out of my mouth! You're stealing it right out of my mouth!"

Durocher was paid for a five-minute WGN-Radio show, "Durocher in the Dugout," with Lou Boudreau. When others sought to interview him on tape, he demurred. Red Mottlow, dean of Chicago sportscasters, asked Durocher for a couple of cuts for Mottlow's WCFL-Radio sportscasts. "Sorry, kid, I have my own show," he told Mottlow, then in his early 40s.

In addition to the pre-game radio show, Durocher also was slated to make appearances on WGN-TV's live 9:30 PM Monday panel/call-in show, "Sports Open Line." But Durocher demanded his $22,5000 fee (he also received a car in the deal) for all WGN work upfront before he ever did his first show. That upset Brickhouse, who also was in charge of negotiating rights fees and other major contracts for the two stations. The tension between the pair never went away. Brickhouse, of course, tried his best to hide the rift when he was obligated to interview Durocher. But once in a while, a glimpse of their real relationship was made public.

Brickhouse hosted "Sports Open Line" before a live audience on June 12, 1967. The previous day, the Cubs launched a tremendous home-run barrage against the Mets, including four round-trippers for Adolfo

Phillips, in sweeping a Wrigley Field doubleheader 5-3 and 18-10. The homers were replayed on "Sports Open Line," leading into this exchange between Brickhouse and panelist Durocher.

Brickhouse: "Do you realize the Cubs in that ballgame yesterday hit probably as many homers as you did in your whole career? (Audience laughter)."

Durocher: "So?"

Brickhouse: "I suppose you were going to say next, 'Well, how many did you hit?' I was going to answer, 'None, and that makes us pretty even.'"

Durocher: "You're very funny tonight."

The manager wasn't very funny in his dealings with the beat writers covering the Cubs on a daily basis. Supremely arrogant by nature and mistrustful of the writers' inevitable probes into his private life, he treated them coldly from the start. During the first spring camp in Long Beach, Ray Sons, starting on the Cubs beat that year for the *Chicago Daily News*, introduced himself to the manager as the latter was sorting through mail in his office. Durocher hardly looked up at Sons.

"He gave me the most limp handshake I ever got from a human being," said Sons, now retired in Ft. Collins, Colorado. The affable Sons got along with everyone—except Durocher. "I couldn't stand the fellow," he said. "He was the most selfish, arrogant guy I ever knew. He was totally self-centered and impossibly arrogant.

"'Amoral' was a good way to describe Leo. His absolute idol was Frank Sinatra [and the way Sinatra dealt with people]. He kissed the ground on which Sinatra walked."

Durocher sometimes purposely fed incorrect information to the beat writers. One day, Jerry Holtzman of the *Chicago Sun-Times* confronted Durocher on his lies. The two nearly came to blows. "Leo said, 'Go ahead and hit me. I'll sue,'" Sons recalled.

On one plane trip, Durocher yanked the pipe out of WGN-Radio play-by-play announcer Vince Lloyd's mouth and threw it into a toilet bowl after Lloyd bested him at gin rummy. On another flight, the manager grabbed the first page of a writer's story out of his typewriter, looked at it, and then crumpled it into a ball. "I don't like it. Write me a new one," he roared.

The manager even recorded a gag, obviously unaired "Durocher in the Dugout" show with Boudreau—who often had to do multiple takes due to Durocher's profanity—in which he accused the beat writers of sexual depravity, conspiracy-mongering and all other kinds of real and imagined transgressions. Somehow, he called Sons "a nice boy," but in the same breath dismissed *Daily News* editor Roy Fisher. "He can go fuck himself," Durocher bellowed.

No wonder even as the Cubs soared in first place in 1969, the media crowd covering the Cubs took their best shots at Durocher in Tom Fitzpatrick's Sunday-magazine feature. The Durocher critics had to seek anonymity as they returned Durocher's venom.

"I think he's the most unprincipled man in all of sports," said one, described as "one of the town's most prominent telecasters." "If I had my way I'd like to see the Cubs win three straight in the World Series, and then fire Durocher that night and not even give him a chance to buy a ticket for the fourth game."

Another sportscaster also wished he had the power to ax Durocher. "I'd love to have the deciding vote on the Cubs' board of directors," he told Fitzpatrick. "I'd just love to see the look on Durocher's face as I voted to fire him after this season is over."

At least the media members only had to spend a hour or so a day around Durocher. The manager's relations with players reflected both his roots in the grungy baseball world of the 1920s and 1930s, and his own arrogance and self-centeredness.

Ernie Banks was his first target in the spring of 1966. Covetous of Banks' status as "Mr. Cub" and believing he was nearly washed up, Durocher did everything he could to belittle Banks. He repeatedly made snide remarks about Banks and tried to experiment with several candidates, such as John Boccabella and John Herrnstein, to replace him at first base. But with his sunny disposition and the patronage of Phil Wrigley, Banks held on. He'd go on to have three more productive seasons from 1967 to 1969 before age and bad knees, not Durocher, got the best of him.

Adolfo Phillips suffered next. A moody player who was socially isolated in Chicago as the Cubs' only Latin player, Phillips began flinching when opponents noticed that he was intimidated by inside pitches. That was like waving a red cape in front of Durocher; the player was displaying weakness of character. By 1968, the Durocher-Phillips relationship began to sour while Phillips' hitting fell off dramatically. His combination of speed and power went to waste. Phillips further angered Durocher with an apparent hypochondriac personality, missing time due to a variety of ailments and injuries. Most prominent was ulcer-like stomach pain which gave the appearance of "jaking." Decades later, former Cubs pitcher Bill Stoneman, now Anaheim Angels general manager, said Phillips stomach problems were real, not mental.

"He had a muscle problem in his stomach, similar to what has been a problem for hockey players," said Stoneman, who became familiar with the NHL maladies in his years in the Montreal Expos front office. "The problem doesn't go away. Everyone thought Claude Lemieux was faking it when he had the injury. But he had a legitimate problem."

Phillips was never the same. After another injury-marred start in 1969, he was traded to the Expos for infielder Paul Popovich two months into the season, spewing invective back at Durocher.

The old-school manager had little use for the attitudes of the modern player.

"Leo was outraged by a bunch of things in baseball," said Lynne Durocher, now living in Highland Park, Illinois. "One thing he said was that younger players were making too much money. He felt they were a bunch of sissies out there. They're overpaid, not hungry enough. Today, it's like they were doing you a favor. He believed they don't appreciate the game like he did [in the 1920s and 1930s]."

A Man Out of His Time

But Durocher wasn't just tough on young players. He was so counter-productive that he seemed like he worked for Cubs opponents. Such a style immediately brought clashes with independent-thinking men like Jim Colborn, who had been signed as a non-drafted free agent in 1967 for $400 out of Whittier College, Richard Nixon's alma mater, by scout Gordon Goldsberry, in his first of two tenures with the Cubs. Colborn was the most outstanding example of a string of young Cubs pitchers who were badly mishandled by Durocher and could only blossom after going elsewhere.

"I always thought he was on the cusp of two generations," said Colborn. "He was from an era when no one questioned authority and no explanations were needed for subordinates.

"I had a theory that Leo didn't like college graduates, young people or extra men." Colborn qualified on all three counts.

But the kids were very wary of a man old enough to be their grandfather. Most of the pitchers were advanced prematurely from the minors by John Holland, and had to produce immediately or else be banished back to Triple-A. They weren't allowed any period of adjustment in making the big jump to Wrigley Field.

"We were pretty much scared to death of what Leo might do," Colborn said. "You were trying to learn desperately. But the expectations were that you know it [already]. Do it or you were out—no explanations."

"Leo demanded performance immediately," Dick Selma said. "He was not going to wait around for development."

The kids were warned when they came up. "We told them, 'Swing the bat, Skip's going to use you,'" said Blake Cullen, then traveling secretary.

And there were to be no questions asked. After going up and down from Triple-A Tacoma and pitching out of an underworked bullpen, Colborn in early 1971 sought a meeting with Durocher to ask why the younger pitchers weren't being used more in the wake of poor performances by the Cubs' veterans on a West Coast trip.

"You think you're a better pitcher than Fergie Jenkins...Ken Holtzman...Bill Hands," Durocher barked at him. "If you want to start, I'll send you to Tacoma."

"We were liked puppies who were being whipped," Colborn said.

Durocher went so far as to inform Cubs opponents what was coming. Gary Ross, a promising righthander called up in 1968, angered Durocher because he apparently wasn't hiding the ball well enough in his glove in a game against the Giants.

"He was screaming at Ross, and yelling out the pitches he was going to throw so the Giants could hear," said ex-catcher John Felske. "Gary was so shook up he had to leave."

Felske, up briefly in 1968, incurred Durocher's wrath because he didn't get "underneath" the hitter as well as Randy Hundley. "I was a lot taller than Randy and I couldn't do it as well," Felske said. "Joe Torre kept hitting my shinguards as he swung the bat because I was so close to him."

Other little things irritated Durocher. Ray Culp, acquired via trade from the Phillies for Dick Ellsworth before the 1967 season, had been NL rookie pitcher of the year back in 1963. He had twice won 14 games in Philly. Only 26 years old in '67, he should have been a rotation mainstay for years. "Ray kept going 3-and-2 on a lot of hitters, and that upset Leo," Fergie Jenkins recalled. When Culp slumped to 8-11 in the second half of the 1967 season, he was as good as gone. Durocher ordered Culp traded to the Boston Red Sox after the season for a minor-leaguer. Culp went 16-6, 17-8, and 17-14 the next three seasons in Boston.

Another of the promising kids of '67 was Joe Niekro, who went 10-7 as a rookie before winning 14 in '68. He went on to a productive 20-year career, picking up the knuckleball that had made brother Phil Niekro so effective. But he didn't get a chance to try the fluttering pitch much in Chicago. "Everything was the same speed," Randy Hundley said of the young, unpolished righthander.

Like Ross, an idiosyncrasy on the mound bothered Durocher. "He always fiddled with his cap, after every pitch," Hundley said. "It drove Leo berzerk; it was irritating to him. Leo kept hounding on him. He finally said, 'Get him out of here,' and Joe was traded."

"It was Yosh Kawano [clubhouse manager] who told me I was traded, not the general manager [John Holland]," Niekro said of the deal sending him to the San Diego Padres for Dick Selma early in the 1969 season. "I came into the clubhouse and found my bags were packed."

A former shortstop, Durocher also fancied himself an expert on pitch selection. One day in 1968, Bill Stoneman threw a curveball late in the game with shadows creeping onto Wrigley Field. The Pirates' Manny Sanguillen hit the ball off the wall for a game-winning double. Durocher screamed at him in the dugout. The next day, the two met. "They didn't give you that $100,000 signing bonus for your curveball. They gave it to you because of your fastball," Durocher yelled at Stoneman, confusing him with Dean Burk, the Cubs' No. 1 draft pick in 1966. He continued his train of thought: "I want you to throw your fastballs late in the game until they hit it off the [scoreboard] clock in center field."

Durocher also quarreled with an excitable Joe Decker and did not pitch lefthander Larry Gura, the Cubs' No. 2 pick out of Joliet in 1969, regularly when he was called up. The end result was a waste. Durocher and Holland had no room as young players as starters. Putting them in the bullpen caused them to rot. The GM did not package them in trades for needed help in 1969 or 1970. Only after the Durocher-era teams passed their prime were they dealt away, and they became successes elsewhere.

Culp, of course, won with the Red Sox. Joe Niekro bounced around before settling down with pitching-conscious Houston, where he perfected the knuckler and had back-to-back 20-win seasons in 1979-80. Stoneman had several decent years, employing the curveball Durocher disdained, with mediocre Expos teams. Colborn had his 20-win campaign for the Brewers in 1973, then won 18 to go along with his no-hitter for the Royals in 1977. At Kansas City, Colborn was re-united with Gura, who was 16-4 in 1978, 18-10 in 1980, and 18-12 in 1982; the Cubs got him back as a washed-up, 37-year-old in 1985. Decker was 16-14 for the Twins in 1974. Ross had a couple of good seasons as a reliever in San Diego.

Durocher's, and almost to the same degree, Holland's mishandling of quality young pitchers was as critical to the failure to reach the World Series in this era as the management's stewardship of the famed 1969 team.

The failure to capitalize on the talents of the pitchers hurt the Cubs all throughout the 1970s. In the shorter term, the failure of the 1969 Cubs, who were for the most part kept together over the next four seasons, was far more dramatic and outwardly painful. An entire generation of Baby Boomers grew up with the nucleus of Ernie Banks, Ron Santo, Billy Williams, Fergie Jenkins, Randy Hundley, Bill Hands, Ken Holtzman, Don Kessinger, and Glenn Beckert. They had the same pull on Chicago as the old Dodgers did on Brooklyn. Young fans could depend on the same players, frequent All-Stars during the area, in the lineup year after year. The majority of the players kept their off-season homes in Chicago; they were part of the community. You could drink with the Cubs at Ray's Bleachers behind the center-field scoreboard or watch their off-season basketball team perform. That's why their failure to get to the World Series is so painful, and explains why the dashed-on-the-rocks fate of that all-time favorite Cubs entry has been micro-analyzed for three decades as the principals have aged and, in several cases, have died off.

Bottomline, there wasn't much the 1969 Cubs could have done to have changed their ultimate fate. They simply were the victim of a once-in-a-generation miracle finish, by the New York Mets. The stark fact was that the Mets captured 38 of their final 49 games, winning 100 games. The Cubs had reached a season (and post-1945) high point of 84-52 on September 2. That means Chicago would have had to finish 16-8 to have held off the Mets.

The two teams played only four head-to-head games in the season's final month, the first two before howling Shea Stadium mobs of nearly 60,000 screaming for Durocher's scalp. The Cubs would have had to sweep the Mets, an unlikely prospect. Then they would have had to depend on others to slow the onrushing New Yorkers, who already had closed to within five games in late August. That was not an insurmountable deficit by any means, as numerous pennant races in previous and subsequent decades have proved. In the end, the Cubs were left in the Mets' dust, finishing eight games out at 92-70, a record that would have been good enough to win or contend to the last day in a majority of seasons.

Oddly enough, the Cubs had an 18-11 August despite a sluggish finishing homestand to finish the month. Durocher's minions, whose lead over the Mets had reached nine games at one point, would have had to push the edge to 13 or 14 or even 15 to have knocked the wind out of New York. The '69 Cubs were good, but not *that* good.

"I don't think Leo could have done anything with a magic wand to change the fate of that team," said Ken Holtzman. "I thought if Leo could have used all 25 guys more and trusted them, I think it might have shown in a little bit better performance in September. Don't get it wrong — the players have to perform. I'm taking the blame as much as anybody for a bad September. But the conditions might have been a bit better."

A Short Roster in '69

Durocher gets most of the blame for playing his regulars into the ground, trying to shorten his rotation to three pitchers at the end, and using virtually only one reliever (Phil Regan) in critical situations rather than spreading the work among Regan and a still-effective Ted Abernathy and lefty Hank Aguirre. But Holland, handling the nitty gritty of trade talks and waiver deals, also had to take responsibility for leaving the Cubs almost two starting outfielders short going into the season, a situation that was partially resolved by right fielder Jim Hickman's hot August. Durocher had to employ nine different center fielders in 1969, the position going up for grabs by Adolfo Phillips' injuries and subsequent trade to Montreal. That's why a ne'er-do-well like Don Young became the center of so much controversy when he misplayed two ninth-inning flyballs in a July 8 loss to the Mets. The Cubs' bench had no reliable backup catchers to give Durocher an option to rest the always-eager Randy Hundley. The only two capable backups were utility infielder Paul Popovich and first baseman-outfielder Willie Smith.

Holland complained on Lou Boudreau's "Leadoff Man" radio show on Opening Day, April 8, 1969 that NL opponents desired the Cubs' regulars in deals. He was not going to trade any part of the nucleus, of course. Holland never explained why he couldn't have traded any of his promising young pitchers, for whom there was no room in the rotation or bullpen, for veteran help.

But another factor might have been at work here: Durocher's reputation. With the Cubs now in an unaccustomed pose of looking down at the rest of the league, The Lip's disagreeable personality apparently came home to roost. Few other teams would do anything to help the Cubs. That's Randy Hundley's theory: the '69 Cubs were a marked team because of Durocher. And, supposedly, a whole mess of general managers and managers wanted Durocher to get his just desserts.

At least for that season, they did not possess the lovable-loser image. They were envied. And when the upstart Mets came out of nowhere, the country had an underdog for which to root.

"Everybody hated the Cubs," said Blake Cullen. "In Cincinnati or Pittsburgh, they'd put a Mets score up, people would cheer. It was the only year it's been that way; otherwise, you'd see Cubs fans everywhere, all over the country. That season we were the enemy, the bad guy."

Late-season deals weren't as common as today. The trade deadline was June 15. If the Cubs desperately needed a center fielder or extra pitcher around August 1, waivers were required. And all other NL teams had first dibs on talent before the first-place clubs. Some "blocking" of waiver deals may have taken place. Besides, Holland's innate conservatism and Durocher's devotion to his starting lineup and rotation probably quashed some potential trades.

Surprisingly, the '69 Cubs regulars also get some criticism. Over the decades, I have asked almost every one whether they needed a rest. None said they wanted to come out of the lineup for a breather despite the long, draining season that featured no breaks in homestands through almost all of July and August.

The players' competitive juices got the best of them. In this respect, Durocher failed. If he prided himself in a near-despotic control of the Cubs, why would he continue to allow players, some of them obviously slumping from overwork, to continue to play until they dropped?

The issue of the players' tiredness did not crop up only in retrospect. It was an ongoing subject as August 1969 proceeded. The lineup, so productive in the first half, tallied just 31 runs, never more than four per game, in a 13-game span between August 8 and 22. Effective starting pitching kept the team winning.

While the batting slump continued, Durocher rarely started Paul Popovich—who was hitting more than .300 as a Cub and was capable at third, shortstop, and second—or Willie Smith at first to spell his regulars. In fact, the only plan floated in August was starting Popovich at third so Santo could shift to left field, and Williams going to his frequent 1960s home in right, with the idea to get more hitting in the lineup. The

Popovich at third/Santo in left array did take place in several games in 1970 and 1971. But in the Dog Days of 1969, Popovich was largely limited to scattered pinch-hitting appearances while Santo's and Kessinger's offensive production dipped steadily. Ernie Banks was another of the second-half slumpers, his age (38) and bad knees taking their toll. But he ended up starting 153 games, including both ends of doubleheaders, in 1969.

Durocher actually desired to rest his regulars for the August 18, 1969 Boys Benefit Game with the White Sox at Comiskey Park. That was the only day off from regular-season play between August 15 and September 4. But the manager bowed to pressure to start his regulars and let them have a couple of at-bats each in the exhibition, played before a ton of Cubs fans in the crowd of 33,333.

By the end of the same week, the Cubs had looked bad in dropping three in a row at Wrigley Field after Ken Holtzman's no-hitter on August 19. After the Cubs' 8-2 loss to the Astros on August 22, one insightful beat writer asked a tight-lipped Durocher while he was shaving: "Is anybody tired on the ballclub? Do you plan to make any changes, give anybody a rest?"

Outraged, Durocher put down his razor, led all the writers out of his office into the cramped clubhouse, and ordered the players out of the shower. Turn off the water, please.

"Now ask them what you asked me," Durocher bid the writer.

The writer sheepishly obliged. "Not one ball player stood up and said he was tired," wrote Jack Griffin in the *Chicago Sun-Times* the next day. "Leo turned triumphantly and went back and finished shaving."

But Durocher couldn't escape questions, not even at home. Wife Lynne Durocher once asked him why he didn't go to his bullpen more. "What does the press want me to do, not use my best players?" he responded. "I don't know if these other players can do it. I have to go with my best."

In private, the players could have asked Durocher for a rest.

"He trusted that lineup," Jenkins said 30 years later. "He would post that lineup coming out of the dressing room. The only change was the pitcher. If they told him they couldn't go, he would have rested them." Williams said Durocher felt the "urgency of winning" in making out the same lineup, day after day. But apparently none of the regulars was going to question his own baseball manhood by asking for a breather.

"You have to blame the players," said '69 pitcher Dick Selma. "Maybe there was something going on with an ego trip. Randy [Hundley] couldn't stand to sit, he'd go nuts if he didn't catch. He refused to rest in the second game of doubleheaders on Sundays. [Ron] Santo said he didn't need any rest."

"They hustled, they played hard," Colborn said. "This wasn't a coasting-type team."

Hundley was hospitalized for a severe ear infection when the Cubs came home for the late-August homestand. He dropped eight pounds while laid up. Upon his release, Hundley stopped by the clubhouse, and despite his woozy condition was drafted into service into the lineup. He couldn't say no. On Sunday, August 25, 1969, Hundley sat in front of his locker, holding his head in his hands, in pain after catching part of the first game and all the nightcap of a Cubs-Astros doubleheader. The catcher, who had set the all-time record by catching in 160 games in 1968, may have suffered from the worst after-effects of illness and overwork. Hundley was hitting .284 with 16 homers and 59 RBI on August 22; he finished 1969 at .255 with 18 homers and 64 RBI.

The only player who refused to automatically overwork himself was Fergie Jenkins. He was bombed out after three and two-thirds innings, yielding six runs and eight hits, in the first game of the Sunday, August 24, doubleheader with the Astros. Durocher asked him to start on Tuesday, August 26, against the Reds. With 17 wins and a season's worth of innings pitched already under his belt, Jenkins said no. Durocher was willing to risk his ace's health with more than a month to go in the season.

"I told them that I needed the extra rest because I felt tired," Jenkins said at the time. "My slider was backing up and my fastball wasn't effective. I had been pounded for 11 runs in about eight innings in my two previous starts.

"Sure, if you haven't pitched much you can go with only two days' rest once in a while, but not if you've pitched over 250 innings like I have."

Durocher seemed willing to gamble with Holtzman, too. In the ninth inning of the August 24 game, as the Cubs clung to a 10-9 lead, Durocher had starters Holtzman and Hands warming up in the bullpen. Holtzman had pitched a complete-game victory over the Astros the previous afternoon, four days after his complete-game no-hitter.

"Kenny couldn't get his arm loose," Hands told Rick Talley in *Chicago Today*. "But I was next if they needed me." Talley surprisingly wrote not one word of criticism about warming up Holtzman.

Durocher finally succeeded in pitching Jenkins on short rest when the season got desperate. After being knocked out in the third inning of the Cubs' 13-4 defeat on September 6 at Wrigley Field, he was summoned on two days' rest against the Mets in the rubber game of the crucial September 8-9 series at Shea Stadium. Jenkins was roughed up again in the 7-1 loss that cut the Cubs' first-place lead to one-half game. The Cubs fell out of the NL East lead the next night in Philadelphia, never to return in '69.

Behind the scenes, grumbling about Durocher's handling of the pitching staff had been heard throughout the season. In mid-June a prominent Cub warned of trouble, even as the Cubs soared high in first place. He was prophetic. "Something has to be done," he said, "because we can't win the pennant with Durocher. He just doesn't know how to handle pitchers."

In the end, Durocher was a 1940s manager going up against the emerging 1970s managers, represented by the Mets' Gil Hodges. Durocher played the hot hand and ignored part of his roster. Hodges, realizing his regulars weren't as good as the Cubs', platooned at four positions to maximize the players' chances for success. While Durocher shortened his rotation and bullpen down the stretch, Hodges used one of the first five-man rotations, led by Tom Seaver and including a young Nolan Ryan, and developed depth in the bullpen with Tug McGraw and Ron Taylor.

Soon Durocher and Holland would go up against not just a cutting-edge manager, but also a color-blind organization, the Pirates, that went everywhere in the Western Hemisphere to recruit talent. But that was a little down the road. The fallout from 1969 was huge, and it's still circulating to a small degree more than three decades later.

The Fallout from '69

As October 1969 ended, the Mets enjoyed their fluke world championship and Chicago settled into a gloomy autumn made worse by the 1-13 Bears. Some media notables wondered if Durocher's "handling" of pitchers didn't have a sinister side. The Lip's background of hanging around with shady characters and high-stakes cards and craps games led to suspicions that Durocher had somehow "thrown" the pennant race to the Mets by gambling on the game. The most serious accusation, according to Rick Talley in *The Cubs of '69,* had Durocher allegedly winning $60,000 betting against his own team in the September 9 game in which

Jenkins not only started on short rest, but also batted for himself in the fifth with the Mets leading 6-1.

Baseball commissioner Bowie Kuhn, fearing another Black Sox-type scandal, launched an investigation. Joining in was the Internal Revenue Service. Chicago's top newspaper investigative reporters jumped into the fray. Talley caught wind of Kuhn's probe, but was asked by the commissioner to not publish anything in order to protect baseball. And nothing ever did get into print. Durocher eventually was cleared, although Bob Glass of *Chicago Today* claimed that Phil Wrigley had paid off "thousands of dollars" in gambling debts the manager had run up in Las Vegas in order to clean Durocher's slate. The Lip later claimed in his autobiography, *Nice Guys Finish Last*, that the investigations were a setup, with the *Chicago Tribune* seeking his hide partially because of the feud with Brickhouse.

Lynne Durocher said her then-husband could not have done anything but have managed on the up-and-up. She said Leo wanted to win badly, perhaps in the case of 1969 too badly. Joey Amalfitano, then Durocher's first-base coach, seconds that notion.

"I spent a lot of time with Leo privately before and after games [in 1969] when the media wasn't around," Amalfitano said. "There were two different Leos—the tough, hard guy the public saw and the other person I got to know. I felt sorry for him because I know how heartbroken he was."

Lynne Durocher said the couple had taken great pains to avoid being seen with organized-crime types who were attracted to the bright lights of his flashy persona.

She said notorious Mafioso Sam Giancana came up to a table the Durochers were sharing with Dean Martin and wife Jeanne in Acapulco, Mexico. "Leo was at my right and Dean was on my left," Lynne Durocher said. "All of a sudden I felt Leo freeze. Giancana came up to the table. He gave Dean a read shot in the arm. Dean put his head down and he had his hand in a fist. Leo had no conversation with him, he wanted nothing to do with him. Leo told me later that this is how he got thrown out of baseball once (by being seen with gangland types).

Another time the couple were on a California golf course. A gangster nodded to Durocher. "We tried to walk quickly off the green," Lynne Durocher said. "The gangster said hello. Leo felt really terrible about it."

"Never in my 10 years of marriage to Leo did he ever have a [gangland] connection."

With the Kuhn-led investigations out of the public eye in the winter of 1969-70, Durocher said his mea culpas. He set out to work on fine-tuning the Cubs for the following season. He hunkered down with Holland on November 17, 1969, working on a deal with Phillies GM John Quinn to land right fielder Johnny Callison.

Eager to move the socially overactive Oscar Gamble, Durocher and Holland dealt their best everyday-player prospect and Dick Selma for Callison. Their public reasoning: The Cubs needed a veteran outfielder and left-handed hitter like the 32-year-old Callison.

But the trade was supremely flawed. The Cubs already had an effective right fielder in Jim Hickman, whose clutch power hitting had kept the Cubs alive going into September. Trading Gamble meant the Cubs now would have to look for a center fielder. Holland promised he would attempt to land a veteran at the winter meetings; he came up with none and Durocher had to employ eight different center fielders, including second baseman Glenn Beckert in one game, during 1970. Hickman also was employed in center, and with a lack of speed looked like he was running on a treadmill on the Houston Astrodome's artificial turf.

"I'm not too worried about center field," Durocher said then. "We're giving up a good center-field prospect in Gamble, but you can't get a solid front-liner without giving up something. And at this point, Gamble still lacks experience." Durocher did not explain why he and Holland brought up Gamble in the first place at age 19, throwing him into center in the middle of a pennant race only three months earlier.

The departure of Selma, who began 1969 12-4 before Durocher shuttled him to primarily bullpen duty, meant Durocher would have to use Joe Decker, one of his accursed young pitchers, as the No. 4 starter in 1970. Selma went on to save 22 games for a mediocre Phillies' team in '70.

The deal also symbolized the Cubs' plight for the remainder of Durocher's tenure: a lack of speed and a weak bullpen. Durocher and Holland failed to address these deficiencies, costing the Cubs an even better shot at the NL East title in 1970.

The next season started out much the same as 1969. The Cubs won 11 in a row on their opening homestand. In mid-June, they were in first place with a 35-25 record. But Durocher could not manufacture runs with slow players all over the lineup. Callison also proved his best years were behind him in Philly. The Cubs lost 12 in a row from their season high-point, dropping under .500 going into July. The manager could not brake that slump, and the losing streak cost the Cubs in the end.

Despite the additions of slugger Joe Pepitone, who was inserted in center for the final two months, and righthander Milt Pappas, the Cubs simply could not get a head of steam going in the second half. Locked in a close three-team race with the Mets and Pirates, the Cubs either lustily outslugged opponents or lost close games due to lack of speed and the shaky bullpen. The team did not stage an eighth- or ninth-inning come-from-behind win between June 3 and August 28. At the same time, Phil Regan, who was 4-1 with 10 saves in June, finished 5-9 with 12 saves, giving up a series of back-breaking homers in the late innings.

For all their power and solid Big Four starters, the little things and Durocher's increasingly conservative style did the Cubs in. After stealing just 30 bases in 1969, the Cubs swiped only 39 in 1970, both figures easily NL lows.

Their 1969 record would have looked great transposed to 1970, but the Cubs fell short in the end, going 84-78 and finishing five games behind a beatable Pirates team.

Worse yet, rifts began to widen between Durocher and his veterans. Ron Santo, previously one of Durocher's top boosters, was angered when he was dropped to seventh in the lineup without any warning.

Missing the Boat on Re-Tooling

The winter of 1970-71 would have been the ideal time for Phil Wrigley to fire Durocher and start to gradually re-tool the Cubs while enough of a productive nucleus remained and talented young pitchers could have brought value in trades. But the owner was oh-so-loyal to the manager who had given the Cubs four years of excitement and uncommon profits (more than $900,000 in 1969). Santo appealed to management to keep the team together, and the hierarchy obliged. The die was cast.

"We had index cards, rating all the players by position in the league," Blake Cullen said of John Holland's files. "We had this conversation at the time: Who's better at third than Santo? Who was a better shortstop than Kessinger?"

Still hampered by the same problems of lack of speed and a shoddy bullpen, the 1971 Cubs started poorly, but rallied in mid-summer to amass a 68-55 record, only four and a half games behind the Pirates on August 20. *Sports Illustrated* featured a Cy Young Award-bound Fergie Jenkins on the cover with the headline "Here Come the Cubs." The article also had a foreboding angle: the creeping thirtysomething age of the regulars.

The Cubs' momentum stopped right there. The worst clubhouse explosion in Cubs history wrecked the season on August 23, before a game with the Cincinnati Reds at Wrigley Field. Durocher ripped into Milt Pappas for throwing a pitch to the Astros' Doug Rader that cost the Cubs the game the previous day. The team meeting quickly degenerated into a shouting match between Durocher and his veterans. The manager accused Santo of asking Holland to stage "Ron Santo Day" six days later before a game with the Braves. Enraged, Santo tried to choke Durocher before he was pulled off by teammates. Durocher briefly threatened to quit as Holland was called to the clubhouse. Clearly, the time was past for a housecleaning of the manager and some players.

The Cubs went into a tailspin, losing eight of their next 12 on the make-or-break homestand to fall to nine games behind the Pirates. On September 4, Phil Wrigley took out his famous newspaper ad defending Durocher and admonishing his players. But Wrigley refused at that point to commit to Durocher for 1972.

A knowledgeable baseball man would have thanked Durocher for his efforts and sent him packing during the 1971-72 off-season, especially since Holland finally landed some players who could run in outfielders Rick Monday and Jose Cardenal, and with young pitchers like knuckle-curve specialist Burt Hooton and farmboy control artist Rick Reuschel knocking on the door of the majors. But Durocher stayed on. He was aging, but so was his team. Both were living on borrowed time.

To soothe all the embittered feelings, Wrigley summoned his contrarian style to hire an "information and services" coach, another baseball first, in ex-reliever Hank Aguirre for '72. Aguirre was charged with acting as a liason between Durocher and the players and media. Briefly, it appeared to work. The Cubs rebounded from a 1-8 start to go into a three-game series with the first-place Pirates on June 23 at Wrigley Field with a 34-22 record, just two games out. But the Buccos, whose free-swinging bats overwhelmed the Cubs' control pitchers in the early 1970s, swept the three-game series. The Cubs fell apart again, dropping to 46-44 at the All-Star break.

Durocher's time finally was up. Summoned to a meeting at Phil Wrigley's apartment on July 24, 1972, the two agreed to part ways. Wrigley refused to call the 66-year-old Durocher's departure an outright firing.

A good era had gone to waste.

"If we had a different type of leadership, we would have had a better chance of winning," said Jim Colborn. "I'm fairly confident that there was more to be gotten from those Cubs teams than we showed. It wasn't a product of the effort. What they had to give was diminished. From the physical side, they were tired. Mentally, the resentment of the leader kept the team from winning. Subconsciously, you don't want to win. The last thing you want is someone you resent getting accolades. Durocher ran that team to aggrandize himself."

The Cubs seemed to respond immediately to new manager Whitey Lockman, recycled by Wrigley from elsewhere in the organization; Lockman had been director of player development, running the mediocre farm system. Players praised Lockman for using his entire roster. Without Durocher, the '72 Cubs finished 39-26 after the All-Star break, their final record a respectable 85-70, second-best winning percentage during this era. But it was only a stay of execution.

The Cubs' core was another year older and less effective in 1973 as Holland, eyeing retirement two years down the line, opted to stand pat. And some of the same communication problems still existed. Although Lockman got some praise publicly, players chafed under his leadership, too. You cannot get Fergie Jenkins and Billy Williams to say nice things about Lockman's managing style today. More problems developed when newly-acquired lefty reliever Dave La Roche was upset when he came down with arm troubles. He claimed management expected him to throw at Nolan Ryan speed when he merely possessed an above-average fastball.

The gas tank finally ran empty after the Cubs got off to a 46-31 start with an eight-game lead at the end of June 1973. The Pirates slumped, apparently shocked after the plane-crash death of Roberto Clemente on a mercy mission to earthquake-stricken Nicaragua the previous December. But the Cubs could not grab a for-the-taking NL East. The lineup stopped hitting, the Cubs developed a hole at first base when rookie Pat Bourque flamed out after a month on the job, and Beckert was hobbled with an arthritic ankle. The Cubs nosedived with a 10-33 record, falling to 56-64, six games out in fifth place by mid-August. The mega-slump seemed impossible to duplicate until the '99 Cubs outdid their '73 forebears, going 10-40 in one stretch in August and September. The Mets pulled off a mini-miracle, going 22-9 down the stretch to snatch a cheap divisional title in 1973 with an all-time worst 82-79 record. The Cubs could have played 10 under .500 from their high point and still won the NL East. But they couldn't even do that due to old bones and tired attitudes.

Wrigley publicly ordered Holland to clean house. That was another bad tactic. Other teams knowing that a GM is under orders to dump players won't give equal value. Holland had to revamp the roster all at once rather than filtering out the players one by one over a span of years. Jenkins, Santo, Beckert, Hundley, Hickman, and Pappas were sent packing. Williams and Kessinger brought up the rear of the departures after the 1974 and 1975 seasons. Somehow, Holland managed to land some good value in return with the likes of Bill Madlock, Manny Trillo, Jerry Morales. But with little homegrown everyday-player talent complementing the imports and constant shuffling of pitching coaches confusing the young hurlers, the Cubs once again became an NL bottom feeder.

The organization had rotted at the core. Wrigley would have opened the checkbook with profits from a perennial winner had the 1969-era team been properly managed. The owner would have been thrilled had the Cubs been restored to the powerhouse-status enjoyed by his father's teams at the end of the 1920s. Instead, with team fortunes and attendance plummeting straight down, he slashed the budget amid the horrible economy of the mid-1970s.

The window had closed on ending the million-to-one era. Durocher, who specialized on opening windows of baseball opportunity in the past, got it stuck halfway through with the Cubs. In tandem with Holland's pedestrian player moves, The Lip's onrushing managerial senility of 1969 to 1972 is worth almost 100,000 to one of the odds.

Chapter 7

Wrigley's Out, Tribune's In

TO BE A CHICAGO CUB in the 1970s was to experience a weird combination of hope, frustration, and desperation.

You'd be a member of a team that got off to some impressive starts, even contending well into August. The fan adulation revived by the Leo Durocher era was dampened a bit, but never plummeted to franchise-threatening depths in the manner of the crosstown White Sox. Beautiful Wrigley Field was your place of employment.

Or was it so beautiful? Some of the most negative attitudes within and about the Cubs organization originated in the 1970s, a depressing decade that nevertheless has been happily commemorated as a time of disco, easy sex, and overall fun and games by nostalgia mongers.

The end of the Leo Durocher managerial tenure and the subsequent collapse of the aging Cubs contender eliminated the positive atmosphere that had enveloped Wrigley Field. Now, more players wanted to leave the Cubs than join the organization. Ken Holtzman was the first one desiring a happier home, asking for a trade late in 1971 and getting his wish fulfilled with a winter-meeting deal to favorite Cubs' trading partner Oakland. Word got around baseball about negative, penny-pinching management and constant changes in managers and coaches. Worse yet, the playing conditions of all-day baseball came increasingly under fire from players who believed the summer heat and constant switch from days at home to nights on the road was tiring them out over the long season.

By the end of the decade, as contracts became laden with all kinds of clauses in the onset of the free-agency era, a host of players blackballed the Cubs. They instructed their agents to insure they'd have "no-trade clauses" that prohibited deals with certain clubs they wished to avoid. The Cubs showed up more than not on the blacklist.

Often now the Cubs were being linked with the one of the cheapest teams in late 20th century baseball—the Calvin Griffith family-run Minnesota Twins.

"Minnesota and the Cubs have always operated along the same lines: no free agents, no big contracts, frugal operation," said agent Steve Pierce in 1981.

Clearly, a change in ownership and philosophy was needed as the decade wore on. But the Cubs were not going to get that, at least not yet. When Phil Wrigley died on April 12, 1977 and son Bill Wrigley, who had been peripherally involved in team management, took over. Only the consequence of $40 million in estate-tax problems brought on by the deaths of Phil Wrigley and his wife, Helen, just two months apart would force the biggest change in franchise history since the early part of the century.

The economic and philosophical culture of the Cubs changed little when Bill Wrigley succeeded his father as owner. Although the two generations shared an affinity for the low profile, Bill Wrigley was not as conservative in his personal life. Before he died in 1999, the younger Wrigley was married three times and, according to a *Chicago Magazine* article reporting on controversy over his estate, had extra-marital affairs. He aggressively built up the Wrigley Co.'s international reach. Revenue and profits soared. But that dynamic business stance did not extend to the Cubs.

Although *Chicago Magazine* said Bill Wrigley loved baseball ownership and was reluctant to surrender control of the Cubs, he did not improve upon his father in putting more resources into the franchise or hiring dynamic executives. In spring training 1997, Cubs president Andy MacPhail escorted Bill Wrigley around the new HoHoKam ballpark in Mesa, Arizona. Wrigley said the visit was the first time he had attended spring training since he sold the Cubs to Tribune Co. in 1981. That was not a sign of a man passionate about the game in the manner of his grandfather, William Wrigley, Jr.

At the time of the sale, the team had been buried so far down that continued status as a big-league club could have been questioned. The Cubs had been stripped down, worse than an expansion club, with few prospects for improvement. But the Cubs hadn't just suddenly arrived there. They had been sliding down a long, slippery slope for the better part of seven years.

The Cubs should not have dipped so far. Even as the Durocher-era gang was broken up, the Cubs could field a quartet of homegrown young pitchers who seemed to form the nucleus of a good rotation: Rick Reuschel,

Burt Hooton, Bill Bonham, and Ray Burris. All had enjoyed some degree of success breaking into the majors between 1971 and 1973. With a still-competitive lineup comprised of batting-champ Bill Madlock, Rick Monday, Jose Cardenal, Jerry Morales, Andre Thornton, and Manny Trillo behind them—the Cubs tied for third in the NL in runs scored in 1975. The makings of a halfway-decent team seemed at hand.

Hooton seemed the most sensational, striking out a Cubs' record-tying 15 in his second major-league start, pitching a two-hit shutout over the Mets in his third start, and hurling a no-hitter against the Phillies in his fourth. Reuschel was 10-8 with a 2.93 ERA as a rookie. Burris had a 2.91 ERA as a rookie reliever with just one year of pro ball under his belt. Bonham, possessed of perhaps the best stuff of all—"That cat can pitch," the Phillies' Dave Cash said in 1974—pitched well as a reliever and sometime starter in his second and third years, with ERAs of 3.10 and 3.02.

"I looked at Hooton, Reuschel, Bonham, and Burris, and I thought we were pretty well set," said Blake Cullen, who by the early 1970s had become John Holland's unofficial assistant general manager.

But like their pitching forebears Dick Drott, Moe Drabowsky, Glen Hobbie, and Bob Anderson, the quartet never coalesced into a winning rotation. Reuschel was the only one of the foursome to have long-term success as a Cub. The negative surroundings and constant change in pitching coaches hampered their development.

Hooton had to take some of the blame himself. He perhaps had been too successful too soon with the sensational starts right out of the chute. The University of Texas product's knuckle-curve never duplicated its tricky early success as Bruce Sutter's split-fingered fastball did. The pitch merely had the effect of a sharp sinker; Hooton would never rack up big strikeout totals that the 15-whiff triumph over the Mets seemed to forecast. "Once I got around the league once or twice, the strikeouts dropped dramatically," he said. "I had to start learning how to pitch, to stop expecting to strike these guys out and just get them out any way I could."

Without strong direction from management, Hooton became overweight and undermotivated. A demotion to the bullpen in the second half of a lost 1974 season in which he finished 7-11 seemed to send his attitude straight into the dumper.

"We cut Hooton 10 percent after that season, and he was pissed," Blake Cullen said.

Leave it to master motivator Tommy Lasorda to concoct a trade with the Cubs by his employers, the Dodgers, while assuaging Hooton's feelings and whipping him into shape in winter ball while the pitcher was still Cubs' property. Then Los Angeles' third-base coach, Lasorda served as Hooton's manager in the Dominican winter league in 1974-75.

"Tommy had a hard time believing a guy had gone downhill that fast," Hooton said. "It wasn't tampering; he was genuinely interested. He told me you just had to do it on your own, that you had to get yourself mentally prepared to pitch in the big leagues."

Lasorda, a gourmand by nature and practice, somehow disabused Hooton of his love of extra portions. The righthander lost 20 pounds during the winter. All the while, Lasorda talked to his front office about setting up a trade to get Hooton. LA general manager Al Campanis made contact with John Holland. Eventually, the deal was done on May 2, 1975, the Dodgers dispatching lefty Geoff Zahn and righthander Eddie Solomon.

The Dodgers, who had stocked their bullpen in the 1960s with home-grown Cubs lefties Ron Perranoski and Jim Brewer, had raped Chicago again. Re-united with Lasorda, working under LA manager Walt Alston, Hooton was 18-7 in 31 games the remainder of the 1975 season. He peaked at 19-10 with a 2.71 ERA in 1978, going on to win 151 games in the majors. Meanwhile, the soft-tossing Zahn had arm problems, while Solomon was a clubhouse problem in his brief Cubs stint. He resurfaced a few years later with the Pirates, changing his name to Buddy Jay Solomon.

Reuschel's development was normal, the portly righthander getting better each season until he won 20 games in 1977. But Bonham went the opposite direction. He actually pitched better in 1974 when he went 11-22 with a 3.85 ERA than in succeeding years that featured 13-15, 9-13, and 10-13 records. Bonham, almost a flower child from California, was non-combative; he did not like to pitch inside. He also suffered from elbow problems that prevented him from breaking off his slider, according to Blake Cullen.

Sure enough, when Bonham was traded to the Reds for pitchers Woody Fryman and Bill Caudill after the 1977 season, he responded with two decent years—11-5 and 9-7—before petering out.

Burris may have been overrated somewhat from the start. As a rookie, he was nicknamed "Little Fergie" because, like Cubs ace Fergie Jenkins, his teammate in '73, Burris was 6-foot-5 and black. But that's where the similarity ended. Burris did not possess Jenkins' wide variety of pitches and razor-sharp control. Sometimes Burris' control was *too* good. After 15-10 and 15-13 seasons the previous two years, Burris was battered for 270 hits in 221 innings in 1977, a hits-to-innings ratio that was horrific even by Cubs standards. He was in and out of the rotation the next season, and moved on to the Yankees in an early-season 1979 deal that actually helped the Cubs, who landed reliever Dick Tidrow. Burris was little more than a journeyman pitcher wandering through the game until he retired after the 1987 season.

Still, when the likes of Hooton, Bonham, Bill Madlock, Andre Thornton, reliever Buddy Schultz, and several others are considered, the Cubs gave away another crop of promising big leaguers during the period.

"From 1974 to 1977, you look at the amount of young talent we had that went on to succeed with other clubs," Burris said. "We didn't maintain that nucleus."

The Kennedy Administration

No nucleus could be maintained if the leadership was changing. The Cubs went from John Holland to Salty Saltwell to Bob Kennedy in the general manager's chair during the period. Anyone in that job operated under the tight Wrigley financial constraints. Kennedy showed signs of aggressiveness in his trades, but always fell short of rounding out the roster with talent due to the modest player payroll. He also had a temper that sometimes got the best of him in dealing with agents, players, and dissenting fans.

The Opening Day 1977 Cubs lineup was paid as follows: Burris ($75,000), first baseman Bill Buckner ($100,000), second baseman Manny Trillo ($50,000), shortstop Ivan DeJesus ($30,000), third baseman Steve Ontiveros ($20,000), catcher Steve Swisher ($50,000), left fielder Jose Cardenal ($150,000), center fielder Jerry Morales ($80,000), and right fielder Bobby Murcer ($250,000). Total payroll was $805,000. The defending world champion Cincinnati Reds had a payroll of $1.7 million. The two NL teams who would win the division titles in 1977 were the Los Angeles Dodgers (payroll $1.443 million) and the Philadelphia Phillies ($1.386 million). The eventual world champion New York Yankees had a $1.495 million payroll.

Somehow, the '77 Cubs caught fire, on the strength of Bruce Sutter's magic split-fingered fastball in relief, Reuschel's 15-3 season start, and opportunistic hitting. The Cubs charged into first place during a three-game Memorial Day weekend sweep of the Pirates at Wrigley Field. By June 29 the Cubs were 47-22, eight games in front. Then Sutter, suffering perhaps from the effects of overwork—manager Herman Franks sometimes used him for three-inning stints—developed a sore shoulder in July. Other players got hurt. Still, the Cubs gamely hung on to first place, for 69 days, a longer period of time between 1945 and 1984 than any other Cubs team save for the 1969 entry. Wrigley Field fans gave the team a standing ovation every time they took the field before the first pitch.

The Cubs needed to add a long-ball hitter and any kind of decent reliever to fill in for Sutter. Kennedy allowed big bopper Cliff Johnson to get waived out of the NL, going from the budget-cutting Astros to the first-place Yankees on June 15, 1977. Kennedy did end up landing Johnson— in 1980, when the Cubs had plunged to the cellar and his bat couldn't help them. The only outside relief help Kennedy landed in mid-summer '77 was the washed-up Dave Giusti, whom A's owner Charlie Finley dumped on the Cubs, big thanks for all the talent Chicago had sent to Oakland.

The lack of moves created unease and dissension in the Cubs' clubhouse—a feeling that would always be close at hand for the remainder of the Wrigley family ownership.

"I feel that was a team that could have won," 1977 outfielder Gene Clines said. "Management didn't back us, and that was one of the most disappointing aspects of that season. We just wanted them to give us some help. There was a big stink about it. So we got away from focusing on what we wanted to do."

The powerful Phillies blew past the Cubs into first place in the first week of August and never looked back. The Cubs continued sinking like a rock. Going into the last week of the season, Chicago still had an 81-76 record, with a chance for the respectability of an above-.500 finish. The weakened, demoralized team couldn't even do that. The Cubs lost their final five games to finish 81-81, in fourth place, 20 games out.

Despite a slew of trades over the next two years, Kennedy made the clubhouse chemistry even worse by adding Dave Kingman, the team's first major free-agent signee, to a locker room that included Bobby Murcer and his rocking chair, and Bill Buckner with his devotion to his statistics. When center fielder Jerry Martin, second baseman Ted Sizemore, and right fielder Mike Vail donned pinstripes, the locker room oozed with negativity. Herman Franks only added to the grumpiness quotient.

Kingman, of course, was the worst offender. Beset with some kind of demons that made him hostile to the majority of humans who tried to deal with him, Kingman thrilled Cubs fans with his 48-homer burst of power in 1979. But he frittered away the city's adulation. Kingman refused to talk to the media through most of his great year, angered by a humorous, tongue-in-cheek story in spring training by the *Chicago Sun-Times'* Joe Goddard. The beat writer had polled Cubs players on their worst- and best-dressed teammates. Kingman easily won the "worst" dishonors, but he took it the wrong way.

"There were some personal clashes," said former outfielder Scot Thompson, then by far the Cubs' best homegrown everyday-player prospect. "I don't think Dave cared that much about baseball. He'd rather be doing something else. Buckner was very egotistical about his statistics. He cared more about Bill Buckner than the Cubs. That 1979 team was the closest I was on. There were a few bad seeds in there, and they were a prominent part of the offense."

Thompson remembered a clubhouse meeting the following season in Philadelphia, in which Rick Reuschel, normally the strong, silent type, spoke up about the need for Kingman to take more of a leadership role. The slugger didn't respond, missing half the 1980 season due to injuries and ennui. He did not even show up for his own T-shirt day at Wrigley Field while on the disabled list. Kingman also displayed a knack for juvenile behavior, tossing a bucket of ice water on *Daily Herald* beat writer Don Friske's head in spring training amid other idiotic episodes.

Thompson, several other regulars, and the pitchers were indeed close, but that wasn't enough for the bad atmosphere to crash another Cubs season. Chicago was squarely in contention in 1979 with a 67-54 record going into the last week of August. But another nightmarish September dropped them quickly out of the race to a final record of 80-82.

Franks had quit with a week to go in the '79 campaign. After the season, a newspaper poll asked Cubs fans who they'd like to succeed Franks as manager. A pre-Cardinals Whitey Herzog, then between jobs, was the overwhelming choice. Kennedy choice old warhorse Preston Gomez instead. Gomez lasted just half a season.

The Downward Spiral

The negatives only increased in the months ahead. Bruce Sutter had won the Cy Young Award for his 37-save season in 1979. He and Kennedy had reached a tentative agreement for a $400,000-plus annual new contract. But the GM had to run the deal past Bill Wrigley first. Wrigley nixed the contract. Angered, Sutter went to arbitration. The Cubs, represented by then-assistant scouting director Andy MacPhail, just 26, offered $350,000. Sutter asked for $700,000. Sutter won. Cubs fans booed him on Opening Day 1980 at Wrigley Field while Wrigley planned ways to dump his salary.

The Cubs soon began spiraling down to one of the all-time franchise low points. Attendance, nearly a record at 1,648,587 Kingman-crazy fans in 1979, plummeted dramatically to a little more than 1.2 million in recession- and inflation-wracked 1980. Kingman's frequent absences, other lineup holes and injuries, and poor starting pitching condemned the Cubs to a last-place finish at 64-98, despite an 11-6 start. Joey Amalfitano, who took over from Gomez as manager at mid-season, started a pitcher's nightmare of a lineup one August day in an attempt to get more hitting without Kingman. To accommodate the statue-like Cliff Johnson at first, gimpy-ankled Bill Buckner moved to left, while slow Iowan Larry Biittner played right. The only trace of speed was Scot Thompson, moving from right field to center for this game.

Playing out of position was the least of Thompson's problems in 1980. In that atmosphere of gloom, the Cubs screwed up a potentially good hitter by messing with his mechanics.

Possessing a Mark Grace, line-drive left-handed style, Thompson hit .300 for much of the 1979 season before finishing at .289 as a platoon right fielder. But management wanted Thompson, who possessed some natural strength at 6-foot-3, 195 pounds, to dramatically improve his two-homer production. Billy Williams, named hitting coach for the first time in 1980, was assigned to change Thompson's swing.

"Billy said he they wanted me to have a fuller swing," Thompson recalled. "He said he didn't know why they were doing this, that with time I would hit more homers. But this was what they were asking me to do. There was a certain feeling that we would try to appease them, but we really didn't have our hearts in it.

"I had two separate swings. One was the swing they wanted me to do. The other was my own. I abandoned it [the imposed swing] fairly early in the season."

The dangers of tinkering with one's natural swing caught up with Thompson. And when he lost even a semi-regular's role, he suffered even more. The natural hitter batted just .212 in 1980. And he was even worse in 1981, batting just .165. He revived as a pinch hitter and sometime center fielder in 1982 with a .365 season, but Thompson would never be more than a part-timer and pinch hitter the rest of his career that moved on to San Francisco in 1984.

Thompson wasn't the only one whose career crashed in 1981. Kennedy, who had traded Kingman to the Mets for outfielder Steve Henderson in spring training, resigned as GM in May after the talent-depleted Cubs got off to a 6-28 start.

In true Wrigley style, the owner recycled another figure from the team's past, naming Herman Franks as "interim" GM. Having apparently recovered from the disgust that led him to resign as manager one and a half years previously, Franks continued cutting the payroll. In a bizarre trade, he dealt Rick Reuschel to the Yankees for pitcher Doug Bird, young infielder Pat Tabler, and $400,000. Nobody could remember when the Cubs needed to scrounge for that amount of money in a deal. Even stranger was the fact, according to the *Chicago Sun-Times'* Joe Goddard, Franks rousted an unnamed sportswriter out of bed and invited him to sit in on the Reuschel trade discussions. When the second major players' strike began on June 12, 1981, the Cubs were virtually out of the league with a 15-37 record despite having shown signs of life by winning five of the last six games.

Clearly, the Cubs needed new ownership who could spend money. Typically, Bill Wrigley had kept his estate-tax problems out of the public eye. But the sharply declining on-field fortunes and shaky management got the wheels turning among a host of business groups. By the spring of 1981, they believed the Cubs would finally be put up for sale. The Cubs' front office began receiving unsolicited purchase offers.

Amid his myriad of business and philanthropic activities that made it seem like there was a cloned version of him, Andy McKenna sensed back in 1980 that Bill Wrigley might be on the verge of selling. President of Schwarz Paper Co. in suburban Morton Grove by day and a sports activist in most of his other waking moments, McKenna had been part of the Bill Veeck ownership group that ran the White Sox from 1975 to 1981. Active on the Notre Dame board of directors, he also had once operated a minor-league baseball team in Michigan City, Indiana. Many years later, he and fellow Chicago magnate Pat Ryan bought 20 percent of the Chicago Bears. So he had a sixth sense about the shifting sands of sports-team ownership.

Shopping-center magnate Edward J. DeBartolo scuffled with Major League Baseball in his attempt to buy the White Sox in the winter of 1980-81. His cash-flush bid was hung up due to other business interests that the baseball lords of the realm believed were questionable. All the while, another group of investors led by real-estate syndicator Jerry Reinsdorf and TV sports impresario Eddie Einhorn group was poised on the sidelines to rush in. While the DeBartolo issue festered, McKenna told Reinsdorf he had a potential other ownership opportunity.

"I remember telling Jerry, 'You know, there's another team in this town you ought to think about buying,'" McKenna said. "At that point, Jerry would be the first to tell you he was a Cubs fan." Reinsdorf, who grew up a diehard Dodgers fan in Brooklyn before moving west to attend Northwestern University, later said he rooted for both Chicago baseball teams in the 1970s.

When the DeBartolo bid was rejected, Veeck, McKenna, and the other Sox owners almost immediately sold to Reinsdorf and Einhorn. Then McKenna talked to Cubs president William Hagenah, Jr.: "We talked about it [a potential sale]," McKenna said. "He told me, 'It could happen.'"

Bill Wrigley was buffeted by the $40 million estate-tax obligation. Although close to a billionaire in total assets by this time, the $40 million was still a healthy bite of liquid assets to tender to the IRS. He did not want to lose any control of the Wrigley Co., his core business. And the marketplace for baseball teams in 1981 had moved into the $20 million range. The tax obligation could be partially satisfied by a sale of the Cubs.

Another factor may have been motivating Wrigley, McKenna theorized. "He also saw that baseball was beginning to be a very expensive undertaking," he said. "When you think that free agency was in its early days, he had the vision to think about what baseball was like in 1981. What would be it be like in 1986 or 1991 and so on?"

But there would be no public auction of the Cubs, McKenna learned. "Bill Wrigley would never wait for a group of guys to get together to syndicate a deal," he said. "He'd have to sell it to one buyer who put down one check, very quietly, without any fanfare. Bill was a very private person and didn't want to go through all that."

McKenna himself could not have bought the Cubs on his own. The market for baseball teams had been established in the $20-million range in 1981, a considerable sum at the time. "I would have had to syndicate it, and Bill Wrigley would not have waited for that," he said.

White Knight on Michigan Avenue

McKenna then realized the "mostly likely" buyer was Tribune Co. "For a lot of reasons," he said. "The historical significance of the two buildings (Tribune Tower and the Wrigley Building) being across the street from each other. They were the two anchors of Michigan Avenue as it grew northbound. Bill was a very traditional guy. There were all kinds of connections. Two old-line, Chicago-based companies."

The strongest connection, of course, was through WGN, flagship of Tribune Co.'s broadcasting arm. The TV station, which had signed on just before Opening Day 1948, had never operated without a full complement of Cubs home games, increased to more than three-quarters of the road schedule in 1968. WGN-TV also was a "passive" superstation in 1981, its signal picked up by satellite and fed nationwide to subscribers of the burgeoning cable-TV industry. Jim Dowdle had just taken the helm of Tribune Broadcasting. A mover and a shaker, Dowdle saw the increased revenue possibilities in the future for cable-borne sports telecasts. On the radio side, WGN, a 50,000-watt clear channel owned by Tribune Co. since 1924, had possessed the Cubs rights since 1958. The Cubs may have stunk to high heaven in 1981, but they had been a perennial revenue stream into Tribune Co. coffers.

But there were perceived threats to that cash flow in the spring of 1981. The Sox's Einhorn was conceiving SportsVision, Chicago's first nontraditional broadcast carrier of sports teams. At the same time, Marshall Field's Field Enterprises owned WFLD-TV (Ch. 32), a potential carrier of baseball. Several 50,000-watt Chicago radio stations would have jumped into the fray to land the Cubs' radio rights had they been put up for bid.

Soon after his meeting with William Hagenah, Jr., McKenna visited Tribune Tower. He had personal relationships with many of the top executives. In the middle of a general conversation, the subject of the Cubs came up. The consensus was to quietly pursue the purchase. "The fact is that there was interest on their part," he said. "Both of us felt something could be done."

While Tribune Co. negotiated with Wrigley and his representatives behind the scenes, two groups of entrepreneur types who grew up rooting for the Cubs tendered offers that seemed to go nowhere.

One group was headed by Jim Anixter, whose family ran a publicly traded cable-TV wire and equipment distribution business based in

Chicago's northern suburbs. He was joined by Jenner & Block attorney Tom Mandler and Chicago insurance executive Charles Balkin. Much of their stake money came from the windfall other group members, headed by Anixter's brother Scott, had made on the Chicago Board of Trade in the 1970s and into the 1980s.

Anixter is as intense a Cubs fan as they come. Almost every room of the basement of his mansion in Highland Park, Illinois, is crammed with framed Cubs souvenirs and newspaper and magazine clippings. He purchased Ron Santo's old wire-mesh locker cubicle from the old Cubs' clubhouse among the stash he has collected. What little space isn't devoted to the Cubs features Chicago White Sox, Milwaukee Brewers, and Chicago Bears items, among others. He even sent a Cubs pennant to Pope John Paul II in 1984 and received a written thank-you from the Vatican.

Anixter loved his Cubs so much that at age 19 in 1964, he and a buddy went to Phil Wrigley's Lake Geneva estate to offer to buy the Cubs. Dismissed by Wrigley as an impetuous youth, Anixter never let go of the desire to run the Cubs. In 1977, after establishing himself in business, he sent another, serious purchase offer to Wrigley. Prompting him this time was the trade of Bill Madlock. Wrigley sent him a reply, not responding to the purchase offer, but instead defending the Madlock trade on the grounds of maintaining fiscal sanity for the Cubs.

"We could have rounded up $20 million in 1977, but we never made an offer because Wrigley didn't respond to it," said Anixter, now out of the cable-TV business, but still running a wire and cable distribution firm for other industries. "We would have had up to 20 people in the ownership group.

"We seriously considered buying the team again in 1981 because we heard they didn't do proper [estate] tax planning," Anixter said. "We offered $22 million. The next day the Cubs were sold for a million and a half less to Tribune Co."

Anixter said he planned to hire Billy Williams as manager. In the mid-1980s, he employed Williams as a sales representative in the cable-TV firm.

Another potential purchase group of businessmen was represented by Drexel Burnham Lambert vice president Joseph Siegman of north suburban Deerfield. Siegman refused to identify the group members other than the fact they were avid Cubs fans who grew up on Chicago's North Side. "Anyone who would deal with the Wrigleys would not want to do it in a flamboyant style," he said. He claimed the group had been trying to buy the Cubs for the previous two years. Nearly two weeks prior to the announced Tribune Co. purchase, Siegman said he had contacted Hagenah and was told the team was not for sale. I ran a story on Siegman's group in the June 9, 1981 editions of Chicago's *Lerner Newspapers*.

In an accompanying story by *Lerner* staffer Stan Zoller, Hagenah pulled off a sly misdirection play, throwing off attention from the obvious behind-the-scenes Tribune Co. negotiations—and the real fact Bill Wrigley was not going to sell to a syndicate of nouveau riche businessmen. "I'm sure Mr. Wrigley told him [Siegman] what he has told other groups interested in buying the club—that if and when he considers selling them team, he will let them know," he said, repeating his insistence the Cubs were not for sale. "'I've been keeping the records for 25 years. I've got a file filled with the names of people wanting to buy the club. It's huge."

While Hagenah kept buyers and curious media types at bay, Anixter hoped to combine his group and Siegman's.

All the while, diehard Cubs fan Mike Royko, Chicago's top newspaper columnist, floated the idea of a purchase of the Cubs to *Chicago Sun-Times'* co-owner Marshall Field. In turn, Charlie Finley, who had disposed of his longtime ownership of the Oakland Athletics the previous winter, had been interested in buying the Cubs, but required a financially robust partner. Finley planned to meet with Field on June 17, 1981—the day after the Tribune Co. purchase.

Although Finley had been a favorite trading partner of the Cubs, he seemed too brash and public to be involved in a deal with Bill Wrigley. In effect, McKenna reasoned, none of these groups would have been seriously considered. But in hindsight, he wonders why no other large Chicago corporate colossus stepped forward, quietly, with that one-check offer.

"I'm surprised more people didn't think about doing it," he said. Jack Brickhouse later said he knew of a dozen individuals who had the resources to buy the team in 1981. Perhaps the Wrigley family's longtime refusal to sell had dampened the desire to pursue what would have been a fruitless purchase effort. And a lot of corporations had other fish to fry in 1981, a year that featured double-digit interest rates, raging inflation, and an oncoming deep recession. Adding a money-draining baseball team did not seem an overwhelming priority.

But Tribune Co. always had weathered economic down times. The paper had been in business since 1847, while the broadcasting arm had been a cash cow. Corporate quarterly profits ranged into healthy double digits even in recessionary times. Col. Robert R. McCormick had avoided layoffs during the Great Depression by putting his staff on half-pay in the trough of the downturn. Former Cubs announcer Vince Lloyd told a story of how the fanatical conservative Republican McCormick, unwilling to pay additional taxes to the Democratic administration of Harry Truman, maneuvered the neophyte WGN-TV's financial status around so it lost money at the cusp of the 1950s and thus was a writeoff. As soon as Republican Dwight D. Eisenhower took office in 1953, WGN-TV began making money.

The $20.5 million Tribune Co. paid for the Cubs turned out to be a near-steal. The media conglomerate could have paid $30 million or whatever if necessary if Wrigley had seriously entertained other bidders like Marshall Field, Charlie Finley, or the north suburban entrepreneurs. In the end, bidders like Jim Anixter believed they didn't have a chance with Tribune Co. in the picture. "I honestly think they were able to consummate that deal because of relationships, and with the WGN connection, Wrigley wasn't going to sell them out," he said.

Bill Wrigley had owned 81 percent, a controlling percentage, of the stock. That pre-empted minority stockholders from successfully challenging the Tribune Co. purchase if they themselves wanted to bid. Some dissent was briefly heard, but died down quickly. Tribune Co. often got what it wanted in Chicago and the Midwest. The sale was approved two and a half months later by Major League Baseball. McKenna was appointed team president, squeezing another role out of his jam-packed schedule; he has continuously served on the Cubs' board of directors ever since. As the 1981 season drew to a close, McKenna set out looking for a dynamic executive to revive the moribund franchise.

Fans had almost unanimously cheered when the deal was announced. At last the Cubs would bid along with other teams for expensive free agents. No longer would the team suffer from their owner's penury. Tribune Co. was considered a savior among the majority of baseball followers in town.

The rooters' intuitions would turn out to be right. The Wrigley Field scene would dramatically improve. Three years later the Cubs would be three innings away from a World Series and ending the million-to-one era once and for all. But there would be some unforeseen caveats waiting in Tribune Co.'s stewardship. The proverbial light at the end of the tunnel was a trick sight. It included both salvation and an oncoming freight train, the latter overtaking the former.

Chapter 8

DALLAS ANNEXES CHICAGO

ANDY MCKENNA WASTED no time finding his man to jolt the Cubs out of their slumber. Within days of the end of the 1981 World Series, the high-decibel Dallas Green was installed as Cubs general manager, striding with his 6-foot-5 frame into Chicago like the marshal coming to clean up the town.

Having received most of his fame for bullying and blustering the 1980 Phillies to a World Series title, Green's background in player development wasn't well-known outside baseball's tight circle. Green had been the Phillies' minor-league director in the 1970s. Philadelphia's farm system was regarded as one of baseball's best in the decade.

"I was a scouting and development guy from Philly. I knew that was at the root of the problem," said Green, now a roving minor-league scout for Phillies GM Ed Wade. He now has plenty of time to decompress from his decades of baseball travels at his farm in West Grove, Pennsylvania.

"We had guys like Lee Elia and Ron Clark as managers and coaches," said mid-1980s Cubs center fielder Bob Dernier, a '70s Phillies product. "There were a lot of people who had a little renegade in them. There was no BS. They told you here's the things you've got to do. They told me to steal bases and catch everything. We weren't overcoached. It was a good system."

That's what Green tried to replicate in the fall of 1981 as he looked around the Cubs' organization and found a lot of things he didn't like.

Green immediately got off on the wrong foot with a slew of Cubs fans and some media when he damned practically everything that came before him under the Wrigleys, imported a platoon of his Phillies' personnel, proclaimed his slogan "Building a New Tradition," and suggested Wrigley Field should have lights for night games. Chicagoans believed Green was in some way belittling their world-class city, while community activists in the neighborhood around Wrigley Field, worried about newly-raised property values of the re-gentrified area, began organizing against night games. Green's bombastic manner and basso profundo voice hammered his ideas home for effect. But the bull-in-a-china-shop approach was necessary. Green simply desired to bring the Cubs up to the standards of the best player-development organizations in the game.

Dallas Green had a lot of faults. He did not show good judgment in some of his hirings. Appointing the droll Gene Michael as manager in 1986 after seeing his name stick out "like a sore thumb" from the American League guidebook was the worst. He overpaid several key players or showed blind loyalty in order to keep them as Cubs, in some cases past their primes. He fired pitching coach Billy Connors while he was laid up in the hospital. With the exception of the breakthrough 1984 NL East title season, the Cubs underperformed at the major-league level under his stewardship.

But the end result of his six years as general manager was the changing of the image of the Cubs. No, they'd still have their lovable loser's persona; only the complete rendering of the million-to-one era to history will purge that from Wrigley Field. But under Green, the Cubs were no longer regarded throughout the game as a sad-sack, laughable operation run by an eccentric, distant gum magnate. Budgets were increased to a competitive level with the better-paying teams in the game. Players no longer blacklisted the Cubs. They now clamored for a spot on the Cubs roster. Even pitchers wary of cozy Wrigley Field in the past gladly signed free-agent Cubs deals.

The long-term financial stability of the Cubs was dramatically improved. Tribune Co.'s potential resources were augmented by increased revenue generated from Wrigley Field. No longer would the owner not care if he made money from paid attendance and broadcast rights. The dark side was a rise in ticket prices and decrease in ready availability of seats, especially the ever-popular bleacher benches.

Bottom line, Green was proactive. He wasn't afraid to make a move, to gamble. Players, fans, and media knew who was in charge. He was a leader. Underlings who worked hard and productively were prized. He even ordered the lunchroom to serve breakfast for early arrivals who put in long hours as part of his effort to turn the Cubs around. Several long-time hands still on the job at Wrigley Field say Green was the best boss for whom they ever worked.

"I was fortunate to be around Dallas around most of his successful times," said Dernier. "I was convinced when he walked in the room that he had a general's veneer, like Bobby Knight. People ask me who was the best coach I ever had. Well, the smartest player I ever played with was Pete Rose. The smartest baseball man I knew was Dallas Green. The smartest coach I ever had was Don Zimmer. All their records speak for themselves."

While crediting McKenna with "having the guts to bring me aboard," Green set out with the monumental task of lifting the Cubs from their bottomless pit at the big-league level while rebuilding scouting and player development.

Mind you, despite Green's criticisms of the time, the Cubs' cupboard wasn't totally bare at the minor-league level. The minor leagues featured outfield prospects Joe Carter, the No. 1 pick in 1981, along with Mel Hall, Billy Hatcher, Darrin Jackson, and Henry Cotto. Scott Fletcher was a plucky middle-infield prospect. Carmelo Martinez had power potential at first base. And Craig Lefferts was an up-and-coming left-handed reliever. All were recommended by Bob Kennedy's scouts and drafted between 1978 and 1981 by Vedie Himsl, whose top January and June picks earlier in the 1970s had usually been busts. However, this little talent surge would not come up fast enough to prevent the Cubs' slide into ignominy in 1980-81. And the system by which these players were produced was antiquated and undercapitalized.

Gordon Goldsberry, the Cubs' Most Valuable Person

To effect a turnaround, Green hired a kind of Phillies Mafia. Longtime Philadelphia operative Lee Elia was tabbed to manage the Cubs. More importantly, Phillies scouting chief Gordon Goldsberry was placed in charge of the scouting and player development system. The hire turned out to be one of the key positive moves of the million-to-one era.

The courtly, dignified Goldsberry, who died as a result of heart trouble while getting ready to go to spring training in 1996 as a Baltimore Orioles scout, worked in sharp contrast to the emotional, outspoken Green. Opposites attracted, and complemented one another in this case.

"I had ultimate faith in Gordy," Green said. "We both had the same philosophies. I'd pop off and be emotional, and Gordy was always able to talk some sense, give advice."

Years later, Goldsberry told of some knock-down, dragged-out arguments with Green that ended with the GM accepting some of Goldsberry's ideas.

"I felt comfortable with Dallas," he said in a 1988 interview with the Cubs' newspaper *Vine Line*. "I knew his philosophies, but that didn't always mean we agreed. Hey, we used used to argue a lot back and forth in Philadelphia, but I always knew where I stood with him. He was very aggressive, but it was a very open situation.

"I knew that he was going to get some things done in Chicago—or at least he was going to try very hard to do it the best way he could. And with new ownership, I think we both felt we had an 80 percent chance of turning things around.

"We knew, however, it would be a long process."

Contrary to popular belief, Green and Goldsberry did not clean out the entire roster of Wrigley-era personnel. Some of the Social-Security age scouts in whom Bob Kennedy had placed a goodly amount of confidence were retired. Roy "Hardrock" Johnson, Billy Jurges, Pete Reiser, and Harrison Wickel were among those who departed. But Goldsberry had known some of the more productive veteran scouts from his own 1967-69 Cubs tenure, which had been his first full-time scouting job, based in the Los Angeles area. Gene Handley, who had originally brought Goldsberry into the Cubs' organization 15 years earlier, was made the western regional scouting supervisor. Buck O'Neil, Bill Capps, Frank DeMoss, Rube Wilson, and Walt Dixon were retained for the long run.

Goldsberry dismissed C.V. Davis, who had been farm director under Kennedy, but retained Himsl as scouting director working under him. John Cox, hired in 1976, had been assistant to Kennedy and was retained in the same role for Green. And on the business side, Salty Saltwell's knowledge of Wrigley Field's daily operations was regarded as invaluable. He was retained as a business-operations executive and consultant, and continued working for the Cubs until 1990.

"Vedie was an outstanding organizer and administrator," Green recalled. "He used those skills to allow Gordy to go out and be an evaluator. Vedie was a strong proponent of central scouting [the Major League Scouting Bureau], but he had to sever that umbilical cord. John Cox was there, and he was a salt of the earth guy."

Green didn't care about ruffling feathers. He found that Ernie Banks was still drawing $25,000 a year for unspecified community relations work. Trying to pin Banks down proved difficult, as many others had discovered. Green reluctantly dismissed "Mr. Cub" from the payroll, knowing the criticism he would draw.

Green and Goldsberry had to change the organization's image, within and without.

"It had to change," Green said. "It wasn't successful. They [the Cubs] were not respected in any phase of their work."

Phil Wrigley's philosophy of loyalty had created a Chicago-style patronage system in which a roster of employees drew checks as an entitlement.

"The Cubs had a bunch of loyal people, but many were former players or coaches who were hired by the Wrigley family," Goldsberry said in *Vine Line*. "And some of these men were in their 60s and 70s. They had a lot of experience, but they weren't the type of people I felt you needed if you were going to come in and emphasize youth.

"Trouble was, a lot of them [scouts and other baseball employees] thought of their jobs as *lifetime* jobs. That was the kind of atmosphere the Wrigley family permitted...It was not a win-at-all-costs type of atmosphere."

Green and Goldsberry knew they would need the equivalent of a five-year plan to get the talent flow going again. But they dared not mention a five-year plan as a slogan; too many baseball executives were hoisted on their petards through the decades opening their mouths like that.

"It would take five drafts to get things going," Green said. "You never see the results of a draft for three to five years. It was going to take us longer.

"We had come from a successful organization. We had the blueprint. Even though we had some stumbling times, we had the game plan of what we exactly we wanted to do. Regardless of what we did at the major-league level, we couldn't hurt ourselves. We could do nothing but improve."

While player development was re-tooled, Green retained many Wrigley front office employees during the transitional year of 1982, inflating the budget. Then, on October 4, 1982, the day after the season's final game, Green axed a slew of the holdovers he deemed unworthy of continued employment. At the same time, he helped supervise the creation of the Cubs' first full-scale marketing program. Under Phil Wrigley, Chuck Shriver, the media relations director, had to double as coordinator of the few special promotional days that were scheduled. Bill Wrigley signed off on staffing one promotions director, first Marea Mannion, then Buck Peden, the latter shifted over from media relations director in 1981. Now Green hired Bing Hampton—who, with his wife Patty Cox Hampton, had run the Phillies' Oklahoma City Triple-A team—to head up the Cubs' first-ever multi-employee marketing department. Within two years, Jeff Odenwald, assisted by eventual present-day marketing chief John McDonough, took over the promotion efforts. The Cubs had moved from ground zero to modern times in marketing the club's considerable natural attributes.

"Largely because of the Wrigley philosophy, it was open the doors and they will come out," Green said. "Bing came up with the 'Building a New Tradition' idea and the idea for the ballgirl [Marla Collins]."

Money from Mother Tribune

To execute his program and continue maintaining the old ballpark, Green needed money, the kind of money that did not exist in the Cubs' own coffers. He said Tribune Co. gave him a multi-million-dollar appropriation to hire the additional staff and step up the re-furbishing of Wrigley Field. Eighteen years later, Tribune Co. had spent $35 million on the old ballpark.

"Sometimes Tribune Co. frowned on what we wanted to do," Green said. "Everything we did cost money. I had to follow guidelines and budgets. But Gordy and I put our budgets up, and they seldom turned us down."

With McKenna acting as a kind of go-between, corporate interference was minimal in the early going. Stanton Cook was Tribune Co. CEO at the time, while former investment banker John Madigan was the No. 2 man in the Tower.

"John and Stan were fans, but they absolutely had no knowledge of [the inner workings of] baseball," Green said. "They let me do the baseball stuff at first."

With one big exception, which did not auger well for the long-term relationship of Tribune Co. to the Cubs. Green had worked out a monster deal, "seven or eight players on each side," with old boss Paul Owens at the 1981 winter meetings in Hawaii. To this day Green won't identify the players involved, but it's probably safe to say two subsequent smaller deals probably included the players under discussion. Sent packing to Philly in the winter of 1981-82 were pitcher Mike Krukow and shortstop Ivan DeJesus. Coming back in return were Ryne Sandberg, Larry Bowa, and Keith Moreland. Bill Buckner might have been in the original deal.

"I came to Chicago under the premise I had total control," Green said. "Andy [McKenna] said we don't want to go ahead with the deal, but I told him I had already shaken hands with Paul Owens. The deal needed the OK of Stan Cook, who was on the Concorde somewhere in Europe. We couldn't get ahold of Stan in time. Gordy and I were pissed. I had to call Paul Owens and tell him the deal was off. It was very embarrassing for both of us. We both went to Molokai and got stinkin'-assed drunk.

"When we got back, we demanded an audience with Stan and McKenna. Gordy was tremendous when he talked. He said we came here with the thought to make Chicago better and we couldn't do it with this kind of interference. They understand, and backpedaled, and agreed from that point on that was fine."

At least for enough years for Green to bring a dramatic winner to Wrigley Field while reviving the farm system. The GM did not lack for funds in trying to import a big-name free-agent like the Dodgers' Steve Garvey in the winter of 1982-83. Garvey elected to stay on the West Coast with the San Diego Padres, to the Cubs' eventual detriment when it seemed the million-to-one era was about to end in '84. Green turned around and gave the money to Garvey's LA infield bookend, third baseman Ron Cey. The Penguin may have been overpaid in both dollars and contractual years (five seasons), but that was the price to be paid for getting prominent veterans to come to Chicago as Green tried to wipe away the negative aura of the Wrigley years.

In the first two years, McKenna served as the conduit between Green and the Tribune suits. But the time-consuming demands of running a modern baseball team were too much for McKenna to continue in the same role. He was not going to give up Schwarz Paper Co. to take over the Cubs for 50 to 60 hours a week.

McKenna and Tribune Co. cast around for a true, full-time team president. A local big name became available in the late summer of 1983. Bears general manager Jim Finks had resigned after nine years on the job, his power diminished in the early Mike Ditka era even while rebuilding the Monster of the Midway with young talent in the early 1980s drafts. Finks had developed an almost universal respect throughout the Chicago sports community for his professional manner. He was hired as Cubs president on September 21, 1983.

Finks, who had briefly played minor-league baseball in 1949 and 1950, operated well in clashing worlds. He got along with the voluable Green and the low-key, bottomline moguls at 435 N. Michigan Avenue. He was equally comfortable in jockspeak and the language of the corporate report. Finks was skilled in dealing with the media and public. He went out for beers with anti-lights activists, lending an open-minded ear to their concerns. I remember my own meeting with Finks in the Wrigley Field pressbox on a 90-degree Sunday in 1984. He appeared crisp and cool in a gray suit despite the heat, and his attitude was the same.

Finks' presence enabled Green to concentrate on what he did best—moving and shaking up the baseball side of his organization—1984 got underway. Green liked working with Finks, contrary to the popular belief at the time.

"The setup with Finks and me was outstanding," Green said. "I loved Finksey. He was great with the entire administrative staff. His football administrative experience helped him. He was super with me because he allowed me total operative freedom."

"Jim was a career sports executive," McKenna said. "I had a feeling Jim and Dallas would get along well. They did, and not just well. Very well. Jim came in as president. I stayed on as chairman and Dallas was executive vice president and general manager. It was a great combination. Jim was happy for Dallas in what he wanted to do."

Others in Tribune Co. liked the way Finks and Green played off one another.

"Dallas just had a problem handling the presidency," Jim Dowdle—then head of Tribune Broadcasting who later became the Cubs' corporate overseer—said of Green's eventual appointment to succeed Finks after the 1984 season. "Dallas needed day-to-day supervision, with someone he would listen to. Had Finks stayed, that would have been a very good mix because Dallas really listened to Finks. Finks didn't really have an ego. Dallas was good until we put him in a position where it hurt him.

"He and I got into it a couple of times on issues. He could just be extremely bull-headed. You had to do the yelling and shouting at him to get some sense in him. I really liked him, we both got along very good. But there were times when he just needed to get screwed down a little bit."

Finks did not support the Tribune Co.'s position on night baseball. He could not continue running a team straight through a white-hot issue with which he did not agree. Behind-the-scenes discussions between ABC-TV and the Cubs on possibly bringing in portable lights for a night game at Wrigley Field took place as early as the spring of 1983, but were tabled because the Cubs weren't scheduled to play on the projected date of the Monday night telecast. The lights controversy really flared up in the 1984 playoffs, when the Cubs had to give up a home game in the National League Championship Series because Wrigley Field did not yet possess lights for scheduled weekend-night games.

"Jim was not in favor of lights like I was," Green said. "But Jim had worked very, very hard to gain concessions from Major League Baseball for Wrigley Field. Tribune Co. sided with baseball."

Finks was pushed out following the '84 season, eagerly returning to his first love, football, in taking over the New Orleans Saints with an ownership stake. Preparing to receive the NL Executive of the Year Award, Green was given the additional title of president. Dowdle's analysis was correct. Green's personality was now directly exposed to the far-more-reserved businessmen in Tribune Tower. But the combination might have worked if the Cubs had somehow bottled their 1984 magic over the next few years.

The Deals That Made a Division Champion

After appointing former Royals manager Jim Frey to the Cubs job in late 1983, Green pulled off the most dramatic series of deals in modern Cubs history, trades that shaped the '84 NL East titlists. He snared Bobby Dernier and Gary Matthews—two-thirds of a starting outfield—from the Phillies for two players he was not going to use, reliever Bill Campbell and infielder-catcher Mike Diaz. Two months later, on May 25, he dealt a benched, unhappy Bill Buckner to the Red Sox for righthander Dennis Eckersley, who nicely plugged up one starting rotation hole. The last link in the success story was completed on June 13, 1984, when Green took his biggest gamble. He sent top outfield prospect Joe Carter and right fielder Mel Hall—who had finished third in the NL Rookie of the Year Award voting in '83, but had started to wear out his welcome in Chicago—to the Cleveland Indians for righthander Rick Sutcliffe.

Surrendering Carter, the prized No. 1 draft pick in 1981, was a big gamble. A true baseball gentleman, the outfielder had a fantastic 1983 at Triple-A Iowa with 22 homers, a .307 average, and 40 stolen bases. He was headed straight for the baseball stardom that he would enjoy for the next 15 years at various outposts in the majors.

Gordon Goldsberry, appreciative of baseball "tools" in young players, resisted giving up Carter. Jim Snyder, then the Cubs' minor-league field coordinator, remembered a big meeting at the Cubs' spring-training offices in Mesa, Arizona, with Carter the focal point of discussion. "Most of the minor-league staff opposed the Sutcliffe deal," Snyder said.

Green prevailed. He was lambasted for a decade afterward for giving up Carter for a pitcher. But the critics had ignored Cubs history. Green's predecessors, all loyal servants of Phil and Bill Wrigley, had either traded for the wrong pitchers or allowed other talented hurlers to pass through their hands. The '84 Cubs would not have finished first and had a chance to end the million-to-one era without an ace-quality pitcher. As June began, the Cubs' rotation was shaky. The team ERA was 4.02 after the first 84 games; the Cubs had become competitive on robust hitting alone. With Sutcliffe enjoying the hottest spell of his career on his way to a 16-1, Cy Young Award-winning record and Eckersley finishing the second half 8-3 with the Cubs, the team ERA was cut to 3.75 at season's end—no small feat. Sutcliffe also would later serve as the veteran steadying influence for the Cubs' other NL East title in 1989.

The strong starting pitching, rounded out by Steve Trout in his best season and Scott Sanderson (when healthy) was backed by a lineup that should serve as a model for any Wrigley Field-based team. The '84 Cubs could either bludgeon opponents with power or manufacture runs in a low-scoring game. Both talents are required in Wrigley Field, where the climate and prevailing winds can change by the hour. Bob Dernier and Ryne Sandberg, the "Daily Double" at the top of the lineup, combined for 77 steals. Gary Matthews then served as almost a second leadoff man, batting third with an NL-leading 103 walks. Sandberg, Matthews, first baseman Leon Durham, Jody Davis, Ron Cey, and Keith Moreland each drove in 80 or more runs.

That lineup suited Frey to a tee.

"We had two guys upfront who could run, and they both had big years with the bat," said the ex-manager, now retired and living in Naples, Florida. "Then you had five guys behind them who could hit the shit out of the ball. It was a great spirit of those guys, who wanted to play hard. I've argued with people [philosophically] about the game. First, you get starting pitching. Then you get three of four guys who can knock the shit out of the ball. Then get speed in a lineup. And a top reliever.

"It's the most comfortable thing to say pitching and defense wins. But you can say this: Name the teams that have won championships that didn't have good offense."

Frey's philosophies would come back to haunt the Cubs years later when he served as GM. But in 1984, everything clicked, particularly when he gave the green light to run to Dernier and Sandberg. The two proved that a running game does not take away from the power to follow in Wrigley Field. From Day One of his managerial tenure, Don Baylor had vowed to revive the oft-neglected concept of speed in the Cubs' lineup.

"I stole over 70 bases three years in a row in the minors," Dernier said. "The Cubs always were designed with the three-run homer looming. They had to budget their running and be cautious. But if you have the threat of speed, the pitcher has to pay attention to us when he should be paying attention to hitters. If I was building a lineup, I'd have two speed guys at the top, and another guy in the eight-hole."

The NL-leading 762 runs tallied by the '84 Cubs, 42 more than runner-up Philadelphia, prove the balanced speed-and-power theory. Combined with good-enough pitching, the end result was 96 victories, the apogee of the million-to-one era. And it would have been enough to get the Cubs through the minefield of the five-game National League Championship Series against the Padres except for some little issues: waking up the sleeping dogs, possible overconfidence, and, a point still debated now, Frey's starting pitching choices.

The Cubs made it appear like the long-delayed World Series appearance was at hand with 13-0 and 4-2 victories in the first two games of the National Championship Series on October 2 and 3, 1984 at Wrigley Field. All the Cubs needed was one victory in the three possible remaining games at Jack Murphy Stadium in San Diego.

However, the normally placid Padres fans were riled up like never before. Emboldened by the Cubs' regular-season success and with his sense of satire always at the ready, *Chicago Tribune* columnist Mike Royko made fun of California baseball fans, calling them the usual California stereotypes of surfers and quiche eaters. Royko had never been fond of Californians. He had few good things to say about the city of San Francisco and its residents when I talked to him as he sat in the auxiliary media section of Wrigley Field's right-field upper deck during the NLCS against the Giants in 1989.

When the Cubs took the field in San Diego on the night of October 4, 1984, they were greeted by an uncommonly loud decibel level from the fans, angered by the Royko column. Suddenly, the Padres had a 10th man to help out. Earlier, a much-larger-than-expected crowd turned out to greet the Padres plane at the airport upon its return from Chicago.

On the Cubs' flight to the West Coast, several players recalled some overconfident talk about walking right in to a sure thing at Jack Murphy Stadium. No player in his right mind today would believe a two-game-to-none lead with one game to go is a lock. History is chock full of abrupt comebacks, the latest being the Red Sox's rally from an 0-2 deficit in the five-game AL divisional series against the Indians in 1999.

Then there was the matter of Frey's rotation. After Dennis Eckersley had made the Game 3 start and got bombed, Frey could have come back with Rick Sutcliffe, who had pitched seven innings in the opener, and Steve Trout—both on three days' rest—in Games 4 and 5, respectively.

Frey held off Sutcliffe to Game 5, perhaps believing that the Cubs would clinch before that point. Then Sutcliffe and Trout would be available for the first two games of the World Series against a powerful Detroit Tigers club that was overwhelming the Kansas City Royals in the ALCS. In a worse-case scenario with the Padres series going the distance, Trout would open up the Series with Sutcliffe still available for two starts.

Scott Sanderson drew the Game 4 assignment against San Diego. While the righthander had pitched well overall with an 8-5 record and 3.14 ERA, he had been in and out of the rotation due to injuries, making just 24 starts, in 1984. A pitcher whose endurance had been in question often is skipped over in post-season, especially if an off-day as the Cubs enjoyed on October 5, 1984 had been scheduled.

Cubs players wondered then, and to this day, why Frey did not go for the jugular and schedule Sutcliffe and Trout to pitch the final two games in San Diego. They speak in a near-consensus.

"You bring back your best to pitch," said Bob Dernier.

Frey has second-guessed himself over the years, but has not lost sleep over his decision.

"Have I ever thought about it? Yes," he said. "But if you pitch Sutcliffe in the fourth game, are they 100 percent sure we're going to win?"

Those percentages dropped dramatically when a less-than-sharp Sanderson was pulled in the fifth. Meanwhile, Steve Garvey began amassing a night to remember at the plate while the Cubs squandered several great opportunities to score.

"We should have won Game 4 anyway," Dernier said. "I'm standing on third base, the bases are drunk and [Craig] Lefferts punches out (Ron) Cey on a bad pitch."

That gave Garvey an opening to get the Padres back into the Series and grab the momentum with his two-run homer off Lee Smith in the bottom of the ninth to win the game, 7-5, capping a five-RBI night. And the second-guessing only intensified when the Cubs, behind Sutcliffe, coughed up a 3-0 lead going into the bottom of the sixth, so agonizingly close to the World Series. Tim Flannery's grounder through first baseman Leon Durham's legs in the bottom of the seventh is one of the most infamous plays in Cubs history, but the series had been slipping away at that point anyway.

Despite the crushing near-miss, the Cubs had wiped away much of the negative hubris of the million-to-one era as a result of the 1984 season. The team had finally made Vince Lloyd's 1969 projection come true, shooting over the two million attendance mark for the first time. Ticket sales during the winter of 1984-85 were like a gold mine; the season-ticket count jumped from 6,000 to nearly 25,000, ensuring a string of two million-plus season gates well into the future. Flush with revenue and positive momentum, Dallas Green re-signed all his potential free-agent pitchers with the exception of reliever Tim Stoddard. Sutcliffe and his rotation mates wanted to perpetuate the winner, and there was no more worry about debilitating day games or the tight dimensions of Wrigley Field in their decisions.

Lame Players Lead to a Lame Franchise

Green, Frey, and the Cubs felt good about their club going into 1985. And why not? They had the best pitching in the second half of '84 returning virtually intact. And despite the age of Cey and Gary Matthews, the balance of the lineup was comprised of young veterans supposedly entering their primes, along with rookie shortstop Shawon Dunston.

The lineup was underproductive at the start, but the pitchers more than held up their end in the first two months. The Cubs again led the NL East, peaking with a 34-19 record. But Sutcliffe had torn a left-hamstring muscle running out a grounder on May 19, 1985 in Atlanta. He came back, in retrospect, too soon, in two and a half weeks, pitching well over a five-start period, including a two-hit shutout over the Pirates. But in the process, Sutcliffe subtly changed his mechanics to compensate for his sore leg, hurting his shoulder. He went on the disabled list two more times, including a season-ending stint beginning July 29. Big Red was followed in short order by the rest of the rotation with assorted maladies. At one point in August 1985, the entire starting five—Sutcliffe, Trout, Eckersley, Sanderson, and Dick Ruthven—was on the disabled list. No one around Wrigley Field ever could remember when an entire rotation was shelved at the same time.

Green's minor-league system could not come up with quality replacements to replace even part of the fallen rotation. Frey was forced to start the likes of Steve Engel, Derek Botelho, Reggie Patterson, and Ray Fontenot in an attempt to fill in for the injured pitchers, with disastrous results. An out-of-control 13-game losing streak had begun to spin the Cubs out of contention in June. Injuries to Dernier and Matthews, and a gastrointestinal infection suffered by Jody Davis depleted the lineup at the same time the pitchers were falling one by one. Only Ryne Sandberg and Keith Moreland performed at or above par. The '85 Cubs were cooked, and quickly fell out of the race. Up in Tribune Tower, there was a collective furrowed brow over the sight of millions of dollars of payroll being shelled out to players in the whirlpool or on the trainer's table.

"If those pitchers had stayed healthy, the Cubs would have been a contender the rest of the decade," Frey said. "We ended up winning 77 games losing five starting pitchers. [Jim] Riggleman would have died to win 77 [in 1999]. Tell him to try to win 77 losing five starting pitchers."

The injuries snuffed out the afterglow of 1984. Like John Holland 25 years before him, Green erred by not opting to gradually re-tool. He was stuck with the fourth year of Cey's five-year contract, while he re-signed Gary Matthews. Cey was 38 in 1986 while Matthews was 36. Their production continued to decline. The pitchers did not re-gain their 1984 form. Sutcliffe ended up 5-14 with another five-week stay on the disabled list. Eckersley was 6-11 while Trout was 5-7.

Worse yet, Frey lost the team emotionally in 1986. He began platooning the aging Cey and Matthews. Rumors began surfacing that the team quit on their manager. When the Cubs started out 23-33, Green fired Frey on June 12, 1986.

Frey had taken writers into his confidence and privately wondered whether several veterans were undermining his early '86 season work. In turn, these players questioned Frey's choice of lineups. Years later, Matthews looked back at his application for the Cubs radio color announcer's job in 1988. He questioned whether Frey, by then the team's general manager, had somehow held him responsible for rallying the team against him in '86. And, as a result, Matthews reasoned, ex-White Sox coach Davey Nelson—who had no past connections to the Cubs—was hired for the radio gig instead.

"After the '84 season, I had said a lot of good things about Sarge," Frey recalled. "I told him personally how I felt he had been instrumental with his spirit and team leadership. If there was a leader on the '84 team, it was Matthews.

"But when the heat was turned on [in '86], I felt he didn't exert it [leadership]. Guys that I had respected and I had a certain regard for, when the heat was on, they became scarce. I had a great amount of respect for Keith Moreland and Jody Davis."

Green had no backup plan to replace Frey. When he cashiered the manager, he also fired third-base coach Don Zimmer because of his close association with Frey. He tabbed coach John Vukovich as his interim manager for the Friday, June 13, doubleheader against the Cardinals at Wrigley Field. In retrospect, Green probably wishes he had made Vukovich, one of the slew of Philadelphia imports four and a half years previously, the permanent manager.

Instead, Green impulsively chose Gene Michael, who was part of George Steinbrenner's large paid entourage of former managers/managers-in-waiting.

"The key mistake I made was bringing in Gene Michael," he said. "He was not a National League guy. He really didn't want to manage, and didn't put his heart and soul into it. I didn't talk to my people about him. That was the beginning of the problems."

The Cubs continued to flounder under Michael, finishing 70-90 in 1986. Stan Cook and John Madigan grew restless at the Tower over the well-paid team continuing to lose. Baseball was entering its management "collusion" period, in which owners tried to hold down salaries by informally agreeing not to sign free agents.

Montreal Expos émigré Andre Dawson ran smack dab into the wall of collusion when he attempted to sign with the Cubs as a free agent in the spring of 1987. Dawson had talked of his desire to come to the Cubs as early as September 1985, and was continually urged by right-field bleacher fans to sign with Chicago. The Hawk's love affair with the Cubs offered absolute proof that Green had forever changed the image of the franchise; prime players now gravitated toward Chicago. Fighting collusion, at first fruitlessly standing outside the gate at the Cubs' Mesa, Arizona, spring training complex, Dawson had to agree to a blank contract for 1987. Green wrote in a $500,000 base salary, surely one of the greatest bargains in Cubs history after Dawson slugged 49 homers, drove in 137 runs, and won the '87 NL Most Valuable Player Award. In 1999, Dawson was named as one of two right fielders on the Cubs' All-Century Team.

Collusion in the mid-1980s suited the Tribune Co. bottomline types very well. They were becoming hardened veterans of labor wars. At the same time, they had endured a years-long strike by their longtime union Tribune newspaper production workers in an attempt to cut labor costs. Stan Cook had known many of the strikers in his years as Tribune production director. Oddly enough, courts eventually awarded damages against baseball due to the collusion while awarding back compensation to the printers who had picketed outside Tribune Tower year after seemingly hopeless year.

Dandelions No More

Court rulings didn't discomfort the Tower executives as much as the state of the Cubs. But Green had pegged his bosses correctly as not knowing all the nuances of baseball. If Cook and Madigan had truly done their homework, they would have realized Green's management style had paid off in a way that was nearly invisible in a major media market like Chicago.

The increasingly negative vibes around both Wrigley Field and Tribune Tower in mid-1986 obscured one of the most positive developments of the million-to-one era—the revived player development system supervised by Gordon Goldsberry. As Green had projected, five drafts starting in 1982 were required to get a consistent talent flow going. Shawon Dunston had been the first No. 1 pick of the Green/Goldsberry regime in 1982. Through all the Cubs' poor finishes in the first 17 years of the draft, they had never had the first overall pick. They took Brooklyn high school star Dunston over Dwight Gooden, whose overall career turned out better than Dunston's. However, scouts' opinions were split on Gooden's upside potential in 1982, and the Cubs opted for the everyday player with raw baseball tools centered around speed to fit Goldsberry's mold of a good prospect.

Dunston was the first of Goldsberry's draft picks to make it to the Cubs, on Opening Day 1985. He stumbled after a few weeks, was demoted to the minors, then recalled for the season's final two months, holding forth as a creditable shortstop on the North Side for the next decade.

Goldsberry's first good drafting year was 1984. A competitive high school pitcher out of Las Vegas named Greg Maddux was his No. 2 pick.

Crafty lefty Jamie Moyer was the No. 6 pick. Switch-hitting catcher Damon Berryhill and hard-hitting outfielder Dwight Smith were top picks in the January draft.

In 1985, Goldsberry landed top Mississippi state hitter Rafael Palmeiro as his first pick. The following year, first baseman Mark Grace and catcher Joe Girardi were picked in June, while center fielder Jerome Walton was drafted in January. The flatlining performance of the parent team led to the major-league debuts of Maddux, Moyer, Palmeiro, and Martinez during the 1986 season.

"The minor leagues were *stocked* with guys ready to play and ready to go," said Grace. "The worst players in the Cubs' organization in the mid-1980s were in the big leagues. Of course you have Andre [Dawson], Ryno [Sandberg], and Rick Sutcliffe. But you have all these guys ready to come up.

The wave of talent didn't just happen by accident. Goldsberry's leadership of both his scouting and player-development staff set the tone. The Cubs did not have a man of his stature prior to his arrival—or ever since his departure.

Early on Goldsberry had changed the modus operandi of the Cubs' scouting staff.

"Work habits, that's where we started to draw the line," he said in 1988. "We wanted to work *harder* than other organizations. Be more aggressive. And become more factual and accurate in our evaluation of players.

"In the [Wrigley] regime, scouts only sent in reports. The decision about how much a prospect would be paid or where he should be drafted, these decisions were made from within the front office in Chicago. I wanted to change that. I wanted my scouts to tell me what *they* thought a prospect was worth. This was a difference in attitude and sometimes that's kind of hard to accept. I just wanted our people to be true scouts, not just reporters."

Goldsberry operated almost autonomously from Green.

"I knew what Dallas wanted, and he let me pretty much alone to do my own thing," he said. "He told me had had plenty to do in Chicago, what with the big league club and running the front office. He left the minors to me. Dallas would tell me, 'You know what my thinking is. You do it.'"

Taking advantage of the greatly expanded player development budget, Goldsberry hired pitching coaches for each Cubs' minor-league team for the first time in history. He also installed Jim Snyder as the organization's first-ever coordinator of minor-league instruction. With enough staffers to run a modern player development system, Goldsberry could go out in the field regularly to see amateur prospects and visit the minor-league clubs.

Friendly and tending more toward the soft-spoken side of the decibel level, Goldsberry could do the good cop/tough cop routine, but preferred the former. He effected change through positive reinforcement. He believed that a conciliator, running both the scouting and player development ends, was necessary. Too often scouts and minor-league managers and instructors in the same organization act like they were opponents, sniping at each other for the shortcomings of young players. A firm hand that nevertheless worked with a velvet touch was needed to unite such often squabbling factions. That same hand worked to encourage, not offer damnation.

"He empowered the people who worked for him," said ex-Cubs pitcher Jim Colborn, who worked as Goldsberry's minor-league pitching coordinator 15 years after Goldsberry, as a scout, signed him for virtually a song. "He allowed them to have authority and responsibility on their own. It's almost like having stock options. When you have a say in an organization, you have a greater commitment to an organization."

"Gordy was very detailed in his approach to scouting," said Jim Snyder, Goldsberry's minor-league coordinator of instruction from 1983 to 1986. "He was a great listener, not someone who was talking all the time. He had a great rapport with scouts and development people. One thing that he and I got across to our instructors was that we cared about them, and we cared about the players.

"What makes it work was the guy at the top allows the guys at the bottom to do the job, and you have good people at the bottom. Gordy used to have seminars on the West Coast, Midwest, and East Coast."

Goldsberry got to personally know as many of his minor leaguers as possible. He encouraged them. In a game of pretenses and phoniness, he was as genuine as they came.

Often a new minor-league director will take over an organization and verbally downgrade the talent he inherits. Goldsberry went against the baseball grain. He saw the talent in Joe Carter and fought against his trade to the Indians for Rick Sutcliffe. He also gave Wrigley-era holdover players that had less of an upside than Carter a fresh start.

"I was told, 'Don't worry about it. You're one of our players now,'" said former minor-league pitcher Stan Kyles, a 1979 Cubs draftee out of Chicago's inner-city Wendell Phillips High School. Kyles had struggled mightily in his first three seasons in the farm system.

"That gave me confidence," Kyles said. "I went out and had my best-ever year in 1982 [11-5 with a 2.51 ERA at Class A Salinas, California]." Kyles never did make it to the majors, but he carved out a nice career as a minor-league pitching coach, the latest with the 1999 Lansing Lugnuts, the Cubs' prospect-laden Class A Midwest League club.

If Goldsberry's system had a "tough cop" character, it was Snyder, yet another of the Philly imports. He worked almost like a Marine Corps drill instructor, verbally pushing his young charges to work hard and master the game's fundamentals. Almost to a man, the products of the Goldsberry farm system said they became better players from the experience of being put through the paces by Snyder, who held the same job with the White Sox farm system in 1999.

"To be successful, you had to have discipline in the organization," said Snyder. "You have to have structure. Young people will work better with structure. I also implemented a drug program Dallas and Gordy OK'd. We let them know we cared about them. There were consequences for everything, and I was the enforcer."

The minor leaguers were worked, and worked again, on baseball's basics. The results showed up in the major leagues in a few years.

"The work ethic started with early work in the mornings," said Snyder. "Hitting, infield, baserunning. That stuff doesn't get better just by the players showing up. Gordy and I talked about it, that it was rigorous, but if they get used to it, they'll come to the bar for you. If they benefit from the work, they'll be championship-type guys, while the others will be second-division type guys.

"I demanded they work. I said we wouldn't put up with guys not doing it. I pushed and shoved all the time in a way to be successful. I tried to give them the best information I could. The managers made fun of [that style], they'd say, 'Here comes the man with the yellow pad.'"

Jamie Moyer recalled the Snyder approach working first with coaches and managers. "The coaches instilled it [discipline] in themselves, then they instilled it in us," he said. "They didn't put up with a whole lot. What I see now in the game, there's not a lot of discipline. I think it made a lot of difference in my career.

"The coaching staff worked very, very hard. They expected the same thing out of you. If not, you were on the outside looking in. Jim Snyder demanded respect. But to get respect, you have to give respect. The prime example was Dwight Smith. He came into mini-spring training [in 1984] with the new draftees. He was very green as far as talent. He had a lot of tools—he could throw the ball the length of the field, he could run like crazy, but he struggled at the plate. They worked with him on hitting, and worked and worked and worked. He developed into a pretty decent hitter."

The peak performance of the farm system took place in 1987. While the parent club hovered around the .500 mark most of the summer, the Cubs fielded one of the game's best minor-league teams in 1987. The Class AA Pittsfield [MA] Cubs of the Eastern League finished 87-51 as Grace won the league's MVP award with 101 RBI and a .333 average. Dwight Smith batted .337 with 60 stolen bases. Further up, at Class AAA Iowa, catcher Damon Berryhill and outfielder Darrin Jackson (who had done most of his development under Goldsberry after being drafted as a 17-year-old by Vedie Himsl in 1981) knocked on the door of the majors with good power seasons.

Within two years, the Cubs could field an all-homegrown battery of Greg Maddux and Joe Girardi, with other farm system products like Smith in left, Jerome Walton in center, Grace at first, and Shawon Dunston at shortstop. Along with veterans Andre Dawson and Ryne Sandberg, they formed the nucleus of the 1989 NL East champions. The kids took the kudos in '89, but the man who brought them there was largely overlooked in all the media hype.

"Very few people gave Gordon Goldsberry the credit he deserves," said Ned Colletti, then the Cubs' media relations director, now San Francisco Giants assistant general manager. "When he was in charge of the draft, it was a pretty strong list. You'll get perhaps a Hall of Famer or two out of all those players. He produced a lot of players who played in the big leagues. Gordy had a great run in Chicago. It was kind of lost in the shuffle."

Looking back on the 80s Cubs player development system, longtime scouting guru Paul Snyder, who built up the Atlanta Braves vaunted scouting and farm system at about the same time, said the Cubs could have been ranked near the top in productivity in grooming their own players during that era.

But in the hit-and-miss world of scouting, no one bats 1.000. Not remotely close. Some of Goldsberry's drafting and development strategies missed the mark. In reality, only two of his No. 1 picks—Rafael Palmeiro and Shawon Dunston—became longtime major-league producers. His edict to have his scouts work harder and smarter paid off with success with lower-round picks like Grace. Looking back, Goldsberry felt no blow to his ego to be self-critical. A few years before his death, Goldsberry lamented that he and his scouts had not produced enough quality and quantity in pitching.

Maddux' record, of course, speaks for itself. Jamie Moyer had some good moments on the mound as a Cub, but did not blossom as a pitcher until the mid-1990s with the Mariners, after wandering through several organizations and the minor leagues. Les Lancaster, an undrafted player who had signed in 1985, spun off an astounding 30 2/3 innings of shutout relief for the 1989 NL East titlists, but overall was just a journeyman pitcher.

Goldsberry could have developed a second ace after Maddux in Mike Harkey. A big hard-throwing righthander, the Cal State-Fullerton product was the Cubs' No. 1 pick in 1987. Harkey even was under consideration for a while as the draft's No. 1 pick by the Seattle Mariners, even ahead of schoolboy star Ken Griffey, Jr. The White Sox, who picked Jack McDowell No. 1 in '87, would have taken Harkey instead had he been available.

"I wrote that he has the best chance to get to the majors faster than any other player I had ever scouted," said Gene Handley, who signed Harkey for the Cubs. Harkey blew through Double-A and Triple-A with a combined 16-4 record in 1988 before making his Cubs debut in September. But subsequent injuries and surgeries sandwiched around Harkey's 12-6 record in 1990 thwarted a potentially great career. Harkey had suffered the cumulative bad effects of a career-long mechanical problem the Cubs tried to correct — throwing across his body.

Striking Out on Roger Clemens

Goldsberry missed big-time on one of modern-day baseball's greatest pitchers. His spring, 1983 scouting reports had good news about high school pitcher Jackie Davidson of Everman, Texas. However, in a 15-day stretch prior to the draft, Davidson made seven starts in an attempt to pitch Everman into the Texas state high school tournament. He strained tendons in his right elbow due to the overwork.

Meanwhile, a tough competitor named Roger Clemens also was coming out for the draft from the University of Texas.

191

Dallas-based Cubs scout Bill Capps experienced a sense of déjà vu. He had lobbied unsuccessfully 18 years previously for the Cubs to draft Johnny Bench. Now he struck out in trying to bend Goldsberry's ear toward Clemens.

"I had Clemens rated ahead of Jackie Davidson," Capps said. "There were seven No. 1 picks out of my area, and Davidson was at the bottom of all of these. I tried to talk him [Goldsberry] out of that deal, because Davidson already had hurt his arm before he was drafted."

Red Sox scout Danny Doyle wasn't fooled. He liked Clemens all along. The BoSox waited for 10 other pitchers to be selected, including Davidson, in the first round prior to Clemens, then pounced on the Rocket-in-construction.

Davidson had a sore elbow from the first day he played pro baseball. "He came into Pikeville [Appalachian rookie league], threw on the side and you could see the ball wasn't popping very well," said Jim Synder "Erskine Thomason [minor-league pitching coordinator] said he couldn't air it out. I called Gordy to send him home and let him rest. Gordy was sold on him; the [scouting] supervisors liked Davidson."

Davidson recovered from his sore elbow, but peaked out with an 8-3 record in the first two months of the 1986 season at Class AA Pittsfield. He never even sniffed the majors. The same year, Clemens won his first Cy Young Award, striking out 20 in one game, for Boston. The Cubs did obtain two Texas Longhorn teammate of Clemens, though. Righthander Mike Capel was picked in the 13th round in 1983, but he only surfaced for a 22-game relief stint in 1988. Fellow righty Calvin Schiraldi, originally rated by many higher than Clemens, came over from the Red Sox in the Lee Smith trade late in 1987, doing virtually nothing over the better part of two seasons.

Goldsberry also drafted pitchers No. 1 in 1984 and 1985—lefthander Drew Hall and 6-foot-9 righthander David Masters, respectively. Hall pitched for the Cubs only sporadically before being shipped off to the Rangers in the Mitch Williams trade in 1988. Masters had good won-lost records in the high minors in 1987 and 1988, but never pitched in the majors.

"Drew Hall had a little hook, a problem with his delivery," said Snyder. "That caused him control problems, although he threw 93 MPH and had a great body. Masters for some reason didn't develop the way you wanted him to."

"When you're hurt, you can't compete and can't gain experience,"

Moyer said. "People start passing you by. Before you know it, you become a journeyman-type pitcher."

Still other pitchers for whom Goldsberry had hopes, such as Len Damian, Jeff Hirsch, Carl Hamilton, and Bill Danek, also faded before they got close to Wrigley Field.

In 1986, Dallas Green noticed that his minor leaguers did not include any real power prospects. Rafael Palmeiro was a line-drive, gap-type doubles hitter at the time. Goldsberry tried to rectify the situation by drafting high schooler Derrick May No. 1 in '86. May did reach the majors as a regular in 1992, but never slugged more than 10 homers in a season as a Cub before settling in as a backup player elsewhere. The perceived lack of power would help lead to the firing of Goldsberry and years of instability and lack of production in player development.

That was in the future. Even while the minor leagues blossomed, disquieting signs had been appearing in the front office for several years. The long arm of Tribune Co. was slowly wrapping itself around the independent-minded Green and his minions.

When Green was appointed team president, Tribune Co. treasurer Don Grenesko was shifted over to Wrigley Field as executive vice president of business operations. Grenesko's background was business and numbers, not baseball. A certified public accountant, Grenesko had an undergrad degree in chemistry and an MBA from Northwestern University.

"I think Donny was a fine businessman," Green said. "He knew absolutely nothing about baseball. He was born and raised in Tribune Co."

Richard Babcock related the inevitable conflict between numbers-crunching execs and old-fashioned baseball people in a 1996 *Chicago Magazine* article on the Cubs. He quoted an unnamed former Cubs official, recalling a weekly staff meeting held during the Cubs' 13-game losing streak in June 1985: "We go around the meeting, everyone giving his report. And when we get to Grenesko, he says, 'This is one of the great weeks in Cubs history. We sold out every day.' And Dallas kicked me under the table, as if to say, 'Look what we're up against.' The whole thing was, we made money."

At around the same time, John Madigan, then Tribune Co. executive vice president and a Cubs' board member, began representing the team at baseball ownership meetings.

Green still plowed ahead despite the corporate encroachment on his bailiwick. "Hell, they had made me president," he said. "I still had enough faith in my abilities to not worry about who was working with me."

By the end of 1986, Tribune Co. honchos ordered Green to cut the $15 million payroll—which at the time ranked No. 3 in the majors—after the two seasons of well-paid stumbling on the field and crowded training rooms. Green complied, dumping Ron Cey and Dennis Eckersley in two separate deals to the Oakland Athletics (where a timely conversion for Eckersley to late-inning relief awaited) for three minor leaguers and a utility infielder before the 1987 season began. Gary Matthews, reduced to pinch-hitting status, finally departed for the Mariners on July 11, 1987. Two days later, fresh from pitching two straight complete-game shutouts, Steve Trout was traded to the Yankees for a lame-armed Bob Tewksbury and two minor-league pitchers.

"Trout had a huge deferred contract," Green said. "George [Steinbrenner] took it all. He [Trout] was an accident waiting to happen. Stick [manager Gene Michael] was pissed."

Another move by the business side of Tribune Co. raised Green's eyebrows. Less than six months after he was fired by Green as manager, Jim Frey returned as full-time Cubs radio color announcer, replacing a retiring Vince Lloyd and taking an aging Lou Boudreau's place on the road. The move was curious. Frey had no previous broadcasting experience. He had not expressed a burning desire to break into the field.

"Bringing Jimmy Frey back was the start," Green said. "They asked me if I minded Jimmy coming back to do radio. That probably was their preparation to replace me. There was really no one who could take my place from within. When I did get fired and he immediately was named GM, two and two gets to be four.

"But I never worried about getting fired. I work my ass off and do what's necessary."

The skids were greased for Green as September 1987 began. Despite terrible overall pitching and a lack of clutch hitting, the '87 Cubs were 67-64 on September 1 that season. But a disgruntled Gene Michael soon resigned as manager, opting to jump before he was pushed. Green aide Frank Lucchesi became interim manager for the rest of the season. The Cubs simply cashed in the season, finishing 9-21 in another astounding last-month collapse to end up in the NL East cellar.

Angered at the team's drooping on-field demeanor, Green first thought of going back on the field as manager. He thought of turning over the general manager's roles to Gordon Goldsberry and John Cox. Green claimed his Tribune Co. masters liked the idea of the 6-foot-5 gunslinger going into the dugout. But, at the same time, he recalled the Tower suits wanted to bring in their own man to run the front office.

Green and the honchos went back and forth on the new management structure. Green even suggested he would train his replacement. "We had three or four head-to-heads [meetings] with Stan Cook and John Madigan."

Finally Green decided he would name third-base coach John Vukovich manager. A press conference was set up for the afternoon of October 29, 1987 at Wrigley Field. Vukovich flew back to Chicago from the Philadelphia area to supposedly go through a final interview with Green and Madigan, then be introduced at a late-afternoon press conference.

The press conference would have an entirely different subject matter. After the meeting with Vukovich, Green and Madigan conferred. The end result was the two men could no longer work together. The *Chicago Sun-Times* reported that Madigan vetoed the choice of Vukovich, an act Madigan denied. The *Chicago Tribune* wrote of the behind-the-scenes meetings about management changes that would include corporate review of all contracts Green negotiated and limiting him to baseball personnel moves.

"He said there's a philosophical difference," Green said of Madigan. "He threw this piece of paper at me that said I resigned."

Green was floored, but took the bullet as he announced his departure to a stunned media. He was never given an explanation for the axing. He still does not know why his Cubs tenure was terminated.

Madigan will not shed any light on that event. He declined an interview request for this book when approached by the Wrigley Field batting cage before one late-season game in 1999. On the day Green departed, Madigan, who praised Green overall, including his payroll-cutting acts of the previous year, said, "It was mainly about how the organization would be shaped in the future. I wanted to go one way and Dallas the other way and we couldn't resolve it...I know Dallas and when he makes up his mind, he makes up his mind and that's it."

"The puzzling thing was that I assumed John Madigan was a friend," Green said. "I thought we had a good relationship. We were together [at an owners' meeting] in Toronto, walked around during breaks and talked about our families. There was never one hint that Dallas Green was in trouble. I never had an inkling of what their desires were. I didn't perceive any problems.

"I wrote him a letter after I had time to digest what happened. I told him I always considered you a friend. If I had any inkling something would happen to him or his family, I would have quickly knocked on your door. He didn't have enough guts to write me back. I've got more respect for guys who call me an asshole than someone like that."

Green won't criticize Tribune Co. as a whole. "In fairness, I can't knock Tribune Co. for what they did for my family," he said.

Now the corporate takeover of the Cubs had been intensified. Like Phil Wrigley decades before them, Madigan and Cook seemingly did not have the ability to network themselves to hire a quality baseball executive. Or they may have eyed Frey all along. Frey was soon named GM. He had no significant front-office experience. All his post-playing career had been spent on the field as a manager or coach, save for three years in the late 1960s as a Baltimore Orioles scout.

The Tower suits did not realize how much damage they were beginning to inflict on the Cubs. Despite the problems at the big-league level, the Cubs' organization, from a financial and player development standpoint, was in the best condition in decades. A paragon of management stability as a corporation, where change moved at a glacial pace, Tribune Co. went against its own style, inadvertently de-stabilizing the Cubs baseball operation at a critical point in its history.

"Everyone was in their right position with the front-office team," said Ned Colletti. "Had everyone been patient with the [pitching] injuries, let it run its course, that team from '84 to '90 could have been a strong team. You would have had young players like Palmeiro, Grace, and Maddux to go along with Sutcliffe, Eckersley, Dawson, and Sandberg. There was a tremendous surplus of talented people."

"Unfortunately, before all of us got up here to make our mark on the big leagues, they fired Dallas," said Mark Grace. "They got rid of the people who made the young players what they are today. That was the big mistake, that we didn't get a chance to make a youth movement with a bunch of kids who were ready to play. With Dallas still running the team, they would have added free agents around us.

"Had that happened, this team would have been a winner for the last decade, no question about it. I think they know that [made a mistake]. Dallas and the people working for him had this organization going in a championship direction. The people that were running the show knew a lot about baseball and cared a lot about winning. That was the main thing they taught us in the minor leagues—winning. If you win, everything will be taken care of."

Green licked his wounds, retreated to his farm in West Grove, Pennsylvania, and later re-surfaced as manager of the Yankees and Mets. He could only shake his head from a distance as two different front-office regimes, under different corporate overseers, helped undo the best organization the Cubs had built up in the million-to-one era. The corporate savior of the Cubs of 1981 would become something entirely different by 1991. By then, men with training in investment banking, newspaper production, and accounting were making major baseball decisions.

"I can tell you in no uncertain terms that they have very little feel for the game of baseball," Green said of Tribune Co. "They have a lack of respect for people in baseball. That translates into bad decisions. It started with firing me and hiring Jim Frey."

His bluster is still loud. But he has the black-and-white record of the post-Green Cubs in the 1990s to prove his point.

The hulking man from Delaware could have done a lot of things better on his watch. But Green still was the best the Cubs had for a long time. More than a decade later, the Cubs still struggled to recover the momentum lost when prim and proper corporate executives couldn't reconcile themselves to outspoken baseball men.

Chapter 9

"It Wasn't Too Hot" to Win

DALLAS GREEN AND his corporate masters bullied and blustered for lights at Wrigley Field, their effort getting more vociferous as pressure from Major League Baseball and the TV networks seeking the ability to broadcast prime-time games from the North Side grew. Faced with a buzzsaw of community and political opposition, Green and Co. subtlely hinted around 1985 at moving out of the Friendly Confines to a new stadium with all the trimmings, possibly at a huge tract of vacant land Tribune Co. owned, housing the WGN-Radio transmitter site, south of the Woodfield Mall in northwest suburban Schaumburg, Illinois.

The pro-lights effort stalled until 1987, when Chicago mayor Harold Washington quietly threw his support behind night baseball. With Washington consolidating his power after his successful re-election, the political worm started to turn. Green was fired and Washington died within a month of each other in the fall of 1987, but the momentum was established. Laws that effectively banned night baseball were repealed, and by the spring of 1988 the legislative green light was given for the lights.

Thus the gala opening night for lights, cut short by a fifth-inning monsoon, on August 8, 1988, ended a four-decades long debate about the lack of lights. Oddly enough, the franchise-wide attitude change for the better, brought about by Green, had dampened down a concurrent controversy about the supposed negative effects of the all-day schedule on Cubs team performances throughout the million-to-one era.

Stereotypes about Wrigley Field's environmental factors in relation to the Cubs had been debated for decades. The talk grew a lot louder after the infamous 1969 collapse, in which a slew of Cubs regulars tired down the stretch, and through most of the 1970s amid a mostly gloomy atmosphere that had enveloped the franchise.

The stereotypes were broken down as follows:

• The Cubs couldn't win playing all home day games, because the players would wilt in the oppressive summer heat and humidity, or get worn down by the constant change from day to night ball on the road and back to day games at home.

• The wind usually blew out at cozy Wrigley Field, making it impossible to sustain a good pitching staff over an entire season.

Green's regime inherited all these ingrained images when it assumed power in the fall of 1981. The talk continued through two losing seasons. Suddenly, the joy of winning replaced the bitching about the sun and wind in 1984. Then-manager Jim Frey summed up the lifting of that longtime burden when he bellowed, "It wasn't too hot this year," as he celebrated the clinching of the NL East title against the Pirates in Pittsburgh.

Through the ensuing decade and a half, very little grousing has been heard from Cubs players about the home schedule, which remained predominately daytime when 18 night games were annually permitted by law starting with the 1989 season. Nor did pitchers continually lambaste the ballpark and its short dimensions as they had done in previous decades when a trade to a pitching-friendly ballpark like Busch Stadium or Dodger Stadium was coveted.

In fact, Wrigley Field's environment basically ceased to be a topic of any ongoing conversation until the summer of 1998, when *Chicago Tribune* Cubs beat writer Paul Sullivan reported some behind-the-scenes management talk of increased night games, possibly up to 30 annually, when the 15-year agreement on night baseball and its 18-a-year-quota expired in 2003. Sullivan also followed up with an extensive feature on July 21, 1999, in which the pros and cons of day baseball were debated once again by Green and others. Meanwhile, Cubs manager Jim Riggleman theorized about how Wrigley Field was a tougher park than normal in which to win, and attributed part of his 1999 pitching staff's collapse in June of that season to the supposed change of wind pattern to the hitter-friendly south and southwest.

But at the dawn of a new millennium, the night-game issue is not a front-burner topic in the manner of decades past. The Cubs' fortunes center more on management's willingness to bear a top-of-the-line payroll and the revival of the player development system, which had gone into sharp decline soon after Green's departure.

The issue of lights, or the lack thereof, had been simply the epitome of Phil Wrigley's eccentric stewardship of the Cubs up until 1969. After committing full throttle to lights for 1942 after big drops in attendance the previous two seasons, Wrigley donated the raw materials to the military after Pearl Harbor. Wrigley unsuccessfully attempted to use portable lights during World War II. After the war, a string of one million-plus annual gates at Wrigley Field apparently satisfied him that he had the right combination to lure crowds during the day. All the while, the last holdouts for day baseball had put up light towers, the Detroit Tigers bringing up the rear in 1948 at Briggs (later Tiger) Stadium.

Fans criticized Wrigley throughout the 1950s for his anti-lights stance. In the climate of the times, many were unable to take off from work to attend weekday games at Wrigley Field, and falling attendance reflected that sociological fact. And more astute fans began to suspect some of the Cubs' drooping fortunes on the field were somehow connected to the all-day schedule at home.

Wrigley held fast in spite of financial losses due to poor attendance for weekday games. He insisted that he was not going to hurt the surrounding residential neighborhood by installing lights, but conveniently left out his own plan to play night games in 1942 and his periodic rental of Wrigley Field for night boxing and wrestling matches, and a Harlem Globetrotters game, all using portable lights. He also forgot to remind fans about how he staged several June and July games in the middle of the war with 6 PM start times and several hours of daylight left in an attempt to attract more war workers just coming off the job. The owner suggested he'd install lights to finish off long games or provide more illumination on cloudy days.

Is the Heat Really on the Cubs?

The '69 season became the demarkation line. Players, media, fans, and even several Cubs officials began to question whether the all-day schedule hindered the team. Subsequent second-half collapses in the 1970s added more fuel to the fire.

When the Cubs began struggling in August 1969, then followed up with an 8-18 finish, part of the blame game centered around Leo Durocher continually using the same lineup, including catcher Randy Hundley, lean-and-lanky shortstop Don Kessinger, and 38-year-old Ernie Banks, every game under the Dog Days sun. Kessinger and pitcher Ken Holtzman later claimed the heat simply wore down the Cubs, and they were joined by a chorus of other players. Holtzman, who had conflicts with Durocher, asked to be traded in 1971, partially because of the environmental conditions at Wrigley Field.

Joining a world championship-calibre team in Oakland, Holtzman, the only Cub ever to toss two no-hitters, said he could see the difference in the physical playing environment between daytime Wrigley Field and cool nights at the Oakland Coliseum.

"The psychology of winning? The A's played all [weekday] games at night in a big ballpark," said Holtzman, now health and physical education director of the Marilyn Fox Jewish Community Center in Chesterfield, Missouri, a St. Louis suburb. "There was a big change [with the Cubs] going from day games to night games on the road, and back to day games at home.

"The Cubs play too many day games. I saw what it took to win. You need 40 night games. You get run down the latter part of the summer. The constant changing of the schedule hurts. It's the change of the body clock. Pro athletes are highly disciplined athletes. They have constant routines.

"In order for the Cubs to be on a more equal footing with other teams they have to play more night games. I'm a fan of Wrigley Field as much as anyone. But one thing that has remained constant for 54 years [since the last World Series] is the predominately day games at home. It's radically different than anyone else."

Prominent opponents like Reds slugger Frank Robinson and Astros pitcher Larry Dierker also believed the Cubs wore out over the long season due to day games.

The Cubs themselves possessed some apparently damning evidence. Team trainer Gary Nicholson, who worked from 1972 to 1976, noticed how his charges often seemed beat in August and September. He compiled an informal study about the apparent negative effects of day games and presented it to general manager John Holland. Nicholson was told to keep a lid on his findings.

During hot spells on Nicholson's watch, players actually made matters worse when they tried to quench their thirst.

"When it's hot like that, the players drink more—they have more beer, for instance, but that flushes you out, you become more dehydrated and you lose potassium and salt," he said. "You lose more energy and have more of a chance of injury, or getting sick because you're tired."

Both Blake Cullen, Holland's assistant, and then-Cubs media relations director Chuck Shriver were aware of Nicholson's study.

"Everybody sort of conceded that it was correct, but nothing was ever going to happen, so nothing was to be gained by making a big deal about it," said Shriver, remembering the Nicholson conclusion about the constant upheaval in the schedule. Nicholson recalled he wasn't going to be a crusader; he said the key to continual, if not lifetime, employment with the Cubs was going along with the brass without dissent.

Nicholson also said that the cramped clubhouse down the left-field line contributed to the players' discomfort. Now used by the grounds crew after Dallas Green built a much larger clubhouse behind the dugout in 1984, the locker room was so small the players were "butt to butt" by their lockers and had to "shower in shifts," Nicholson said. The air conditioning was poor; "it was hard to cool off in there after games," he added.

"There were rats everywhere," former outfielder Pete LaCock said. "It hurt your preparation being in there. When the minor leaguers came up in September, they were put in a back room, like an equipment room. They were crammed in there."

Plans for a new clubhouse were on the drawing board, but always took a back seat to Phil Wrigley's continual renovation of the seats and parts of the lower and upper deck. Holland was not going to push Wrigley to shift resources to a new spacious clubhouse with room to breathe and modern training equipment.

"John was a product of an era when baseball didn't have a lot of money. He was tight," Shriver said.

The Wrigley Field dugouts under Phil Wrigley also were small and cramped. If players needed to go to the bathroom during the game, they had to walk down the left-field line to the clubhouse. On the hotter days of the year, they could not walk down a short passageway leading from the dugout, as they do today, to cool off in the clubhouse.

While the Cubs practiced self-censorship, the media and several dogged researchers exercised their First Amendment rights. The best numbers-crunching was by Don Zminda, now vice president of publishing products for Morton Grove, Illinois-based STATS, Inc., one of Major League Baseball's statistical services. In the June 1987 *Sabermetric Review*, a baseball analysis newsletter, Zminda revealed the Cubs had a lower winning percentage in September compared to every other National League team between 1969 and 1984.

Between Opening Day and August 31 during 15 years surveyed (the fractured 1981 season was left out), Zminda said the Cubs had a .499

winning percentage, ranking seventh among the 12 NL teams in existence during the period. But from September 1 to the end of the season, the team's winning percentage dropped to .439, the biggest falloff of any team. The next greatest percentage drop after the .060 of the Cubs was by the Braves at .025, followed by the Cardinals at .024. Biggest gainer from September 1 on were the Montreal Expos, of all teams, from .460 prior to .511 after (a .051 gain). Best post-September 1 winning percentages were by the Pirates (.583), Reds (.560), and Dodgers (.553).

The numbers were closer when all Cubs teams from 1946 to 1984 (1981 excepted) were factored in—no doubt due to the overall poor quality of the host of Cubs teams prior to 1967. Zminda started with 1946 due to the preponderance of lights for night games with the resumption of normal baseball after World War II. For all games from April 1 to July 31, the Cubs had a .467 winning percentage, worst of the eight NL teams in operation in 1946. The only big-league team faring worse was the Philadelphia/Kansas City/Oakland Athletics with .462. The Cubs and A's also brought up the rear of their leagues with post-August 1 winning percentages, respectively, of .451 and .444. Best 1946 to 1984 winning percentages for full seasons were no surprise—the Yankees (.577) and Dodgers (.568).

"A September decline doesn't mean the Cubs are doomed to failure—but it does mean that they are extremely unlikely to come from behind to win a close pennant race," Zminda wrote.

More research showed the Cubs' decline in performance for road night games from 1969 to 1984. The Cubs had a .475 winning percentage for road day games, fourth best in the 12-team NL. But that dropped off sharply to .425 for road night games.

Zminda even broke down the batting performances in the first game of a road trip, usually at night, for the famed slugging troika of Ernie Banks, Billy Williams, and Ron Santo for 1960 to 1971. The abrupt adjustment from seeing the entire baseball during the day to possibly just half the ball at night was seen as the cause of the dropoffs. Williams hit .277 with a .462 slugging average in the first game of road trips compared to .297 and .507 in all other games. Santo hit .245 with a .378 slugging average in the first game away from home compared to .281 and .480 for all other games. Banks, Mr. Cub, dropped the most. He hit just .220 with a .430 slugging average, compared to .264 and a .489 slugging average at all other times.

Overall, from 1946 to 1989, the Cubs had winning records at home in 25 seasons, but on the road in just three years (1969, 1984, and 1989). Some of the dropoffs from home to road records were astounding. In 1953, the Cubs were 43-34 at home, 22-55 on the road. Other big disparities took place in: 1954 (40-37 home, 24-53 road), 1956 (39-38 home, 21-56 road), 1961 (40-37 home, 24-53 road), 1983 (43-38 home, 28-53 road), and 1986 (42-38 home, 28-52 road).

Some contrary trends, in the tradition of Phil Wrigley, also are at work here. Zminda's survey, of course, was completed long before the 1989 and 1998 seasons, in which the Cubs showed staying power at night, factoring in 18 after-dark games at Wrigley Field.

In 1989, the Cubs were nearly dominating in night games on the road: 35-24. With a 10-7 record at home (one game was rained out) after dark, the 45-31 night-game record was a spur to the NL East title. The hitting dropoff continued for night games: a .247 team batting average compared to .273 during the day. But to prove that the baseball is harder to see at night, the Cubs' team ERA was 3.24 after dark compared to 3.59 during the day. Overall, the '89 Cubs hit .250 and had a 3.31 ERA on the road compared to .272 and 3.54 at home.

But Zminda's thesis had to be updated based on the 1998 results. The Cubs actually hit better at night (.268) than during the day (.262), while pitching less efficiently after dark (4.57 ERA) compared to during the day (4.39). The '98 Cubs were 38-32 in night games and 52-41 in day games.

When the causes for the historic dropoff in performance on the road and down the stretch were first debated, the supposedly hot, sultry weather present for months on end at Wrigley Field drew the lion's share of the blame. But a review of the stats shows the heat was hardly any worse than other outposts throughout the majors in mid-summer, and in many cases was a lot more comfortable than many cities. The months of April and May are often frigid, more chilly and wet than October and November in Chicago. September is usually a moderate month with a few hot spells, but without the peak of summer humidity. That leaves three months of supposedly beastly weather. But Wrigley Field's location on Chicago's North Side gets some consistent breaks from the worst of summer heat and humidity in mid-summer.

The ballpark is located just a half mile from Lake Michigan, which acts like an inland ocean in generating its own weather. Temperatures often are cooler near large bodies of water due to prevailing winds carrying cooler air from lake or ocean. On summer days when the temperatures are up to 90 at O'Hare Airport, Chicago's official weather recording station 12 miles inland, the thermometer often doesn't get out of the mid-70s at Wrigley Field.

Players, fans and media remember the extremes, be it temperatures, or windy days at Wrigley Field, and believe they're the norm. But they're wrong.

You can sweat at Wrigley Field, all right, but not like sultry near-tropical climes like St. Louis and Atlanta. Former third baseman Terry Pendleton, who also played in Atlanta, said day games at Wrigley Field were not as hot as night games in mid-summer at St. Louis' Busch Stadium, particularly in the era of artificial turf. WGN-TV weather anchor Tom Skilling said St. Louis' summer climate, frequently featuring daytime high temperatures pushing 100 (achieved during batting practice for 7 PM night games at Busch Stadium, in the center of the heat island of downtown) with humidity readings not far behind, is different than Chicago's. Few St. Louisans have ever campaigned for an air-conditioned domed stadium for their Cardinals, who have survived numerous sauna sessions to win a slew of NL pennants.

In 1999, exactly one 90-degree gametime temperature was recorded at Wrigley Field—a blistering 98 on July 30, when Cubs catcher Jeff Reed almost fainted at the plate due to the heat combined with the effects of a bad cold. The three previous seasons—1996 to 1998—each recorded just one 90-degree gametime temperature at Clark and Addison.

In contrast, during summer's three hottest months, June, July, and August, each of the four seasons between 1996 to 1999 featured frequent moderate summer temperatures during games. The number of June through August games featuring first-pitch temperatures under 80 was 25 in 1999. The comparable under-80 figures for 1996 to 1998 were, successively, 29, 31, and 29.

Want to wear a jacket at Wrigley Field? You could have with 68-degree gametime highs on June 29 and August 8, 1999. Other under-70 June through August gametime highs for 1996 to 1998 were: 68 on June 18 and June 19, 1999; 69 on July 30, 1996; 67 on August 5, 1997; 68 on June 26, August 25 and August 28, 1997; 69 on July 23, 1997; 54 on June 5 and 57 on June 7, 1998 (the first Cubs-White Sox regular-season series); 67 on June 15 and 69 on June 16, 1998, and 69 on July 4, 1998.

Specific temperature records going further back are not as readily available. But a temperature track for the lakefront between 1975 and 1979 showed only one truly blistering month—an average high temperature of 87.7 in July 1977. Other summers can be much cooler. The next year, 1978, average July lakefront high was 81.2. The weather can turn, too. After that sweaty July 1977, the lakefront high did not crack 84 between August 11 and 25. In 1979, the lakefront high did not get above 78 between August 11 and 18.

The late Jack Brickhouse told of an unexpectedly chilly experience in his welcome to Chicago after moving from Peoria.

"My first year in Chicago, on July 3, 1940, I was standing on the Morse L platform in Rogers Park [a lakefront neighborhood] and I could see my breath," Brickhouse said. "I figured, what kind of town is this where I can see my breath in the middle of summer?"

Brickhouse always carried a black topcoat along in his car just in case he needed it in the Wrigley Field broadcast booth. And he did several times in mid-summer. He remembered a Sunday doubleheader against the Pirates in the 1940s. "They had 40,000 at the game," he said. "The temperature started at 75, then dropped to 45 by the nitecap. The crowd went down to 10,000 by the middle of Game 2."

Our perceptions of heat have been inflated by years. And maybe it just *seemed* hotter. Homes, offices and cars did not feature as much air conditioning in the 1960s as today. My family did not purchase window air conditioners until the spring of 1970; prior to that we suffered with fans on the third and top floor of a six-flat apartment building in Chicago's West Rogers Park neighborhood. For the ballplayers, factor in that cramped, hot Cubs clubhouse.

Don Kessinger said it "seemed 1969 was the hottest summer ever. Every day you'd go out to the ballpark, and you couldn't breathe." Interestingly enough, Kessinger hails from the Memphis area, one of the most torrid and humid summer climates in the country. Even the most brutal Chicago summer would not compare with the relentless, months-on-end sauna bath of the mid-South.

Kessinger no doubt remembered some individual series in June and July 1969 when the temperatures soared into the 90s. But, as a whole, 1969 was not out of the ordinary, temperature-wise, for a Chicago summer.

The average summer temperature (in a range from June 21 to September 21) for 1969 was 73.3, according to a survey provided by Chicago-area forecaster Richard Koeneman, who works with Tom Skilling at WGN-TV and the *Chicago Tribune*.

During Kessinger's Cubs tenure (1965 to 1975), the average summer temperature topped 1969's figure in 1966 (73.9), 1970 (73.6), 1973 (73.5), and 1975 (73.6).

In fact, the long-term trend showed some cooling in the 1980s. In only one year between 1951 and 1981 did the average summer temperature fail to reach 70. That was 1967, the Cubs' breakthrough season under Leo Durocher, with 69.5. But between 1981 and 1986, the average was under 70 five times, with a low of 68.7 in 1982. The Cubs swept a crucial four-game series from the Mets to solidify their hold on first place in early August 1984 amid 90-degree heat and boiling-point emotions from play-ers and fans, but otherwise played in a temperate summer with the av-erage temperature at 69.5.

Hottest average temperatures of the million-to-one era were 1955 with 76.9, 1959 with 75.0, and 1995 with 74.9 (featuring the killer heat wave in July, including a 104-degree 7 PM gametime temperature on July 13 at Wrigley Field). The '55 Cubs started out 46-37, but then went 1-19, mostly on a death-march eastern road trip around the All-Star break. They played .500 the rest of the way to finish 72-81. In '59, the Cubs were 50-48 at the end of July, lost seven in a row, and again played .500 the rest of the way to finish 74-80. In strike-shortened 1995, after a roller-coaster season of winning and losing streaks, the Cubs had enough left to win eight in a row from September 22 to 29 at Wrigley Field, climbing to 73-69 and the cusp of wild-card contention before losing the last two games of the season.

There can be a correlation between cooler summers and winning Cubs seasons and/or good pitching performances. The 1989 NL East title season sizzled on the field but not in the thermometer as Chicago re-corded only seven 90-degree or more high temperatures the entire sum-mer. And in 1992, when the record-low post-war average temperature was recorded, the Cubs led the NL in ERA before the inevitable September collapse.

Summer temperatures can vary wildly. Just one year before the tem-perate '89 season, the Cubs experienced a beastly environment in one of the hottest Chicago summers ever. Although the average summer tem-perature was highest in 1955, the city experienced its most 90-degree or more days with 47, including seven with 100-degree or more highs, in 1988.

"You just died playing out there in the daytime," Mark Grace said of 1988. "All you wanted to do after a game was go home and sleep."

Brutally hot weather alone would not account for the frequent Cubs collapses or the disparity of home and road records. In some cases, some of the abrupt September nosedives, like in 1979 and 1987, may have been psychologically-based. Bad clubhouse chemistry and players who simply cashed it in with a month left to play were obvious factors. A number of Cubs teams played .500 or above baseball consistently through Labor Day, only to have the bottom fall out overnight. If the team was truly tired due to the heat, the decline in performance would have been more gradual and prolonged, starting in July, in the manner of spectacular second-half collapses in 1973 and 1977. Despite a hitting slump, the '69 Cubs were 18-11 in August, including a six-game winning streak that began at the end of the month.

Still another reason was the majority of Cubs' teams roster makeups as lead-footed, power-oriented teams, designed for Wrigley Field. Possessing the last at-bat at home, the Cubs always could try to outhit opponents. They could not employ such a strategy on the road, where the bottom of the ninth always would expose weak Cubs pitching. And throughout the 1960s and 1970s, the opening of bigger ballparks with artificial turf throughout the NL put a premium on speed and outfield defense, two qualities the Cubs usually lacked.

The Circadian Rhythm and Day Games

Most likely the biggest culprit of sagging second-half fortunes are the day-to-night-to-day schedule changes, which would affect athletes requiring to be at optimum physical and emotional peaks much more than an office worker changing from 8 to 5 to 4 to midnight. Here is a situation in which Cubs players got used to banker's hours — at the "office" around 9 AM, go home at 5 PM. Suddenly, they go on the road to start revving up for a game when they normally knock off the job. In the most extreme case, a Sunday day game that ends a long homestand precedes a four-hour flight to the West Coast. The result is a two-hour time change, and a Monday night game in Los Angeles, San Diego, or San Francisco that begins as late as 9:30 PM Central time, when the players' body clocks have been tuned on the homestand to start winding down for the night.

Negative effects of the reverse-commute back from the West Coast used to hurt the Cubs prior to the installation of lights. After playing a 3 PM (Central) time Sunday afternoon game to wind up a West Coast trip, the Cubs' chartered plane would not get back to Chicago until after midnight. If the NL schedule makers could not carve out an off-day the next day, the team had to quickly turn around, get up after short rest, and play a day game Monday afternoon.

"Coming back from Los Angeles on Sunday, we often told the players not to show up for batting practice [Monday morning], they were so tired," said Gary Nicholson. "They'd still come dragging in. They drank an awful lot of caffeine and Coke as a stimulant to keep 'em going."

But after the lights were turned on in 1988, the Cubs typically scheduled night games at home for the first game back from road trips so the players could get their proper rest. "You'd be surprised at the difference three of four hours' extra sleep made," Mark Grace said of the ability to sleep in on the days after the end of road trips.

Most baseball players live on an entertainer's schedule—working nights, staying up until 3 AM, sleeping until 11 AM or noon, with "breakfast" at midday, lunch in mid-afternoon, and dinner after their performances at 10:30 or 11 PM. The only exceptions are the Sunday afternoon or occasional weekday game, in which managers often cancel mandatory batting practice to allow the players to sleep in and not arrive at the ballpark until as little as 90 minutes prior to gametimes. Such a schedule is perfect for the night-crawlers among the single players, as former reliever Bill Caudill was as a Cub, or night owls like the Phillies' Curt Schilling, who fiddles with his computer until nearly dawn. Former Schilling teammate Mickey Morandini, a Cub from 1998-99, said the ace pitcher wouldn't likely come to Chicago as a free agent because he usually snoozes until early afternoon, and sometimes had to be roused to get out to the ballpark by 3 PM.

Cubs players are different. They're 9-to-5ers at home; entertainers on the road.

"It's as if one week you have the day shift and the next week you have the night shift," White Sox trainer Herman Schneider said in a *Chicago Sun-Times* article examining the issue on June 13, 1982. "You have to be very disciplined to go to bed at a normal hour. Especially if you're a regular. If people think it's easy, they're barking up the wrong tree."

In the same article, behavorial ecologist Dr. Suzanne Marcy talked about the effects of constantly trying to alter the "Circadian Rhythm," the body's natural 24-hour clock. "During a particular day you will have highs and lows," she said. "You might see behavorial aberrations if you continually upset eating and sleeping habits. One of those aberrations is increased irritability."

Even with 18 night games, the constant schedule changes is a challenge.

"It's entirely possible," Cubs trainer Dave Tumbas said of the wearying effects of day-night-day. "A shift worker operating heavy machinery can adjust faster. A player has to take his time. They have to get their rest. It goes back to preparation."

More of an issue at present are the widely varying starting home gametimes—usually to accommodate TV—which irritate the players the most. The typical 1:20 and 7:05 PM starting times are supplemented by 2:20 PM starts on Fridays, some 3:05 PM starts on Saturdays to avoid being blacked out on WGN by the competing Fox Game of the Week, and 12:15 PM Saturdays when the Cubs are selected as the Game of the Week.

Day games also provide a dilemma for proper nutrition. Cubs players need to have a sizable breakfast to get enough nutrients in their systems before they go through batting practice. Those who missed out on breakfast traditionally ended up noshing on junk food and caffeine in the clubhouse. Doughnuts and coffee used to be mid-morning locker-room stables—hardly the breakfast of champions. Dallas Green began trying to introduce healthier foodstuffs into the clubhouse.

Even if a good, nutritious breakfast is consumed, that can't hold a player through a long afternoon of work. Billy Williams remembered when the clubhouse had no light-lunch food at all; the Cubs tried to play all their home games semi-fasting. A full lunch an hour prior to gametime is not recommended. Tumbas said he tries to encourage starting players to eat a bowl of soup and half a sandwich, or soup and a salad, after batting practice—something to tide them over to late afternoon without slowing down their energy by diverting a lot of blood to the digestive system. "You could have a regular meal no sooner than three to four hours before a game," the trainer said. "But one and a half meals by gametime is all right."

When it all shakes out, the supposedly negative effects of day games have hardly been uniform. The 1984 Cubs, who were 52-31 from July 1 on, were not the only entry to defy the stereotype of slumping second halves or horrid Septembers. The '89 NL East titlists were 52-32 from July 1 on, including 18-11 to finish out the season starting September 1. The wild-card winner of 1998 was 47-34 from July 1 on. The '98 Cubs reached a high point of 87-67 on September 18 and would have easily won 90 or more games if not for a 2-6 finish that necessitated the wild-card qualifying playoff game against the Giants at Wrigley Field.

In 1972, the Cubs were 39-26 (including an 18-12 September-October) after the All-Star break. In 1982, after starting out 40-65, including a 13-game losing streak, the Cubs finished 33-24 from August 1 on. In 1993, with only the ultimately unsuccessful salvation of manager Jim Lefebvre's job to play for, the Cubs had a 20-10 finish from September 1 on. Buried in the race in ninth place due to a 48-inning scoreless streak in late June, the 1968 Cubs revived with a 23-7 streak in July and August, winning their final five in a row to finish 84-78 in third place. And after being accused by Phil Wrigley of "playing like clowns" in a 43-59 start, the 1976 Cubs finished 32-28.

The majority of Cubs I've spoken to in the 1990s said they liked day games, particularly if they had families. They appreciated living a normal life half the baseball season, being able to go home to eat dinner at a normal time early in the evening. And the prospect of the constant schedule shifting was not too daunting to free agents when successive Cubs managements have opted to loosen the pursestrings.

Mickey Morandini has pointed out another interesting advantage of life as a Cub—easier travel. With Chicago's central location, the longest flights are four hours to the West Coast, with a little more than three hours in the air to Phoenix. But the great majority of other flights are two hours or less. The Cubs can drive the 90-minute trip to Milwaukee, while flights to St. Louis, Cincinnati, and Pittsburgh are about an hour's duration. So in comparison to teams on either coast, who sometimes must endure nearly six-hour cross-country hops, the Cubs' travel burdens are lessened. They hardly compare with the Seattle Mariners, whose closest foe, the Oakland Athletics, is two hours distant by air.

Manager Don Baylor wants to use the day games to the Cubs' advantage, stressing rest and preparation in contrast to the party-time proclivities of many visiting teams. With evenings usually free to pursue nightlife and good eatin' and drinking, many Cubs foes regard Chicago as their favorite road city. From the standpoint of a former opponent, Baylor said visiting players tend to stay out later in Chicago.

Former 1960s Cardinals third baseman Mike Shannon used to play a day game, go back to the hotel to sleep a few hours, then went out on the town on his rounds as midnight approached, earning the nickname "Moonman." With dawn around the corner Shannon went back to catch a few more hours' sleep, and came out to kill the Cubs with grand-slam homers and other clutch hits. Baylor hopes a slew of foes follow Shannon's schedule, but don't possess his endurance and come to the ballpark bleary-eyed and off their games.

Cubs management will have to choose between baseball and marketing concerns when they apportion their quota of night games in the early 21st century. City politicians and the community are not likely to agree to 50 night games. Besides, the Cubs will ruin the basic appeal of Wrigley Field if the old ballyard becomes a predominantly nighttime venue.

Night games are now scattered throughout the schedule. The three or four games usually played in April and May should be shifted to mid-summer. Weeknight games in mid-season usually don't draw more than day games, but they are certainly uncomfortable for non-luxury box fans and players in the usually frigid evenings of spring. Night games relatively early in the season usually do not result in full houses. A few more night games during the summer's dog days will give the players the additional rest they say the need.

Cubs management also will need to somehow get an amendment on the present ordinance to permit a Friday night game at home if the Cubs are coming off a road trip ending on a Thursday. The short turnaround after the team flies home into the wee hours, only to have to play a 2:20 PM. Friday game, takes its toll. In the past, the Cubs have been caught playing Thursday night games in Pittsburgh, St. Louis, Cincinnati, and even in Phoenix on one occasion, only to be forced to sleep fast after the flight home to play the next afternoon at Wrigley Field. Neighborhood activists had succeeded in prohibiting Friday night games period, and limiting other weekend night games to two, as a result of worries over drunkenness and other anti-social behavior from fans letting loose at TGIF time.

If the Cubs have the right blend of talent, and aggressive management in the dugout and front office, they'll win whether they play morning, noon, or night, shifting from days to nights and back to days again.

Everyone Knows It's Windy, Right?

The same thinking that states the Cubs can't win playing day games at Wrigley Field also suggests the team will always have trouble holding down the opposition due to prevailing winds blowing out at the cozy ballpark.

That's another stereotype carried over by decades of players and media who have paid scant attention to longtime trends and basic Chicago meteorology.

Wrigley Field has gotten its bandbox, homer-happy reputation from a couple of handfuls of football-score slugfests, the run orgies more often taking place early in the season during unusual warm spells. A succession of mediocre pitching staffs has mightily contributed to the image.

If the naysayers looked closely enough, they'd find the real prevailing breezes more commonly offer a deterrent to batted balls—all season long. It's no free lunch for hitters during the supposedly hot months of June, July, and August. The same moderate temperature readings at Wrigley Field in mid-summer correlate to winds blowing in from the north or off nearby Lake Michigan.

The Friendly Confines are by no means a mecca for sluggers, even in the hitting-friendly era of the new millennium. The presence of frequently inblowing winds put a premium on the Cubs' fielding a competitive pitching staff. Any representative of management who insists the Cubs simply cannot build up some of the baseball's best pitching due to Wrigley Field is either blowing smoke or is ignorant of history.

Combining the inblowing winds and historically high infield grass, cagey pitchers actually could thrive in Wrigley Field. "When the wind blows in here, it's like pitching in the [Houston] Astrodome," said four-time Cy Young Award winner Greg Maddux, the greatest pitcher the Cubs ever let get away.

Fergie Jenkins, who the Cubs managed to keep during his prime years, actually performed better in Wrigley Field than on the road during his six consecutive 20-win seasons from 1967 to 1972. Kevin Tapani was 15-4 at Wrigley Field in his first two seasons as a Cub, allowing only nine earned runs in 49 innings in 1997 and featuring a lower ERA (3.80) at home than on the road (5.81) in 1998. Maddux allowed just seven homers during the entire season in his first Cy Young Award year (1992), which featured a 20-11 record and 2.18 ERA. Dick Ellsworth had a 2.11 ERA to go along with his 22-10 mark in 1963.

As a staff, the Cubs have thrived when they've had the talent and right approach to pitching in Wrigley Field—control and keeping the ball down. On July 30, 1963, the Cubs, led by Ellsworth, allowed the fewest runs (337) of any major-league team, even less than the pitching rich White Sox (348) and Dodgers (371) of Sandy Koufax and Don Drysdale. The team ERA, which had dropped as low as 2.69 on July 16, 1963, was 2.88. The '63 Cubs ended the season with a team ERA of 3.08, second in the NL to the Dodgers.

Spurred by great years from Maddux and Mike Morgan, the Cubs team ERA dipped as low as 2.98 on September 5, 1992. The NL-leading figure was below that of the second-ranked Montreal Expos at 3.23. At that point in the season, the Cubs had surrendered 27 fewer runs than the Expos, had allowed the fewest hits of any big-league team, and had allowed the third-fewest number of homers. But the ERA inflated to a final figure of 3.39, fifth in the NL, due to yet another of the team's patented final-month nosedives, this time 11-21 from September 1 on.

In 1972, the Cubs' team ERA was 3.22, fourth in the NL. Of the five rotation starters, Jenkins, a 20-game winner, had the highest ERA (3.21). In 1969, the Cubs' ERA of 3.34, which inflated during that season's September swoon, was fifth in the NL.

Homer-hungry hitters have noticed the scoreboard flags blowing out, changing their swings to the uppercut mode. That plays right into the hands of any smart pitcher. In contrast, at least one observant Cubs player, former left-handed-hitting outfielder George Altman, changed his swing to an inside-out style, going to left field to avoid pulling the ball into a predominantly east wind coming in over the right-field wall.

"Everyone remembers the days when it blew out and you'd have lots of homers," said Altman. "But I remember a crosswind that would blow all the time from right to left field. I learned to hit the ball the other way, to left field. I'm surprised Billy Williams hit as many homers as he did to right field in his career here."

The homer-filled games to which Altman referred included the Phillies' 23-22, 10-inning batting practice exhibition over the Cubs on in 1979; the Phillies 18-16, 10-inning win in which Mike Schmidt slugged four consecutive homers in 1976; the Cubs' 16-15, 13-inning victory over the Reds that featured 11 homers in 1977, and the Cubs' 16-12 victory over the Cardinals in 1980. All but the win over the Reds took place on unusually warm, windy days in April and May; the 1980 Cardinals win was played on April 22, when the all-time high for the date, 91 degrees, was set.

These games are well remembered and help set the stereotype of Wrigley Field as a wind-blown bandbox. But the numbers over the decades suggest otherwise.

The Cubs media relations staff has kept track of wind direction and speeds at Wrigley Field since 1982. Periodic studies of these numbers show the winds uncommonly blow out, hindering the pitchers, for even a few days in a row. In contrast, the inblowing wind can be a pitchers' delight. During one nine-game stretch in May 1988, not one homer was recorded by either the Cubs or opponents in Wrigley Field. Winds blew in as hard as 31 MPH in one game, almost bending the panes of glass in the old pressbox windows.

The record shows that between 1982 and 1988, winds blew in from the north, northeast, and east for 263 games. Crosswinds from the southeast or northwest that could serve as deterrents to batted balls hit to right and left, respectively, were in evidence for 99 games. The homer-friendly south, southwest, and west winds were recorded for 194 games.

In the warmest months of June, July, and August in 1982-88, a potential pitcher-friendly wind was predominant. Factoring inblowing breezes and crosswinds together, the three-month period over the seven-season span showed 71 playing dates for this category in June, 50 in July, and 75 in August. In contrast, outblowing winds were present for 26 dates in June, 38 in July, and 28 in August.

Maddux and Morgan were particularly helped by the wind in the cool season of 1992, featuring the lowest average summer temperature (67 degrees) of any year in the million-to-one era. During a 33-game span from April 23 to July 8, the wind did not blow out once. Through games of September 5, 1992, the wind blew in a total 43 times, was a crosswind eight times and blew out 15 times.

More recent statistics continued the trend. All but a few games were recorded during the four-year period from 1996 through 1999. In the latter year, the wind blew in 50 times, was a crosswind 11 times, and blew out 11 times. The figures for the previous three seasons were: 1996, in 34, crosswind 14, out 31; 1997, in 47, crosswind eight, out 19, and 1998, in 53 (including the wild-card qualifier game against the Giants), crosswind six, out 19.

The June through August figures, again combining inblowing and crosswinds into one category, were: 1996, eight in June, six in July, and 10 in August; 1997, 12 in June, 12 in July, and 11 in August; 1998, 11 in June, nine in July, and nine in August; 1999, nine in June, five in July, and 14 in August. Outblowing winds for the same period were: 1996, eight in June, six in July, and 10 in August; 1997, one in June, three in July, and four in August; 1998, five in June, three in July, and three in August; 1999, two in June, six in July (the only mid-summer month in the four years in which outblowing was in the majority), and five in August.

The inblowing wind even saved a Cubs' no-hitter. On August 19, 1969, Henry Aaron lost potential homer No. 756 when he connected in the seventh-inning against Ken Holtzman. The ball passed over several rows of bleachers before the wind pushed it toward left field. Gravity then drew the ball to earth into the waiting glove of Billy Williams, backing himself into the vines by the curvature of the wall at the end of the bleachers. Relieved, Holtzman then went on to hurl his first career no-hitter, amazingly recorded without a single strikeout.

Inblowing winds are present for two reasons, according to WGN-TV weather forecaster Tom Skilling. The presence of Canadian high pressure systems north of Chicago, importing cooler air, is one factor. The other, cooler summer temperatures near the lakefront compared to inland areas, is what Skilling termed a "local wind regime." That is caused by the absence of any pressure system near the city. The lake winds work inversely in winter, keeping lakefront areas warmer than inland regions.

South, southwest, and west winds are caused by an organized high pressure system over Chicago or to the south of the city. These systems are the bearers of the unwelcome summer heat and humidity. But unless the summer is on the warm side of normal, the high pressure systems have less of a cumulative effect than the other factors promoting winds that are a potential deterrent to batted balls.

Home-run hitters, flexing their muscles like never before and working against increasingly inferior pitching, were able to more easily conquer inblowing winds in the late 1990s. And a weak Cubs' pitching staff cooperated. The '99 Cubs allowed a record 221 homers, including 124 at home. Cubs hitters slugged just 98 at home. Seemingly everyone was getting into the long-ball act in far greater frequency, wind blowing in or out, even compared to the 1980s.

But the longtime track record showed the Cubs were hardly the perennial league leaders in allowing homers and runs at home. In the period from 1947 to 1989, the Cubs allowed the most opposition homers of any team at home 11 times and the most runs nine times. Cubs batters led in homers eight times and runs scored eight times. No Cubs pitcher has ever come remotely close to the 50-homers-allowed record set by the Twins' Bert Blyleven.

Allowing hits of all shapes and sizes along with a surfeit of baserunners, and not pacing the league in serving up homers, was the weaker Cubs pitching staffs' main problems. In 1974, all five rotation starters, such as they were, allowed more hits than innings pitched. Burt Hooton gave up 214 hits in 176 innings pitched. Bill Bonham gave up 246 hits and 109 walks in 243 innings. When the team ERA inflated to 4.56, alarmingly high for the times, in 1975, the Cubs collectively allowed 1,587 hits in 1,443 2/3 innings. Again, Bonham led the way with 254 hits and 109 walks allowed in 229 innings.

Among the most ignominious baserunner-allowed statistics by Cubs starting pitchers were Dick Ellsworth with 321 hits allowed in 269 innings in 1966, Ray Burris with 270 hits allowed in 221 innings in 1977, Doug Bird with 230 hits allowed in 191 innings in 1982, and Steve Trout with 217 hits allowed in 180 innings in 1983. In the period of 1971 to 1985, the Cubs' pitching staff collectively allowed more hits than innings pitched in every season except 1972.

Wrigley Field itself became a supposed home-run haven in the mid-1950s, after the center-field bleachers were closed off to fans. The absence of their white shirts increased overall visibility for hitters. Between 1931 and 1949, the Cubs hit more than 100 homers just once. And the clock had to advance all the way to the lively-ball season of 1987 before the Cubs hit more than 200 homers as a team. The 1978 Cubs slugged just 72 homers, 28 by Dave Kingman. In 1975, the Cubs hit 95 homers as Andre Thornton was the team leader with just 18.

Meanwhile, despite overall mediocre pitching staffs, during the late 1940s and early 1950s Cubs annually ranked at or near the top of the NL in fewest opposition homers allowed at home.

Members of the Pirates 1970s "Lumber Company," such as outfielder-first baseman Al Oliver, said they saw the ball well during the day at Wrigley Field, and thus were able to consistently defeat an otherwise-dominating pitcher like Fergie Jenkins. But other prominent hitters said they had some trouble hitting during the day at Clark and Addison. Andre Dawson reported a "glare" that was absent only on an overcast day. The Dodgers' Pedro Guerrero said: "I never hit good in Wrigley Field...It's the sun."

The long grass also bothered several of the best hitters. Perennial batting champ Tony Gwynn said he would never have wanted to play in Wrigley Field as his home ballpark; the infield grass robs him and other line-drive specialists of hits.

But, like the issue of the heat and day-to-night-to-day, talent is the deciding factor. If the Cubs have good pitchers, they'll win in Wrigley Field.

If they have muscle-bound sluggers, they'll outhomer the opposition. If they fall short in both categories, they're in trouble in Wrigley Field.

The sun, the wind, the elements, all of Mother Nature's sideshows are nice backdrops to Wrigley Field. But they were not the cause of the million-to-one era. Man has conquered nature in some cases; Wrigley Field can be one of them given a management adept enough to do so.

Chapter 10

"FREY-ED AND ZIMMER-ED"

ALMOST EVERYTHING else they do in business turns to gold. But Tribune Co.'s decision to fire/force the resignation of Dallas Green could not have come at a more inopportune time. Good timing was never a strong feature of the million-to-one era.

A few days after Green announced his departure on October 30, 1987, the major league general managers meetings were held in Florida. John Madigan, the Tribune Co. executive VP who finally codified the divorce with Green, ended up representing the Cubs at the meetings along with assistant GM John Cox. Madigan was the only man with investment-banking experience who circulated among the wheeler-dealers.

At the same time, Madigan assumed the title of Cubs chairman. He announced he was looking for "a good strong baseball guy, not a corporate guy" to run the Cubs. "What we don't need is one of those [corporate people]. We've got enough of those. We need a baseball guy."

Madigan meant a baseball guy to run the Cubs, but at the same time said the team would do without a president. "I don't intend to move out there [to Wrigley Field]. I will definitely be more involved. We don't normally run our subsidiaries from downtown. We'll have a baseball guy who reports to me and [then-executive VP Don] Grenesko."

Two of the last three sentences in that quote summed up how Tribune Co. would run the Cubs until the mid-1990s. While Madigan professed that the team wouldn't be run from Tribune Tower, he admitted any general manager in this management structure would be under the thumb of corporate executives who had little experience in the personnel side of baseball. Tribune Broadcasting chief Jim Dowdle would seek to loosen this umbilical cord of control when he took over as corporate overseer in 1994. But in the interim, years of management chaos very much unlike the rest of normally stable Tribune Co. would ensue and turn the Cubs into a near-laughingstock.

Green and others suspected Jim Frey was part of some contingency plan to replace Green when he was named WGN-Radio color announcer for the 1987 season, less than six months after he was fired as Cubs manager. That theory stated Frey was hired for radio to become even more familiar with Cubs personnel over the long season in preparation for the coup against Green. But judging from both Cubs history and the lack of baseball acumen by Tribune Co. executives, Frey's eventual appointment as GM on November 11, 1987 was simply a matter of convenience. He was already on the premises working for WGN and had the high profile as the only manager to run a first-place Cubs team since 1945. The accessible Frey worked very well with the media. If Green's departure had been choreographed months in advance, he would have been fired immediately after the end of the 1987 season and not nearly a month later.

Madigan had to scramble around to find Green's successor. A long negotiation process and especially lucrative contract would have been needed to snare a well-established GM. With the winter meetings, the free-agent signing season, and the need for a new manager urgent issues, the Tribune Co. brass couldn't have afforded a long, drawn-out search process, made more difficult by the lack of insider's standing in the game by the corporate crowd.

The sudden departure of Green provoked a sense of unease in the Cubs' organization, which had finally stabilized in the 1980s. Player development chief Gordon Goldsberry had to send letters to his staff assuring them their jobs would be safe, at least for another year. This would turn out to be not the first time over the next few years that the front-office staff, scouts, and minor-league personnel had to worry about a change of management affecting their job security.

Goldsberry would have been a good choice as GM. Green already had involved the player development guru in a number of major-league decisions. Respected throughout the game, he would have been a great choice as GM. But Goldsberry said on November 7, 1987 that he wanted a certain level of control. And Madigan wasn't likely to name Green's right-hand man as GM after showing Green the door.

Former White Sox GM Roland Hemond, then working for the commissioner's office, expressed keen interest in the Cubs' job. Madigan also contacted Dave Dombrowski, Hemond's former No. 1 Sox deputy and then a rising front-office star, for a conversation. Dombrowski soon became Montreal Expos GM and moved on to the same job with the Florida Marlins, where he won the World Series in 1997. Kansas City Royals GM John Schuerholz was rumored to be restive. Schuerholz eventually would move on to a decade's worth of success with the Atlanta Braves.

Frey had dreamed of running a front-office, even though he had no middle-management experience as a stepping stone to a GM's job. One report in the fall of 1987 had Frey calling then-Baltimore Orioles owner Edward Bennett Williams in an effort to return to the team for which he had worked as a scout, minor-league manager, and big-league hitting coach from 1964 to 1979.

But Frey had not obtained the necessary experience in wheeling and dealing as a front-office middle manager. A good baseball man, savvy as a hitting coach and down-to-earth in an often verbally profane classical baseball manner, Frey started out overmatched as Cubs GM. And he had to operate under the corporate thumb of Tribune Co., first with John Madigan's oversight from five miles away at Tribune Tower, then Don Grenesko serving as team president on site at Wrigley Field.

Once Frey was given the nod as GM, Don Zimmer, his chum from their teenage days together at Western Hills High School in Cincinnati, was an automatic choice as his manager and top baseball advisor. But Zimmer wasn't the only qualified managerial candidate available in the fall of 1987. Joe Torre, then biding his time as an Anaheim Angels announcer, had reportedly interviewed with Green before the latter's sacking, but all indications were that Green had settled on John Vukovich as his manager all along. Cubs bench coach Johnny Oates also was interviewed. Of course, Torre and Oates went on to rank in the top five of the most successful American League managers in the 1990s.

During his introductory press conference on November 11, 1987, Frey vowed he would not clean house among the front-office staff. Goldsberry's minor-league organization continued almost unchanged for 1988, while his major-league scouts stayed on the job for the first year, too.

But the tenor of the organization changed, and not for the better, in the eyes of many baseball people.

"Is Jim Frey the type who empowers people?" said Jim Colborn, a Goldsberry hire who stayed on for two years as minor-league pitching coordinator. "It's the same style as protecting your ass. Your people only echo what you think. The organization is like a schizophrenic organization."

Colborn hit on something. If anything was common in the Jim Frey-Don Zimmer era, it was more of a negative reinforcement filtering down from the top throughout the Cubs' organization. Frey and Zimmer were good baseball men, but they did not operate in the manner of tough cop-good cop complement of Dallas Green and Gordon Goldsberry. The Cubs organization just wasn't the same. There wasn't that same energy, that reaching for championship-calibre standards, that was fostered under Green, even if the won-lost record at the big-league level didn't reflect that.

"I had a good working relationship with Jim Frey," recalled Scott Reid, another holdover who continued on as a major-league scout under Frey. "Jim was a good manager, but the responsibilities of a GM are so wide, things like dealing with agents. It's very time-consuming. Jim was a grassroots guy who had a lot of ability to manage players. But his experience in things like scouting and running a farm system were very limited. And Jim wasn't as detailed as Dallas [Green]."

"Dallas and Jim were different personalities. Jim had a great understanding of what puts winning team together. But when Dallas walks into a room, you know his presence is there. Jim Frey takes over, a lot of scouts didn't know him. If Dallas wasn't sure about what a guy said in a [scouting] report, he'd call him. Jim never did get that involved in scouting."

Frey desired to imprint his personal philosophies on team makeup. From Day One as Cubs GM, Frey publicly expressed his thirst for long-ball hitters, one that would eventually backfire on him and the Cubs.

"A lot of great players aren't speed merchants," he said. "In this park [Wrigley Field], in the middle of summer, you put six or seven singles hitters out there and the other team will keep going ahead with three-run innings."

Tinkering with the pitching staff became Frey's first priority, however, when he and Zimmer attended their first winter meetings as the management duo in December 1987 in Dallas. Frey had come into the flesh-peddling market armed with a request for a trade from Cubs closer Lee Smith, first reliever ever to save 30 or more games four years in a row. Less effective in 1987, Smith increasingly heard Wrigley Field boo birds. He saved 36 games, then a career-high, but blew 12 games and lost 10 others. He said later he believed the fans designated him up as the villain while they annointed Ryne Sandberg the local hero, in Great White Hope fashion. A normally funny, even ribald fellow whose loud clubhouse repartee with Leon Durham was true Triple X-rated material, Smith became increasingly surly around the locker room in 1987 as Frey looked on as an announcer. Five years later, Smith said he enjoyed smaller, low-key St. Louis better than Chicago; fans left him and his wife, Diane, alone to eat dinner without besieging him for autographs and conversation.

Smith had been virtually set up to aggravate the masses. With a nearly-100 MPH fastball earlier in his career, he had to be handled carefully. But a succession of Cubs managers often used him for two or more innings in save opportunities. That gave batters a better opportunity to time Smith's heat. Jack Clark and Keith Hernandez in particularly wore out Smith. The stopper did possess a breaking pitch, a tricky slider, that could have mixed things up and made him less predictable. But one day in 1986, Smith received orders from the front office to not use the slider after he hung one to Candy Maldonado for a game-winning homer. In his later years, the slider would become a bread-and-butter pitch for Smith.

Wary about Smith going into the last season before free agency and fearful of his sore knees and back, Frey sought to deal the reliever. With Smith's reputation and still-formidable fastball, he could have been auctioned off to the highest bidder, the Cubs receiving star-quality players in return. The Dodgers and Mariners were interested. But Frey, who privately along with Zimmer were not Smith fans, jumped at an offer from the Boston Red Sox—pitchers Calvin Schiraldi and Al Nipper.

Scout Charlie Fox, a longtime Green aide, laid the groundwork for the Smith deal with the Red Sox. Gordon Goldsberry, who was with the Cubs contingent in Dallas, later said the deal with the BoSox went down in "half an hour," a fact confirmed by others in the know. Frey apparently grabbed at the first two names offered for Smith instead of holding out for a better deal.

Years later, the GM said too much impatience in making deals was his biggest regret running the Cubs. Impatience would be the byword throughout the tenures of Frey and Zimmer. The Smith deal was the worst example with the longest-lasting repercussions. In settling quickly for just Schiraldi and Nipper, Frey not only gave up baseball's most prolific reliever ever, but set in motion a domino effect of moves that eventually robbed the Cubs of one of baseball's best hitters of the 1990s.

Schiraldi, a former teammate of Roger Clemens at the University of

Texas, re-joined the Rocket with the Red Sox in 1986. He threw as hard as Smith. But he had pitched shakily in the '86 World Series against the Mets, losing two games. Despite 38-degree cold, Schiraldi was sweating bullets coming off the mound and seemed to express unease in pressure situations. Much to his chagrin, Frey learned of this personality trait soon after the deal. He was not going to entrust late relief to a Nervous Nellie. Thus Frey signed an overripe Goose Gossage to fill the stopper's role, while Schiraldi, still uncomfortable at times on the mound, became a starter for 1988. Nipper was a warm body with a cold arm, virtually a batting-practice pitcher with ERA's more than 5.00 his final two Red Sox seasons; "we look at Nipper as a journeyman fourth or fifth starter or long [relief] man," Frey said after the trade.

While Schiraldi and Gossage struggled much of the time in 1988 and Nipper took up space on Zimmer's roster, Frey made another curious trade. He dealt promising center fielder Dave Martinez, one of Goldsberry's prized farm-system products, to the Montreal Expos for switch-hitting outfielder Mitch Webster. Semi-committed already to the youth movement that the farm system offered, Martinez had hit .292 in his first full season in the majors in 1987. His production was down at .254 in '88, but he was still just 23. Webster had enjoyed two and a half decent seasons in Montreal, his peak being 15 homers, 63 RBI, a .281 average, and 33 steals in '87. But Webster, older at 29, was not a natural center fielder. The Expos used him in either left or right. He made an error in center in his first game as a Cub. By the start of 1989, Webster was shifted to left.

In 1987, Frey had predicted that Martinez and Ryne Sandberg would combine for 100 steals one day. But Frey and Zimmer soon became upset with Martinez's perceived lack of aggressiveness on the bases. He had stolen 16 bases in 24 tries in 1987 and seven in 10 tries in '88. One time in San Francisco in early July, Martinez was given the green light to steal. He stayed planted at first base, aggravating the brass, who already displayed quick-on-the-trigger proclivities.

Webster eventually became a part-time player with the Cubs before departing after the 1989 season. While Martinez never became a star, he stuck around the entire 1990s as a complementary-type player with a number of teams, including the White Sox. He most recently has played with Tampa Bay.

If Frey was miffed by Martinez' supposed lack of aggressiveness, he was doubly dissatisfied by left fielder Rafael Palmeiro's lack of power. First of two Cubs No. 1 draft picks in 1985, Palmeiro hit .307 with 41 doubles in his first full big-league season in 1988. But he slugged just eight homers in 1988 after belting 14 in just 221 at-bats in 1987. Palmeiro drove in just 53 runs, including just one in July 1988. He batted in only 43 of the 208 runners in scoring position when he was at the plate during the entire '88 season.

Frey and Zimmer failed to realize the National League had taken the juice out of the baseball in 1988 after a homers-and-runs-filled season in '87. Only seven NL teams hit at least 100 homers. The Cubs tied for third in the NL with 113 homers; the Mets were the league leaders with 152. Andre Dawson's home-run total fell from 49 in his MVP season in 1987 to 24 in '88; Dawson dropped from 137 RBI to 79 (in 591 at-bats). Ballhawks on Waveland Avenue said that despite a hotter-than-normal summer with a string of 90-degree days, 1988 was the worst year they had ever experienced for airborne souvenirs. A dropoff in power wouldn't be unusual for even the best players. A younger hitter like Palmeiro could be excused for not having a linear progression to big-bopper status amid the deadened-ball season.

Power is not necessarily heaven-sent. The technique of muscling up can be taught. The player can change his batting style or lift weights to become stronger. That was Palmeiro's fate by the early 1990s, but Frey couldn't see far enough into the future—or wait for the future to arrive. But the ability to hit .300 is natural; it cannot be impressed in a player. Forgetting all these facts and desiring a "guy who can do some [offensive] damage, a thumper," Frey began peddling Palmeiro at the winter meetings in the first week of December 1988 in Atlanta. Being packaged with him was lefty Jaime Moyer, whose finesse style had fallen out of favor with Zimmer amid a string of low-run losses. Moyer had a 9-15 record with a 3.48 ERA in '88.

Frey eventually landed Mitch "Wild Thing" Williams for Palmeiro and Moyer. The GM was forced to look for a reliever with Gossage nearing the end of the road. Williams went on to save 36 games in nerve-wracking style for the 1989 NL East titlists, then got hurt and became disgruntled. One train of thought was that the Cubs would not have won in '89 without Williams. Another was that the Cubs could not keep both Palmeiro and Mark Grace, if both ended up as first baseman. However, Palmeiro was no Dave Kingman in left field; he would have been an acceptable defensive player given his eventually productive bat.

Strangely, Williams wasn't even in the original trade talks with Texas.

"We were trying to help our bullpen and get a utility infielder," Frey said. "The trade started out with us talking about [infielder] Curtis Wilkerson. At the winter meetings, we found out we had a chance to expand the deal. Mitch [Williams] wasn't in the conversation when we were ready to make the final deal. We rejected an offer the night before that didn't have him in there. We finally talked about getting a starter or reliever, and Mitch came into the deal."

Giving up Palmeiro did not sound good to media pundits at the time.

"No one can feel good about losing Palmeiro," the *Chicago Sun-Times'* Joel Bierig wrote on December 6, 1988. "The guy can hit .299 in his sleep. He's a safer bet to become Don Mattingly than Williams is to become Lee Smith...Jim Frey remains a steak-and-potatoes guy in an age when many of his peers are discovering there's nothing wrong with a little quiche and pasta."

The Palmeiro and Martinez deals turned out badly for the Cubs in the long run. By 1992, none of the players Frey had received for either young outfielder were still Cubs. The way in which both players were seemingly rushed out of town so early in their careers led to urban-legend stories— still commonly gossiped about among cynical fans and media more than a decade later—of non-baseball reasons for the trades. No logical reason for dumping prime young homegrown talent could be offered other than colossal misjudgment and impatience by Frey and Zimmer. That's why the multitudes believed there was a story behind the story.

Palmeiro, hurt by the deal, wore a T-shirt in his later travels that read "I was Frey-ed and Zimmer-ed." His trade was the second of two big moves that backfired on Frey and the Cubs after the 1988 season. He fired Gordon Goldsberry over supposed philosophical differences on how the player development system should be run.

Goldsberry had demonstrated loyalty to the Cubs and his scouts and minor-league staff in opting to stay on after Green was cashiered. "I feel comfortable with [Frey's] background," Goldsberry said when Frey was hired. "He has an outstanding background in scouting and a deep appreciation for it." In turn, Frey acknowledged the revival of the minor-league system. "All my friends have made it clear the Cubs' minor-league organization has a lot of prospects and the scouting and player-development departments must have been doing a good job."

But as 1988 progressed, Frey found out that no power prospects awaited promotion to Wrigley Field. Goldsberry had signed smaller, faster players. Looking at the likes of 5-foot-8 outfielder Doug Dascenzo, whom Goldsberry had compared to Lenny Dykstra, and speedy center fielder Ced Landrum, Frey said the farm system was stocked with "midgets." Goldsberry's responsibilities were reduced; he no longer oversaw the minor-league system. He was restricted to supervising the scouting department while Bill Harford, his youthful deputy, was put in full charge of administering the minor-league clubs. Another issue, in which Frey was upset over the productivity of several scouts to whom Goldsberry was loyal, was reportedly part of the growing rift.

The September 1988 issue of *Vine Line* featured a cover story with the banner headline, "Farm System Yields a Bumper Crop," with another headline, "Gordy's Gang," above photos of Goldsberry, Palmeiro, Grace, Moyer, Greg Maddux, Darrin Jackson, Shawon Dunston, Damon Berryhill, and Les Lancaster. Hearing of editor Bob Ibach's plan to put the story on the cover, Goldsberry responded, "Don't do that. You'll get us both fired." Sure enough, Goldsberry was soon shown the door, and Ibach, another Green appointee back in 1981, followed soon afterward.

The player development system has not fully recovered yet from the departure of the popular Goldsberry. Eleven years later, Cubs corporate overseer Jim Dowdle verbalized the folly of the firing.

"They never should have let Frey get rid of Goldsberry," Dowdle said. "That's baseball: 'He's not my guy.' That probably was not the smartest thing to do."

Basically, Cubs' player development was de-stabilized. Two more changes in leadership in Goldsberry's job would condemn the Cubs to bottom-feeder status in player development by the mid-1990s.

"No question that a lack of stability in upper management has a trickle-down effect," said Texas Rangers assistant general manager Dan O'Brien, Jr., who ran the productive Houston Astros scouting system through much of the 1980s and 1990s. "Whenever you have a change in management, there's always going to be a step back, an initial step back, while there's a period of adjustment. The question is, What is size of adjustment? If it's significant, it definitely can be felt all the way down to rookie level."

Goldsberry's departure was considered "significant."

"The Cubs were considered one of the best," O'Brien said of player development in the 1980s. "The results support that. You could tell that from the outside, from the way the organization was put together. Gordy was very well-respected. He had a significant track record."

"You have to focus on leadership," said David Rawnsley, a former Astros scouting official who now is a columnist for *Baseball America*. "Goldsberry would have been better than who they had after him."

While Harford offered some continuity in Goldsberry's philosophy in administering the farm system, he did not have the same impact in Jamie Moyer's eyes.

"Was his voice as strong as Gordy's?" the lefty asked. "His responsibilities were split, while Gordy ran both [scouting and the farm system]. He was real young compared to Gordy and Dallas."

Goldsberry could only watch from afar when, with Maddux pitching, eight products of his scouting and player development system stocked the 1989 NL East champion lineup. They included Grace at first, Dunston at short, NL Rookie of the Year Jerome Walton in center, rookie-award runner-up Dwight Smith in left, and a succession of Berryhill, Joe Girardi, and Rick Wrona catching. More talent was yet to come up from the minors.

But problems were starting to develop in the player development system. Crucial momentum was lost due to Goldsberry's firing, and the Cubs needed it when his final draft in 1988 turned out to be a bust. Goldsberry selected second baseman Ty Griffin, a 1988 U.S. Olympic player from Georgia Tech and a natural "tools" athlete, over a slower-footed player with a questionable glove, but surefire bat from Oklahoma State. His name? Robin Ventura. The White Sox, drafting in the position immediately after the Cubs, jumped for joy when the Cubs passed on Ventura.

With Ryne Sandberg entrenched at second and Vance Law a stopgap-type player at third, the Cubs needed a third baseman who could come up quickly. Griffin, used to the aluminum bat in college and possessed of a questionable glove at second, was shifted to third base in the minors having only played two games at the hot corner, in high school. Later he was tried in the outfield. He was found sorely lacking at both positions. After a promising start at the plate in 1989, Griffin's performance tailed off quickly. Bill Harford later wondered whether Griffin ever tried to mentally step up his game to meet the demands of pro baseball.

"I'm the type of player who, when I'm on the field, is more fluid than others," Griffin said early in his pro career. "I was brought up always to be a relaxed type of player. It may seem like I'm just going through the motions out there when I'm really not."

Griffin advanced no further than Class AA, where he hit just .164 in 42 games in 1991. He was demoted back to the lower minors, and was traded to the Reds on March 31, 1992. Meanwhile, Ventura was the White Sox third baseman on Opening Day 1990 and enjoyed his best overall season with the Mets in 1999 after signing a lucrative free-agent contract.

Eventually, only two products of Goldsberry's 1988 draft ever reached the majors. Switch-hitting slugging outfielder Kevin Roberson had a few glorious pinch-hitting moments for the Cubs in 1993-95 before moving on. Lee Smith-like reliever Jessie Hollins, a 40th-round pick, seemed poised to move up to the big-league staff in 1992, but hurt his shoulder, underwent surgery, and was released early in the 1995 season. The third-round pick, pitcher Roberto Smalls, advanced only as high as Class A, endured personal problems and was released in 1991.

The string of unproductive drafts had only just begun.

"Scouts are like independent contractors," said David Rawnsley. "They do the same job no matter who's the boss. The decision-making process in the draft is concentrated in one or two hands. You have a wrong direction or bad leadership on draft day, and you'll have trouble."

To replace Goldsberry's scouting supervisor position, Frey hired former Mariners GM Dick Balderson, who he had remembered from his managing days in Kansas City. Balderson had been a longtime Royals farm-system administrator, then was promoted to director of scouting and player development in 1981. In 1985 he moved on to Seattle, where he presided over the drafting of Ken Griffey, Jr., before being fired and re-placed by Woody Woodward. Frey called up John Schuerholz in Kansas City and Mariners officials to get a scouting report on Balderson.

"In every instance they said good things about his character and about all the things he had done from a professional standpoint," Frey said.

But Balderson represented a radical change from Goldsberry. He didn't have the all-encompassing control and supervision of his prede-cessor. And he did not actually go out in the field to crosscheck prospects in contrast to Goldsberry, who relished getting out of the office. The stick-in-the-office style actually was practiced by others and was not consid-ered by baseball insiders a right or a wrong way to run a scouting department, just a style of management. Some wonder, though, whether not going out to see potential top picks, as another set of eyes could bring a fresh perspective to the scouting process, was a detriment in the Cubs' choice of players in this period.

One of the more forthright, honest, and accessible men in player development today, Balderson now is director of the famed Braves' farm system after tenures with the Colorado Rockies and as a Braves' big-league scout. He's honest to a fault about the drafts he supervised in 1989 and 1990 that put the Cubs' farm system in a bigger hole.

Other than a few changes in the scouting staff and the hiring of famed Latin scout Luis Rosa by Frey, Balderson used most of the same Goldsberry scouts.

"I think the change was a non-factor," he said. "I inherited Gordy's staff. There was a little philosophical difference between Gordy and I, but the main objective still was to get the best players. We had the same guys. Scott Reid was our national crosschecker, and I'd trust Reid to the ends of the earth. We had the same East Coast scouts."

Although Madigan and Grenesko had kept control of the Cubs' player payroll through 1990, keeping it under the levels achieved under Dallas Green, Balderson said he always had the budget he needed.

"I did the budget for the minor leaguers, and we always accounted for an annual increase of 5 to 10 percent," he said. "The budget was always approved. It was never cut. The scouts got raises based on tenure and position, and got bonuses every year here."

Prompted by Frey to find a power hitter in his first Cubs' draft in 1989, Balderson selected raw high schooler Earl Cunningham No. 1 out of rural Lancaster, South Carolina, one position in the draft behind the White Sox, who picked Frank Thomas. Another Goldsberry hire, scout Billy Champion, had first spotted Cunningham, projecting the 6-foot-2, 224-pound right-handed hitter as a cross between former Sox out-fielder Carlos May and Bo Jackson.

Cunningham would go on to endure weight problems. Coming from a rural, Southern background, he scarcely knew how to take care of himself in bigger cities, so the Cubs sent Cunningham to DePaul University to take classes in an effort to educate him on adult life. Worst of all, he simply had trouble making contact, his few prodigious minor-league homers more than canceled out by strikeouts at a rate of one for every three at-bats. For five minor-league seasons, with a relatively short stint in Class AA Cunningham's highest stop, the Cubs tried to get him going, but he eventually was released early in the 1994 season.

"We just didn't draft the right guy. Sometimes you make a bad judgment, and in this case we made it," Balderson said.

"Cunningham was right there on our list. Earl simply didn't have the aptitude to learn to be a major-league player. He had some tools to work with, great makeup, but did not have the aptitude. He couldn't go out there, live from day to day and control his money. The process we used to select Earl proved to be the incorrect process. If he doesn't hit for power, he's got to have some other tools. Earl could run for a big man, but his arm was short, his defensive abilities were short."

Perhaps the Cubs got ahead of themselves in projecting Cunningham's power.

"The least predictable tool is power," Rawnsley said. "You go after the best athlete when you draft."

If the Cubs wanted to project long-term power along with enthusiasm in a raw player in 1989, they could have gone close to home to draft a fellow named Jim Thome from Peoria. A devoted Cubs fan growing up, Thome once sneaked into the Wrigley Field dugout in an attempt to get Dave Kingman's autograph while on a youthful excursion with his parents to Chicago. Before the Indians' first interleague game against the Cubs on June 22, 1998, Thome sat in the visitors' dugout—this time on legitimate business—and stared almost open-mouthed at the sights and sounds of Wrigley Field revving up for the first pitch. He would have been a natural Cub. But, playing for Illinois Central College, Thome was drafted in the 13th round by the Cleveland Indians in '89. The Cubs' area scouts, John Hennessey and Toney Howell, either missed Thome completely or had nothing good to say about him. Thome was a project, but seemingly worth at least picking in the high middle rounds.

"You could see the raw strength, but he was an off-field [left field] hitter, a shortstop but slow afoot," said Dan O'Dowd, now Colorado Rockies GM who ran the expanding Indians' scouting program in 1989. "I don't how you could have missed him. His mother and father are big people. He had strength potential. Jim was 190 pounds then, now he's 235, 240 pounds."

While Cunningham stalled out in the lower minors, Thome simply got better, responding to the Indians' minor-league instructors, as he progressed through pro baseball. By the mid-1990s, he was one of baseball's top left-handed power hitters, his home runs to dead center truly of Ruthian dimensions.

Selected No. 2 after Cunningham in 1989 was third baseman Gary

Scott, whose career crumbled after being rushed up to play third base for the Cubs after a sensational spring training in 1991. After hitting well in the lower minors in 1989 and 1990, Scott spent just five weeks in Double A to finish out the latter season. A legitimate prospect, his career was ruined in the same manner as Roy Smalley's 40 years previously. Scott was traded out of the organization after the 1992 season—when he should have been merely completing his minor-league apprenticeship prior to getting a shot at Wrigley Field.

"Scott had the tools, but he got rushed," Balderson said. "He fell into that old Ron Santo trap at third base, where we haven't had a third baseman since Santo. He had such a great spring [in 1991] and made the club. Everyone wanted to send him down for more experience, but they looked at his numbers and there was nobody else at third base. If we could have had anybody who could have started at third base, we could have justified sending him down.

"It wasn't the draft with Scott, the wrong player being picked, but the process that allowed him to get to the major leagues so quickly led to his downfall."

Scott's premature promotion to the Cubs should not have happened. Experienced third basemen Terry Pendleton and Gary Gaetti, both free agents in the winter of 1990-91, both wanted to sign with the Cubs, but got nowhere with their pitches to Frey. Spurned in Chicago, Pendleton signed with Atlanta, where he won the NL's Most Valuable Player Award.

Two other '89 draftees, right-handed pitchers Dave Stevens and Dave Swartzbaugh, had brief Cubs appearances later in the 1990s. Two other righthanders, relievers Aaron Taylor and Travis Willis, had good minor-league seasons, but never got near the majors and left the organization by 1994.

With a hole in the talent flow already opened by the '88 and '89 drafts, Balderson tried to concentrate on pitching in 1990. This time, injuries and just plain bad luck went hand in hand with overrating prospects' talents.

"We had a bad-year, injury-wise, and it all fell apart," Balderson said.

Six of the first seven picks were pitchers—lefthander Lance Dickson out of the University of Arizona was No. 1, followed by righthanders Ryan Hawblitzel, Troy Bradford, Tim Parker, Sean Cheetham, Tyson Godfrey, and Adrian Sanchez. Concentrating so many high picks on pitchers who did not work out cut a further hole in the talent flow through the farm system. As a result of the emphasis on pitching at the top, there were scant numbers of everyday position players rated good enough to be legitimate big-league prospects. By the mid-1990s, the Cubs would be woefully short of middle infield prospects, among other positions.

Mike Harkey, the No. 1 pick in 1987, was bit by the injury bug starting in 1989. Dickson proved the bug was a true epidemic when he went down after breezing through the minors like he was a man among boys in 1990.

Dickson possessed just an average fastball. But his curveball was special. First baseman Mark Grace said Dickson's curve, coming out of college, would have been one of the best in the majors already. Signing quickly, Dickson started out at low-A level Geneva (NY), striking out 29 batters and walking just four in 17 innings. Moved up to Class A Peoria of the Midwest League, he whiffed 54 batters while walking 11 in 35 2/3 innings. Then he packed his bags again, going to Class AA Charlotte, where he fanned 28 and walked just three in 23 2/3 innings.

Beset by ineffectiveness and injuries to the Cubs' pitching staff, the Chicago brass was desperate—and, once again, impatient. They looked in the direction of Dickson, all of 20 years old in 1990.

"Don Zimmer called me when Lance was at Class AA," said ex-Cub Jerry Kindall, Dickson's college coach and now advisor for USA Baseball. "Zimmer asked if this guy can help us now. I said if he could get the curve over, he can help you. He had enough of a fastball to keep you competitive."

Dickson came up on August 9, 1990, just two months after he was drafted, and took the loss in a 3-1 Cardinals victory at Wrigley Field. But in his next start, he was hit below the right knee by a one-hopper off the bat of the Astros' Eric Anthony. A week later, an infection developed in the same area. Dickson's whirlwind season was over.

It proved to be too much, too soon. Maybe Dickson shouldn't have been up in Chicago, getting hit in the knee.

"I thought Dickson went through the minor-league system quickly, maybe too quickly," Balderson said. "It was incredible what he did in the minor-league system. It was no contest. We had no pitching. We thought we were justified in making the decision [to promote him through three levels]."

Jack Brickhouse would have described Dickson as "snakebit" in ensuing seasons. In 1991, he lost two and a half months due to a right foot stress fracture while at Class AAA Iowa. In 1992, he suffered torn cartilage in his left shoulder, undergoing season-ending surgery on May 20. Rehabbing in 1993, he had three stints on the disabled list due to left-shoulder soreness. Poised to make the Cubs' pitching staff in spring training 1994, Dickson hurt his shoulder again. After two more surgeries, he threw in the towel.

"We were all pulling for him," Kindall said. "His arm went bad, and it was a huge disappointment. Here was a great young pitcher. I don't think Cubs abused him. That's just baseball. Every organization has that regrettable example."

The Cubs could not look for solace from the pitchers drafted after Dickson. Parker, talked up constantly by Balderson at the time, retired in 1992 after a myriad of elbow, shoulder, and knee injuries. "Who knows how good a Tim Parker could have been?" Balderson said. Cheetham hurt his back, never rose above Class A, and was released in 1994. Bradford proved to be a bust. Hawblitzel performed well in the minors record-wise, but fell short of expectations and was let go in the 1992 expansion draft. "Hawblitzel never got faster," Balderson said. "I thought he would, but he didn't.

"Three bad drafts in a row hurt you. You don't have too many strong fish in the barrel. History tells you that you've got to have guys coming all the time, at different stages and at different levels."

"If you have three or four years where things don't turn out well in your drafts, you're hurting," former Astros general manager Bill Wood. "It will cost you big time four years down the line. You'll have to go out and get expensive free agents. You get in a downward spiral."

Balderson's 1991 draft would turn out to be far more productive—but too late and too little to plug up the gaping hole moving through the farm system. No. 1 pick Doug Glanville, No. 3 pick Terry Adams, and No. 8 pick Steve Trachsel all made it to the majors with the Cubs in some kind of regular role, with Glanville headed for stardom now with the Phillies. 1991 Venezuelan free-agent signee Jeremi Gonzalez made it into the Cubs' rotation in 1997 and 1998 before getting hurt. Outfielders Ozzie Timmons and Robin Jennings and Dominican free-agent signee pitcher Amaury Telemaco reached the Cubs in limited roles.

Telemaco's presence also displayed another weakness of Cubs player development. He is the only Dominican player ever signed by the Cubs to ever make it to Wrigley Field. The Cubs still lagged behind most other big-league clubs in landing players from talent-rich Latin America as the 1990s got underway. Combined with the unproductive drafts of 1988 through 1990, the plugged-up Latin pipeline is considered one of the reasons for the farm system's precipitous decline as the decade progressed. The lack of quality Latin players really stuck out to David Rawnsley when he looked at the Cubs' farm system throughout the 1990s.

Luis Rosa, famed for his work for the Texas Rangers earlier in the 1980s, "was as good of a Latin scout as there was on the face of the earth," Balderson said. But he turned out to be far less effective as a Cubs scout. A Puerto Rican, Rosa possessed all the angles on landing talent on his native island in the manner of a classic old-time scout being able to outbid and outtalk his competition. But when the June amateur draft began including Puerto Rican players in 1988, "that nullified some of Rosa's aggressiveness," Balderson said. And Rosa was not as effective flying over to the Dominican Republic and Venezuela to procure talent because of the different personal styles in each country. He was the only full-time Latin scout employed in 1989, and the holes in coverage south of the border showed up immediately.

An obvious solution to boosting the flow of talent from the Caribbean was to start a training academy to house, feed, clothe, and teach baseball fundamentals to young Dominican and Venezuelan players. The Dodgers had been the pioneer in setting up a Dominican academy under the supervision of scout Ralph Avila. The Astros established a beachhead in Venezuela at the dawn of the 1990s with two academies in the South American nation. Other teams followed the lead of the Dodgers and Astros. The Cubs didn't, by Balderson's choice and without any encouragement from higher-ups. The lack of cutting-edge baseball knowledge and adherence to the bottomline by the Tribune Co. executives in charge again would hurt the Cubs.

"I thought there was a fine line," Balderson said. "There were two approaches. Approach A, you could walk in and get your feet wet and come out with a little bit of talent. Plan B, sign a boatload of players and hope you get one guy. I just didn't think the boatload theory was the way to go for the amount of money it would take. Throw in the academy, hire 15 scouts, the boarding of the players, the maids.

"I don't know if this team was ready for that when I was there. I don't think they were willing to commit 'X' amount of dollars. I didn't think that was the way to spend the money at the time. Maybe I should have pushed harder. But a lot of clubs spend hundreds of thousands of dollars [in a Caribbean country] and they don't have a pot to pee in. To try to succeed, you've got to think 'Latin.' It's like herding cattle through the trough. You have to jump in with both feet and can't nitpick. It takes time, it takes patience, it takes money, it takes failure."

Like the revival under Goldsberry, the struggles of the farm system and tardiness in jumping into the Latin market weren't readily apparent to fans and media concentrating on the fortunes of the big-league club. Once again, the Cubs' future looked promising when the heavily home-grown team got hot in the second half and won the 1989 NL East title with a 93-69 record, second-best since the 1945 pennant year. Except for Andre Dawson and third baseman Vance Law, every regular had a great year, and the one-two rookie punch of Jerome Walton and Dwight Smith helped the Cubs lead the NL in runs scored. Mark Grace, establishing himself as a top contact hitter with a .314 average, called Smith the Cubs' "best offensive athlete." Looking to the future, Grace said "there's a chance we eventually could have the best lineup in the majors. You're looking at a team that will put runs on the board and make things exciting."

That lineup showed its inexperience and impatience in the five-game loss to the Giants in the 1989 National League Championship Series. The younger players didn't display the relaxed, got-nothing-to-lose style of the regular season. Andre Dawson struggled mightily trying to carry the load. Giants coach Dusty Baker had told Dawson prior to the playoffs that his team's strategy was to prevent the slugger from beating them and concentrate on the rest of the lineup. Dawson later admitted he should have displayed more patience, drawn his walks, and taken what the Giants were willing to give him.

Pitching also provided some cracks appeared in the positive scenario of the division-winning team. Don Zimmer had no consistent fourth and fifth starters, having gotten a lot of mileage out of big years from Greg Maddux, Rick Sutcliffe, and the surprising Mike Bielecki. At one point in mid-season, Zimmer—never an adept handler of pitchers—tried a four-man rotation. He eventually went back to a five-man rotation as Bielecki and Maddux narrowly escaped coming down with sore arms. It was too late for Sutcliffe, though. Thousands of innings pitched had taken its toll on Big Red. After a 7-3 start that kept the Cubs afloat in the first half, Sutcliffe began showing the wear and tear down the stretch. By 1990, he had broken down, undergoing season-ending shoulder surgery.

With his pitching staff appearing shaky going into the 1989-90 off-season, Frey had to make a significant move, even with the prospect of a healthy Mike Harkey ready for the 1990 rotation. Money shouldn't have been the object after a then-record 2,491,942 million fans streamed into Wrigley Field to see the Boys of Zimmer. But Frey's sum total of off-season pitching moves was a ne'er-do-well righthander named Jose Nunez, acquired from the Toronto Blue Jays for lefthander Paul Kilgus, one of the failed fifth starters of '89. The lack of fresh faces on the pitching staff would come back to bite Frey and Zimmer in 1990 as a rash of injuries, led by Sutcliffe, and ineffectiveness wracked the Cubs' pitching staff and wrecked the season. Even Harkey broke down in September after amassing a 12-6 record. He was never the same.

All the while, Frey continued his quest for long-ball hitters. He and Zimmer tried to change Grace's hitting style to produce more power early in the 1990 season. The results were nearly disastrous, and after the All-Star break Grace was told to go back to his natural swing. He had his usual .300 season. Frey, though, was proud of Ryne Sandberg's 40-homer campaign that led the NL (60 or more homers was still a science-fiction concept in 1990). One day, I sat down with Frey in the Wrigley Field lunchroom to recall, for an article, the GM's work with Sandberg that unleashed the second baseman's power back in 1984. Frey waxed eloquently. At one point I tried to ask a follow-up question. "Shuddup and keep on writing," came Frey's retort as he continued his train of thought about Sandberg's power.

Frey did finally land his authentic outfield big bopper to complement Sandberg and Andre Dawson at the 1990 winter meetings in Rosemont, Illinois. Flush with profits from two big attendance seasons, team president Don Grenesko and the Tower higher-ups allowed Frey to increase his payroll from $14 million to $27 million. So Frey landed free-agent slugger George Bell from the Toronto Blue Jays, immediately on the heels of signing left-handed pitcher Danny Jackson from the Cincinnati Reds. By mid-December 1990, he signed free-agent reliever Dave Smith, escaping a payroll-slashing Houston Astros franchise.

The trio of acquisitions established the Cubs as a pre-season favorite to win the NL East in 1991. But there were some hidden problems that did not become evident until the season got underway. Bell was a potential clubhouse problem and disruption. His arrival also prevented Dwight Smith, who had slumped in 1990, from developing into a reliable regular player; the brass' impatience had struck again. Jackson also was an iffy clubhouse presence. Worse yet, he was brittle, suffering through groin and other injuries that robbed him of his previous effectiveness. And

Smith's declining effectiveness over the past season or two had been masked by the spacious Houston Astrodome. He would pay for hanging breaking pitches in smaller Wrigley Field. Signing all three players had virtually used up the player payroll increase; there was neither the bucks nor the apparent interest to sign a Terry Pendleton or Gary Gaetti to fill the gaping hole at third base. The impatient management settled on rookie Gary Scott instead.

Almost everything backfired on the Cubs in the spring of 1991. Jackson, battling injuries, and Smith were ineffective. The latter had to shoulder the entire late-inning relief load after Frey traded Mitch Williams to the Phillies at the start of the season for relievers Chuck McElroy and Bob Scanlan. Williams, like Rafael Palmeiro, spent some of his waking time ripping Frey and Zimmer. Meanwhile, Scott stumbled badly at third base and was eventually demoted to Triple-A. The pressure to produce a winner enveloped top management.

Zimmer inflamed the situation by demanding a contract extension after Grenesko dawdled on a new deal coming into the season. The relations between the two men became contentious. Previously content to ride herd on the overall budget and keep the Cubs' business operations running as smoothly as ever, Grenesko suddenly injected himself into the baseball-end of the operation by going over Frey's head, firing Zimmer on May 20 with the Cubs 18-19 on the season.

From his retirement home in Naples, Florida, Frey remembers being angered at Grenesko and Tribune Co. at the usurping of his supposed authority.

"I told him that when I was hired, you told me I was going to run the baseball club," he said. "I was told I had to fire Zimmer. And if I was not going to fire Zimmer, he'd go down there and fire Don himself. I felt as if that was possibly the beginning of mistrust (between Frey and Tribune Co. management). I found it hard to go to the ballpark with the same resolve, without the same respect."

The Cubs' season degenerated when Grenesko named Jim Essian, the Cubs' Triple-A manager, to replace Zimmer. Not a major-league quality manager, Essian never gained control of the clubhouse. His biggest contribution seemed to be enthusiastic dugout clapping of the type needed to turn on a nearby light or electrical appliance.

While turmoil enveloped the front office, the Cubs' future was neglected. In June 1991, Greg Maddux told me in one dugout conversation that he fully intended to re-up with the Cubs if negotiations would be conducted in good faith. He later said he was promised by top management that his deal would be done later in 1991. But the loose ends were left untied, allowing a disastrous situation to develop.

"If I don't sign anything by next spring [1992], there's a very good chance it will be my last year in Chicago," Maddux said in my interview, published in *Chicago Sports Profiles* magazine. "However, if I do sign something by the spring, then I'll probably look to buy a place here in Chicago.

"Longevity and security are probably the most important things. Two years ago, when they guaranteed my money for this year [1991], I told them I would talk to them. I would negotiate with them openly and freely. That was part of the deal two springs ago, so I'll hold up my end of the bargain."

The sands were shifting. Grenesko's firing of Zimmer was not part of some long-term grand plan as Cubs president. He was not going to hold the job long-term. He would return to the Tower with a promotion as vice president of finance for Tribune Co. later in the fall. Meanwhile, Stanton Cook, who upon his retirement as Tribune Co. CEO, had taken over from Madigan as Cubs chairman on August 1, 1990 and began to assert his influence.

A 1949 Northwestern graduate with a degree in mechanical engineering, Cook also began immersing himself in baseball-wide issues, including blocking the Cubs' re-alignment to the NL West in order to protect WGN-TV prime-time ratings. He was nicknamed "The Senator" for his distinguished gray visage and bearing. After reaching the mandatory corporate retirement age of 65 in 1990, Cook simply didn't want to walk away with his gilded old-age package from Tribune Co. He desired to stick around in some capacity. So he was given the sinecure of running the Cubs, a visible part of the company, but nevertheless a small part where his decisions wouldn't radically impact the overall corporate bottom line. One observer of the management structure of the time said Cook was a "lone wolf" heading the Cubs where he wouldn't be in the mainstream of Tribune Co.

With Grenesko set to depart, Cook began to look for a new team president. But unbeknown to Frey, his job was in jeopardy, a year ahead of the expiration of his contract in 1992. Frey had simply planned to retire at contract's end; he always said too many baseball executives and field personnel stay on longer than they should.

Even so, Frey said Cook initially offered him a three-year contract extension over lunch one day. Frey told him he would mull it over. At the same time, Cook continued his search for a team president. On October 25, 1991, the Cubs asked for permission to interview Blue Jays GM Pat Gillick for the job. Gillick journeyed to Tribune Tower to talk to Cook and others on October 30. But on November 1, he withdrew his name from consideration. The prospect of corporate interference had left him cold. He opted to stay with the Blue Jays to see if some big-name player moves would finally propel Toronto to a World Series victory. Gillick ended up with two consecutive rings in 1992 and 1993.

"I don't think the Cubs wanted to win," Gillick, now Mariners GM, recalled. "That's part of the marketing plan. Some of the mystique of the Cubs is ineptitude. If they win, there might be an expectation level to win again. It's not a big deal to the company. The Cubs are a pimple on the Tribune Co.'s financial statement. They're not a core business."

With Grenesko a lame duck, Frey could not make any major moves. Cook and Tribune Co. attorney Dennis Homerin were basically running the team. Maddux and tough-guy agent Scott Boras mulled over a contract offer: five years for $25 million. Confirming his feelings of mid-season 1991, Maddux fully intended to stay a Cub past his free-agent season of 1992. He said later he went against Boras' advice and struck a no-trade clause from the proposed new contract to move the agreement along. The length and finances were fine with Maddux. But he didn't agree to the deal fast enough for Cook's and Homerin's tastes. The corporate boys pulled the deal off the table, angering Maddux and Boras. Now the Cubs would have to come bowing and genuflecting to them, with the concept of a $25 million deal that would have ended up a monster bargain years later now consigned to history.

"If I would have been there, Maddux would still be there," Frey said.

But he didn't get the chance. Somewhere along the way, Cook changed his mind on Frey. He stumbled upon Larry Himes' name in a media guide. The former White Sox GM, Himes had spent 1991 scouting games at Wrigley Field for the Cleveland Indians and Texas Rangers. While toting a laptop computer to the scouts' seats behind the plate, Himes was desperate to keep his name in front of the baseball lords of the realm. He had few job prospects since he was fired amid a cloud of acrimony from the White Sox on September 15, 1990, the implication that he could not get along with Sox chairman Jerry Reinsdorf and other team officials.

In Joey Reaves' 1997 book *Warsaw to Wrigley—A Foreign*

Correspondent's Tale of Coming Home from Communism to the Cubs, Himes' resume was described as "dozens of pages long, printed in booklet form."

Cook was impressed. Frey was John Madigan's hire. Cook would now make his own imprint on the Cubs, despite the fact many baseball insiders believed Himes' attribute was scouting, not running a front office. And Himes himself said he was not a people politician, a skill needed in managing the disparate egos of a baseball front office.

Frey was summoned to a meeting with Cook on November 13, 1991. He was informed he would be moved out of the GM's job. Frey would serve out the final year of his contract as a "senior vice president"—a makework position of minor scouting duties out of his home in Baltimore.

The stealthy recruitment of Himes left Frey with a bad taste in his mouth. "They're very secretive, it's a CIA mentality," he said of the corporate crowd.

Cubs front-office staff were shocked the next morning when they learned Himes was the new GM. So were most of the attendees as a Wrigley Field Stadium Club press conference was called to announce the appointment. Himes passed by me on the way to the podium. I was as surprised as anyone, but for a different reason. "Team president?" I asked, but got no answer. That *was* the open position, but Himes seemed an odd choice to become president. Moments later, another management change for change's sake commenced.

Frey said a hushed conversation took place between Cook and Grenesko a few feet away from the podium. "Cook said to Grenesko, 'Don't let Frey talk today, don't let Frey grab the microphone,'" the deposed GM said. "Despite that, I grabbed the mike. I thanked everybody for eight great years. They [Cook and Grenesko] were greatly relieved."

Relief would not be the predominant feeling around the Cubs over the next few years. Himes and his organization came in with the stellar reputation of stocking the White Sox with four quality No. 1 draft choices. They would do nothing of the sort with the Cubs. In fact, the organization continued moving backward. The end of the million-to-one era would be nowhere in sight.

Chapter 11

PEOPLE POLITICS, EYE TESTS, TIRES, AND BALANCE BEAMS

LARRY HIMES WASN'T quite the ogre he was popularly portrayed. At least that's my interpretation. I didn't deal with him every day as a subordinate or beat writer until the last of his three years as general manager, so I didn't catch the full flavor of the emotionally-swirling atmosphere in which he operated. I did not start working Wrigley Field every game for *The Times of Northwest Indiana* until about a month into the 1994 season.

But I had few complaints about my dealings with Himes. He returned my calls more promptly than any other top Cubs executive with whom I've dealt. He always was opinionated, blunt, and logical-sounding to make for good quotes. "There should be a gulf between marketing and baseball," he had said back in 1988, when I first interviewed him as White Sox GM.

He kept his own confidence. Himes didn't bestow off-the-record nuggets on the traveling beat writers like some other executives in the game. I got no information "for background" from him. He flipped off ambitious, scoop-hungry writers in Chicago when he didn't give them advance breaks on stories. When players with whom the writers were chummy began grousing about Himes, he had no shot for a fair hearing in the many parts of the Chicago media.

Unfortunately, where there's smoke, there's fire. When Himes was given a three-year contract as Cubs GM in November 1991, he took a job for which he was ill-suited. The Cubs had become the equivalent of show-biz in sports. The team also had the burden of climbing out of the million-to-one era. A special kind of personality, dynamic and open, a politician and a mover, almost a showman, was needed to head up the Chicago National League Ballclub. A politician and a showman Himes was not.

A talented scout and lifelong baseball man, Himes succeeded in turning around the low-profile Chicago White Sox in the late 1980s. He wasn't under a microscope at old Comiskey Park, though. Himes did not have to play for the masses watching on a superstation and court expensive free agents. He could afford to lose for several years while taking a $7 million budget for the entire operation and squeeze every buck out of it. Few paid attention to his management style.

Himes simply had trouble dealing with the myriad of personalities and egos that make up a big-league team's clubhouse and front office, and accompanying corps of media. That got him into trouble on the South Side, and he was fired near the end of the 1990 season, the Sox' most successful campaign since their American League West title season in 1983. He'd run into even bigger problems with the high-profile Cubs, already in turmoil after the management changes from the Dallas Green to the Jim Frey regimes. Big names were upset by his persona. Even Andre Dawson, one of the classiest men in modern baseball who rarely ripped anyone, was upset at Himes. The Hawk claimed Himes repeatedly walked right past him in the Cubs' locker room, never acknowledging him, while talking only to Sammy Sosa, his prized acquisition. Mark Grace, another prominent Cub who is slow to publicly criticize others, years later called Himes "Satan." The clubhouse was a cauldron of dissension during his tenure as general manager.

Himes' alleged office behavior became the stuff of locker-room gossip and fodder for talk shows. All-sports WSCR-Radio talk-show host Mike Murphy, a former Wrigley Field Left Field Bleacher Bum who ended up hosting a talk show on all-sports WSCR-Radio in Chicago, repeatedly told a tale—originating with a Philadelphia writer—about Himes' supposed temper. As the story went by Murphy's on-air accounts, Himes, a fitness buff, ordered half a sandwich from his assistant while working for the White Sox. When the assistant mistakenly brought back a whole sandwich, Himes allegedly threw it back at her. Informed of Murphy's continuing on-air storytelling in 1998, Nancy Nesnidal, the longtime assistant to Himes and successor Ron Schueler, vehemently denied the sandwich-throwing incident ever took place. So did Himes himself.

And he caught grief when Ryne Sandberg suddenly retired in 1994, claiming he had lost the zest for the game, Sandberg inferred the bad ongoing Cubs season and negative clubhouse atmosphere under Himes was driving the all-time second baseman out of baseball. In reality, Sandberg and wife Cindy, their marriage long the subject of rumors, were on the verge of divorce. A devoted father, Sandberg's retirement as a traveling baseball player would help protect his claim for at least shared custody of his two children. In later years, Himes would express bitterness that he took the blame for Sandberg's departure when personal problems were at the core of his decision.

Himes couldn't catch a break anywhere. To be sure, his personal style brought some of the criticism on himself. But a lot of the blame also can be laid at then-Cubs chairman Stanton Cook's feet for hiring Himes without carefully considering his fit for the Cubs' job. Cook would have taken great care in hiring a top executive for Tribune Co. But, like several of his Tower cohorts and Phil Wrigley before him, Cook was not plugged into baseball's close-knit network to find the right person.

Himes had been the longtime scouting director of the Anaheim Angels before the White Sox hired him as GM late in 1986 to replace Hawk Harrelson. He always had been renowned for his scouting prowess. When he was deposed as GM in 1994, he was kept on the Cubs payroll by new team president Andy MacPhail as a special-assignment scout. It was not a make-work position; he was dispatched all over the game to report back to MacPhail and successor Ed Lynch. More than five years later, Himes toils in the exact same job for the Cubs. MacPhail and Lynch value his scouting expertise. MacPhail also insists that Himes should not be ripped for everything that happened on his watch.

He now works out of his Mesa, Arizona, home. Himes doesn't have to manage people, doesn't have to administer a big-league team budget, doesn't have to deal with stifling corporate dictums from Tribune Co. brass.

As GM, without the oversight and guidance of a baseball man on the premises working as team president, Himes did not apportion his financial resources to the best ends for the Cubs. Always fascinated by gadgets and technological advances that would seem to help develop players faster, he approved expenditures on these near-exotic programs while the Cubs still lacked a development academy/training base and extensive scouting network in the Caribbean. Himes insisted that the game's foundation was the minor leagues, but he could not rustle up the money to hire a hitting coach—or "offensive coordinator" in top aide Al Goldis' words—for each Cubs minor-league team. Worst of all, he did not have the power to spend whatever it took, or jawbone Cook to do the same, to keep Maddux in the fold once the door was open again for a long-term deal at mid-season 1992.

In fairness to Himes, he was financially hamstrung through much of his tenure. Dallas Green's free-spending ways had given Tribune Co. execs the attitude of "once burned, a million times careful." The higher-ups kept reins on Jim Frey. Now, with Cook operating out on his own as Cubs chairman, Himes' team budgets not only had to go through Cook, but also were funneled even further up to Tribune CEO Charles Brumback and his cohorts for review. Like all other Tribune Co. subsidiaries, the Cubs were under a mandate to make money or break even at the least.

When he was hired, Himes' White Sox record was played up. Himes and player development chief Goldis had earned plaudits for their nearly unprecedented drafting success with the White Sox from 1987 to 1990. Four consecutive No. 1 picks—Jack McDowell, Robin Ventura, Frank Thomas, and Alex Fernandez—became impact players, the cornerstones of the Sox early and mid-1990s contenders. Not as well-publicized was the lack of depth in the first three of these drafts. Although the top picks became stars, there had been little production from lower picks until the last draft Goldis supervised, in 1990, when he picked Ray Durham, Jason Bere, and James Baldwin well behind Fernandez.

Given a parsimonious operating budget by Sox chairman Jerry Reinsdorf in the late 1980s, Himes was able to pare down the club to next to nothing, then begin to build it back up with the top picks and other younger players, such as Lance Johnson and Roberto Hernandez, he and Goldis obtained from different organizations. He desired to do the same thing with the Cubs. "I wanted to strip it down and start over, but I couldn't do it because of the effect on WGN-TV," he said of Tribune Co.'s commitment to protect its superstation's ratings.

Before the corporate controllers quashed his strip-down idea, Himes even began exploring a trade of Sandberg in the winter of 1991-92. But instead of a deal, Sandberg was soon re-upped by Stanton Cook to a record annual contract—angering much of baseball's hierarchy—while Greg Maddux remained unsigned.

Although Himes had scouted the National League at Wrigley Field on behalf of the Indians and Rangers during the 1991 season, he wasn't all that familiar with the Cubs' organization, history, player tendencies, or opposing talent. During one game early in the 1992 season, I interviewed Himes in his private suite above first base in Wrigley Field. The Phillies' Darren Daulton launched a homer over the right field wall. Himes profanely criticized Daulton's ability as a hitter. But he was unaware of Daulton's history as a Cubs Killer in Wrigley Field. I told Himes that Daulton had been going wild against the Cubs since 1985; the Phillies catcher had been a productive hitter overall during most of that time.

Himes was unaware of Andre Dawson's dignified hold on the Cubs clubhouse, especially his steadying influence on former trash-talking shortstop Shawon Dunston. After he let Dawson go as a free agent following the 1992 season, Himes pointed to statistics that supposedly showed the Cubs' outfield, with the gimpy-kneed Dawson playing right, had the worst range in the league that year. But Dawson, whose MVP season in 1987 had started the bleacherites' "salaam" salute to slugging feats, had been invaluable just for his clubhouse presence. He was worth keeping around as a team leader. A more politic Himes could have helped retain Dawson.

Similar schmoozing techniques might have reeled Maddux back in. But Himes did not, or could not, offer olive branches to Maddux and agent Scott Boras once Stanton Cook had pulled a $25 million deal to which Maddux had agreed off the table the previous winter. An emboldened Boras demanded $32.5 million over five years at 1992 the All-Star break; the Cubs countered with a deal potentially worth $29 million over the same period of time. The gap could have been breached with some skillful people skills and the ability to significantly sweeten the contract.

Maddux would have been worth $40 million off his 1992 Cy Young Award-winning performance alone—20-11 (he could have won as many as 25 games given the poor run support he got through the first half of the season) and a 2.18 ERA, second lowest by a Cubs starter since World War II. He had trouble with his mechanics pitching out of the stretch during periods of inconsistency in 1990 and 1991, but smoothed that out superbly for 1992. Teams very rarely develop an ace of aces, and the Cubs had one in Maddux, No. 2 draft pick back in 1984, the pride of Gordon Goldsberry's farm system.

If Stanton Cook knew anything about such intricacies of the game, if he was the avid lifelong Cubs fan he always claimed he was, he would have ordered Himes to re-sign Maddux no matter what the cost. But Cook had spent most of the previous four decades as production manager of the *Chicago Tribune* and later CEO of Tribune Co. The blue-blood trappings of such positions, all the time spent managing billions of dollars of assets from the 23rd floor of Tribune Tower, didn't leave much time for numbers-crunching of Cubs history and understanding of the inner workings of the game.

Maddux was the smartest and toughest pitcher in baseball. Once veteran Rick Sutcliffe departed after the 1991 season, he seemed to blossom as the team guru, his quiet personality transforming for the better. Maddux not only knew the hitters' weaknesses cold, but also dissected his fellow pitchers' tendencies. He said the action on southpaw reliever Chuck McElroy's pitches made him more effective against righthanders than lefthanders. Maddux even occasionally called pitches for teammate Frank Castillo through a secret set of signs relayed from his seat in the dugout. Castillo admitted the sign system existed, but always Maddux stonewalled; "that's team business," he said.

When a Maddux pitch knocked down a hitter, it was intentional. His control was *that* good. He once said that if a hitter needed to prove his baseball talents by coming out to the mound to start a row after being low-bridged, then come on. Maddux gave away a potential victory (which would have given him 21 wins) with a month to go in the 1992 season to protect Ryne Sandberg. Earlier in the game, Sandberg had been knocked down by a Padres' pitcher. Picking his spot to retaliate, Maddux decked a Padres' hitter in the seventh inning with two runners on, two out and the Cubs leading by one. He was immediately ejected without so much as a warning. The plate umpire explained that Maddux was such a strong competitor that he knew what was on his mind; hence the lack of a formal warning prior to the heave-ho. Cubs reliever Jeff Robinson then entered the game, gave up a three-run homer and the eventual loss was charged to Maddux. But if Maddux had stayed in, he likely would have held on to the lead to win the game. Giving himself up to protect a teammate only increased the respect of his fellow Cubs.

All along, Maddux' first choice was to stay in Chicago. Even when the Yankees, with a $34 million offer, and the Braves entered the picture in the autumn of 1992, Maddux tried a back-channel approach through teammate and Las Vegas buddy Mike Morgan to get back with the Cubs at the last moment. Himes already had spent most of the Maddux money on free-agent pitcher Jose Guzman. Maddux signed with the Braves for $28 million, virtually the same amount of money he would have gotten in Chicago. The first free agent signed by Himes late in 1991, Morgan later said that he would never have come to the Cubs if he thought Maddux was going to leave.

Himes' snaring of Sammy Sosa from the White Sox for a troublesome George Bell, a cagey move in its own right, couldn't make up for the loss of Maddux, which might have been worse than the trade of Lou Brock in 1964. Everyday impact players are easier to sign as free agents or even develop in the farm system compared to finding four-time Cy Young Award winners who could put the baseball wherever they want around the strike zone.

One day in 1995, Maddux easily dispatched the Cubs in a victory at Wrigley Field. "Every time I see him out there, I see Larry Himes," said shortstop Shawon Dunston. Although Cook with his power of the purse deserved the lion's share of the blame for Maddux, Himes had to take most of the bullets in ensuing years.

Himes also couldn't get plaudits for his deals for Sosa or third baseman Steve Buechele, the latter of which he added a much-needed bat and rid himself of Danny Jackson and his injury track. A younger, more immature Sosa quickly drew clubhouse criticism as a supposedly self-centered "hot dog," allowed too much freedom as Himes' pet acquisition. Buechele quickly fell in with the clubhouse dissenters, who began mumbling around their lockers and to friendly media members from Day One of Himes' GM tenure. Hearing the gripes all around him didn't help Maddux' outlook on signing a new deal as he seethed over the contract shenanigans in the winter of 1991-92.

The players couldn't have been happy over Himes' bizarre roster construction for the 1993 season. He substituted outfielder Candy Maldonado as the right-handed power threat for Dawson. He didn't last the entire '93 season, traded with six weeks to go for Glenallen Hill. Aging Willie Wilson was signed as the primary center fielder. Wilson spent a lot of his time lounging and complaining in a clubhouse easy chair by his locker. One day after a game he got into a verbal row with Derrick May and Dwight Smith in the shower area, prompting manager Jim Lefebvre to rush from his office to break it up. When Wilson finally was released in 1994, the enmity that he left behind was enormous. As Wilson stalked out of the clubhouse for the last time, WMVP reporter Bruce Levine shouted at him, "Don't let the door hit you on the way out."

Worst of all was Himes' signing of not one, but *two* left-handed relievers, stopper Randy Myers and setup man Dan Plesac. Himes negotiated with both at the same time without informing each party of the concurrent talks with a fellow southpaw. Although he hailed from northwest

Indiana, Plesac would have never signed if he knew Myers also was coming aboard. And if Plesac was disconcerted, imagine the chagrin of Lefebvre when he opened the '93 season with four lefties and just two righthanders in the bullpen. The two additional southpaws were Chuck McElroy and veteran Paul Assenmacher. The righties were Bob Scanlan and Jose Bautista.

Himes figured he'd trade Assenmacher for good value after landing Myers and Plesac. But he was stuck with the bearded veteran due to his unusually rich, long-term contract for a setup man; Jim Frey had signed Assenmacher for closer's money when he had become disenchanted with Mitch Williams two years earlier. Himes could not move Assenmacher until the trade deadline, July 30, 1993, with the pennant-panting Yankees taking the big contract off the Cubs' hands in exchange for center fielder Tuffy Rhodes. In the meantime, Lefebvre had no need for three southpaw setup men with Myers the closer. Plesac lost effectiveness from disuse, while Scanlan temporarily suffered a sore arm from overwork early in '93. Not trusting Bautista as yet, Lefebvre had no other reliable righthander and was forced to use Scanlan almost every game until his arm nearly fell off.

Lefebvre was fired by Himes soon after the 1993 season. Lefebvre claimed Himes gave him no reason for the dismissal; Himes later said Lefebvre had not fulfilled certain expectations about the style of the ballclub, such as running more. He believed Lefebvre was a veteran's manager who didn't properly handle the younger players.

Himes then spent the off-season of 1993-94 dumping payroll like ballast out of a sinking balloon. Despite the cash flow from another record Wrigley Field attendance—2,653,763—Cook ordered Himes, going into the last year of his contract, to cut payroll and other team expenses across the board. The roller-coaster ride of Tribune Co. expanding the payroll, contracting, expanding again, and cutting back continued. The corporate parent, a hawk on the growing labor dispute at the time, was battening down the financial hatches for the inevitable players' strike. Dutiful soldier Himes carried out the slashing by knocking out almost every middle-level salary he could find.

Greg Hibbard, the Cubs' leading 1993 starter with 15 wins, and outfielder Dwight Smith were allowed to leave as free agents. Pitcher Mike Harkey was let go. Scanlan was traded to the Brewers for two minor leaguers. Worst deal of all was trading still-promising southpaw McElroy to the Reds for two minor-league pitchers and a catcher.

I wondered why Himes was committing career suicide, carrying out the payroll-slashing when that would only cement his fate after the 1994 season. Himes agreed to meet with me in the team weight room, empty during the winter, during his mid-day workout. As he labored on a treadmill, I told him he was falling on his own sword by decimating the Cubs' roster. Himes did little more than shrug in response. He didn't believe he was in trouble, but the signs were all over the place.

The combination of off-season personnel dumpings and the hiring of new manager Tom Trebelhorn—who with a one-year contract had all the earmarks of a lame duck like Himes—made the Cubs' atmosphere almost intolerable as the 1994 season got underway. Sure enough, the Cubs lost a record 12 games in a row at home, requiring the services of barkeep Sam Sianis' hex-busting billy goat parading around the fringes of the playing field to effect a 5-2 victory over the Reds. Trebelhorn staged his "firehouse talk" with agitated fans outside Wrigley Field. Stan Cook even descended from his Brahman's perch to the dugout to tell the media that all wasn't lost.

Conceptually, not at the major-league level. The Tower guys could order the cash spigot opened. The Cubs could have replaced every departing player except Maddux with a quality free agent or product of a trade. What they couldn't do is properly groom their own homegrown players if they were looking for the wrong prospects, not fully exploring the foreign market or embarking on unusual programs impeding the development of minor leaguers.

That was the legacy of the Larry Himes administration. The Cubs farm system already was troubled as 1992 turned to 1993. Himes was given less than three years to turn things around. That wasn't nearly enough time.

Unfortunately, Himes and his top aides made matters worse with eye tests, batting drills atop rubber tires and balance beams, and other time-consuming tactics that tempered many minor leaguers' hunger to reach the majors. How many minor leaguers were set back by these programs, criticized later by Andy MacPhail when he took over as Cubs president, isn't known. But when twinned with a terrible 1994 draft, the sagging Cubs' player development system would spend the rest of the decade climbing out of a hole that only got bigger under Himes, Al Goldis, and assistant general manager Syd Thrift.

When he became GM in 1991, Himes could not at first hire Goldis, who was contractually committed to running the Milwaukee Brewers' player development department. He then named veteran baseball man Thrift as assistant general manager. The drawling Virginian always was chock full of visionary ideas that married technology to baseball, but rarely found an organization in which to implement them. He discovered a kindred soul in Himes.

"Dr. Jonas Salk [developer of the polio vaccine] said all answers in the universe are discovered by answering the right questions," Thrift said early in 1992. "We start doing that in baseball, but we always get side-tracked. We get tired of trying new things in two or three years. Like the rest of the country, we suffer from a lack of long-range planning."

Himes had a noble goal in mind. "I wanted to find ways to increase the success ratio of drafted players," he said. "I wanted to increase the number of players coming to Wrigley Field [from the minor-league system]."

Given the green light by Himes, Thrift embarked on a program of eye exams for all players to determine depth perception problems. Then he began a program of exercises, designed to strengthen vision and perception. Players peered into a "vectogram," several pieces of plastic containing an imprinted image. The further the player pulled the pieces apart, the more he had to focus on the image of the middle.

Others in the organization became suspicious of Thrift. They thought he came off like Professor Harold Hill in *The Music Man*. Cubs employees saw a fast talker at the least, a slew of wacky ideas at the worst.

Gary Mack, an Arizona-based sports psychologist who had worked for the Cubs since the early Dallas Green era, watched Thrift's entrance into the organization. "He was like a snake-charmer," Mack said. "It was like a baseball trade show out there with the odd stuff he was showing off that he wanted to players to do."

"He had too much input," then-outfield instructor Jimmy Piersall said. "He had stuff in his car like he wanted to sell it."

Thrift also prompted Himes to install state of the art video equipment to be used in visual training. Meanwhile, Himes appropriated $750,000 for the construction of a video analysis room just outside the Cubs' clubhouse. The room, still used, had enough monitors and switches to stock a TV remote truck.

Traditionalists were aghast. "That's wasted money," said Dick Balderson. "If you spent $100,000, that's all right. Otherwise it's cosmetic surgery."

Balderson was in no position to express his dissent. He and minor-league director Bill Harford worked on borrowed time once Himes was hired. They would last as long as Goldis was not available. Besides, Balderson was too far along in his 1992 draft preparation for Himes to fire, not just yet. Balderson ended up picking Pepperdine righthander Derek Wallace No. 1. Wallace had been severely injured in an auto accident while in college. He would hurt his arm while in the minors. Two and one-half years later, Wallace would finally provide value to the Cubs—as trade bait for center fielder Brian McRae. Balderson had no No. 2 pick in '92; it had been ceded to the Dodgers in compensation for signing Mike Morgan as a free agent. Brant Brown, the only member of the '92 draft class to ever make any tangible big-league contribution, was the No. 3 pick.

Balderson dutifully went ahead and signed Wallace. Then Himes lowered the boom, canning Balderson and Harford. Goldis had finally freed himself of his obligations to the Brewers. He was named the player development chief on September 18, 1992. In a pressbox conversation soon afterward, he told of his dream of a championship parade down Michigan Avenue, with the fruits of his scouting and player development system a major impetus for the future glory. His long decades of scouting seemed to be reaching a climax.

Based on his drafting feats with the White Sox, Goldis' arrival was hailed. He hired some of his trusted instructors, such as Rick Patterson and Joe Tanner. A group of scouts had moved with Goldis from team to team—Danny Monzon, Ed Ford, Preston Douglas, and Jesse Flores, among others.

Goldis promised to teach the nuances of offense to his minor leaguers, such as bunting, hitting behind the runner, proper baserunning and, above all, basestealing. Desiring "burglars" on the bases, he opened a "School of Thieves" during his first spring training in 1993.

"I want us to run the bases better than anybody," Goldis said then. "I want to be a daring club. I want people to come out to the ballpark, see the young kids and wonder, 'Is this guy gonna steal home, or will they pull off a double steal?' I don't want a blah kind of ballclub."

Goldis never graduated the class of thieves because of distractions. In addition to the eye tests installed earlier by Syd Thrift, the Cubs' minor leaguers now had elongated work days in spring training and before games during the season. The players were upset with extra work that went beyond the basic drills on fundamentals with which Jim Snyder had so much success a decade earlier under Dallas Green.

Goldis brought in some low-tech props to help in training. He believed that players standing atop rubber tires and 2-by-4 pieces of plywood could improve their balance in their batting stances. Minor-league equipment manager Michael Burkhart requisitioned some 25 old tires along with the wood for the program.

At one point Goldis even toyed with the idea of using soccer balls as part of his conditioning.

"What's a better way of teaching middle infielders how to use their feet? Have you ever seen a soccer player with bad feet?" Goldis theorized in 1994.

Pele's pride never appeared on a Cubs' field. But the tires and balance beams remained. In addition to batting and infield practice with the requisite fundamental workouts, the players now had to perform the additional balance drills. To many, Goldis was mandating quantity over quality.

"It got so a lot of them hated coming to the ballpark," recalled Cubs minor-league pitching coordinator Lester Strode, at the time a pitching coach in Goldis' system.

"In theory, the balance beam and tires could be very important things to do," said outfielder Robin Jennings. The left-handed hitter was a 1991 draftee who played in the system for eight seasons amid cameo appearances with the parent team, prior to leaving via free agency in the winter of 1999-2000.

"But when a minor-league player is trying to make the team and impress the staff, I don't think balancing yourself on a 2-by-4 piece of plywood is the way to do it.

"Spring training is supposed to get you in shape for the season, not wear you out. You'd start at 7:30 AM, go through all these drills, have lunch, play a game and then more drills after the game. I never saw the training room so filled the first few days of spring training."

The balance beams and tires were circulated throughout the farm system for use during the season.

"We'd be doing these drills in the heat at 2 PM in the heat in Florida before batting practice," Jennings said. "When it's 95 degrees and 100 percent humidity, you're doing all this early work and with all the minor-league travel, it takes away from your concentration. To have it mandatory to do these extra things was too much. It's not like you have plush clubhouses to take a break in after these drills."

"It got to be a little tiresome," said outfielder Brant Brown of the drills when he played at Class A Daytona and Class AA Orlando in 1993 and 1994. "I think it did affect the play, how guys recovered, their rest. Toward the end of the year, everyone was so spent."

With an engineering degree from the University of Pennsylvania, outfielder Doug Glanville said the Goldis system was "interesting, to say the least. They had so many different ideas and different gadgets to try to work on aspects of the game. I understand what they were getting at. They were going to the root, trying to say, 'Balance is important to a hitter, so let's come up with balance drills.' But the bottomline in the game is the game. There's certain fundamental things by playing that you have to develop. If you get too far away from it, you might lose that focus. His [Goldis'] philosophy is probably the most unique I've ever seen. It turned out it didn't work well with that organization."

Jennings, Glanville, and others don't fault Goldis for working hard. "Al was a very nice man; I just think he was a little gung-ho with his regimented spring training," Jennings said.

In response, Goldis, now a scout for the Cincinnati Reds, said the players weren't used to working hard.

"I know they were tired," he said. "We tried to build them up to where they were physically and mentally strong. They were never conditioned to playing an entire season. A lot of guys [in other organizations] worked harder than the Cubs guys. Do hockey players get tired? In the long run these guys built up their physical and mental endurance."

To this day, Goldis defends the concept of the balance drills. "People never thought of these things," he said. "Ernie Banks thought it was tremendous. He said if he had that stuff, he would have hit 600 homers."

While the players complained, Goldis and several key members of his minor-league staff were at loggerheads. The controversial Jimmy Piersall, who most of the players liked as the roving outfield instructor and a kind of senior baseball advisor, thought Goldis had "wild ideas." Piersall also said he fell asleep in meetings Goldis held for the coaching staff between 5:30 and 9 PM.

"He didn't get to the field until 12 noon, and we had been there since early morning," Piersall said. In response, Goldis said he was up to 2 AM handling paperwork.

"Piersall thought it was a lot of shit," he said. "He had his own philosophy. He had a contract. I couldn't hire all my people and we couldn't get rid of these contracts. You always had Piersall saying things behind the scenes. They were afraid of him. You had the obstacles of people who didn't believe in your philosophy."

Several prospects also didn't measure up to Goldis' standards of dedication. At the time, he questioned Glanville's aggressiveness. A slew of organizational types were down on the former 1991 No. 1 pick while he amassed only fair-to-middlin' seasons in Class A and Class AA.

Piersall, constantly working with Glanville on his center fielding, claimed Goldis said Glanville "didn't have any guts, that he'd quit. He had to fight his way through problems with managers Goldis hired. They were on him." Seven years later, Goldis said he "was one of the few guys who believed in him" and that he "spent a lot of time with him. I was from Columbia and he was from Penn. I tried to make a connection that way. I tried to talk positively to him. A lot of people were down on him."

Glanville won't say any bad things about Goldis to this day. But the fact remains that Glanville believes his career did not get into gear until Tom Gamboa, later the Cubs' third-base coach, instilled confidence in him as his manager in the Puerto Rican winter league in 1994-95, after Goldis had been shifted away from administering the minor leagues by new team president Andy MacPhail. In 1997, Glanville hit an even .300 for the Cubs before becoming a star-in-the-making in center for the Phillies.

While Goldis unsuccessfully tried to win the loyalty of holdover players and coaches, he and his scouts focused in on trying to change the Cubs' June draft fortunes. Goldis fell in love with University of Texas slugger/ pitcher Brooks Kieschnick. Scouts opinions were split on Kieschnick, a gifted hurler who had tremendous raw power, but few other tools. "Al's the only one who thought Kieschnick was a No. 1 pick," said one scout. Others believed Kieschnick was legitimately a No. 1 choice. Goldis went ahead and picked Kieschnick in the first round. In the meantime, a financially struggling team that could never match the Cubs dollar for dollar took a chance on a smallish lefthander out of Division III Ferrum (VA) College. After the Cubs passed on him in favor of Kieschnick, the Astros picked the flame-throwing Billy Wagner, acquiring one of the cores of their late 1990s contending pitching staff.

Goldis also selected shortstop Kevin Orie out of Indiana University as a "sandwich pick" in between the first and second rounds, along with college righthander Jon Ratliff. High school catcher Pat Cline was a sixth-round choice, while hulking righthander Steve Rain was chosen in the 11th round.

At least Goldis' 1993 picks enjoyed a sniff of the major leagues. After much hype, Orie enjoyed a slightly-above-average rookie season at third base for the Cubs in 1997 before fizzling out the next year and being traded to the Marlins. Kieschnick and Rain had brief Cubs appearances.

The 1994 draft was another story. Although Dan Evans, assistant general manager of the White Sox, said the '94 and '95 drafts were "thin," they were a starvation diet of talent for the Cubs. The utter lack of production of '94 is a major single reason the upper levels of the farm system of the late 1990s was strapped for players. The only '94 draftee to make the majors in a significant way was a near-afterthought—47th round pick Kyle Farnsworth, who was promoted prematurely to the Cubs' starting rotation in 1999. Pitcher Richard Barker, a 37th-round pick, had a five-game cup of coffee with '99 Cubs.

And, once again, the savvy Astros ended up with a productive pitcher while the Cubs ended up holding the bag.

In '94, the first 10 Cubs picks, starting with high school righthander Jayson Peterson of Denver, were pitchers. Overall, Goldis and his scouts picked 43 pitchers, compared to 14 outfielders, 12 infielders, and six catchers.

"A lot of these guys have legitimate arms," Goldis said a few months later in *Vine Line*. "So I'm really happy with that. If I had enough guts and a long-term contract, you know what I'd do? I'd do the same thing next year. Take the 10 best players, but really load up on the best pitchers. We'd have a dynasty with pitching for the next 10 years."

Goldis got the opposite of a dynasty. Instead, the 1994 draft laid the groundwork for the Cubs sinking to the bottom of rankings of minor-league systems a few years later, crippling the parent club's ability to replenish its roster with homegrown talent when a youth infusion was badly needed. None of the first 10 picks from 1994 ever threw a pitch for the Cubs. And the overemphasis on arms further shorted the farm system of position players, in the same manner as the 1990 injury-riddled draft.

The Cubs took Peterson with the No. 15 pick in the '94 draft. "This guy can be a No. 1-type on our staff," Goldis said then. Ten picks later, the Astros chose pitcher Scott Elarton, who had pitched against Peterson in Colorado youth leagues. The fortunes of the two clubs can probably be summed up by their '94 draft strategy.

Peterson was a hard-throwing righthander who Elarton said had as good an arm as he did. But Peterson didn't possess Elarton's character. Peterson had assorted personal problems that only got worse after he was drafted. Meanwhile, Elarton was valedictorian of his senior high school class in Lamar, Colorado. Both his parents were educators; his father was a local superintendent of schools.

Peterson suffered from arm problems and wildness in the minors. He also became a disciplinary problem. Within three years he had washed out of the Cubs' organization. After dominating in the middle minors, the 6-foot-7, 240-pound Elarton finished 1999 with a 9-5 record, a 3.48 ERA, and 121 strikeouts in 124 innings pitched in a season shortened by a stretched rotator cuff in his right shoulder.

How did the Cubs strike out on Elarton? And how did the Astros land their man *again*?

Peterson and Elarton tricked most talent evaluators. Peterson was rated the No. 11 pitcher in the draft, while Elarton was No. 16, by *Baseball America*. Elarton was perceived to be committed to a baseball scholarship to Stanford.

"Nobody believed Elarton would play minor-league baseball," Astros assistant general manager Tim Purpura said.

But one of the part-time Astros scouts in the area also was Elarton's summer-league coach. He knew the kid's real story.

"I told the scouts all along that my dream was to be a professional baseball player," Elarton said. "If the money was right, I would sign a professional contract.

"We liked Elarton, but he would have cost a tremendous amount of money," Goldis said. "We had a budget. We really couldn't take a chance on a guy we didn't know if we could sign."

The Florida Marlins were one team that shied away from Peterson. "Our scouting department had nothing good to say about Peterson," said Cubs player development chief Jim Hendry, who had worked for the Marlins in 1994. "Jeff Pentland [now Cubs hitting coach] was the area [Marlins] scout in charge of Colorado that year. At the conference call of scouts before the draft, he was very high on Elarton and not high on Peterson. Elarton was more of a signability problem."

Armed with the inside information, the Astros took a catcher, Ramon Castro, with their first pick in the first round. With other teams hesitating, they could afford to wait for Elarton to drop into the lap later in the first round. The Astros gave Elarton his desired bonus money plus a commitment to pay for college at a later date.

The difference between Peterson and Elarton apparently was between the ears.

"We had the same velocity, the same pitches," Elarton said. "The biggest thing is figuring out the mental makeup, what's inside the kid. I guess we've got some special people with the Astros."

There were no special Cubs draftees after Peterson. No. 2 pick Brian Stephenson was hurt most of his career, never moved beyond Class AA, and eventually was traded to the Dodgers to complete the deal for Eric Young and Ismael Valdes in the 1999-2000 off-season. Righthander Javier Martinez, a hard-throwing Puerto Rican, was a pitcher that subsequent management may have made a mistake on by letting him go in the Rule 5 draft to Pittsburgh in 1998. No. 4 pick Jason Kelley was hurt most of his pro career and was released in May 1999.

The tale of woe continued with No. 5 choice Barry Fennell, a lefthander. Another injury-prone hurler, Fennell was still pitching at Class A in 1999. No. 6 pick Neal Faulkner retired in September 1997 after a series of injuries. No. 7 pick Tim Spindler never signed with the Cubs. No. 8 pick Sean Bogle, who never got beyond Class A, was released in June, 1997. No. 9 pick Jason Ryan did pitch well in starting out the 1999 season, and brought some value when he was traded to the Twins for stopper Rick Aguilera. No. 10 pick Shawn Box was released in May 1997 after not rising above Class A.

Perhaps the draft process had some internal flaws. Under Goldis, a preponderance of draftees came from the coverage areas of favored scouts Ed Ford (New York and New Jersey) and Preston Douglas (southern Georgia and northern Florida). Neither area was considered a hotbed of amateur talent in the mid-1990s. In 1994, Fennell, Spindler, and Ryan were recommended by Ford, while Kelley's area scout was Douglas.

The effects of the '94 draft weren't really felt for three years. But the Cubs' overall mess was big enough for the men at the top of the Tower to put the dynamic Jim Dowdle in charge of the Cubs in mid-summer 1994. He added the corporate oversight of the troubled team to his duties supervising Tribune Co.'s broadcasting and publishing subsidiaries. Dowdle quietly began casting around for a new man, steeped in baseball experience and respected throughout the game, to run the Cubs.

The baseball strike began August 12, 1994. Dowdle zeroed in on Andy MacPhail, general manager of the Twins. In his office at Wrigley Field, Larry Himes must have known his time was quickly running out.

Even to this day, he will not criticize Stan Cook for tying his hands or not providing the proper support. He fell on his sword and served his masters to the end.

Himes, an expert in baseball X's and O's, but not its people, was about to take his place in the darker side of the history of the million-to-one era. Another big change was slated to take place. But the era would still not be in range of its conclusion.

Chapter 12

JIM, ANDY, AND ED

SEVERAL WEEKS before Thanksgiving 1999, the wreath displayed above the huge Michigan Avenue entranceway showed that Christmas had come early to Tribune Tower.

It always does, anyway, year-round, quarter after mega-profitable quarter.

Up 23 floors in the gothic-buttressed monolith are the executive offices of the media conglomerate, where good, gray executives count the profits of a company that began with Joe Medill's *Chicago Tribune* 150 years previously. To make double-digit quarterly profits and sate the stockholders during recessionary years was eminently possible; to double or triple that percentage of profits during boom times was now almost expected.

In this nerve center of the tower of maximum power for Chicago, the Tribune Co. bossmen traditionally counted the proceeds from newspapers, TV and radio stations, book publishing, Internet properties, and, more recently, a major-league baseball team and a national TV network. These were happy times except in one respect. The man in a corner office with a northwest view over Michigan Avenue wasn't happy over the artistic performance of the company baseball team in the forgettable season concluded a month previously.

I had never been above the fourth floor in my own *Tribune* copyboy days of the mid-1970s. So I half-expected rich mahogany paneling, humidors, and offices the size of airplane hangars all over the center of the tower of power. An old-line, country-clubbish atmosphere. I found none of the trappings of extreme privilege, nor a chimney for smoke to billow through the roof when decisions were reached.

Jim Dowdle's office was bright, airy, and decked out in modern décor. There was not a surfeit of space beyond his desk. He possessed a small table for conferences. This could have been a VP of advertising or marketing's office, not the inner sanctum of the No. 2 man at Tribune Co.

Less than two months from his retirement, with a successful heart-bypass operation looming, Dowdle set his ol' Notre Dame athlete's frame down in a chair by the table and blasted away a lot of Cubs fans' and media's myths about the tether that ran from the 23rd floor five miles north to Wrigley Field.

"When I hired Andy [MacPhail], we sat in the Minneapolis hotel for seven hours," Dowdle said. "I just told him that I really wanted to cut the cord between the Tower and Wrigley Field. Anytime you want to sit down and talk, I'm 15 minutes away.

"To me there was too strong a connection between the Tower and Wrigley Field.

"They needed an active president who really understood the game. My role was to basically ask questions, to have the president ask me questions. The two of us would set the payroll."

Astounding. From the day Dallas Green was fired in 1987 until the day Dowdle quietly took over corporate oversight of the Cubs nearly seven years later, the Cubs' fate was squarely in the hands of executives who knew everything about good business but little about the emotional ebb and flow of sports. And it became ingrained in Chicago's consciousness, echoed by baseball people who had come into close contact with the Tower power-brokers: Tribune Co. just wanted to make money, and if the Cubs won, that would be all right, too.

But here comes Dowdle granting virtual ownership powers to third-generation baseball man MacPhail. The Cubs president would have such stature as to be able to set a payroll low, middle or high, make a case with one man instead of layers of suits, and usually get his way. A quiet revolution had taken place, buried amid the acrimony of the devastating players strike of 1994-95.

Jim Dowdle's severing of the puppet-strings ties of the Cubs to the corporate parent did not succeed in lifting the team out of the million-to-one era as he retired from his job on December 31, 1999. The Cubs had been sidetracked so badly, the player development system degenerating into one of the game's worst by the middle 1990s that, like an economy sunk into a depression, the recovery process was slow and not linear. Progress one year did not extend into the next, and severe setbacks would seemingly start the process all over again in 1998 and 2000.

Part of the agonizingly slow comeback was by design—MacPhail's. He could set any tempo he chose, having been granted more power and latitude than anyone running the team since Phil Wrigley himself to affect the Cubs' fate.

In choosing MacPhail, Dowdle picked a man who was afforded almost universal respect throughout the game, through both his own efforts and his lineage. MacPhail was the grandson of the mercurial Larry MacPhail, first promoter of night baseball and New York baseball radio broadcasting. He was the son of Lee MacPhail, as dignified as Larry MacPhail was mercurial in his personal behavior, a top executive of successful Yankees and Orioles franchises before ascending to the American League presidency.

Only 41 when appointed Cubs president, Andy MacPhail was a self-proclaimed throwback to old-fashioned baseball values. Thoughtful, low-key and never egocentric like a slew of high-profile baseball moguls in other cities, he would not seek the quickest fix to end the million-to-one era. He would not raise the bar of hyper-inflated salaries on his watch and apply a baseball version of Keynesian economics to the Cubs.

Raised on the East Coast and with just one previous five-year stint in the Cubs' front office to expose him to a little of the hubris of the pennantless decades, MacPhail did not possess the native Chicagoan's emotional sense of urgency to reach the World Series ASAP, damn the torpedoes. The deliberate approach was his style upon taking office, amid snickers from fans and media who watched as lesser-light players were signed in an attempt to control the payroll.

"I have to be careful not to put myself in a position where I feel that pressure and do things not in the best interests of the organization," MacPhail said in the winter of 1994-95. "Give our current set of circumstances, we have to lean toward the slow, steady and unspectacular [method of improvement]. We are not predisposed toward making the big splash. We have to be careful not to try to hit the six-run homer in the first inning."

MacPhail's hand-picked general manager, Ed Lynch, echoed the same sentiments in analyzing the Cubs' cycle of losing.

"A new general manager would come in, feel the pressure to win now, took whatever prospects he had at the upper [minor-league] levels, tried to move them for players to win right away, and those players you bring in don't work out," he said. "You lose the players you bring in, and the prospects you traded. The cycle starts all over again. We wanted to have patience with some of our young players—patience enough to understand it was foolhardy to go out and try to win everything when you're not even in a position to compete."

Five years later, MacPhail echoed his earlier statements.

"The past is the past," he said. "I can only take responsibility for the past five years. While I intellectually understand the hubris that went along with the franchise, until you live it and become sort of a focal point for it, you really can't appreciate what it is. It can create problems where you're so anxious to do something through the next season that it comes at a long-term cost."

That stance, looking at the Cubs' problems cerebrally as an outsider who never experienced the woe of the 1969 collapse and other tales of woe would not sit well with fans looking for the end of the million-to-one era. Whoever runs the Cubs, it seems, has been detached from that experience, dampening down the emotional reflex to build a winner ASAP.

"The real shortcoming in this organization is that nobody's from Chicago," said Bruce Miles, Cubs beat writer for the northwest suburban-based *Daily Herald*. Miles grew up on the South Side as a Chicago baseball fan; his late mother, Bette, was upset the day the Cubs traded Lou Brock in 1964. Bette Miles accurately saw Brock as an up-and-coming star.

"They fail to understand there's an urgency here of Cubs not winning a World Series since 1908 or be in it since 1945," Miles continued. "It's kind of a passionless organization. They lack the passion of people who grew up as dyed-in-the-wool Cubs fans. Their attitude is all of that happened before we got here."

MacPhail's cautious approach to rebuilding led so many outsiders to accuse him of being "Tribune-ized," of simply allowing more of the same corporate bottomline approach to running the Cubs. True to his personal style, MacPhail would not adamantly refute the mistargeted criticism nor campaign for his program through the media.

His five years would be marked by some adept trades concocted by Ed Lynch, who resigned on July 19, 2000 amid another Cubs collapse, with MacPhail himself taking over as general manager at least through the end of the 2001 season. But the good deals would be counterbalanced in many instances by overevaluation of talent—particularly the 1995 starting rotation and the veteran makeup of the ill-fated 1999 team—along with an aversion to big-ticket free agents. Second-tier free agents usually were signed, the end result often being good money being thrown after bad. All the while, MacPhail and Lynch were hampered by the lack of production from the battered farm system, forcing them to continually go outside the organization for talent. And that was a case of "let the buyer beware."

MacPhail had been hired by Dowdle on the basis of his work as Twins general manager, overseeing two World Series winners in the Metrodome in 1987 and 1991. He had been aggressive via free agency and trades with monies puny compared to even the worst Tribune-mandated budget in building around a homegrown nucleus groomed by Twins farm director George Brophy under the old Calvin Griffith ownership. MacPhail inherited the core of Kirby Puckett, Kent Hrbek, Gary Gaetti, Tom Brunansky, Greg Gagne, and Frank Viola—a collection of talent that would have been hyped to the heavens had they come up as Cubs. He then added the likes of Jeff Reardon, Don Baylor, Kevin Tapani, Rick Aguilera, Jack Morris, and Chili Davis at various junctures to round out the winning formula.

But was MacPhail, who loved the promotion to the presidency of a big-market club, actually more suited to be the general manager—in name—of the Cubs on the basis of his dealmaking skills and with a better budget at his fingertips? MacPhail consults with Lynch when the latter comes up with a trade or free-agent signing. But some wonder if MacPhail's real effectiveness wasn't in aggressive player moves. He might have been more qualified to be the GM in name, rather than in inference. Meanwhile, Lynch, who had just four years of front-office experience coming into his Cubs' job, would have been perhaps his vice president of player personnel, training for a GM's job.

"There's a layer [of management] between him and every personnel decision," said Dan Barreiro, sports columnist for the *Minneapolis Star Tribune*, who covered MacPhail's Twin Cities tenure. "Andy's not in a hands-on role as in Minnesota. He's not necessarily making every decision himself. The puzzling part for me is if I'm Tribune Co., I'd have wanted him to run it [as GM].

"MacPhail is a guy who likes being in baseball business. But he doesn't want to be in the trenches. He's done the in-trenches thing. He is reflexively conservative. He doesn't really care for throwing money at problems."

"He did a very good job with resources here. He'd make moves. There was a black hole at second base for the Twins. He traded Tom Brunansky for Tommy Herr. It was a disaster, but at least he tried."

"A Backslapper and Dealmaker"

Whether MacPhail and Lynch were hired to positions one level above their best effectiveness in 1994 is somewhat moot now. What matters is that Jim Dowdle took action in a better-late-than-never stance to restore autonomy to the Cubs' front office. MacPhail had been on the 23rd floor of Tribune Tower only "two or three times" in five years, Dowdle said. Much more commonly, Dowdle journeyed to the ballpark for financial and other business meetings. He never turned down a MacPhail team budget.

Establishing a team president who had power and believed in staff stability ended years of upheaval as both the Cubs' corporate overseer and general manager turned over on an every-three-years schedule, barely ahead of the merry-go-round of managers on the field. No baseball team can survive such constant changes at the top. There is hope, again taking its front-row-and-center position at Wrigley Field, that this kind of management structure will continue under Dowdle successor Dennis FitzSimons.

"This is the biggest reason why I went out and hired a president," Dowdle said. "I felt continuity was needed. When we hired Jim Riggleman, I told him I hope you were the only manager I see in my regime. He was.

"I had the advantage of looking back at the first 12 years of Tribune [ownership], learning from both positive and negative experiences. Were some mistakes made? You'd better believe it."

The Cubs' history might have turned out for the better had Dowdle been in charge during the late 1980s and early 1990s. He knew how to aggressively grow a business. And, as a former Notre Dame athlete, he was the most sports-minded executive under the corporate umbrella, but was one notch too far down the chain of command to have had the Cubs under his wing until 1994. He possessed uncommon candor for a Tribune Co. top executive, but also had a corresponding uncommon background that brought him in touch with people as much as spread sheets. And that experience was crucial in dealing with the baseball side of the Cubs.

A native Chicago South Sider, Dowdle's background had been in sales and TV station management as he moved around the country, from Chicago to Oklahoma City to Minneapolis-St. Paul to Tampa. Finally he came aboard in 1981 as head of Tribune Broadcasting, then basically a Chicago company that owned a few stations scattered around the country.

His first major move was his best—hiring Harry Caray away from the White Sox. Dowdle and Dallas Green had cautioned Caray to tone down his act working for the more conservative Tribune Co., compared to the guerrilla theater of the air Caray and sidekick Jimmy Piersall staged under Bill Veeck's White Sox ownership.

Dowdle then concentrated on empire-building. Tribune Co. paid $500 million for KTLA-TV in Los Angeles in 1985, then gravitated toward program production and syndication through the new Tribune Entertainment division. By the late 1990s, Tribune Co. was a 25 percent owner of the youth-oriented WB Network. Dowdle was now in charge of all Tribune media operations, including newspapers, along with overseeing the Cubs.

"He's a backslapper and a dealmaker," said one prominent Chicago-based media observer. Working a room during a Cubs' press conference or related event, Dowdle was the archetype who could talk to anyone. Unlike his gray-suited cohorts who were comfortable crunching numbers, Dowdle gave off the image of a fella you could hoist a few with. He seemed even more the voluable, outgoing baseball man than MacPhail.

He even got along with Dallas Green, although several rows in which the two large, opinionated men engaged would have been worth box-seat ticket prices.

"Dowdle was very supportive of what we were doing," Green remembered. "But he was never in decision-making roles for baseball."

Dowdle's corporate oversight even gave confidence to the one Cub who had lived through the myriad of front-office and managerial changes.

"It's unfortunate he was retiring," said first baseman Mark Grace, who was in his 15th year in the Cubs' organization in 2000. "He's an ex-athlete, straightforward, honest and a good man. He's a sports fan. He wanted the Cubs to win. He wanted to make money. By the same token, Jim Dowdle wanted to make money with the Cubs being good. He was the first guy since I've been here who thought that we'll make money by winning. The purse strings are a lot more open than they were five years ago when Jim Dowdle took over. The Cubs will miss him."

How far those purse strings draw open is up to MacPhail. From Day One of his team presidency, he insisted he and his corporate bosses wanted to win—and took responsibility for the end results.

"That doesn't make any sense," he said in 1994-95 about the stereotype that Tribune Co. didn't want to win. "If you want to think about it for five minutes, you know that can't be true. They [Tribune Co.] have more at stake than does the customary owner. They have more ways to profit that Carl [Pohlad, Minnesota Twins owner] ever did. That kind of criticism falls flat on its face.

"If we don't do well, it will be *our* fault, not anyone else's. If we don't do well, it won't be because we were denied resources."

So then, armed with bottomline authority from Dowdle, it became MacPhail's call not to tap Mother Tribune to give the Cubs a huge shot in the arm as teams tried to financially recover from the 1994-95 strike. He would not try to win immediately with free agents, resulting in what he projected were even higher annual losses during the strike-recovery period. At the same time, he chose not to unload his veterans, strip the team down, start over again, and build a contender back up in the successful manner of the Atlanta Braves, Cleveland Indians, and Houston Astros. Charting the resulting kind of twilight-zone middle course would be enough to keep the fans interested and the turnstiles clicking, but it would not result in improvement at the big-league level. It seemed like a way of biding time until that projected early 21st century day when improvements in scouting and player development would deliver more homegrown players to Wrigley Field.

"One of the major jobs that confronted was rehabilitating it [financially] through the strike period," MacPhail said. "One hand is trying to patch up here [at the major-league level], this one here is trying to develop and progress your [minor-league] talent. There are clubs that still haven't recovered from the strike. Look at Cincinnati and Oakland in 1999. Both came close to the post-season, but that wasn't mirrored in their performance at the gate. Cincinnati had been a great baseball town, but they did not get the bang they expected. Oakland had drawn in the past, but had scuffled more recently.

"The choice we took was to try to keep the product on the major-league field reasonably entertaining while we did what we had to do that is not visible to the general public [improving scouting and player development]. I think tearing it down and going young would have been two broadsides to the ship. I'm not sure how many broadsides the ship could stand.

"I just didn't want to give up a major-league season. I didn't want to say, 'We're going to retool and have an arbitrarily low payroll; just go with kids, build from the ground up and see what happens in four or five years.' I just didn't feel like after the strike and with this particular club's history, we could do that."

Former Cubs GM Larry Himes said he had wanted to strip the Cubs down and start fresh, but was prevented from pursuing that tact by Tribune Co. because of perceived negative effects on WGN-TV ratings and ad revenue. Told of that statement, Jim Dowdle replied, "I don't know what Larry is talking about." But if MacPhail had come to him with a strip-down idea, Dowdle said he might have signed off on it despite the obvious problems with other Tribune Co. subsidiaries.

MacPhail may have underestimated Cubs fans. They'd been waiting a long time anyway. If an executive of his reputation and record had come to them and told the fans that a total rebuilding was the only sure way to build a winner, that the idea had worked countless times in baseball, they might have been willing to follow MacPhail to hell and back.

"Andy rode into Chicago on a shining horse," said Bruce Miles. "In hindsight, not stripping it down in '95 was a bad move. He has been patching every year since. He had license to do it. He could have said, 'This is a mess. It will take a few years.' It was a terrible mistake. I disagree with Andy's view. He could have done it because of all this positive publicity he came into town with. If they gave the city's baseball fans credit, they could have sold it better."

The Low-Profile Approach

Indeed. Despite his eloquent, articulate personality, MacPhail has studiously avoided campaigning about his plans in the Chicago sports media. He prefers to stay in the background while Lynch acts as management spokesman. Forty-two-year Cubs fan Al Fujara, a disabled Chicago police officer, calls MacPhail "The Ghost" for his low-key, background-craving persona. In a kind of throwback to Phil Wrigley, MacPhail is accessible to the regular beat writers covering the Cubs, but usually avoids broadcast interviews, particularly on sports-talk radio. He rarely comes down to the dugout or clubhouse at Wrigley Field to schmooze the media before games. But he's more accessible when he makes road trips, typically covered only by the three regular traveling beat writers for the *Chicago Tribune*, *Chicago Sun-Times,* and *Daily Herald*.

MacPhail, in fact, likes the trendy nature of giant media-market Chicago, in which the hot team of the time garners the emphasis of coverage of both print and broadcast outlets, and where the NFL's Bears will always eat up gobs of airtime and column inches no matter what the team record. In an interview with Dan Barreiro of the *Minneapolis Star-Tribune* in the fall of 1999, MacPhail said he rather liked being nearly invisible in Chicago, where a lot of attention was drained away from the Cubs during the Bulls' championship runs. In contrast, in Minneapolis-St. Paul, MacPhail said he could hardly go anywhere without being approached to talk about the Twins.

But the Twins don't have the history or special relationship with their fans of the Cubs. The fans would feel more confident if the man with the power of the purse told them where the franchise is going. In a sports-media column in the *Chicago Sun-Times* in 1997, Jim O'Donnell said the time was right for MacPhail to directly address Cubs fans. The plea went unheeded.

"If I felt that I could get my message adequately and accurately through the media, I would do it more consistently," MacPhail said. "I don't go out on a campaign with it, because I don't have any confidence that the message, from my perspective, would be adequately carried through.

"You're not going to be favorably perceived if you're in a management or owner's role by the media in this town. There is a kind of focus here where I can watch a team [the Bulls] win six championships in this town 'despite the ownership,' which delivered every player except one.

"Going out and trying to make your case in the media is not likely to come out with a good end result. I'm just somewhat skeptical that I'd get a great shake here. I've never withheld my opinion [when asked]. I just don't go out and try to campaign and articulate the case. Sports-talk radio is not [real] sports. That's just Jerry Springer with a sports motif. Their ratings are not keeping people from going to Wrigley Field. You've got no chance. Why would you bother?"

MacPhail also chose not to toot his own horn on the improvements in scouting and player development that began on his watch—namely, the hiring of Pacific Rim scout Leon Lee and hitting coaches for each minor-league team, and the opening of training facilities and expansion of scouting in the Dominican Republic and Venezuela.

"It's in my best interests that they [other big-league teams] don't know where we're making inroads," he said.

MacPhail wasn't going to campaign—and he was willing to take criticism for his modus operandi.

"To act unfettered and get the job done, sometimes you just have to walk through a little flak," he said. "That's just the nature of the game."

But the vacuum in information and perspective from the top allowed decades of misconceptions and stereotypes to continue to be perpetrated by a Chicago sports media that often only superficially examines the state of the Cubs. A top honcho doing the Harry Truman plain-speaking routine was needed to make up for holes in media coverage of the Cubs that existed in 1995 and continue unfilled today.

Beat writers for the five Chicago-area newspapers—the *Chicago Tribune, Chicago Sun-Times, Daily Herald, Daily Southtown,* and *The Times of Northwest Indiana*—who are present at all Cubs home games are as competitive as anyone in the country in covering the behind-the-scenes, inside story of the team. That means working the Cubs' clubhouse, dugout, and batting cage before the game, and talking to scouts and other baseball people as they come through town.

But the city's corps of newspaper sports columnists and broadcast personalities often come up short. Baseball is not the favored sport among a large chunk of sports-media types, both reporters and supervisors. With the exceptions of the *Tribune's Skip* Bayless and the *Sun-Times'* Jay Mariotti, the columnists work Wrigley Field only on a scattershot basis, as baseball season is used to burn off vacation time, and for coverage of golf tournaments and NFL training camp. Once September hits, however, the columnists very rarely miss a Bears' game or another NFL assignment on Sundays.

Less than a handful of radio reporters, most notably Bruce Levine of WMVP-Radio (AM 1000) and David Kaplan of WGN-Radio (AM 720), regularly work the pre-game clubhouse and talk to the top executives. Les Grobstein, overnight talker on WSCR-Radio (AM 1160), rolls out of bed in time to attend the majority of home games. Cubs players have long complained they take brickbats from radio sports-talk show hosts who rarely show their face at the ballpark. The hosts, most of whom are football- or basketball-oriented, don't typically offer the fans a perspective on the Cubs they can't already get from other media. The gabbers are often under a management edict to provide "entertainment" on their shows, giving legitimacy to MacPhail's Jerry Springer analogy. And without a conduit to the locker room and front office, they'll sometimes air inaccurate information about players, managerial strategy, and executive decisions.

Meanwhile, TV stations usually make just cameo appearances at Wrigley Field. Camera crews, often accompanied by producers—not reporters or anchors—holding the microphones, typically show up just to get post-game locker-room sound bites.

While the first-string media gang-tackle Bears games and radio and TV stations offer all-day coverage on NFL Sundays, broadcast outlets sometimes do not staff weekend Cubs games even with update announcers. Those that are dispatched are often inexperienced or out of their league. One young producer for WFLD-TV (Channel 32) called Cubs outfielder Doug Glanville "Lance Johnson" after one 1997 game. Another young radio intern-type called Cubs manager Jim Riggleman "coach" after another game in 1996. "Well, coach, who's going to start at running back next week?" I asked Riggleman when the kid departed.

As fans received more of their news from the broadcast media or the Internet, the conduits for in-depth Cubs coverage and analysis were lessened. With MacPhail circumspect about his total verbiage for public consumption, that meant a continuation of decades-long misunderstandings about the Cubs as "lovable losers" and "cheap Tribune Co." as MacPhail and Lynch established their roster of their first Cubs team in 1995.

Lynch batted .667 in the hastily-arranged strike-delayed spring training of '95. He traded oft-injured former No. 1 draft pick Derek Wallace and another minor leaguer to the Kansas City Royals for switch-hitting center fielder Brian McRae, plugging up one gaping lineup hole. Then he snapped up bargain-basement pitcher Jaime Navarro, let go by his original team, the Milwaukee Brewers. Yet as he and MacPhail rode herd on the payroll with strike-induced losses looming, outfielder Glenallen Hill was released rather than being tendered a $1 million deal. A terrific team player who loved playing for the Cubs, Hill couldn't understand his dumping. His loss hurt, but Lynch made up for his penny-wise, pound-foolish mistake by re-acquiring Hill in mid-1998. He was still a Cub going into 2000.

The brass attempted to go with rookies Ozzie Timmons, who showed power potential in the minors, and Scott Bullett in left field in place of Hill as the truncated 1995 season got underway. The Cubs got off to a 20-11 start, but left field and third base in the form of an end-of-the-line Steve Buechele, were offensively impotent positions as June got underway and the first big Cubs' slump knocked the team back in the pack.

Rookie GM Lynch continued on his roll, dealing extra starter Mike Morgan to the Cardinals for third baseman Todd Zeile. That was the first Chicago-St. Louis trade since Bruce Sutter-for-Leon Durham and Ken

Reitz in 1980. Days later, Lynch traded slumping catcher Rick Wilkins for left fielder Luis Gonzalez and catcher Scott Servais. In the process, Lynch probably sacrificed any momentum for the now-benched Timmons, who had just started to hit for power in the week before the deal.

One rumored trade Lynch did not make was Sammy Sosa to the Baltimore Orioles for young reliever Armando Benitez and outfielder Alex Ochoa. Sosa was upset by the talk, peaking around the 1995 All-Star break. Former Cubs player-development maven Gordon Goldsberry was by now working as a special assignment scout for Orioles GM Roland Hemond. I called Goldsberry to check out the report. Goldsberry, one of the game's most honest men, said Sosa's connection to the Orioles was only on a list of "impact" big leaguers Hemond had asked Goldsberry to compile. Sosa was not leaving Chicago. I took the slugger aside in the Wrigley Field dugout to re-assure him he was staying put.

Starting with McRae, the deals proved Lynch's ability to swing deals without years of experience—and without a real stock of minor-league prospects to entice trading partners.

Membership in an old-boys' GM club wasn't necessary, Lynch said, the image of the cigar-chomping, back-slapping, wheeling-and-dealing GM having been "overrated."

"It's a stereotype," he said. "Sure, a lot of it is relationships away from the office. Relationships are obviously strong among certain general managers.

"But when it comes to trades, all bets are off. Believe me, you're not there playing poker and bluffing with no hand. Your negotiating style is something that can help you or hurt you, obviously. The bottomline is if you're in the market to acquire a certain player, and they want a certain type of player you don't have to offer, there's nothing you're going to say or do or bluff or be aggressive enough to take something they don't want. Other people are a lot smarter than you think."

There is little verbal dancing around when a trade is discussed.

Lynch said after a bit of "pleasantries" and "small talk," he tries to get to the point quickly. "You say, 'Hey, I'm trying to add bullpen help or left-handed hitting help in the outfield. Would you talk about player X on your team?'"

Once again, MacPhail's actual role was blurred in a slew of stereotypes and the team's president's lack of high-profile posturing. Too many media types believed MacPhail was the real general manager with Lynch doing the scutwork. When assistant general manager David Wilder left to become VP of player personnel for the Milwaukee Brewers after 1999, one media cynic cracked, "He didn't want to be the assistant to the assistant any more."

But when pressed on the issue, MacPhail said he does not talk to general managers about trades.

"That's Ed's job," he said. "I don't go to the winter meetings. Ed's job is major-league player personnel. That's his baliwick. I've been a GM for nine years. His responsibility is different than mine. I'm not the guy working the phones or making the trades. His job is to be able to explain to me and articulate why it makes sense. He is good at articulating why.

"There have been trades Ed made that I haven't been ecstatic about. He had to convince me why the [Jon] Lieber deal was a good deal. Once he does that, I say do what you have to do. My job is to ask questions, like can you get a better deal elsewhere? The only reason you nix something is if you know something he doesn't know about a player or if the due diligence hasn't been done. These are the only reasons. It's never been an issue."

MacPhail agreed with Lynch that GM-to-GM relationships aren't the crucial factor in sealing a deal.

"Clubs are like foreign countries. They do what they perceive to be in their best interests regardless of relationships. They would deal with the devil himself if they believed they could get a starting pitcher out of it."

There would be times in later years when Lynch's lack of dealmaking would cause controversy. In turn, Lynch criticized his critics. But in the immediate post-strike aftermath, he was one of the more proactive GM's. And the effect of his deals would have been greater had usually productive hitter Zeile not hurt his hand, affecting his swing and crimping his long-ball production. Gonzalez and Servais had come through with good seasons after arriving in Chicago.

A rollercoaster season of slumps and surges ended with the Cubs flirting with the wild-card playoff berth in the final week of 1995 due to an eight-game winning streak. The team fell short, but the 73-71 finish (the Cubs lost the final two games) seemed to put a glittering fringe on the start of the MacPhail-Lynch regime.

Wasted Opportunities in '96?
Yet MacPhail cut the payroll rather than increasing the budget in an

attempt vault the Cubs into serious contention for 1996. He told *Chicago Magazine* that the team lost $14 million. The '95 payroll of nearly $36.8 million would drop to $32.6 million the following season. The belt-tightening and misjudgments on talent in the off-season would hurt the Cubs even up to the present time.

After a decade as the Cubs' shortstop, Shawon Dunston was allowed to leave as a free agent rather than be paid $10 million over the next three years. Dunston had been the Cubs' best clutch hitter in '95 with a .296 average, 14 homers, and 69 RBI. MacPhail and Lynch also bid good-bye to stopper Randy Myers, unwilling to cough up a multi-year, megabucks deal to a reliever they believed showed significant slippage in his performance in the second half of '95. And they declined to re-sign Zeile, despite the need for another productive bat in the lineup. Zeile was perceived as weak defensively at third base.

The players the Cubs did not pursue in the winter of 1995-96 would come back to haunt them.

With his first free-agency rights staring him in the face, sparkplug second baseman Craig Biggio of the Houston Astros said late in the '95 season that he loved Wrigley Field and wouldn't mind playing in Chicago. In a bidding war, the resource-laden Cubs could not fail to beat out Texas entrepreneur Drayton McLane, the Astros owner who always has had to watch his pennies. Biggio wasn't keen on leaving Houston, his original organization, but money and the prospect of employment in the Friendly Confines would have talked. The Cubs passed on Biggio, apparently picking up signals that Ryne Sandberg—who had remarried the previous summer—was itching to return to baseball. But Biggio was entering his career prime, while Sandberg was on the back nine of his baseball lifetime.

MacPhail and Lynch also chose to stand pat with their starting rotation of Jaime Navarro, Frank Castillo, Kevin Foster, Steve Trachsel, and Jim Bullinger. This was the first in a series of over-evaluations of talent, combined with an eye toward payroll control. Of the quintet, only Navarro had an above-average year at 14-6. Castillo pitched well much of the time, but the changeup pitcher could not afford to be off-kilter with his control at any time. Foster had trouble keeping the ball in the park, Trachsel had an off-season, and Bullinger, who some in management believed was a big overachiever, had finished 12-8 after starting out '95 at 10-2. Clearly, there was room for a bona-fide No. 1 pitcher to come aboard to improve the rotation while creating trade bait with one of the returning '95 starters being deemed surplus.

A perfect pitcher for Wrigley Field was probably available in the $4 million range. He threw the hardest sinker in the game. MacPhail would have had to stretch his careful budget to land him, but he would have been worth it for the rest of the 1990s. His name was Kevin Brown.

A 21-game winner with the Texas Rangers in 1992, Brown had a disappointing 10-9 season in his one year as a Baltimore Oriole in 1995. On December 2 of that year, Brown signed with the then-undistinguished Florida Marlins as a free agent. "But I wasn't locked into going to Florida," Brown said years later, adding that he would have seriously considered pitching in Wrigley Field. MacPhail also later realized the missed opportunity. On September 29, 1996, the final day of a season that had ended in a whimper at Wrigley Field, MacPhail admitted that "in retrospect," the Cubs should have pursued Brown, who was 17-11 with a 1.89 ERA for the Marlins.

The Cubs did sign away an Orioles' pitcher, all right—slowballing Doug Jones. Virtually throwing a changeup off his changeup, Jones was tabbed as Randy Myers' replacement. MacPhail and Lynch also inked slap-hitting free-agent third baseman Dave Magadan. The moves were regarded as thoroughly unappetizing, almost sleep-inducing, and could not have improved the Cubs at all. They didn't. Jones was a flop, allowing 41 hits in 32 1/3 innings before being released. Oddly enough, the reliever then revived for the better part of two years with the Milwaukee Brewers. Magadan was hurt and hit just .254 while Orioles reject Leo Gomez took over at third. Sandberg had a decent comeback season with 25 homers, but overall the Cubs lacked game-breaking power beyond Sammy Sosa. Predictably, the seasons of three of the five holdover '95 starters—Castillo, Foster, and Bullinger—crashed.

The pedestrian off-season moves did not sit well with the mainstay Cubs players. The team lurched along around the .500 mark much of the summer, but still were within hailing distance of the first-place St. Louis Cardinals. MacPhail and Lynch made no deals as the July 31 trade deadline approached. Brian McRae began wondering aloud about the lack of action. Mark Grace also expressed dissent from the company line. Even Jim Riggleman privately wondered what was going on. When the manager chimed in with his puzzlement behind closed doors, I couldn't wait any longer, finally calling MacPhail and Lynch for their take on the situation. Admitted almost immediately after contacting executive assistant Arlene Gill, I found Lynch in MacPhail's office talking over personnel moves. I informed them of the clubhouse verbal cauldron. They were unaware of the mounting dissent on their club. Their response was something like, "We're upset that they're upset."

One player who didn't dissent publicly was Sammy Sosa, whose lineup "protection" was 15-home-run producer Luis Gonzalez. Privately, he was mildly frustrated by the lack of power up and down the lineup. "I need some help. I can't do it all by myself," he told me.

Later in August, Lynch tried to swing a waiver deal. He offered young reliever Terry Adams and minor-league pitcher Steve Rain to the Pittsburgh Pirates for lefty hurler Denny Neagle. Although the Pirates liked the hard-throwing Adams, they liked young Atlanta Braves starter Jason Schmidt even better. The Braves simply had more and better young players to offer the Buccos, surrendering youngsters Corey Pointer and Ron Wright, with Schmidt the player to be named later in the deal completed August 28, 1996. Later that day, Riggleman said the Cubs were prepared to pay a heavy price for Neagle, but refused to identify the players in question. Several months later, Adams was privately confirmed as the main commodity the Cubs offered.

"We were competitive in '96 until September," MacPhail recalled. But in reality, the Cubs merely lingered on the fringes of contention until St. Louis pulled away at the end. Sammy Sosa broke his hand and was lost for the season on August 20, his 40 homers on a 52-homer season pace at that point. Somehow, the Cubs did not collapse for another three weeks. They had a 74-72 record before an old-fashioned September nosedive— 14 losses in their final 16 games—made yet another season look worse than it should have.

In an attempt to plug up some obvious holes, MacPhail and Lynch signed free-agent pitchers Kevin Tapani and Mel Rojas in the winter of 1996-97. Clearly, another offensive threat to protect Sosa in the lineup was needed. The Cubs did make inquiries into the medical condition of the Braves' David Justice, a productive slugger who had missed most of the '96 season due to shoulder surgery. Justice asked Brian McRae at a California golf tournament in January 1997 if a deal to the Cubs was possible. But no trade ever took place. Justice ended up being dealt to the Cleveland Indians on March 25, 1997, basically in exchange for center fielder Kenny Lofton. Justice went on to slug 33 homers, drive in 101 runs, and bat .329 for the World Series-bound Indians.

The payroll would drop further to $30.7 million, ranked 23rd in baseball. The Cubs opted to throw left field wide open to a plethora of outfield prospects—former No. 1 pick Brooks Kieschnick, Robin Jennings, Doug Glanville, Ozzie Timmons, Pedro Valdes, and Brant Brown. With Mark Grace perennially blocking his way at first base, Brown made a nervous conversion to left in spring training 1997. He expressed trepidation about switching to the outfield. Almost all the candidates hit well in Arizona, and Brown was named the Opening Day left fielder.

Meanwhile, another rookie, Kevin Orie, was slotted in at third amid much hype. The never-ending quest to find a new Ron Santo settled on the back of the tall, quiet Pennyslvanian. Most raved about his gap hitting ability and future power potential. Orie had hit .314 in 82 Double-A games in 1996, a basis for much of the hype. But in the eagerness to annoint a new Santo and promote any kind of prospect with ability from the moribund farm system, almost everyone failed to notice Orie's track record of wrist and shoulder injuries in the minors, and the fact the Double-A stint was his only productive stretch in the farm system.

The combination of the rookies, a seeming emotional hangover from the end of 1996, and actual foreboding about playing the first 12 games against the powerful Braves and Marlins led to one of the greatest embarrassments in Cubs history. The team underwhelmed all its previous ignominy by losing a National League-record 14 games from the start of the season. Of course, that streak set an all-time Cubs record for losses in a row. The 1997 campaign was over practically before it started. One struggling young left fielder yielded to another, while Sandberg finally showed his age at second base. Tapani was lost for the first half due to right index-finger surgery. McRae slumped badly, while Sosa's production was down from 1996. Worst of all was Mel Rojas' utter failure to handle the stopper's role and the expectations of his big contract. Rojas was nearly booed out of Wrigley Field when he gave up 11 homers, several of them game-busters, while going 0-4 with just 13 saves in 54 games.

Lynch did not wait until after the season to try to change the losing mix. On August 8, 1997 he pulled off a waiver deal with the Mets, dumping off Rojas and McRae—by now perceived as a malcontent by management—and receiving center fielder Lance Johnson and starting pitcher Mark Clark in return.

But the Cubs fans let Lynch and MacPhail know their work was far from done. On September 20, 1997, during ceremonies marking "Ryne Sandberg Day" at Wrigley Field, many of the 38,313 assembled booed when MacPhail, making a rare on-field ceremonial appearance, came to the mike. MacPhail told the crowd he deserved the catcalls.

Looking back at the 1997 disaster that ended with a 68-94 record, MacPhail said the ensuing personnel moves of the following winter were logical. "We made a judgment in the off-season that while we didn't play well, with a few patches we'd be competitive," he said. But another emotion was no doubt felt behind closed doors and in meetings with Jim Dowdle—embarrassment. The pressbox consensus of early 1998 was that the honchos were shamed into dramatically increasing the payroll for that season, to more than $51 million, ranking 11th in baseball.

Also, by 1998, MacPhail apparently deemed that the Cubs had sufficiently recovered from the strike to hike the payroll. The end result were trades for second baseman Mickey Morandini and left fielder Henry Rodriguez, and the free-agent signings of stopper Rod Beck and shortstop Jeff Blauser.

What was still lacking was that big-ticket stopper-like pitcher, the type on which franchises risk their financial futures if he blows out an elbow or shoulder. MacPhail insisted he is not philosophically opposed to such megabucks deals. "You can't philosophically take one [avenue to improvement] out just because you don't seem to like it." But he also was hesitant to propose an even bigger budget increase to Jim Dowdle for one more "impact" player. "Can you make the case and are you close enough?" he said. "We haven't gotten to the point where I, in good faith, can look and say, 'We're just about there. One pitcher will make the difference. For that reason, I am recommending we spend 'X' to get there.'"

No $75 Box Seats

MacPhail also said he tries to keep the budget in line with team revenues that rank in the high middle-of-the-pack range among all big-league teams. *Forbes* magazine has confirmed that ranking when it has run annual articles on the financial strength of teams.

"It's somewhat repugnant to me that you and I are sitting here five years from now, and a box seat at Wrigley Field might be $75," MacPhail said.

"We've had only had one price increase while I'm here. I'm kind of proud of it. We try to keep it affordable and entertaining...The idea of moving the ticket price to $75 from $25—what it is today—all for the privilege of paying a guy $25 million instead of $10 million really doesn't sit too well with me.

"This club has done a great job maximizing revenues," he said of Wrigley Field and a new cable deal with Fox Sports Net Chicago. "We were 10th or 11th in attendance, with ticket prices 12th or 13th. We had no naming rights or signage in Wrigley Field. Our revenues are 12th, 13th, 14th out of 30 teams, and that's where our payroll sits.

"If you're going to ask me to sustain losses in range of $20 million to $30 million annually for the privilege of owning a baseball team or jack ticket prices up to $75 a box seat, no. I still believe, old-fashioned that I am, that I can create a farm system that over time can supply us the players in a more efficient manner so we can make selective judgments as to who we make the big commitments, and try to be reasonably conservative in what we do in what it costs a family of four to go to the ballpark."

Despite operating in the nation's third-largest market, MacPhail said the Cubs cannot achieve the revenue stream of the New York Yankees and their lucrative broadcast-rights deal. The annual revenue difference between the Cubs and Yankees? "It's $90 million in the Yankees' case," he said. "Precious few clubs can afford the type of stability that the Yankees and Braves have. But that doesn't preclude you from being a good organization."

First baseman Mark Grace can see MacPhail's logic on one hand. On the other, he realizes that winning at the turn of the millennium requires top-of-the-line spending.

"It's not our money," Grace said. "We can bitch about it. But if it was your money, would you say, 'Goddamn it, I'll risk millions and millions on a pitcher who could blow out his arm'?

"But even today, spending $64 million [the Cubs' final 1999 payroll when deferred payments are factored in] is run of the mill. There are a lot of teams spending a lot more money than that. Occasionally, there's a team that gets hot with a low payroll. But if you win, you've got to pay."

The Cubs' budget is constructed by MacPhail, Lynch, business-operations chief Mark McGuire, and team controller Jodi Norman. Each fall during the MacPhail regime, the team honchos met at Wrigley Field with Jim Dowdle and an associate from either Tribune Entertainment or the corporate accounting department.

"We'll project our revenues, expenses, players who are arbitration-eligible and what their salaries might be, different free agent needs and what they may be, operating income from the stadium, stadium improvements and marketing expenses," MacPhail said. "It's a discipline that Tribune Co. insists on. Not a discipline of spending, but a discipline of knowing where you're going and how you're going to get there and with what means, well before you get into the signing season. Sometimes we project a loss, sometimes we show we'll come in around break-even.

"They approve it, and we go along on that basis. The great advantage is that we're not one of these teams that get into the signing season and really doesn't know where it's going to proceed until the owner approves something in late December or January, when you're behind the eight-ball. The budget is simply how you start. If you have a good season, you add; a bad season, subtract. It's just how you start. If for whatever reason you miscalculate salaries or have some unforeseen expenses and you need to waiver from it, we talked to Jim."

On Opening Day 1999, Dowdle confirmed that the Cubs had the flexibility of increasing the team payroll even more during the season. "It's just a matter of which players you have to give up for the player you want [instead of money]," he said. Sure enough, the payroll went up more than $2 million when the Cubs landed stopper Rick Aguilera on May 21, 1999.

At that point, the Cubs were trying to extend the "shelf life," in MacPhail's words, of the surprise 1998 wild-card playoff team. Sammy Sosa's 66-homer outburst and Kerry Wood's strikeout *wunderkind* season combined with good seasons from all of the off-season acquisitions except for Blauser led to the memorable campaign. The 90-victory season, achieved when the Cubs beat the Giants 5-3 on September 28 in a wild card tiebreaking game at Wrigley Field, actually could have been better than it was.

The Cubs had reached an 87-67 record after a 4-3 win over the Padres in San Diego on September 17. But the team lost six of its last eight games, allowing the hard-charging Giants to tie them. The Cubs survived to play the tiebreaker game at the last possible second, when the Giants blew a 7-0 lead against the Rockies on September 27, the regular season's final day. Kevin Tapani, who had two starts to win his 20th game near season's end, lost them both instead. And the Cubs somehow managed to go 13-11 in September, prior to the tiebreaker, without the services of Wood, shelved with a sore elbow, a precursor to the surgery that would knock him out for the following season.

The unproductive farm system, with Wood—a 1995 draftee—the only "impact" player produced the entire decade, and lack of upcoming Latin talent would come back to haunt the Cubs on two fronts in 1998. Little fresh blood was coming up besides Wood to stock the pitching staff. The retreads and aging veterans making up the middle-inning corps collapsed thoroughly in July 1998. Seeking to re-tool his bullpen on the fly, Lynch was forced to go outside the organization and overpay for middlemen Matt Karchner from the White Sox and Felix Heredia from the Marlins. The price were two former No. 1 picks that had spearheaded MacPhail's attempt to revive the player-development process. Highly regarded right-handers Jon Garland (1997 No. 1) and Todd Noel (1996 No. 1) went to the White Sox and Marlins, respectively. Karchner and Heredia turned out to be alarmingly inconsistent over the next one and a half seasons, and the former repeatedly re-injured his groin to knock him out of much of the 1999 campaign.

Lynch also needed to beef up the starting rotation all along in 1998. When Wood went down for the count after his August 31 start, manager Jim Riggleman was forced to make do with the likes of Don Wengert and retread Mike Morgan in his place in the rotation. Lefty Terry Mulholland, so effective in relief, had to be pressed into service as a starter near the end of '98.

Back in late July, the Cubs actually had a chance to catch Houston for the NL Central title and not worry about surviving a wild-card race. The Cubs were as close as two and a half games behind the Astros on July 27 with a 60-46 record. A kind of behind-the-scenes sweepstakes developed for the services of Randy Johnson, whom the Seattle Mariners were dumping for salary considerations. The Cubs apparently were eliminated early from the Johnson derby. Top trade-bait Jeremi Gonzalez had hurt his elbow and was shelved from the rotation. Lynch had no combination of almost-ready regular-player and starting-pitcher prospects to offer Seattle GM Woody Woodward, a reclusive type. Garland and Noel, still teen-agers, each were still three years away from the majors. But if the financially-inferior Astros were lurking around, the need to prevent the Big Unit from landing with the division leaders became imperative.

When the expected top bids from the Yankees and Indians washed out, Woodward was still left holding Johnson as the midnight Eastern Time trade deadline on July 31 approached. The price seemingly would drop. With minutes to go, as Lynch completed the deal for Heredia with the Marlins, Astros GM Gerry Hunsicker offered two of the products of his Venezuelan scouting machine: second baseman Carlos Guillen and pitcher Freddie Garcia, plus a player to be named later. That turned out to be top lefty prospect John Halama. The clock ticking down, Woodward bit on the deal, and Johnson made the Astros' rotation, superior to that of the Cubs, even better. Within two weeks, Houston had pulled away to a nine-game lead. The Astros eventually were upset in the playoffs, but at least Johnson had given them the chance to win while making Houston a dominating team in the NL Central.

The Johnson trade remained a sore subject with Lynch for more than a year. He didn't like criticism that he didn't do all he could to land Johnson and block the Astros from locking up the division. In a previous book, *Sammy Sosa: Clearing The Vines*, I wrote how Lynch had used up his tradeable material for Karchner and Heredia. "But no one will ever know what might have happened had Lynch, on a hunch, made a late-night phone call to Woodward on July 31," I continued.

That last sentence was like waving a red cape in front of a bull. After Lynch got a copy of the Sosa book, he called me into his office at the training complex in Mesa, Arizona, as spring drills got underway in mid-February 1999. He vehemently disputed my interpretation of the Johnson deadline events. I responded that I was going on information he had given the media the following day—that the Cubs had been eliminated early on from landing Johnson—and now it seemed that he was altering his story of the Johnson talks.

Lynch couldn't get the Sosa book reference out of his head. Several times over the next few months, an irritated Lynch would talk about how Houston gave up prime prospects like Guillen and Garcia whenever the subject of Johnson came up. Later, MacPhail said he would have seriously considered meeting Johnson's long-term financial demands had the Cubs landed the Big Unit. It all became a moot point, though, when Johnson, desiring to play at home in the Phoenix area, spurned a generous Houston contract offer to sign with the Arizona Diamondbacks.

Disaster for That Ol' Gang of Ours

Not landing Johnson turned out to be not as serious as the decision to bring back the aging 1998 team virtually intact for 1999 while not adding a significant pitcher as a free agent.

Re-signing Gary Gaetti proved to be a disaster. In a kind of last hurrah at 40, Gaetti hit .320 in 37 games down the stretch to help the Cubs to the wild card playoff. MacPhail had known Gaetti well from his younger days with the Twins. But to expect Gaetti in his baseball dotage to produce over the long season at third base was a case of talent misevaluation. The Cubs also dialed up wrong on catcher Benito Santiago.

Lynch did obtain Jon Lieber for outfielder Brant Brown, but the Cubs needed yet another starter with Wood's elbow a question mark after 1998. Jim Dowdle had believed that if Wood was healthy, the Cubs already had their heavy-duty ace. "When we had the opportunity [to contend coming into] last year, we put some additional money on the line," he said. "We had Kerry Wood. Why should we go out and pay for these guys [ace pitchers] if we already have one? [Randy] Johnson or [Roger] Clemens, would that have made much of a difference?"

Had Wood not required "Tommy John" tendon-transplant surgery, the Cubs' rotation would have been that much stronger with a second veteran pitcher. With Wood out, the extra pitching acquisition could have plugged up the hole. The pitching shortage became even more acute when Kevin Tapani pitched with a sore back, his ineffectiveness mounting, most of the summer before being forced onto the disabled list in September 1999.

The '98 Cubs turned out to be a one-year wonder who got iron-poor blood and clubhouse ennui all at once, on top of an epidemic of injuries and pitching ineffectiveness. The end result was the worst mid-season collapse in Cubs history —a 10-40 record from July 23 through September 14— that made the team's 32-23 start seem like it was from another season.

Players like Santiago and center fielder Lance Johnson had conflicts with the normally agreeable Jim Riggleman much of the second half of 1999. Santiago was benched, while Johnson spent more than two months (June 10 to August 20) on the disabled list with an abdominal strain. The lengthy time Johnson was disabled, on top of previously raised eyebrows over a lengthy hand injury in the first half of 1998, caused the clubhouse tension. Dowdle was angry that several players appeared to take Tribune Co.'s money and not gave much back in return.

"You are paying substantial money for people to perform," he said. "If I came in to this job and performed the way they performed, my ass would have been out of here. You got a bunch of guys who quit. [Their reasoning is] I'm going to get my money. By laying down and being on the injured list, I can get a couple of more years on another contract."

But others in baseball believed the Cubs squandered their highest payroll in history.

Even before the mid-season grand nosedive, a prominent Houston Astros player, who did not want to be identified, explained why his team had the edge on the Cubs despite a lower payroll.

"They spent the money on the wrong people," the player said. "And it's always a question of pitching. They don't have enough."

Still, the length and breadth of the slump amazed the Cubs' brass. A team couldn't have tried to lose as much as the Cubs did in 1999.

"I don't think there's been a team in history that was nine games above .500 on June 9, and at the end of the year had that kind of record (67-95)," Dowdle said. "Usually, these disastrous years start on Opening Day."

And if the collapse on the field and the imitation of a sit-down strike in the clubhouse wasn't bad enough, consider all the other things that went wrong in 1999.

Dowdle had commissioned a statue of the late Harry Caray, unveiled on Opening Day 1999 outside Wrigley Field with Dowdle and Tribune Co. CEO John Madigan in attendance. Oops. Dowdle forgot to include Jack Brickhouse, who had died six months after Caray, in the sculpture. Brickhouse had broadcast Cubs games twice as long as Caray. Older Cubs fans howled in protest when the compensatory Brickhouse tribute, his trademark "Hey Hey" home-run call, was festooned in red letters on the ballpark foul poles.

More than a month later, the Cubs gave a look-see to the famed Hideo Nomo. The team and Nomo disagreed on the number of minor-league starts the Japanese pitcher would get to work back into shape. Seeking assurance he would regain his lost control, the Cubs wanted Nomo to make one or two additional starts beyond the ones to which he and his agent had agreed. Nomo didn't want to spend extra time in Triple-A, so he ended up signing with the Milwaukee Brewers, for whom he was 12-9 in two-thirds of a season.

On the heels of the failed Nomo experiment, the Cubs then stirred a firestorm of protest when they drafted tainted college pitcher Ben Christensen with their top pick in the June 1999 draft. Wichita State righthander Christensen had gained infamy for throwing at Evansville hitter Anthony Molina, hitting him in the eye, while Molina was timing Christensen's pitches in the on-deck circle.

On August 23, the Cubs delayed their scheduled night game with the Giants at Wrigley Field due to the imminent prospect of heavy rain. Problem was, the monsoon didn't arrive for nearly two hours. WGN-TV weather forecaster Tom Skilling speculated that the rain system, moving west to east, stalled out west of Wrigley Field and actually began expanding in the other direction. An official game could have been played before the rains actually hit, causing a washout of the contest. The "dry" rain delay prompted top Giants officials, in attendance, to rip Cubs management.

Everything the team touched turned to stone in 1999, save for the turnstile count at Wrigley Field and a wave of talent moving through the lower minor leagues.

"Despite our tribulations on the field in 1999, our farm system and scouts performed well," MacPhail reasoned. At least there had been some benefit in some of the dreadful finishes of the 1990s. In 1995, the Cubs got the No. 4 pick in the draft, choosing Kerry Wood. In 1998, picking No. 3, they landed outfielder Corey Patterson. The horrid finish of 1999 assured another No. 3 pick in the 2000 draft.

But five years into his regime, the Cubs should have been building to something far different, far more positive, far more hopeful, than what was presented in 1999. All the events uncovered the fact that little actual progress had been made in building back the franchise despite the turnaround from the strike and millions of dollars spent on middle-level free agents.

Even with the negatives-laden wrapup to the 20th century, Dowdle endorsed MacPhail's stewardship. He looked at the big picture.

"Andy's got two World Series under his belt," Dowdle said. "He sure didn't do it with money. He did it with intelligence and feel for the game. Andy has more than filled my expectations for an individual representing the team well. I've told several people that I hope to see Andy MacPhail as (baseball) commissioner. Here's is third-generation baseball man who's very protective of the game."

With the farm system still at least a year away from really bearing fruit, MacPhail and Lynch had to patch again for the 2000 season. To be sure, that strategy got the Cubs only their third playoff appearance since 1945. But, more often, the middle-ground of making a team just competitive enough where it can make the playoffs with a good tailwind behind it has tended to backfire. The Cubs almost stood more of a chance of getting worse, quickly and spectacularly if the negative streaks of 1996, 1997, and 1999 are taken into account.

"I don't think your observations are incorrect by any means. Why not invest in it the Houston way?" MacPhail said of a visitor's suggestion that he should have torn the Cubs down in 1995 in order to build them back up again. There was logic in that strategy. If not pursued, then MacPhail should have moved at 78 RPM to win quickly, which could be accomplished only with one of the game's highest payrolls. Big deficits might have been made up from additional revenue gleaned from the glorious afterglow of a Cubs World Series appearance.

MacPhail chose neither course of action. And, as a result, after five years of his administration, only a glimmer of hope at the minor-league level and in improved foreign talent procurement makes the million-to-one era any closer to conclusion compared to 1995.

Chapter 13

BASEBALL'S DEPARTMENTS OF AGRICULTURE

SIGNING AND GROOMING enough of the right players has been a mystery that has escaped the Cubs during the majority of the million-to-one era.

But a system of good scouting and player development isn't a secret akin to the Manhattan Project. It requires a commitment from ownership, creativity and flexibility in exploring new foreign markets, willingness to shift financial resources from the major-league club, and, above all, patience in waiting for top prospects to develop and stability among the administrators, scouts, and instructors who handle the kids.

For various reasons, the Cubs have lacked some or all of the above prerequisites over the decades. They could have easily fixed the problem. The blueprint for quality player development has been used by a score of teams who have greatly benefited. Top recent examples have been the Houston Astros, Atlanta Braves, and Cleveland Indians. Not so coincidentally, these franchises joined the New York Yankees as the major leagues' most successful teams throughout the 1990s.

The Astros, Braves, and Indians accomplished their development feats with in many ways less advantageous financial and marketing positions than the Cubs.

Houston and Atlanta are football towns, with baseball seemingly only a secondary passion for much of the sport's history. The Astros often have been a financially struggling franchise, having operated under a bankruptcy umbrella at one time and never possessing the most prosperous ownership around. Meanwhile, the Indians were the American League's answer to the Cubs without the glamour and appeal of Wrigley Field. They were a decade-after-decade loser, rumored to be a candidate for a move to another city, away from tiny crowds in cavernous Municipal Stadium.

But with commitments from top brass that filtered down through the organization, the Astros, Braves, and Indians were able to build up scouting and development systems that provided them a core of homegrown players. They established early beachheads in the talent-rich Caribbean while the Cubs had only a halting presence south of the border. When the players reached the major leagues and began to lift the fortunes of the franchises, the respective managements made judicious trades and free-agent signings.

The proof is in the results, after teams had built up their development systems literally from nothing. The Astros may be the best example.

Former Astros general manager Bill Wood, trained in the formerly vaunted Los Angeles Dodgers' farm system, hired on with Houston as assistant scouting and player development director during the late 1970s, a dark period financially for the franchise.

"The club was in bankruptcy under [Judge Roy] Hofheinz," said Wood, now a major-league scout. "Ford Motor Credit Corp. and GE Credit Corp. called in their debts and were running the club.

"We started at zero. We really were a bankrupt ballclub. We weren't drawing, we had no attendance. We had little recognizable talent at the major-league level. We had a stripped-down farm system. We were part of the Major League Scouting Bureau, which would do the majority of the groundwork [on prospects] and then we'd do the crosschecks. We had five full-time scouts. We had no travel jackets, no bags for players to carry equipment in, and our uniforms were hand-me-downs. We didn't have enough talent to fill a Triple-A club."

But when John McMullen bought the club in 1979, the good baseball men on hand, led by Tal Smith, began a process of persuading the owner to put more of the scarce financial resources in scouting and player development. A $1 million annual budget increased to $7 million by the time Wood ascended to the GM's job in 1987. The team merely returned to its original formula of success under founding general manager Paul Richards, who had built up a productive farm system in the 1960s—and who snatched Larry Dierker away from the Cubs by offering him $15,000 more to sign.

"McMullen wanted to show that a team could be competitive with a low payroll," Wood said. "The strong point of the organization would be development and scouting. We could pull this off."

"Under Dr. McMullen, we were always encouraged to be creative to find alternative means of getting players," said Dan O'Brien, Jr., who ran

Houston's scouting efforts from 1984 until he left after the 1995 season to become assistant general manager of the Texas Rangers.

Also influenced by the development-first philosophy was Andy MacPhail. After five years' experience in the Cubs' front office from 1977 to 1981, MacPhail joined the Astros as assistant general manager just as the development effort was revving up. He left to join the Twins in 1985.

Through the 1980s, the Astros beefed up their scouting staff to 15 full-timers. But they emphasized quality over quantity, with O'Brien citing the support of top management as the impetus. Quality everyday player prospects like Craig Biggio, Ken Caminiti, Glenn Davis, Billy Doran, and Kenny Lofton came into the system as it was being built back up.

"We were very focused on the quality of people we hired on the scouting and player development staff," O'Brien said. "It was a mixture of backgrounds and qualifications—diversity. We developed consistency of training, with an emphasis on continuing education, always trying to get better."

At one point the Astros hired former ace Tigers pitcher Hal Newhouser as a scout. Newhouser talked to his scouting comrades in meetings about the art of pitching and his experiences in the game. "It was invaluable. It was a clinic," said O'Brien. "I wish we had foresight to videotape those meetings."

Adding the farm system to his supervisory duties, O'Brien tried to dampen down the inevitable rivalries and backbiting between scouts and minor-league managers and instructors. Gordon Goldsberry had successfully pulled off that tact when he ran Cubs player development in the 1980s.

"That sort of working together doesn't happen naturally in the game," O'Brien said. "So we had a program where we took members of the scouting staff and had them working in the player-development system in the summer. Meanwhile, the player development people would scout in the off-season. That way, each would have an understanding of the other's jobs."

Always emphasizing pitching, O'Brien and his scouts worked off a specific profile of the type of pitcher they would sign, based on "physical prerequisites, ability, arm action and character. The scouts would focus on velocity. If they did not have movement on their fastball, that's OK. The player development people would say, 'We'll team 'em.'"

Such a philosophy produced pitchers like Darryl Kile, a 30th-round pick in 1987; Shane Reynolds, a third-round pick in 1989; and back-to-back first-rounders in Billy Wagner (1993), and Scott Elarton (1994).

Lefthander John Halama, a 23rd-round pick in 1994, emerged with a 13-3 season with Triple-A New Orleans in 1997. He ended up being dispatched to Seattle in the Randy Johnson trade at mid-season 1998, and along with fellow Astros product Freddie Garcia enjoyed some success in the Mariners rotation in 1999.

"They stressed control, not to nitpick and to challenge hitters," Halama said of his instruction in the Astros' farm system. "Control one side of the plate before you try to control both. For a lefthander like me, it was control a pitch away to a righthander, then come in and have an off-speed pitch you can throw anytime in the count."

Working as coordinator of pitching instruction for Houston's minor-league system is Dewey Robinson, a native Chicagoan who grew up four miles north of Wrigley Field.

"I was surprised by the quality of arms we had," ex-White Sox pitcher Robinson said of his debut as pitching coordinator after a long coaching tenure in the Sox system. "All these guys were throwing 90 MPH or better. All big and strong. The next thing I noticed was the quality of curveballs."

Unlike the Cubs' rushing of prospects through the farm system through the decades, the Astros take it slower.

"Gerry [Hunsicker's] philosophy is we don't move guys until they're ready to be moved," Robinson said. "Eric Ireland [second-round pick in 1995] led the Florida State League in ERA and pitched a perfect game. But he spent the whole year in Class A ball. Scott Elarton was moved up step by step."

Hunsicker's background was pitching. He served as both a college and minor-league pitching coach early in his career. "He's got his thumbprint on the organization," Robinson said.

The key move, however, that enabled the Astros to leap nearly a decade ahead of the Cubs in talent procurement was their beach-head in Venezuela. While McMullen and ownership successor Drayton McLane kept tight reins on the big-league payroll, they approved expenditures to establish two training facilities in talent-rich Venezuela while most other big-league teams looked elsewhere in the Caribbean, if at all.

The Astros already had a Latin American presence. Even when they operated with a bare-bones scouting staff in the mid-1970s, they had a presence in the Dominican Republic along with the Giants and Pirates. Legendary Latin American talent maven Howie Haak, who had long funneled talented players to the Pirates, worked for the Astros in the late 1980s. And Bill Wood had a friendship with Venezuelan baseball-team operator Andres Reiner, who had moved to Houston to go into the home-building business.

"He helped me place players in winter ball," Wood said. "He educated me about his country, about why the times were good for the production of players. Most clubs who were in Latin America concentrated on the Dominican, and we were getting beat there. I needed every avenue I could to find and develop players. I felt like it was time to take a chance in the Latin market, and we needed to go somewhere where we could gain an advantage for a while."

Wood proposed going to Venezuela to McMullen in 1989. He also bounced the idea of a training facility off Haak.

"One of the key factors was we wanted to do it with a network of scouts," Wood said. "Andres would be the head guy, and he'd have regional supervisors who'd find players to bring to the academy."

Reiner acquired two sites for academies in Venezuela. Not only would the players get baseball instruction, but they'd also receive English language lessons and instruction in nutrition, social skills, and basic finance.

"We spent $100,000 getting everything started," Wood recalled. "It was a big gamble, but we were cutting back in other areas. We had that money available, and had ownership convinced that it was a good gamble to make. If we could get a leg up on talent in that country, we'd have more than a one in 30 chance of signing players [the number of chances per round in the June draft each team gets to obtain players]."

The gamble paid off. The academies have produced 10 players who have reached the majors. "At a player a year, to have that many reach the major leagues, that's what we wanted," Wood said. "No way could we get a player a year out of the Dominican. Other clubs caught on and saw what we were doing."

The Venezuelan connection resulted in Randy Johnson. Pitcher Freddy Garcia and second baseman Carlos Guillen were the main bait to land the Big Unit. Meanwhile, outfielder Richard Hidalgo is an Astros starter.

Reiner now is special assistant to Hunsicker. The Astros have expanded their Carribean scouting efforts to Nicaragua and Panama, among other baseball outposts.

But no matter if the talent is acquired domestically or from foreign markets, the Astros generally know what to do with it — keep the players in Houston uniforms. Rarely do the Astros make a Johnson-type trade. They realize the benefits of patience and stability in player development.

"Realistically, it will take five to six years for tangible evidence of your work," said Dan O'Brien, Jr. "There is no short-cut [in player development]. You have to keep doing it, year in and year out."

Pitching Experts in Atlanta

The Atlanta Braves possessed a highly paid, underachieving big-league roster in the mid-1980s. Clearly, the franchise had to re-tool, to go down before it could go up again.

The strategy? Pump some of Ted Turner's TBS superstation profits into the Braves' farm system. Several bad drafts had nearly gutted the formerly productive minor leagues, which had produced good players back to the franchise's Boston days.

The idea worked. Although Bobby Cox and John Schuerholz have made shrewd trades and free-agent signings from the general manager's chair for the last 15 years, homegrown players have formed the core of baseball's longest-running contender. The Braves made the post-season every year between 1991 and 1999 (the strike season excepted), including five World Series appearances.

And while some naysayers insist the Braves lived on past player-development reputation at the turn of the millennium, the fact remains that the Braves continued to bring up quality pitchers in the late 1990s despite having drafted behind most other teams for an entire decade.

How 'bout three key contributors to the 1999 World Series team: starter Kevin Millwood (11th round, 1993 draft), stopper and verbal anarchist John Rocker (18th round, 1993 draft), and middle reliever Kevin McGlinchy (fifth round, 1995 draft). Andruw Jones was a 1993 amateur free-agent signee out of the Caribbean island of Curacao. He was out in 1999 due to surgery, but the previous season's 30-games savior Kerry Ligtenberg, an amateur free-agent signee in January 1996, was obtained from the Southern Minny Stars (Austin, MN) of the independent Prairie League.

Even deep into their reign as the NL's top contender, the Braves still hadn't lost their touch, signing and grooming big-league performers to build on an earlier homegrown nucleus of pitchers such as Tom Glavine and Kent Mercker, third baseman Chipper Jones, outfielders David Justice and Ryan Klesko, catcher Javy Lopez, shortstop Jeff Blauser, and second baseman Mark Lemke.

That turned out to be money well-spent by Turner, reversing a decade's worth of questionable financial decisions on free agents and other high-priced players.

Cox has reaped the fruits of his decision to strip down and go young after stepping aside as GM and going back to the dugout as manager in 1990. Schuerholz, who came from a player development-oriented franchise in Kansas City, merely continued the momentum when he succeeded Cox in the front office.

Braves chairman Bill Bartholomay, who along with Turner signs off on the top financial decisions affecting the franchise, pinpointed the exact time of the scouting and farm-system upgrade.

"Near the end of the 1980s, we had pretty good information about our Richmond [Triple-A] team. It was getting better," he said. "Effective with the 1988 season, we increased [player-development] expenditures about $3 million, a 30 percent hike. We had reason to think things could be escalated.

"I think we get a little more bang for the buck."

Meanwhile, the Braves opted to concentrate their minor-league clubs in the Southeast. "We tried to localize the teams, try to get them around Atlanta, in driving distance," Bartholomay said. "It let's our management see the teams without flying 5,000 miles around." A side benefit was acclimating the minor-leaguers to playing in the oppressive heat and humidity of a southern summer, so they could make craft Atlanta into a true home-field advantage when they were called up to the majors.

The Braves also crave stability and experience in their minor-league managers and instructors. Going into the 1999 season, minor-league pitching coaches Bill Fischer, Bruce Dal Canton, Mark Ross, and Eddie Watt each had at least seven seasons working in the farm system at various levels. Fischer and Dal Canton also had experience as big-league pitching coaches. Roger Clemens enjoyed his first success under Fischer in the mid-1980s with the Boston Red Sox. Other minor-league managers and instructors stuck around for years, too.

"You knew who your manager was going to be each level as you went up," said righthander Jason Schmidt, a top right-handed Braves' prospect in the mid-1990s now with the Pirates. "It was the same everything. The pitching coaches were outstanding."

The Braves minor-league personnel are motivated to stay by good compensation.

"The pay scale in the Braves' system is better than most systems," said former Cubs scouting chief Dick Balderson, who took over the administering of the Atlanta system in 1999 under old Kansas City boss Schuerholz. "It is loyalty. They're treated fairly and we trust them. There's not a lot of trust in this game. When I took over, things hardly changed. I fired one guy at the Class A level, re-assigned a pitching coach, hired a pitching coach for the rookie league and one roving instructor. And that was it for openings."

The Braves field more minor-league teams than most. "We have three 'summer' clubs [rookie-league or short-season Class A], compared to most who have two," Balderson said. "We have a total of seven teams, compared to other organizations' five. For a non-drafted player, there are more opportunities to play. High school players have a better chance [to gain basic experience] in a pure rookie league or a low Class-A league."

Major-league pitching coach Leo Mazzone, famed for his rocking back and forth in dugouts, believed in a program where pitchers throw more frequently, rather than less. The system was implemented throughout the Braves minor leagues.

"There's a basic philosophy that the more you throw, the better you'll be," said Balderson.

"It most definitely helped with guys like myself and Bruce Chen," said lefthander Micah Bowie, who was traded to the Cubs in mid-season 1999. "You pitch your game. You have a day off. You throw your bullpen, another bullpen, have a day off and you pitch. You throw between starts two days in a row.

"Their theory works. I did it my whole career. It helps you with your feel, touch and control. You never throw hard on the side, you never air it out and throw 100 percent. It's straight mechanics, feel and touch, nice and easy for two days. You do more repetitious throwing, but you're not doing it at a maximum effort. I think they have fewer arm injuries than other teams."

Headed by renowned talent procurer Paul Snyder during the key moments in the 1980s and early 1990s, the Braves' scouting department went after young pitchers deemed "unsignable" by most other organizations.

"They'll take the guys who are supposed to be top one-to-three round picks," Schmidt said. "The word is out that these guys want to go to school. They want too much money. Instead, the Braves figure, 'Let's take 'em in the eighth, 10th, 12th round, and see what we can do.'

"They have very good scouts who can sign these guys. You see these guys come into the system and ask where do they come from? They were supposed to be a No. 1 pick and they asked for $1 million. Other teams couldn't pay them. The Braves end up getting them for a bargain. They have a winning tradition and it's still hard to turn down the money. It's hard to turn that down when you figure, 'I'll get to play for the Braves and I'll still get a couple of hundred thousand dollars.'

"The scouts never back off due to signability," Balderson said.

Braves scouts also take chances with prospects possessing checkered health histories.

"There will be guys who are supposed to be top picks coming out of high school," Schmidt said. "They get tendinitis or something, and their stock fell. The Braves will take those guys and figure they'll work with them. They'll work it like the stock market. More times than not, it works out."

The Braves have benefited several ways from possessing the Big Three of Tom Glavine, Greg Maddux, and John Smoltz. Their young pitching prospects aren't under any pressure to produce in a big way when they come up to the majors. With the stability in the rotation at the top, the Braves can afford to emphasize drafting high school pitchers and allow them to take their time to develop.

"They give us six, seven years to develop," Bowie said. "The scouts will say, 'Look, he's really developed.' If you were in another system, you might have been brought up too fast. You wouldn't have developed. You may never reach the point you can reach. They look at a Braves' pitcher, and they see a more refined pitcher than they'll see in their own system.

Bobby Cox worked them in as the No. 5 starter or a middle-inning reliever. Or they're used as trade bait, with the Braves' reputation for pitching development sometimes inflating their value.

"The feeling is, these are Braves pitching prospects, they must be pretty good, they'll bring a high price in a trade," Schmidt said. "The Braves will get trades that other teams don't normally get."

Reputation goes a long way in baseball. In fact, once you win, and win again, reputation will feed on itself. That's how the Braves have kept going for a decade.

Major League III *Really is Big-League*

A bigger joke in the middle 1980s than the Braves were the Cleveland Indians. After 102- and 101-defeat seasons in 1985 and 1987, respectively, the Tribe were honored in a left-handed manner by Hollywood with the pair of *Major League* movies. A 105-loss campaign followed in 1991.

The Cubs were still carrying a bit of the aura from the 1984 NL East title, so the Indians were the favorite *Bad News Bears*-type subject for celluloid. There was humor in ineptitude at Municipal Stadium.

Unlike the Cubs, the Indians hadn't even had a sniff of a pennant race or a division title in recent decades. The last meaningful September had been in 1959, when Cleveland was outlasted by the "Go-Go" White Sox in September. But the situation wasn't funny to new owner Dick Jacobs, team president Hank Peters, and the young, aggressive baseball executives they hired.

"Very simply, we decided that the Indians were a patchwork organization of different management philosophies and styles," said Colorado Rockies general manager Dan O'Dowd, who hired on as Indians farm director in December 1987 before being promoted to assistant GM under the dynamic John Hart. His description of the situation sounded eerily similar to the Cubs of the mid-1990s.

"We knew we had to get worse before we got better," O'Dowd said. "We formed a strategic plan with Dick Jacobs."

Peters first tried to field somewhat of a competitive team while the execs tried to rebuild the scouting staff and farm system. But that tact didn't work.

"You either run with the big dogs or be with the puppies," O'Dowd said. "We eventually cut the payroll back to $7.5 million, traded all the high-priced talent, and started developing a core of young players."

The staff took 1988 as a season to identify the team's problems. Minor-league coaches were added. Scouts got pay raises and cars. Two national crosschecker scouts were added. The player-development budget increased totaled $1.5 million for 1989.

Then the Indians jumped in full bore with a training academy in the Dominican Republic. And they went far from the madding crowd.

"We put the academy in Santiago, in the valley of the Dominican mountains, where there are physically stronger players," O'Dowd said. "We didn't have the resources to have an academy in Santo Domingo and compete with the big boys. Young Dominicans ignored by other scouts came down and tried out with us."

The end results of the improved scouting efforts were the drafting and development of outfielders Albert Belle, Manny Ramirez, and Brian Giles; first basemen Jim Thome and Richie Sexson, and pitchers Charles Nagy, Bartolo Colon, Jaret Wright, and Paul Shuey. GM Hart then granted long-term contracts after the young players reached the majors to keep them out of arbitration and increase their satisfaction quotient of playing for the Indians.

"It's cost predictability, and it sends a message to the fans of trust and hope, that there's a long-term plan," O'Dowd said. "For years, Cleveland had been such a layover for players that we sent a message that's going to stop."

The Indians did not rest on their laurels once the pipeline of talent had been established from the minors, enabling the major-league team to elevate itself from laughingstock status in 1991 to the World Series in 1995.

With young Mark Shapiro, son of famed agent Ron Shapiro, on board as director of minor-league operations in 1994, the team was able to implement an individual development plan for each player.

"It creates a roadmap for every player to track his development through the farm system," said Shapiro, who succeeded O'Dowd as assistant GM late in 1998. "It shifts responsibility to the player, instead of having the development done to him."

The program, begun in 1995, features regular assessment of the players' strengths and limitations in their physical, mental, and fundamentals "domains," in Shapiro's words. "It's a program where the player evaluates himself," he said. "It gives him a set of skills and activities for which he can be responsible.

Shapiro claims to have conceived the program. "Dr. Charles Maher [the team's sports psychologist] helped me put flesh into it. It developed from a frustration that the language of [player] evaluations were full of rhetoric. We tell them they've got to throw more strikes. How? Get better command. How? A better release point? We go back to the root of the issue. I'm extremely lucky to have John [Hart] buy into it."

"Although this is more work, it will make us better. We're not trying to re-invent the game. We're just trying to re-focus ideas."

Cubs player development officials were informed of the Indians' system. But after doing away with the Larry Himes-Al Goldis-Syd Thrift program of rubber tires, balance beams, eye and psychological tests, team president Andy MacPhail wasn't likely to stray from the basics of letting the players work on fundamentals before the game and then performing for nine innings.

Shapiro believes a good player-development system has to do more. "A lot of people just throw the bats and balls out there and let them play," he said. "There has to be a more efficient way of developing players."

With signing bonuses spiraling, the Indians usually account on a "natural" five percent increase in their player-development budget each year, Shapiro said. "But if there's something important we can do in player development, we can get the money for it," he added.

No matter how efficient or creative the player development teams like Houston, Atlanta, and Cleveland are, they'll always pale in comparison if the Boss himself, George Steinbrenner, wants to become a farm-system devotee. In many ways, Steinbrenner has moved in that direction in recent years.

"George wasn't successful until he shut up and got suspended for two years, where he couldn't trade all his young players away," former Tribune Co. Cubs overseer Jim Dowdle said.

Indeed, the Yankees could have outperformed all the other farm systems had Steinbrenner not gone for short-term fixes, trading home-grown players for overpriced veterans. The likes of Willie McGee and a host of other prominent major leaguers over the past generation have traced their roots to the Yankees' farm system. But more recently, he has returned such up-the-middle strengths as shortstop Derek Jeter, center fielder Bernie Williams, catcher Jorge Posada, and pitchers Andy Pettite, Mariano Rivera, and Ramiro Mendoza.

Headed by Mark Newman, who is well-respected throughout the game and receives more than adequate funding by Steinbrenner, the Yankees' player development and scouting could potentially outperform all other competitors. The Yankees also have set down specific standards for each of the nine positions on the field, according to GM Brian Cashman. Drafted players and free agents have to adhere to those standards.

Obviously, the Cubs have light-years of catching-up to do in player development with the leaders in the game. The team has made up some ground under MacPhail's administration. Whether they can do it as ef-fectively as those who established the high ground before them will help determine whether the million-to-one era lasts well into a new century.

Chapter 14

LANSING, THE DOMINICAN, VENEZEULA, AND KOREA
A Cubs' Revival?

HEE SEOP CHOI'S smooth, fluid left-handed power stroke was in full bloom on the hot early evening of July 25, 1999 at Oldsmobile Park, a half-mile east of the state capitol building in Lansing, Michigan.

Some 7,000 fans, still baking in the setting sun, were wowed when Lansing Lugnuts first baseman Choi tried to hit the ball straightaway against Ft. Wayne Wizards righthander Ryan Van De Weg. But the result of a smart hitting approach was pure, raw, unadulterated power.

The 6-foot-5, 230-pound Choi pulled the ball instead. It soared past "Turkeyman's" smoked turkey-leg concession stand in right field and over the QD Quality Dairy Co. sign, clearing the 24-foot right-field wall. The ball continued its trajectory over the outside fence, finally alighting on Cedar Street. If the bomb had been transplanted to Wrigley Field, the ball would have been long gone onto Sheffield Avenue, 400-plus feet from homeplate.

Imagine the range of his homers if the 20-year-old Choi had five more years' experience.

"I'm still making the adjustment to the wooden bat," said Choi, the first Korean player ever in the Cubs' organization. "With the aluminum bat, I hit it farther.

"I'm definitely learning as I go along. I've been here a while, and I'm not getting as good pitches to hit. They're now pitching me outside. I've got to make adjustments. I'll try to go to left field more."

Spoken like a cagey big leaguer. Choi's actions and words, the latter conveyed in 1999 through interpreter Jerry Min, are part of a wave of talent that could stock the Cubs' lineup in the early part of the 21st century. At the dragged-out end of the previous 100 years, when many of the parent Cubs players mentally packed their bags with a half a season to go, prime season-ticket holder "hope" temporarily surrendered its front-row Wrigley Field perch to take up residence more than 200 miles away with the Lugnuts, the Cubs' Class A farm club in the Midwest League.

The Lansing accomplishments of Choi, ballyhooed center-field prospect Corey Patterson, catcher Jeff Goldbach, third baseman David Kelton, pitcher Carlos Zambrano, and outfielder Tydus Meadows have provided a psychological lifeline for long-suffering fans to grasp. After so many decades of management upheaval and poor talent selection, the Cubs finally have a wave of everyday player prospects coming up and stable player-development management to groom them.

But the apparent revival, which team president Andy MacPhail admitted was "invisible" to the average fan back home, wasn't limited to the '99 Lugnuts, whose uniforms from afar look like that of an established winner—the Atlanta Braves. Finally, after too many seasons of misfires and neglect, the Cubs have caught up with most of the rest of baseball in modern-day methods of talent-procurement.

Rated "last in Latin America" in scouting in the mid-1990s by player-development chief Jim Hendry, who is directing the revival, the Cubs now have training academies to match other teams in both the Dominican Republic and Venezuela. Five years into the new millennium may pass before the Cubs reap the fruits of their presence south of the border. But at least the development-challenged team is in there pitching.

And the Cubs have contracted with one of the most popular American players ever to perform in Japanese pro baseball to serve as their coordinator of Pacific Rim scouting. Leon Lee, who lived year-round in Japan and learned the language and local customs of both Japan and Korea during his 12-year Japanese pro career, used his knowledge and reputation to sign Choi for $1 million in late 1997. Then Lee landed a second Korean, 6-foot-2, 210-pound catcher Yoon-Min Kweon, a former junior national teammate of Choi, on December 10, 1999.

The steady movement toward Wrigley Field of minor-league players and improvements in talent procurement finally took hold four seasons into MacPhail's presidency. Reviving a crippled player-development system was akin to turning around an ocean liner in a bathtub. The constant changes in management, from Gordon Goldsberry to Dick Balderson to Al Goldis, had a wrenching effect. There was no continuity. And now there would be another period of adjustment as Goldis virtually faded out of his once-promising Cubs tenure in favor of former college coach Hendry, who in 2000 would be the first scouting director since Goldsberry to supervise five consecutive June amateur drafts.

The first two years of MacPhail's regime was basically spent trying to straighten out the mess of past regimes, filtering out non-productive personnel and trying to set a new course for scouting and the farm system. The Cubs would have to suffer a little longer for the constant front-office changes of the 1987 to 1994 period. To fully realize the end results of a stable player development process would require patience into the new millennium. "It's a six-, seven-, eight-year process," MacPhail said.

Of which the first several years were spent getting the new regime's player-development act together—flushing out the old, bringing in the new.

"No question that a lack of stability in upper management has a trickle-down effect," said Dan O'Brien, Jr., assistant general manager of the Texas Rangers and former Houston Astros scouting director. "Whenever you have a change in management, you're always going to have a step back, an initial step back, while there's a period of adjustment. The question is, what is the size of the adjustment? If it's significant, it definitely can be felt all the way down to the rookie-league level. It goes back to a learning curve to see how quickly the transition takes place."

By now, the changes were taking their toll on Cubs' minor leaguers, some of whom would play under their different third player-development regime by the mid-1990s.

"With the constant changes, you'd never have somebody sticking by you and being in your corner," said outfielder Robin Jennings, a 1991 draftee of then-scouting director Dick Balderson. "That hurt a lot of guys. Whatever regime drafts you and brings you up is in your corner. New guys come in and read reports, but they're also getting heresay about people."

With a conservative, deliberate personality, MacPhail was not the type who would arbitrarily fire large numbers of holdover employees from a previous regime when he assumed power. But he discovered some serious flaws in player-development chief Al Goldis' hand-picked top scouts. Almost right off the bat from MacPhail's ascendancy to the Cubs' presidency in September 1994, he fired national crosscheckers Danny Monzon (who also was Latin American supervisor) and Rod Fridley, and western regional scouting supervisor Jesse Flores. The actual firings and the reasons behind them were buried amid the rancor of the ongoing players' strike at the time. However, one reason was an apparent lack of written reports filed by scouts like Monzon.

Goldis, now a scout for the Cincinnati Reds, defended the fired scouts. "They filed reports and sent them in to the computer system," he said. "The reports were lost. Andy wanted to see Danny's reports. They weren't there. So he fired him. Carl Rice [the Cubs' computer-system supervisor] found the reports later."

Rice refuted Goldis' claims. He said he never found missing scouting reports in the computer system.

MacPhail had removed GM Larry Himes and shifted him to an Arizona-based scouting job. Then he offered Goldis, who had run both departments under Himes, the choice of either running the scouting or the minor leagues. Goldis picked scouting, signing a two-year contract. MacPhail also wanted Goldis, who had handled scouting and farm-system duties out of his home in Sarasota, Florida, to be based in Chicago. Some front-office tension had been created by Goldis' far-afield style. Meanwhile, Hendry was hired away from various player-development roles with the expansion Florida Marlins to run the minor-league system. Hendry had been named *Baseball America's* college coach of the year for leading Omaha's Creighton University to a third-place finish in the College World Series in 1991, prior to being hired by the Marlins. He brought some of that collegiate rah-rah spirit to the Cubs organization, a man who was bluntly honest and humorous in a cutting, bench-razzing manner.

While Goldis began preparing for the 1995 draft, MacPhail and Hendry began dismantling the rubber tires-balance beams-eye tests training systems that had been set up under Himes and Goldis. MacPhail reasoned that the previous regime had strayed from basic player development, emphasizing technology and gadgets instead of plain ol' fashioned playing and fundamentals repetition. And despite the financial dislocations of the strike, the Cubs added a hitting coach for each minor-league team, complementing the manager and pitching coach, for the 1995 season. In the previous two years, Goldis had complained he could not add a hitting coach due to budget restrictions.

Running the farm system, Hendry had an immediate problem on his hands in Goldis' 1994 first-round pick Jayson Peterson, who went through his first spring training with the minor leaguers in 1995.

"From the day I got here, he never worked hard, never wanted to go by the rules," he said. "To me, his ability at a young age was going backward. I sent him out of spring training his first year because he didn't want to get in line, didn't want to run, didn't want to do his regular work, and had a very surly 'I can do whatever I want as the first-round pick' attitude. We're not looking for altar boys. But people want to have to work. He didn't put in the time, effort, and energy to become a major-league player."

'95 Draft after Wood Unproductive

With his duties cut in half, Goldis was still entrusted with the 1995 draft. The Cubs picked fourth. Dallas-area schoolboy star Kerry Wood was passed up by the three teams ahead of the Cubs. Goldis pounced on Wood, and the Cubs seemed pleased. To this day, MacPhail will remind you that Wood was not picked by the three other teams. "Al should get credit for Wood," he said. "The scouting director is directly responsible for the draft."

That cut both ways. Goldis was responsible for what followed in '95 after Wood. His 1994 draft has proved almost a complete bust. On the heels of that gaping hole moving through the farm system, the lack of production from '95 draft from Round 2 down compounded the problem. The Cubs thus had little from which to draw from the minors in 1998 and 1999, when the crop of 1994-95 draftees should have been knocking on the door of the majors.

Lefthander Brian McNichol, the second pick in '95, said a number of draftees from his crop were beset by injuries, including himself. McNichol, who made a cameo appearance with the Cubs at the end of the 1999 season, was the only other '95 Cubs draftee besides Wood to make the majors by '99. Righthander Jeff Yoder, the No. 3 pick and a recommendation of Goldis-favored scout Ed Ford, lost a year to injury in 1997. He had made it only as far as Double-A by '99.

Goldis is still miffed that MacPhail did not give him additional money to sign the 1995 No. 4 pick, shortstop Adam Everett, a high schooler out of suburban Atlanta. Everett spurned the Cubs' offer, went to college, and was drafted No. 1 by the Boston Red Sox in 1998. Everett was traded to the Houston Astros after the 1999 season. Hendry later said that Yoder may have been overpaid for what the No. 3 slot in the draft at that time would have commanded, making less money available to offer Everett.

Although Goldis, who was hired by Larry Himes, handled the draft, MacPhail takes the responsibility for the failures of the 1995 post-Wood selections on his shoulders. The selections, and their subsequent development in the minors, took place on his watch, he reasoned.

The Goldis-MacPhail relationship was not fated to last long. Goldis became dissatisfied with top management in Chicago as he was demoted to a national crosschecker position in the fall of 1995 as Hendry replaced him as scouting director. He was labeled a "special assistant" to GM Ed Lynch for the 1996 season, but in reality he was being phased out as the end of his contract neared. He was not invited to attend the 1996 draft, the first one conducted by Hendry. Soon he was out of the Cubs organization altogether, his glory days of drafting Jack McDowell, Robin Ventura, Frank Thomas, and Alex Fernandez in succession now very much past tense.

"They were good baseball people," MacPhail said of Himes and Goldis. "I'm not going to denigrate the people who were here before." Goldis is long-gone from the organization, but Himes in 2000 had spent twice as much time as a special-assignment scout—all under MacPhail—than he did as Cubs GM.

While Hendry prepared for his first draft in 1996, former Braves minor-league official David Wilder was tapped to take over administration of the Cubs' farm system. He found few assets besides Wood, third baseman Kevin Orie, and a platoon of outfielders of almost equal ability—and who all, with the exception of center fielder Doug Glanville, played virtually the same position.

While Wilder supervised the grooming of Wood in Class A in 1996, he also began to be frustrated by the progress of Goldis' top pick in 1993, slugger Brooks Kieschnick. The big left-handed hitter, a slow-footed gent who in reality was a designated hitter, seemingly had a breakout season at Triple-A Iowa in 1995, leading the American Association with 23 homers and 149 hits while batting .295. But the Cubs believed Kieschnick needed more experience after only two-plus pro seasons, and he remained at Iowa for 1996.

Kieschnick's production declined modestly in 1996 as his power-to-all fields swing changed. Hendry said his swing got longer as time went on.

"I liked Brooks a lot," he said. "Brooks Kieschnick in my opinion had a very, very long swing. Some people can shorten their swings. He had a hard time shortening it. Brooks put pressure on himself to hit home runs and get here. They didn't have to go 100 feet out of the ballpark. He tried to hit balls 500 feet. But he had enough power to hit the ball out into left-center field."

Present-day Pittsburgh Pirates coach Rick Renick, who was manager of Triple-A Nashville, an Iowa Cubs' opponent, in 1995-96, also said he liked

Kieschnick. But Renick's analysis is the same as Hendry's: "In his mind, he thought he had to start hitting a lot of homers. He thought he had to get his swing longer and pull the ball more, instead of hitting the ball to left field, which he could do well. I thought he'd do well at Wrigley Field, because he could hit the ball all over. He was a great kid. He played hard."

Kieschnick got a brief shot at the Cubs' left-field job in 1997. But he became caught in a merry-go-round of minor-league outfielders who pretty much canceled each other out as they played the same position. Only the speedy Doug Glanville survived the numbers crunch, and he's now starring in center field for the Philadelphia Phillies.

In addition to slugger Kieschnick, the Cubs' system had Robin Jennings, who was considered the best all-around hitting talent of the outfield prospects. Left-handed hitter Pedro Valdes, a 1990 draftee out of Puerto Rico, had the best pure swing. Right-handed hitter Ozzie Timmons had shown flashes of power both in the minors (22 homers at Iowa in 1994) and with the Cubs. First baseman Brant Brown found his path blocked at Wrigley Field by Mark Grace, so he was shifted to left field, where he nervously donned an outfielder's glove for his first regular stretch in pro baseball. All had double digit homer totals and relatively high batting averages in Triple-A.

"They were all good young talent," Renick said. "They had starting potential. I thought a lot of these kids would play for the Cubs."

Others weren't so sure. Several scouts said none of the players had star quality; they were "fourth-outfielder" types.

The field was too crowded when the Cubs threw open the left-field job for the platoon of outfielders in the spring of 1997. Kieschnick, Valdes, and Jennings were sent back to the minors after brief trials, while Brown bounced to and from Iowa. Timmons was traded out of the organization. Only Glanville stuck (out of position) in left field, hitting an even .300 in a semi-regular role in 1997. Brown filled in superbly for an injured Lance Johnson in the first half of the 1998 season, but hurt his shoulder diving for a ball in an interleague game in Detroit. Kieschnick ended up as fodder for the expansion draft, wandering through the minors as Tampa Bay property in 1998-99. Valdes was let go. Jennings was the last of the outfielders to leave the Cubs via six-year free agency after the 1999 season.

"No one really got an opportunity," Jennings said. "To try out six guys at one position and come up with a surefire winner, it was like pulling numbers out of a hat. You couldn't put all the players into one. They just stuck with it way too long, and used the revolving door way too long. A lot of those guys competing for the job lost out in their careers.

"It's really strange. It's hard for me to believe that guys coming off great minor-league seasons, that if they didn't think they would crack the lineup, why keep them around? They'd wait until they were out of options and leave them back in the minors."

To be sure, opposing teams weren't exactly banging down Ed Lynch's door to trade for the outfield surplus. In the end, the Cubs did not need all the outfielders with basically one position open in Wrigley Field. All the while, the farm system was desperately short of middle infielders and catchers due to the over-emphasis on top-round pitching picks in previous drafts.

Prospects who seemed to thrive at the lower levels of the minor leagues hit a wall as they tried to progress upward through the system.

"You can give the players all the instruction they need, but if they don't have the ability, the skills, or the aptitude to move along and be successful as you planned it to be, it will be a lost cause somewhere down the road," Cubs minor-league pitching coordinator Lester Strode said.

"More so than anything, it seems to catch up with them once they hit that Double-A or Triple-A level. The breaking point is at that Double-A level. It seems that at the Double-A level, most organizations put their best prospects on the field at that particular time. That's where you're going to see what kind of true ability you have out there on the field."

By 1997, after surveying the minor leagues, David Wilder said the Cubs possessed only two "impact" prospects—Kerry Wood and catcher Pat Cline. Wilder defined "impact" by the measure of star-quality players who had made it up to the Atlanta Braves, his former employer: Chipper Jones, Javier Lopez, and Ryan Klesko. The evaluation of Wood was definitely on the mark, but Cline's star began to fade after two good years in Class A in 1996 and 1997. By 1999, he was a slump-ridden Triple-A player who had been shifted to right field.

Looking beyond the Borders

The Cubs weren't alone in among major-league teams in ruing the lack of development of highly touted draftees. With a shrunken overall domestic talent base in the 1990s due to the rise of other sports siphoning off baseball prospects, Hendry did not want to keep relying on the draft alone to fill the Cubs' talent needs. "You cannot, in my opinion, anymore in this country take one pick a round in the amateur draft, without augmentation from the Dominican Republic, Venezuela, and Asia — and think you're going to have a completely well-rounded system," he said. Hendry soon found the people to carry out the Cubs' first comprehensive international scouting program.

A young go-getter who pushed the Cubs to start their Latin-American training facilities is Oneri Fleita, a second-generation Cuban-American. A former player at Creighton for Hendry and a rookie-league manager in the Baltimore Orioles' farm system, Fleita, 33, was hired as manager of the low Class-A Williamsport Cubs of the New York-Penn League in 1995. He shifted to scouting in 1996, based out of his home in Omaha. But he always had a fascination for Latin-American scouting. He asked Hendry to allow him to move to Georgia later in '96 so he could cover that state, Florida, and the Caribbean. Fleita soon became the team's Latin American coordinator.

When he worked in the Cubs' instructional league at the start of his Chicago tenure, Fleita had thought the makeup of the Cubs team was "night and day" compared to the Orioles. "'Where the hell are the Latin guys?'" he asked himself.

He wasn't any happier once he looked around what passed for Cubs facilities in the Dominican Republic. Fleita realized the program needed to be built from the ground up. And more work still needs to be done. As of 2000, only one homegrown Dominican player, pitcher Amaury Telemaco, had ever reached the Cubs' major-league roster.

"We couldn't do any worse than what we were doing," Fleita said. "Our Dominican team was in a co-op situation with two other teams. We didn't have adequate facilities. We just had one field. There were billy goats tied up to stakes in the ground; they were the groundskeepers because we didn't have a mower."

The Dominican facility that Al Goldis had claimed Danny Monzon had begun to set up had never come to pass. Fleita persuaded Hendry, and subsequently MacPhail, that the Cubs should have a training base in the talent-rich country.

He could build on the Cubs' name, familiar to Dominicans due to Sammy Sosa's rising profile and the televised games on superstation WGN-TV. "Then we developed the fact we're out there scouting," Fleita said. "All I heard was negatives [about the Cubs' scouting presence]. I was shocked the Cubs were so far behind."

Fleita then hired former Orioles farm-system teammate Jose Serra, a native of San Pedro de Macoris, Sosa's hometown, as top Dominican scout. In turn, Serra hired two part-timers to increase coverage of the Dominican, while asking Cubs minor-league instructors to come down "to make the kids feel they're part of the organization."

Finally, Fleita got around to building the facility at Santana, an hour from Santo Domingo. "We fixed the holes in the field and had the Cubs logo painted on," he said. "Then we asked the organization to give us batting cages. We then built a 3,000-square-foot clubhouse. It was done as nice as they could have done; the local people helped us out and earned a living in construction."

Fleita then rented two homes where 20 young players could be housed. Two housekeepers, one a cook and another a cleaner, work in the homes. Ultimately, he would like to build dormitories, but the young Dominicans have it better than home now in the rented housing. "The kids get three squares a day," Fleita said. "They grow month by month. We have an English class three days a week with a professor coming in. If they don't make it in baseball, they'll still learn English and be able to work at a hotel. And they can be better people in life."

By the end of 1999, Fleita and his scouts had signed "close to 50 kids. But to me, we won't be successful until we can say we have someone in Class AA."

While he was a whirling dervish in building up the Latin program, Fleita found the time to help scout Corey Patterson and David Kelton, who got off to good starts in their Cubs' organizational careers at Lansing in 1999.

Fleita did not stop with the Dominican. While some financially pressed teams can only afford a training facility or academy in one Latin-American country, the Cubs are finally applying their considerable resources properly. The Astros may have beaten the Cubs to Venezuela by almost a decade, but at least the North Siders are there now.

Fleita is now renting a stadium in Puerto Caballa and has constructed dormitories under the bleachers. "We've divided the country into thirds [for scouting territories]," he said. "We added two new scouts and a manager and pitching coach, and participated in the Venezuelan summer league for the first time in 1999. Hector Ortega's working full-time and will run the whole show. There are four part-time guys in Venezuela."

In Puerto Rico the Cubs employ a full-time scout, Jose Trujillo, along with the requisite bird-dogs. Question, please? How will the Cubs find guys from out-of-the-way places like the Dutch-run island of Curacao, which produced Andruw Jones and Randall Simon for the Braves?

"A lot of kids from places like that play in tourneys all over the Caribbean," Fleita said. "You find out when the tourneys are, and you try to have someone at those tourneys. The Braves just did a good job in scouting guys like Jones."

The development of the training bases and the beefing up of scouting leads Fleita to believe that "out of 30 teams, we're in the top 10 now" in presence in the Caribbean. "We'll create a network. We'll lose players in the process, but in the end we'll come out on top.

"I have no doubt in my mind this will be built up more. The basement of the house has been set perfectly. I think we have a group of guys who care about getting good players to the States."

Jim Hendry estimates that the Caribbean training facilities cost between "half a million and three-quarters of a million dollars a year to operate, not counting who you sign."

The Cubs will need to groom their own kids through the Dominican and Venezuelan training facilities. Andy MacPhail will shy away from expensive Latin prospects, including émigré Cubans, represented by high-powered agent Joe Cubas.

"There are some areas where we're not going to be aggressive, where we don't think we match up and will get the end result," said MacPhail. "We're not as aggressive when Joe Cubas gets his players and takes them from camp to camp, goes to the Yankees and Braves. We'll instead try to open up other avenues. We don't have the resources to be all things to all people."

Although MacPhail sounded like just another Cubs management skinflint with that comment, he is in reality committing dollars to foreign talent. That's been the case with Leon Lee's Pacific Rim work that has netted a possible Mark Grace successor in Choi, just 21 in 2000.

Once again, the Cubs had lagged behind the trend-setters in the game in working Japan and Korea. A scout, Tad Powers, had worked Australia back in the Al Goldis era, but the Cubs scarcely had any other presence in the Far East in the mid-1990s. When asked why he didn't add a Pacific Rim scout, Goldis said, "Why should I have been worrying about that when I couldn't get enough money to sign Adam Everett [in 1995]?"

Meanwhile, the Dodgers under former owner Peter O'Malley established themselves early in the game with the signings of Hideo Nomo out of Japan and Chan Ho Park from Korea. Just like in the 1940s and 1950s, the Dodgers were light years ahead of the Cubs in talent procurement methods despite no advantage in the exchequer.

"O'Malley brought the Dodgers to the forefront," Lee said. "He was aggressive in spending the money. He went to Korea six times before he signed Chan Ho Park."

Even the Montreal Expos fished around on the other side of the Pacific; Lee worked as a consultant for the Expos from 1992 to 1994, after serving as technical advisor to the Tom Selleck movie *Mr. Baseball*.

"It's grown fast," Lee said of Pacific Rim scouting. "There are probably 18 to 20 teams that are active over there. Some specific teams have not followed proper protocol [in scouting and trying to sign players], and they have tough times making progress."

A former minor-league player in the Cardinals' farm system, Lee is the brother of early San Diego Padres outfielder Leron Lee, with whom he was re-united with the Lotte Orions of the Japanese Pacific League. Signing on as the Cubs' Pacific Rim coordinator in January 1998, after the winter meetings, Lee immediately put his contacts and high profile to work.

"I established a reputation for off-the-field activities," Lee said. "I worked with disabled kids and orphans. They said I had a Japanese heart. But you are never really accepted as Japanese.

"I learned Japanese. I made up my mind that I would be there. My interpreter started teaching me some Japanese songs. I actually went on TV, sung Japanese songs, and made a record. I was on TV with a singing contest. I had a sing-off with a Japanese singer. I got 100, he got a 98. I also published a [sports] magazine there. The people appreciated it that here's a guy making an effort to acclimate himself to Japanese culture."

Lee lived in Japan year-round, save for the Christmas holidays, when he came home to visit family.

"I could make money in off-season, making appearances. My kids, including Derrek [a Florida Marlins first baseman], went to school there. I'd do the Japanese World Series in Japanese as color announcer.

"I look at it as going to their country not expecting things to be the same. I'll respect way they do things. I'm the only Pacific Rim coordinator with the kind of background. Because of that stature, I can get in doors. They still recognize me."

Lee typically makes seven scouting trips a year, each lasting seven to 10 days, from his home in Fulsom, California. But it was down among the sheltering palms of Florida where he first spied Choi.

"I already found out the Korean national team was going to train in Cocoa Beach," he said. "Choi caught my eye immediately. There were no other scouts there. I then went to Korea in April 1998 to see him, and I really liked him."

On two subsequent scouting trips to Korea, Lee first took Midwest regional scouting supervisor Brad Kelley, then Jim Hendry himself on the follow-up journey. But Lee worried the effort might be for naught. "They had changed his hand position and had him wrapping his bat really bad. He didn't look good," he said. "I got permission from his coach to change his hands."

But the establishment at Korea University, for whom Choi played, did not want him to depart for the U.S. Top players in Korea are paid to go to college, Lee said. And an initial Cubs' contract offer of $800,000 had been rejected. However, Lee's stature as an ex-pro player in Japan helped bridge the gap. The Cubs had to agree to compensate the university for the money they had paid Choi—and then some. Choi finally got $1 million to sign. "I went to Andy MacPhail and said, 'There's no Korean who's ever been a position player in the big leagues,'" Jim Hendry said. "I want to sign this guy. It will be $1 million or a little over. There was no 'Oh, we can't do that. What are you thinking about?'"

Hope's Box Seat at Lansing

Lee landed an outstanding individual in Choi. He's eager to learn baseball, American style. And if his first year at Lansing was any indication, he got nothing but A's and B's. He batted .321 in 79 games spread over 290 at-bats. Choi had 18 homers, 18 doubles, and 70 RBI. He also scored 71 runs. Choi displayed a good eye at the plate with 50 walks, amassing an impressive on-base percentage of .422. Only a total of 18 errors at first base marred an otherwise stellar line. Despite the bobbles at first base, he seems to have very good agility around the bag for a big man. Brooks Kieschnick also had great minor-league numbers, but Choi appears to be a better overall athlete than Kieschnick.

He dreams big dreams.

"I want to be a left-handed complement to Sammy Sosa," he said through interpreter Min.

Even though he scarcely knew English, Choi eagerly soaked up all the instruction he could get. Before the July 24, 1999 game against Ft. Wayne, then-Lansing hitting coach Steve McFarland used body English to demonstrate good batting form in a little bull session with Choi behind the batting cage at Oldsmobile Park. "Hands and hips together, said McFarland (named the Lansing manager after the season), as he held his hands together, then pointed to his hips. In turn, Choi pointed his index finger to his head in the international acknowledgement that he understood.

The language barrier was the one hole in Choi's game he wanted to close up. He vowed to learn English quickly so he can truly feel a part of the Cubs' organization. He'll succeed if he can pick up the language as fast as he has done with the ways of American minor-league baseball.

"The biggest hurdle right now is learning English and communicating with the other players, off the field," Min said. "The players right now are missing out on how fun he can be.

"He told me about when he went to college in Korea, he was like a team clown," Min said. "He was always goofing around, making practical jokes, trying to make people laugh. He just enjoys life for what it is. Even the time he struggles, doesn't have a good game or two, he doesn't dwell on it."

Choi did not have trouble communicating his feelings with body English. One day after my first conversation, Choi acknowledged my presence again in the locker room as he went to the showers. He gave me a playful punch on the shoulder in the universal language of "How 'ya doin'?"

Otherwise, Choi did not suffer any culture shock traveling among the small cities of the Midwest League.

Min said Choi likes American food. So eating well in meat-and-potatoes mid-America was not a challenge. He'd have his first exposure to down-home Southern cooking when he was promoted to Double-A West Tenn in Jackson, Tennesee. In contrast, many young Latin-American players, already burdened by learning English from scratch, reported missing their staples of rice and beans when they first toured the minor-league outposts.

"He's been around the world with the [Korean] national team," Min said. "He's been to Europe. And he's been to the United States three other times. He's somewhat used to the American culture, the different foods, and the lifestyle. He's adjusted very well."

Choi's easy adjustment to American culture was not all that surprising to Lee.

"Koreans are more outgoing," Lee said. "The Japanese are more culturally shy. The Koreans are more aggressive by nature. They're physically bigger than the Japanese. Korean athletes are a whole lot bigger and stronger. Their diet is more meat-based than in Japan."

Restrictions on talent are tougher in Japan. Pro players must have nine years of service before they gain free agency rights. By then, many have moved past the prime of their careers. Loopholes that allowed Nomo to leave have since been closed.

"That's why we're focusing more on Korea," said Lee, who is in the process of learning the language to complement his Japanese. "In Korea, you become a free agent after seven years as a pro, but compensation [to the Korean team] is needed. It's still easier to get players out of Korea."

Hence the late-1999 signing of catcher Yoon-Min Kweon, to whom the Cubs committed considerable dollars. Lee also had signed a Japanese infielder, Takaaki Kato, out of Keio University, early in 1998, but Kato spent just one year in the low minor leagues before being released.

Like any new-age entrepreneur, Lee wants to continue to open the global marketplace. He'd love permission to get into mainland China, which possesses an embryonic national baseball program. Lee even said he has a connection with a Chinese real-estate mogul who could get him past the Big Brother government regulators in Beijing to establish relationships with the baseball people. Competing Pacific Rim scouts aren't as yet wired in like that. Lee even mentioned a bowler on the Pakistani cricket team who is clocked at 100 MPH, and the fact Singapore is beginning a baseball program.

Lee's dream job would have him operating his own division as an arm of the scouting department to thoroughly cover Asia. "We'd need to have three full-time people out in the field and one behind the computer," he said.

But MacPhail threw some cold water on those expansionist dreams.

"Leon might be a little ahead of himself," he said of Lee's desire to scout China. "There are other areas where baseball is developed well. We have adequate manpower to cover the Pacific Rim now. We're pretty happy scouting in Korea and Japan."

Obviously, an influx in foreign talent had to make up for inevitable misfirings and injuries of draft products, the slow development of other draftees, and the trades of top picks for veteran players.

Hendry drafted top high school pitching prospects Todd Noel and Jon Garland No. 1 in 1996 and 1997, respectively. But GM Ed Lynch had to surrender both kids to plug up a leaky bullpen in mid-season 1998, Noel traded to the Marlins for lefthander Felix Heredia and Garland to the White Sox for righthander Matt Karchner. The No. 2 pick in '96 was naturally-talented outfielder Quincy Carter, who had a split-sports personality due to his quarterbacking talents at the University of Georgia. After three mediocre low minor-league seasons, Carter, good enough to be a Heisman Trophy candidate, opted to stick with football.

The No. 3 pick in '96, pitcher Skip Ames, blew out his arm. As 2000 began, the Cubs were still waiting on the development of pitcher Chris Gissell (No. 4) and infielder-outfielder Chad Meyers (No. 5), a Creighton product who briefly took over at second base at the end of the 1999 season. Lefthander Phil Norton, the No. 10 pick, was on a steady path upward until running into problems at Triple-A in 1999.

The Cubs lost the second-round pick in 1997 to the White Sox in compensation for signing free-agent pitcher Kevin Tapani. No. 3 pick Scott Downs, a left-handed pitcher, made his Cubs' debut in 2000. No. 5 pick Jaisen Randolph, a speedy outfielder, has shown good progress into the middle levels of the system. A surprise was No. 26 pick Mike Meyers, a Canadian right-handed pitcher, who enjoyed a 14-3 overall season in 1999 split between high Class A Daytona and Double-A West Tenn.

Many of these players found improved conditions for development as the Cubs shuffled their minor-league franchises around in the late 1990s. The Class AA team was moved from Orlando, which had a cramped locker room and old facilities on a field next to the Citrus Bowl football stadium, to a new ballpark in Jackson, Tennessee. But the biggest leap forward in facilities and atmosphere was at Lansing. The Cubs previously had owned a Midwest League team in Rockford. But a new stadium was not in the offing in Illinois' second-largest city, and attendance was below expectations at old Marinelli Field. When the opportunity came to re-locate to spanking-new, city-built Oldsmobile Park in Lansing, the Cubs jumped at it.

"Our minor-leaguers play in better environments in Lansing and West Tenn," MacPhail said.

Oldsmobile Park has everything a player development department needs to groom their kids: enthusiastic fans who show up in good numbers, a decent-sized home clubhouse and an indoor batting cage beyond the center-field wall that permits fundamentals drills to continue even in bad weather. The cage features batting tees on which players can practice different aspects of their swing. Indoor pitching mounds can be set up in the cage so the Lansing hurlers can throw when rain or cold weather makes outdoor work off the bullpen mound impractical, or when extra sessions on learning new pitches or mechanics are needed.

In such an atmosphere, Corey Patterson, the No. 1 draft pick in 1998, began to make Cubs fans believe another Lou Brock was in the making in 1999.

Steve McFarland and a few others in the organization believe the 5-foot-9, 175-pound Patterson won't be just a speedy basestealer. Viewing Patterson from afar, he looks like another 1980s-vintage Cardinals fleet-footed outfielder. But McFarland said Patterson has "30-30" potential— the vaunted 30-homer, 30-stolen bases level that only Sammy Sosa has achieved in Cubs history.

"I don't think I'm going to be much of a power hitter," Patterson said. "I like to hit the ball in the gaps. If not, put the ball on the ground and use my speed. If I am a 30-30 guy, that's great. If not, that's fine, too."

Patterson's 1999 pro debut line in Lansing sounded like Brock at his best: a .320 average in 112 games spread over 475 at-bats. The center fielder had 20 homers, 35 doubles, a league-leading 18 triples, 79 RBI, and 35 stolen bases in 42 attempts.

Even before he masters the nuances of hitting, Patterson could help the Cubs with his speed and defense.

"I think I'm a pretty good defensive player right now," he said. "Every day, I come to the park, I think defense and baserunning come hand in hand. You should never have any problems with that. Anyone can play good defense. They may struggle with the bat for a little while as they move up. Defense is a very important part of the game, which may be overlooked sometimes."

Patterson and Brock are linked by an accident of history. Patterson was born on August 13, 1979, the very day Brock collected his 3,000th hit against the Cubs' Dennis Lamp.

"I've seen clips and highlights," Patterson said of Brock's career. "I actually got to meet him [in 1999]. I saw him at the futures [stars of the game] in Boston. He was our manager. I have high respect for him. He's a great guy. It's an honor being compared to him."

Patterson knows all too well the attention focused on him, as a kind

of savior after too many years of non-production from the minors. Few
five-tool players ever come through the Cubs' farm system.

"I knew after I got drafted that the expectations were going to be high
from the fans and other people," said Patterson. "What I try to do is block
all the pressure and tension out and every night just do the best I can and
get better every day.

"I definitely think I can make it fairly quickly, depending on how hard
I work and how better I can continue to improve. I'm not going to set any
timetable on myself. I think if I do improve, it will be left up to the organization."

Patterson is smart enough to know his success won't be automatic—
and it must be earned. Throughout 1999, overeager fans called for
Patterson to simply be handed the Cubs' center-field job for 2000 with just
his one season of Class A experience under his belt. But if they had
watched him carefully in Lansing, they would have understood he simply needed some more experience.

Although Patterson had a fabulous all-around offensive season, he
still made some mistakes of inexperience. In one game against the Ft.
Wayne Wizards, he slashed a sinking liner to center that was dropped.
He motored into second—standing up. The ball arrived at the same time
and Patterson was tagged out. He also needed to close up the holes in his
swing against left-handed pitchers, who are not all that common in the
Midwest League.

Interviewing Patterson in Lansing, I couldn't tell if he was 19 or 29
if I already didn't know his age. He was a polished interviewee even as
a teenager.

"I give thanks to my parents," Patterson said of the source of his
maturity. His father, Don Patterson, is a former NFL defensive back with
the Detroit Lions and New York Giants.

"They did a great job raising me," he added. "I'm sure they'll continue
to do so. I try to stay calm when things aren't going well in baseball. You
have to maintain your composure and not get too overexcited. My biggest
thing is to try to stay calm and not let emotion take over."

Also getting some credit in his development is a member of the Cubs'
All-Century team—Bruce Sutter.

The former split-fingered fastball specialist had settled in suburban
Kennesaw, Georgia, after his career ended with the Atlanta Braves more
than a decade ago. The Pattersons also were Kennesaw residents. Sutter's

youngest son, Ben, is best friends with Patterson. The younger Sutter and Patterson played together, helping capture the 1998 Georgia state baseball title at Harrison High School in Kennesaw.

Ever the supportive parent, Bruce Sutter spearheaded the fundraising drive to improve the baseball facilities at Harrison High. One scout who saw Patterson play on his home field said the Harrison complex is better than a lot of high-school football fields and buildings in football-crazy Georgia. Part of Patterson's development can be credited to the excellent facilities and community backing.

"There were a lot of people who helped out, a lot of hard work," Sutter said. "It was a new school, and we had to build the baseball field, build the pressbox, locker rooms, dugouts, and batting cages. It was all privately funded, and we had to raise a lot of money, did a lot of golf tournaments and other events."

Sutter most likely knows Patterson better than anyone in the Cubs' organization.

"Corey spends a lot of time at our house," Sutter said. "He's a terrific young player and a terrific young man. If he can go to Double-A in 2000 and put up the same kind of numbers he did this year [at Class A Lansing], he will come up to the majors pretty soon.

"He's a kid who can do anything on the baseball field. He's got the right attitude. If he strikes out four times in a game or hits four homers, he's going to be the same when he walks off the field. His mom and dad have done a great job with him. He's going to be a special player."

Modest almost to a fault, Patterson did not set himself apart from his Lansing teammates in 1999. He roomed with third baseman Kelton and catcher Goldbach. Although Patterson was promoted further up the minor-league ladder ahead of Kelton and Goldbach in 2000, the trio remained friends, and looked forward to the day when they could win as Cubs together.

"We had a real good idea that we had a strength here," southern Indianan Goldbach, now the organization's best catching prospect, said of the collection of young talent's cohesiveness on the '99 Lugnuts. Goldbach and Kelton were both taken in the second round in '98 on the heels of Patterson's selection.

"I try not to look at it [the Cubs' long-term catching needs], but I'd lie if I said I didn't," Goldbach said. "I would like to get to the major leagues as fast as possible, and this is a good position to do it in.

"I would like to be a power hitter. If I'm going to be a doubles hitter, that will be fine with me." Goldbach is not the physically biggest catcher, under six feet and 190 pounds, but wants to bulk up to 200 pounds to handle the rigors of the long season at the higher minor-league levels.

Kelton, who hails from West Point, Georgia, has a tall, almost lanky build that gives a hint of Chipper Jones. He knows he has to adjust to off-speed pitches as he moves up. "I feel like I can put up some home run numbers," he said. Defensively, he said he has a "lot of confidence" in handling different third-base situations.

Kelton said he and his teammates "love it" when asked if their group can help revive the minor-league system. They felt challenged when *Baseball America* and other publications rated the Cubs near the bottom in recent years on player development quality and number of prospects.

Meanwhile, Cubs fans seemed to take up seats behind hope's front-row perch in Lansing. Hearing of the Lugnuts' exploits on WGN-TV Cubs broadcasts, Kelton and Co. reported receiving a steady flow of fan mail from Illinois. "It was surprising when I first got to Lansing," he said. "It was fun to come to the ballpark and have mail for you."

As the players rise through the farm system, Hendry said they will not experience a formal, detailed self-evaluation system of the kind practiced by the Cleveland Indians.

"We give each player an off-season conditioning program," he said. "We talk to each player individually about their strengths and weaknesses. But players aren't stupid. Let's not over-analyze this thing. The game is the game. And we have quality instruction, quality roving instruction. We play 140 games. The player is welcome to talk about his situation every day."

Someone is doing something right. Hopelessness is no longer the byword for Cubs player development. The system is starting to rise in the eyes of the baseball world.

"The Cubs system is infinitely better than two years ago," *Baseball America* analyst David Rawnsley said. Hendry draws positive comments from baseball types when you ask about him.

After David Wilder was promoted from farm chief to assistant general manager after the 1998 season, Hendry added the minor leagues to his supervisory duties. The management structure is now similar to that of Gordon Goldsberry's tenure from 1981 to 1988—one Chicago-based man in charge to pull the often bickering factions of scouting and the minor leagues together, while finding the time to go out and scout players himself.

One of these personally scouted players was controversial No. 1 1999 draftee Ben Christensen of Wichita State. Hendry showed he could stand the heat in the kitchen by taking the righthander, who had been suspended for the season after hitting Evansville batter Anthony Molina in the face with a thrown ball while he was standing in the on-deck circle timing pitches. Although the Cubs were widely and vehemently criticized for taking Christensen, Hendry claimed his research had showed the pitcher had an exemplary personal record otherwise, and that the Molina beaning was an aberration. He looked at Christensen, otherwise a possible Top 10 draft pick if not for the incident, falling to the No. 26 spot as an opportunity to be mined, talent-wise and financially. Christensen would cost less further down in the first round.

If Christensen shows the proper contrition and personal behavior over the long run and comes through as a Cub, the beaning will be cast into history. Hendry no doubt will be lauded for taking a gamble amid the firestorm of protest.

That has been the only controversy of an increasingly productive career in the front office that has led to at least one associate to compare Hendry to Goldsberry.

Latin American scouting supervisor Oneri Fleita said the two men are similar, even though Hendry's personality is more rough-hewn than the courtly Goldsberry's. Fleita knew the latter man from his days in the Orioles' farm system earlier in the 1990s.

"Jim and Gordy have a lot of similarities," Fleita said. "These men have huge hearts, check their ego at the door, care about people and take time to care about their families. There aren't many people who can do the job Jim's doing. Pulling together scouting and player development is important."

The crucial test will be if the Cubs can keep the present player development structure intact. At least one prominent Cubs player suggests Hendry should be a good general manager candidate, somewhere. The continuity that has been hard-won again could be broken if Hendry ever gets a better job offer before the rebuilding of Cubs player development is finished.

"You look at Hendry, and you should make sure he has someone good behind him," former Tribune Co. Cubs corporate overseer Jim Dowdle said. "If you know Hendry's going a good job, so do other teams."

Working smartly and efficiently will have to be the byword for Hendry and his staff. They will not be showered with the game's top budget. They will not match dollar for dollar with the Yankees, again by Andy MacPhail's choice.

"I don't look at it as a badge of honor by increasing [player development] expenses," he said. "That should not be the measure of a club's commitment to development and scouting. It's not just what you spend, but how well you do it and where you apply your resources."

Whatever is spent, however it is spent, nothing will matter in ending the million-to-one era until the Cubs begin tapping a talent pipeline from below that has rarely been completely open.

Chapter 15

THE PSYCHOLOGY OF WINNING

HE SOUNDS LIKE a fast-talking salesman or corny Texas business-man, but Drayton McLane seems to have struck on the right mental approach in helping make his team one of the winningest franchises in baseball.

The owner of the Houston Astros is no shrinking violet. McLane will start off games sitting in his field-level seat, then circulate among fans to see how things are going.

"I'll wander through the stands talking to people," he said. "I'll do the first and second inning behind the plate, then work the crowd and come back. We're in the customer service business."

Before and after games, though, he's the Astros' top cheerleader. "I talk to the players about being competitive, being successful," he said. "If you don't have a $90 million payroll and all the best players, you've got to get them feeling good. You go down and sit with the players' wives; we care about them. I'll go out and make 200 speeches a year."

McLane believes you can develop a winning atmosphere, and can talk it up. So while he leaves the trades and drafts and other personnel moves to his hired hands, McLane tries to set the tempo for the Astros. From the mid-1990s on, it looks like he's been successful.

"We talk about being champions," McLane said. "I stole a line from Ronald Reagan, 'It can be done.' We changed a lot of things here. We changed management. We changed uniforms. We changed the clubhouse. We talk every day about winning. Too often in pro baseball, you don't use emotions."

McLane believes the same out-front approach can work with a team that has the most unique image in pro sports.

"If I owned the Cubs, I'd put all that stuff about losers in a bonfire," he said. "You've got to see yourself as a winner, you've got to feel good about yourself, about winning."

But McLane was reminded that his rah-rah style was the exact opposite of low-key, behind-the-scenes Cubs president Andy MacPhail's.

"Then if not with Andy, get somebody else involved to say it around the organization," he said. "Somebody's got to lead the charge. Losing begets losing."

Well, MacPhail himself confirms he is not going to adopt the McLane cheerleading style.

"You can't talk your way [to winning]," he said. "Attitude is a function of the field staff. You have to put the talent on the team. You could put the Dallas Cowboys Cheerleaders out there, and it wouldn't matter. We're breathing our own smoke down there, thinking on that on the basis of our great eloquence you could win 92 games with the same cast that won 67 the year before. That would be taking yourself a little too seriously."

Maybe MacPhail hasn't studied sports psychology enough, or isn't too familiar with Cubs history. After all, he said he is not responsible for the nearly five decades of woe of the million-to-one era that preceded his appointment to the Cubs' job in 1994.

But if the truth be known, winning and losing atmospheres do develop and get perpetuated in sports. Players who have performed on the winningest teams such as the Yankees and Braves, and others in the recent past, could feel the positive vibes and winning tradition ooze out of almost every pore. Losing begets losing, McLane said, and vice versa.

The Cubs' only palpable image for the general public is that of the "lovable losers." MacPhail claims that's a media creation, but now the Cubs as baseball's cuddly also-rans is now ingrained in society. Hollywood is perpetuating the image through the depictions of the Cubs as stumblebums who eventually rise up to win through some fantastic scheme or sometime in the mid-21st or 22nd century. Even McLane's own 1999 team media guide referred to the Cubs as "lovable losers" in a historical summary of their former home, the Astrodome.

In reality, Cubs players aren't battered down by a "lovable losers" image. In baseball's fluid world, few have stuck around for any length of time to experience the constant string of disappointments. Only Mark Grace has more than 10 years' service in the organization. If anything, there is no image at all to feed off. Not winning. Not losing. The Cubs don't seem to stand for anything except sun, fun, and a Wrigley Field that is empty come October.

But Grace has worked for the Cubs long enough to remember a management regime that tried to do what McLane has done with the Astros. Talk the talk, then walk the walk with good player development. Drafted in 1985, Grace remembered how the Dallas Green regime tried to teach the players how to win in the minors, and that a definite winning feeling had filtered down from Wrigley Field due to the 1984 NL East title season.

"Every season, it was typed in your contract, 'Get ready for your championship season,'" said team elder Grace. "Dallas, Gordon Goldsberry, Jim Snyder [coordinator of minor-league instruction] said it. Since then, I've never heard 'championship' used by different managements around here.

"You'd hear, 'bust your balls,' 'bust your ass,' you'd hear 'compete,' you'd never hear 'championship,' or 'championship atmosphere.'"

But talking "championship" is not uttering a dirty word elsewhere in baseball.

"Our mission statement is we want to be a championship team, year in and year out," said Charles Maher, a professor of organizational psychology at Rutgers University who works as sports psychologist for the Cleveland Indians.

Now the Cubs may have join the game's best in talking championship. Even though the front office won't do the cheerleading routine, the Cubs apparently have found a manager to revive the "championship"-thirsting atmosphere that Grace experienced.

Baylor, Hendry "Winning"Advocates

Don Baylor will turn back the clock not only to the Green philosophy, but his own playing days on winners as he takes the Cubs' helm.

Grace said he'll start using "championship" in various contexts when he talks to the media, and he'll be echoed by Baylor. Somebody in charge will actively preach the words that sports psychologists say are necessary to get baseball players properly motivated to win.

Baylor, a veteran of a great Baltimore Orioles organization in the 1970s and three different World Series winners from 1986 to 1988, believes his first few months on the job is not too early to start verbally creating a championship-type atmosphere with the Cubs.

"That's my M.O.," Baylor said of the "championship" concept. "I'll say it, because I believe it.

"I didn't take this job just to be content with just happened in the past. Attitudes have to change. I'll talk about winning every day I step on the field. It's a belief that I had, that the players will find out will be contagious. Losing also is contagious. After a while it becomes acceptable to many. But it's not acceptable to me. I've never played on a last-place team, and I'm proud of that."

Baylor had inherited the baggage of a bedraggled team that had lost 40 of 50 at one stretch in 1999 and had several players quit on predecessor Jim Riggleman.

"I look at it as a challenge like Bobby Cox did when he went to Atlanta [as manager in 1990]," Baylor said. "They had been losing all the time, and now they've won eight consecutive [division titles].

"It's a challenge, no doubt about it. This franchise here is a great franchise with the support they get. I want to change that into a positive, where we can start thinking about winning.

"Once you get into the second half of the season starts [as a non-contender], guys are talking about setting up [off-season] hunting trips, fishing trips. That part of the season I hate the most when you're out of it. I want to take us in a different direction as far as thinking about winning. It won't be going through the motions."

If MacPhail believes the field staff has to establish the winning attitude, then Baylor is up for the responsibility.

"I believe the manager has always set the tone for a team," he said. "The players play accordingly. If the manager is laid back, the players are laid-back. It's a manager's responsibility, as long as there's no interruption and interference from upstairs. If the players believe the manager is running the team, it's more convincing for the players. They can't go upstairs to complain they're not playing."

That's just the type of man Cubs brass wanted after the clubhouse problems of the summer of 1999.

"This is one of the reasons Baylor's here," former Cubs corporate overseer Jim Dowdle said. "He's got a reputation of not taking too much malarkey from too many people. He says what's on his mind, he's a good communicator. Jimmy [Riggleman] couldn't turn into the tough guy after four, five years. But he's a great individual, one of the best."

Baylor said players, fans, and media are imagining things when they talk of a winning atmosphere permeating a baseball organization.

"It trickled down to the minor leagues with the Orioles," he said. "It happened right after they acquired Frank Robinson and won the World Series in 1966. I felt that in 1967, when I signed and played in Bluefield, West Virginia. You played with pride because the Orioles had won the World Series.

"And you had that atmosphere in spring training, 1969, with the Orioles. It was business. You had your fun, but it was still business. You worked on your cutoffs and relays like it was a game. There was no goof-off period."

Maybe the Cubs now are doubly lucky. Player-development chief Jim Hendry, a former head baseball coach at Creighton University who should know something about pep talks, is complementing Baylor with a verbal vision to his young players.

"Learning to win is part of development," Hendry said. "I try to create it [a winning atmosphere] with the concept of it's never been done before. So why don't you people be part of something that's never happened? If you people end up playing in Wrigley Field and you are there when we win, history will take good care of you. The greatest team in Cubs history is the '69 Cubs. The last time I checked they came in second place."

But, at the same time, Hendry insists his youngest, best prospects are not part of the million-to-one era.

"You think Corey Patterson ever hears or cares about the term 'lovable losers?'" he huffed. "David Kelton couldn't give a damn about what happened with the '85 Cubs or the '92 Cubs. This is their career, this is our system, we've only been here a few years, we've got a chance to do it the right way and I think we're building that way. So all that history that the fans and media get caught up in, that doesn't filter down to Corey Patterson and Jeff Goldbach."

Hendry has gauged his players properly. Some of the top prospects said they are self-motivated to win.

"We all love the game, we love coming to the ballpark every day," third baseman Kelton said. "We have fun playing with each other. When we're off the field, we hang out with each other. A lot of clubs don't have that with their organization. We're real motivated to go out and win, and make each and every one of us a better person."

"We have one heck of a competitive group," catcher Goldbach said. "We like to compete. We're self-motivating. We compete every day. I don't think that's going to be a problem in the future. There's not one of us in here that would rather do good themselves instead of winning. That's the whole thing about baseball."

Elementary sports psychology dictates that athletes look to someone in charge to set a positive example.

"Most pro athletes, whether they admit it or not, would rather have a cheerleader than someone who doesn't allow them to know where they stand," said sports psychologist Maher. "These players with the Yankees are indoctrinated from the bottom up. As much as George [Steinbrenner] gets upset and makes others angry, he stands for something. The players notice. You need someone like that. Players want more of George or Dallas [Green] style.

"More often than not, that type of executive is a better communicator and gets better results. Someone who's low-key doesn't juice the players up. Dallas Green's heart was in the right place."

There may not be cheering in the pressbox, but there sure is room for it in the locker room.

"There's got to be cheering in sports," said Bob Schleser, professor of psychology at the Illinois Institute of Technology, who has worked with golfers, Olympic athletes, hockey players, and Memphis State's basketball team.

"There used to be a belief that people are motivated by dollars," Schleser said. "But after a certain amount of dollars, it doesn't make a difference anymore. Athletes will complain about a lack of Dr. Pepper in the locker room. They have the same day-by-day issues as anyone else."

The One Big Guy in Charge

Athletes will pick up on a management's commitment to winning.

"The No. 1 thing that I feel is important is consistency and commitment from the organization," said Arizona-based sports psychologist Gary Mack, who worked for the Cubs for a decade starting in 1984. "Everyone wants to win, but not everyone is willing to do what it takes to win. The greatest risk is to not take a risk, and I don't see the Cubs as a risk-taker."

The attitude of tendering big contracts to players who might get hurt, but might just stand an even better chance of helping you win is best summarized by Arizona Diamondbacks owner Jerry Colangelo: "Nothing ventured, nothing gained." Colangelo drew criticism from other owners for throwing around big bucks to the Randy Johnsons of the world and having to order up a cash call in 1999 from his roster of corporate partners. But the end result was the Diamondbacks making the playoffs in only their second season of existence and establishing some kind of winning tradition for a new franchise.

A passionate individual often must be the one trying to establish a tradition of winning. And these individuals are in the game to win, not to make profits. McLane and Giants owner Peter Magowan both projected at least $14 million losses for 1999 that had to be covered by cash calls or dipping into personal assets. It is a game for fans, not for corporate profit-mongers.

"Baseball is a game, it plays with the heart," Maher said. "People who breed winning are passionate about the game and communicate it. The corporate language doesn't do it. Organizations that are successful are led by one strong leader. It's in the nature of corporations to be conservative."

"The corporate world feels it's better to be safe than sorry," said Mack. "It's a world that doesn't understand sports at all."

"Steinbrenner doesn't fit the corporate image," said IIT psychologist Schleser. "Neither does Ted Turner. Or even Bill Gates. They have passion, they have emotion. That's what's lacking with the Cubs at high levels. There's no one yelling. They need a Steinbrenner type to get angry."

Although the Diamondback's Colangelo needed a huge infusion of Arizona-based corporate money to make major-league baseball in Phoenix become a reality, classic corporate style and baseball management don't mix in his opinion.

"Corporate ownership in running a team like another corporate entity doesn't usually work," he said. "You have to have someone running the show who is doing it instinctively, without being worried about the value of corporate stock. Sports are so different than other businesses with the emphasis on winning."

Indeed, the most successful franchises in baseball have been led by dynamic, voluable individuals at either the ownership or general manager's level. A group of executives, figuratively sending up smoke from the top of Tribune Tower when a decision is reached, has not proven successful.

Colangelo, who grew up as a Cubs fan in south suburban Chicago Heights, is one example of a strongman at the top.

"I don't believe in committee decisions," he said. "I'll take input from everyone in my organization. But you have to have someone making decisions."

And going out on a limb when the checkbook is concerned. "I'm not afraid to fail," Colangelo said. "You can't go into any decision looking at the downside of any big contract. In signing free agents, you do it with eyes wide open, you do it knowing you're one injury away from disaster. But you have to take risks [to succeed]."

The Diamondbacks are the latest of a series of teams who have been able to craft winning from nowhere in the 1990s.

McLane's cheerleading has been one of the final touches for a proud, cohesive roster in Houston. No, the Astros have not made a World Series yet, but the Cubs gladly would trade positions and many of their players for Houston's advantageous perch in the NL Central.

"The leadership has always been here with [Jeff] Bagwell and [Craig] Biggio," Astros stopper Billy Wagner said. "A lot of us have played together in the minor leagues. It's not a stressful environment. The rookies are not coming here saying, 'I got to hit this home run. I got to do this. Do that.' Guys just go out and play.

"I think this team knows how to win. The big thing with this team is at times, we're a bunch of overachievers. We don't have the Randy Johnson, the Trevor Hoffman, the marquee guys that you circle the wagon and say 'Oh, Lord, here they come.' Not until [1998] when we got [Moises] Alou did Houston start gaining a little respect. And Bags and Biggio had been doing their thing longer than Mo.

"Everybody's willing to lay out, play hard and put it all on the line for each other. If someone makes an error, they don't have to come to the pitcher and say, 'Hey man, I'm sorry.' We know they're trying hard. If I give up a home run, they're not going to go up and say 'It's all right.' They know I know it's going to be OK, I got to be ready for tomorrow. Everybody's got that mutual understanding that, hey, we're still playing hard, just because you don't get it done one day, they're pulling for you just as much."

The most palpable tradition of winning in baseball, of course, is with the New York Yankees. Long before Steinbrenner bought the team and issued his regal commands and demands to win, the decades of winning set up a tradition unlike anyone else. Cubs catcher Joe Girardi and his teammates fell into the flow when they became Yankees.

"There can't be any selfish play," Girardi said of the team's World Series-winning formula in the 1990s. "The guys in New York understood that a lot of us should have been playing every day. We could have been playing every day in other places. But sometimes you have to sacrifice to accomplish the team goal.

"We played very much as a team. Both catchers [Girardi and Jorge Posada] wanted to play every day. We had about six outfielders playing three positions who could have been playing every day. We had two DH's who could have been playing every day. Players understood that you sacrifice a little bit, and the rewards of winning are wonderful."

Girardi said newcomers could sense the winning history and the obligation to live up to it when they arrived in New York.

"You feel the tradition and how special of a place it is to play," Girardi said. "When you walk into Yankee Stadium and walk out onto the field, you realize the greatness that has been there. George [Steinbrenner] is very good at bringing a lot of the old-time players around. It's great to hear them talk and listen to all their stories. If you're any kind of historian, you know Yankee Stadium is quite a place to be."

The next-longest run of winning tradition is in Atlanta. Owner Ted Turner is far less involved than he used to be. But players knew he was in charge, while realizing some top baseball folks like Bobby Cox and John Schuerholz had wide latitude to make personnel decisions.

"These guys have been winning for so long, they know what's expected of them," said former Cubs pitcher Terry Mulholland, who was traded to the Braves in mid-season 1999. "They don't get too high or too low. It's a consistent approach to each game. These guys really enjoy playing baseball. I'd say that their whole approach to the game is professional, and it goes all the way from Schuerholz to the clubhouse guys. It's not that they expect to win, but they enjoy winning and that's all they want to do. They really don't let little things get in the way, they minimize distractions."

Not only Baylor and Grace felt the concept of winning filtering down to the minors with the Orioles in the late 1960s and the Cubs in the mid-1980s. Homegrown Yankees products Ricky Ledee and Shane Spencer felt the team's championship tradition being bred down in the farm system. Former Braves pitching prospects Jason Schmidt and Micah Bowie experienced the same feeling while coming up in the Atlanta system.

One team that has cast away decades of losing tradition is the Cleveland Indians. The Tribe have not won a World Series yet in their 10-year revival program, but at least they have made it to the Fall Classic twice, in 1995 and 1997. The Cubs gladly would have taken such a record.

Former Indians owner Dick Jacobs, a low-key man, signed off on the financial moves that led to the Indians' revival. He also gave great power to a dynamic general manager, John Hart.

"John Hart is very outgoing, very easy to talk to, big on communicating," said former Indians reliever Paul Assenmacher, an ex-Cub and

White Sox. "John's always willing to listen to you. He's a very easy person to get along with. He's genuine."

Everyone knows where they stand in Cleveland.

"At least you know with Indians if you don't produce, he'll find someone else who will. John is not one to sit still," Assenmacher said. Sure enough, longtime manager Mike Hargrove paid for the 1999 playoff failure with his job.

"John Hart would probably love to be the manager himself," sports psychologist Charles Maher said.

Hart purged more than three decades' worth of Bad News Bears attitudes from Cleveland. The same can be done with the Cubs, even if players and front office types claim the "lovable losers" tag has not affected the team in the 1990s.

A self-fulfilling losing prophecy did take place in 1997 and 1998, though. In '97, "woe-is-us" worry began to engulf Cubs' spring training camp when the players and staff were faced with the realization the first 12 games of the season were against the Braves and beefed-up Marlins. The Cubs had played well against the Braves in 1996, including being one dropped double-play ball away from sweeping a four-game series at Wrigley Field. But that feat didn't matter. Sure enough, the Cubs ended up dragging their tail in losing a record-tying 14 in a row from the start of the season. Later, manager Jim Riggleman said the negative talk (and it wasn't just media hype) contributed to the mega-slump.

Then, at the end of the 1998 season, the Cubs were considered such an accidental wild-card playoff team that they were not given any chance to beat the Braves in the NL division series, despite being an impressive 6-3 in the regular season against Atlanta. The Cubs ended up being swept in three straight in the series.

"It's the expectancy theory," said sports psychologist Gary Mack. "If you think you can or can't, you're probably right. It's the attitude that some people have that they're going to lose. Beliefs about yourself drive you. Sportswriters feed into it. Guys are human and can't help but get thoughts in their head."

Someone, someway, has to jolt the Cubs into a positive move forward, to create some kind of definite winning atmosphere at Wrigley Field that can filter downward to the rookie-league team in Mesa. It looks like the burden will fall on Don Baylor's broad shoulders and winning-player persona at the major-league level and Jim Hendry's college-coach cheerleading in the minor leagues.

"If you say you're going to do things slowly and unspectacularly, that doesn't breed enthusiasm," sports psychologist Maher said of Cubs upper management's style. "If the focus is always on the budget, you'll usually get more of the same."

In the end, the "lovable losers" image may not be totally purged until the Cubs finally, resolutely, end the million-to-one era. Just listen to a devil's advocate, in this case Jim Dowdle.

"In this kind of media environment, a guy would be shooting himself in the foot to start talking about bringing a championship," he said. "You're driving home every night and you'd be hearing that shit thrown at that guy until hell freezes over...or until he does [win a championship].

"You don't have a tradition of winning here. We're going to be steeped in the tradition of losing until we win. There's not much you can do to instill a tradition of winning until you win."

Chapter 16

MAKING SENSE OF MILLION-TO-ONE ODDS

THROW OUT ALL the stuff about billy goats and curses and too many day games. The only logical conclusion one can make about why the Cubs have defied odds as high as a million- to-one in not appearing in a World Series since 1945 is that no dyed-in-the-wool Cubs fan has been in charge to end the historic pennantless streak.

Think about it. No one Cubs fan who grew up paying 75 cents or $1 to get into the bleachers or got in on free admissions on Ladies Day with Mom packing lunches has ever run the team over the past seven decades. No one at the top has applied the passion of cheering for Hank Sauer or Ernie Banks or Rick Monday or Ryne Sandberg to build a winning organization befitting a world-class city like Chicago.

The Cubs once had a maniacal fan in charge: William Wrigley, Jr. The Cubs were the Yankees of the National League when he ran the show. But his death in 1932 left an ownership void that has never been filled. His son, Phil Wrigley, kept the Cubs out of a sense of family duty. If ol' P.K. really cared about the Cubs, really understood the game and the people in it, he would have written the check and hired the right executives to restore the Cubs to the dominance of his baseball-loving dad's era. Phil's son, Bill, was cut in the same basic low-profile personality mold of his father, and although he liked being around baseball by all reports, was financially handicapped due to estate-tax problems.

Tribune Co. started out as a savior to rescue the Cubs from Wrigley family penury. And Philadelphia import Dallas Green, after a long period of blustering about the Phillies way of doing things, began to fall in love with what made Wrigley Field and Cubs fans so special. Yet the long arm of increasing corporate control cut off Green prior to him completing the player-development rebuilding plan he started.

Subsequent Tribune Co. corporate control of the Cubs was bottomlineoriented. And although team president Andy MacPhail, an East Coast native, has almost as much authority as Phil Wrigley himself under a loosened Tribune Co. oversight to change things, he will proceed at his own philosophically-controlled pace, ignoring the urgency to win as the decades since the last World Series at Wrigley Field mount.

The folks who grew up with and really cared about the Cubs, who have died a thousand times and more through hope and inevitable frustration, have never had a shot at running the Cubs.

Consider the description of a group of Chicago-area businessmen who tried to buy the Cubs in the late spring of 1981, but weren't allowed a legitimate shot to make a bid because Bill Wrigley was secretly negotiating with white-knight buyer Tribune Co.

"They wouldn't be in it for the profit motive," said broker Joe Siegman, who represented the group, at that time. "These people are die-hard baseball fans, crazy Cub fans who were born and raised on the North Side."

If the person in charge had grown up with the Cubs or spent real quality time in the trenches, he'd really know the impact of a Cubs World Series team, and a winner. "It would be the most celebrated championship of our time," former Cubs pitcher Terry Mulholland said. ABC-TV sportscaster Brent Musburger, who cut his career teeth in Chicago, once said a Cubs World Series winner would be bigger than the Bears' Super Bowl XX championship. If the Cubs won the World Series, they would finally become No. 1 in media coverage and fan appeal in Chicago, supplanting the Bears.

MacPhail professes to care about the greater good of baseball. A Cubs appearance, if not a victory, in the World Series, would be so sentimental, so stupendous, that it could do for the game as much, if not more, than the Sammy Sosa-Mark McGwire home-run race of 1998. The fan base would be so energized, and anyone throughout the world who was repeatedly thwarted from achieving a dream would be rooting for the Cubs. The euphoria would be indescribable, radiating in its glow from Clark and Addison for thousands of miles around, across lands and seas. Not to mention, for the bottomliners, the millions more to be made in promotional and marketing value from the long delayed Cubs visit to the promised land.

Problem is, can the Cubs break out of the Tribune Co. bottomline mold to make it there in our lifetime?

At face value, the very reason for Tribune Co.'s ownership of the Cubs no longer exists. The team was bought to protect WGN-TV's ancestral programming. A complement of 145-plus games per year was the core programming of WGN in 1981, when the station was only in its infancy as a satellite-borne station. But in 2000, WGN no longer is a non-network station just filling its schedule with sports, movies, reruns of old network shows, and some syndicated programs.

Now it is a linchpin affiliate of the young-skewing WB Network, of which Tribune Co. is a 25 percent owner. *Buffy the Vampire Slayer*, *Dawson's Creek*, and *Popular* have earned the allegiance of teenagers (and advertisers drooling for the kids' dollars) all over. Baseball is now secondary to the prime-time WB fare, and night Cubs games often are handed off to Fox Sports Net Chicago or even UHF independent station WCIU-TV, which once had bullfights and *Amos and Andy* reruns as its staple fare.

Would Tribune Co. get out of the baseball business if it deems the Cubs aren't synergistic with the rest of the corporate landscape?

"I think Tribune Co. will sell the Cubs in about five years," said Steve Friedman, a 50-year Cubs fan and native Chicagoan who now produces CBS-TV's *The Early Show*. "Baseball is an older, more genteel sport. Tribune Co.'s going for teenagers and young, urban professionals with their new TV programming. Wrestling's more their profile."

So who is wealthy enough and a big enough fan to step forward and buy the Cubs if Tribune Co. ever wants to sell out?

"Paul Allen if he lived in Chicago would be best owner," said Friedman. "Someone who had grown up as a Cubs fan, in his mid-40s, early-50s, someone says before I die I want to see Cubs win. The best teams owned by one guy. It's got to be the vision of one person. Teams are successful if they're run by one guy."

Unfortunately, the one Cubs fan who grew up to be a dynamic sports owner moved away to Phoenix in 1968. Jerry Colangelo is the Southwest's top sports mogul, arguably the most powerful individual in the state of Arizona. Colangelo used to be a high school lefthander, a teammate of Jim Bouton at Bloom Township High, who was a big-league prospect until he hurt his arm. He talks about his days traveling up to Wrigley Field from south suburban Chicago Heights to see Hank Sauer play. The emotional involvement of a Colangelo type in running the Cubs could be immeasurable. Is there another one like him out there in the Chicago area?

Maybe Tribune Co. won't ever sell the Cubs after all. They might want their cake and eat it, too. New FCC ownership rules permit one company to own multiple TV stations in the same market. Tribune Co. could buy a second TV channel in Chicago and designate that their sports station while running WB programming on WGN-TV. If Tribune Co. could pay $500 million for KTLA, Los Angeles' top independent VHF station in 1985, the company could afford megabucks for another channel in Chicago now.

Whoever owns the Cubs will have no excuse to run the team other than a big-market club. So says no less a passionate baseball man than Andre Dawson, the 1987 National League Most Valuable Player for his 49-homer, 137-RBI season with the Cubs and role-model persona. Dawson is a towering power of strength and dignity who doesn't waste words. When he speaks, most anyone within earshot has an obligation to listen.

"Without a doubt," he said of any big-market team in New York, Chicago, and Los Angeles always being in a position to contend. "If you're a big-market franchise, you've got to be right up there among the top. Money isn't going to guarantee you winning, but you can't win unless you spend the money. This is one place [Chicago] where you should always go that extra step to get the key personnel. Until you do that, you're going to be up and down, up and down.

"When you have the resources to do it, you do it. If you don't have the resources, that's another thing. But those organizations [Yankees and Mets] set certain standards. That's why they are where they are. They just don't want to put a product out there that's in the middle of the pack."

Dawson set an example of a premium player who make a little bit of a sacrifice to play in Wrigley Field. He reaped the rewards tenfold for his decision. He said others of his kind will follow suit if asked.

"To be afforded an opportunity to play in Wrigley Field, with the huge following nationwide, I don't think any player would turn his back on it," he said.

One prime player who has thrived in Wrigley Field nevertheless is getting a little edgy about ever fulfilling one important career goal. And in the process, Sammy Sosa speaks for countless Cubs fans. On August 2, 1999, in a heartfelt conversation by his Wrigley Field locker, Sosa spoke of his yearning to play in a World Series.

"If I'm going to stay here for life, I'm looking for them building a good team around me," he said. "I don't want to be here and play all my life without winning a World Series championship. They need to put a good team around me so I can stay here and finish my career."

Obviously, the year 2001 is the key. The Cubs will want Sosa to stay out of free agency going into the following season. His $42.5 million contract, signed in 1997, has a mutual option for 2002, when Sosa will be 33. He can opt out of the last year of the contract if he chooses.

"When it is time to talk about that [new contract], they'll have a good team around me," Sosa said.

But if Sosa wants to leave to try to play on a winner, he'd likely not lack for the contract of his dreams from either the Yankees or Mets, who could depend on thousands of Dominican fans who have settled in New York to whir the turnstiles to cheer him on.

Asked flatly if he would go elsewhere if the 2001 Cubs don't measure up to his standards, Sosa said: "I think so. They know what I want. They know I like to win. I'm not a GM. But I love to win, I love to come to the ballpark happy and do my job. I want to make sure they have a good pitching staff and a good bullpen."

Sosa wanted to hold out hope, but you could pick up some skepticism in his demeanor. Some of the fans are more outwardly resigned to an endless million-to-one era.

"It seems like the Cubs were meant not to be winners," said Al Fujara, a disabled Chicago police officer and 42-year Cubs fan who recorded baseball highlights off the WGN-TV prime-time news with a reel-to-reel tape recorder as early as 1966. "Throughout my entire life I fantasized about the Cubs winning it all. I knew deep down, though, that it was never going to happen in my lifetime. Pure and simple."

Others keep up the faith. And why not, in the case of Joel de la Fuente, the actor who played a Cubs-loving U.S. Marine in outer space in the year 2065 in the old Fox sci-fi series *Space: Above and Beyond*.

"Of course I believe that," de la Fuente said of the Cubs reaching the World Series in his lifetime, prior to 2065. "But whether they do or don't, it's all about the journey. I would much rather they lose well than win badly, if that makes any sense.

"What are the odds, given the dismal nature of our current sports franchises and their respective front offices, of the Cubs being the *next* Chicago franchise to win a championship [not counting MSL and stuff like that]? I think we stack up quite well when viewed from that viewpoint!"

Such prominent Cubs as Mark Grace and Glenallen Hill believe the team will play in a World Series in their lifetimes. But they have the advantage of youth.

Others don't. TV producer Steve Friedman, 53, vows he won't die until the Cubs play in the Fall Classic. *Chicago Magazine* editor Richard Babcock best summed up the travail of the fan running out of lifetime to see a Cubs' pennant.

In a 1996 article on the Cubs, Babcock interviewed MacPhail about his management philosophy. He concluded by posing this angle to the team president: "I did something cruel. I asked him what he would say to an 85-year-old Cubs fan, someone who has been following the team and buying tickets all those years, but who may not have the time left to wait while the Cubs try once again to put together a winning team.

"A faint, wistful smile crossed Andy MacPhail's young face. 'I'm doing the best I can,' he said softly."

Superficially, MacPhail sees that all is well in the appeal of his team. He views the record Wrigley Field attendance in 1999, the club selling tickets up to 92 percent of ballpark capacity, as an accurate measure of fan acceptance. One day a few years back after a Saturday afternoon game, he took one of his sons and walked on Clark Street north of the ballpark to soak in the happy crowds of celebrating Cubs fans. So the adopted Chicagoan can see Cubdom having a good time on a summer afternoon.

But can MacPhail—the man with the power, if not only of the purse, but also of persuasion to profits-counting executives in Tribune Tower—really know the soul of the city, the to-the-gut yearning for a winner that could capture large chunks of baseball fans worldwide for a decade or more if fulfilled?

Somehow, can't there be a real-life repeat of the 1933 movie *Gabriel Over the White House*, where the famed archangel transforms a Herbert Hoover-type president who has uttered the old budget-balancing platitudes about solving the Great Depression? The changed chief exec instead does Franklin Roosevelt several steps further, not only successfully attacking the economic disaster, but also using tanks to smash gangsters and forcing world powers to forge a United Nations-like peace.

Wherever Gabriel is now, he needs to visit the Wrigley Field bosses to let them know the solution is not heavenly interference, but the resolute, aggressive actions of mortal men who have at their fingertips the power to retire the million-to-one era to the history books.